FIFTH EDITION

2

GRAMMAR *in* CONTEXT

SANDRA N. ELBAUM

The cover photo shows the San Francisco-Oakland Bay Bridge over San Francisco Bay in California.

HEINLE
CENGAGE Learning™

Australia • Brazil • Japan • Korea • Mexico • Singapore • Spain • United Kingdom • United States

HEINLE
CENGAGE Learning™

Grammar in Context 2, Fifth Edition
Student Book
Sandra N. Elbaum

Publisher: Sherrise Roehr

Acquisitions Editor: Tom Jefferies

Development Editor: Sarah Sandoski

Technology Development Manager:
   Debie Mirtle

Director of Global Marketing: Ian Martin

Director of US Marketing: Jim McDonough

Product Marketing Manager: Katie Kelley

Marketing Manager: Caitlin Driscoll

Content Project Manager: Andrea Bobotas

Senior Print Buyer: Susan Spencer

Project Manager: Chrystie Hopkins

Production Services: Nesbitt Graphics, Inc.

Interior Design and Cover Design:
   Muse Group, Inc.

For permission to use material from this text or product, submit all requests online at www.cengage.com/permissions

Further permissions questions can be emailed to **permissionrequest@cengage.com**

Library of Congress Control Number: 2009936998

ISBN 13: 978-1-4240-7901-8

ISBN 10: 1-4240-7901-2

Heinle
20 Channel Center Street
Boston, Massachusetts 02210
USA

Cengage Learning is a leading provider of customized learning solutions with office locations around the globe, including Singapore, the United Kingdom, Australia, Mexico, Brazil, and Japan. Locate our local office at international.cengage.com/region

Cengage Learning products are represented in Canada by Nelson Education, Ltd.

Visit Heinle online at **elt.heinle.com**

Visit our corporate website at **www.cengage.com**

Printed in the United States of America.
5 6 7 8 9 10 — 15 14

Contents

Lesson 3

Lesson 4

Lesson 5

Lesson 6

Lesson 7

Lesson 8

Lesson 9

Lesson 10

Lesson 11

Lesson 12

Lesson 13

Lesson 14

Appendices

Index

Acknowledgments

Many thanks to Dennis Hogan, Sherrise Roehr, and Tom Jefferies from Heinle Cengage for their ongoing support of the *Grammar in Context* series. I would especially like to thank my development editor, Sarah Sandoski, for her patience, sensitivity, keen eye to detail, and invaluable suggestions.

And many thanks to my students at Truman College, who have increased my understanding of my own language and taught me to see life from another point of view. By sharing their observations, questions, and life stories, they have enriched my life enormously.

This new edition is dedicated to the millions of displaced people in the world. The U.S. is the new home to many refugees, who survived unspeakable hardships in Burundi, Rwanda, Sudan, Burma, Bhutan, and other countries. Their resiliency in starting a new life and learning a new language is a tribute to the human spirit.—*Sandra N. Elbaum*

Heinle would like to thank the following people for their contributions:

Elizabeth A. Adler-Coleman
Sunrise Mountain High School
Las Vegas, NV

Dorothy Avondstondt
Miami Dade College
Miami, FL

Judith A. G. Benka
Normandale Community College
Bloomington, MN

Carol Brutza
Gateway Community College
New Haven, CT

Lyn Buchheit
Community College of Philadelphia
Philadelphia, PA

Charlotte M. Calobrisi
Northern Virginia Community College
Annandale, VA

Gabriela Cambiasso
Harold Washington College
Chicago, IL

Jeanette Clement
Duquesne University
Pittsburgh, PA

Allis Cole
Shoreline Community College
Shoreline, WA

Fanshen DiGiovanni
Glendale Community College
Glendale, CA

Antoinette B. d'Oronzio
Hillsborough Community College-Dale Mabry Campus
Tampa, FL

Rhonda J. Farley
Cosumnes River College
Sacramento, CA

Jennifer Farnell
University of Connecticut American Language Program
Stamford, CT

Gail Fernandez
Bergen Community College
Paramus, NJ

Irasema Fernandez
Miami Dade College
Miami, FL

Abigail-Marie Fiattarone
Mesa Community College
Mesa, AZ

John Gamber
American River College
Sacramento, CA

Marcia Gethin-Jones
University of Connecticut American Language Program
Storrs, CT

Kimlee Buttacavoli Grant
The Leona Group, LLC
Phoenix, AZ

Shelly Hedstrom
Palm Beach Community College
Lake Worth, FL

Linda Holden
College of Lake County
Grayslake, IL

Sandra Kawamura
Sacramento City College
Sacramento, CA

Bill Keniston
Normandale Community College
Bloomington, MN

Michael Larsen
American River College
Sacramento, CA

Bea C. Lawn
Gavilan College
Gilroy, CA

Rob Lee
Pasadena City College
Pasadena, CA

Oranit Limmaneeprasert
American River College
Sacramento, CA

Linda Louie
Highline Community College
Des Moines, WA

Melanie A. Majeski
Naugatuck Valley Community College
Waterbury, CT

Maria Marin
De Anza College
Cupertino, CA

Michael I. Massey
Hillsborough Community College-Ybor City Campus
Tampa, FL

Marlo McClurg-Mackinnon
Cosumnes River College
Sacramento, CA

Michelle Naumann
Elgin Community College
Elgin, IL

Debbie Ockey
Fresno, CA

Lesa Perry
University of Nebraska at Omaha
Omaha, NE

Herbert Pierson
St. John's University
New York City, NY

Dina Poggi
De Anza College
Cupertino, CA

Steven Rashba
University of Bridgeport
Bridgeport, CT

Mark Rau
American River College
Sacramento, CA

Maria Spelleri
State College of Florida Manatee-Sarasota
Venice, FL

Eva Teagarden
Yuba College
Marysville, CA

Colin S. Ward
Lone Star College-North Harris
Houston, TX

Nico Wiersema
Texas A&M International University
Laredo, TX

Susan Wilson
San Jose City College
San Jose, CA

A word from the author

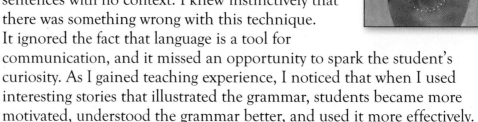

My parents immigrated to the U.S. from Poland and learned English as a second language. Born in the U.S., I often had the task as a child to explain the intricacies of the English language. It is no wonder that I became an English language teacher.

When I started teaching over forty years ago, grammar textbooks used a series of unrelated sentences with no context. I knew instinctively that there was something wrong with this technique. It ignored the fact that language is a tool for communication, and it missed an opportunity to spark the student's curiosity. As I gained teaching experience, I noticed that when I used interesting stories that illustrated the grammar, students became more motivated, understood the grammar better, and used it more effectively.

In 1986, I published the first edition of *Grammar in Context* and have continued to search for topics that teach grammar in contexts that are relevant to students' lives. The contexts I've chosen each tell a story: practical ones about technology (social networking and e-books), interesting people (Tiger Woods), and events that made history (the election of President Barack Obama). Whether the task is a fill-in grammar exercise, a listening activity, an editing exercise, an interactive conversation activity, or free writing, the context is reinforced throughout the lesson.

I hope you enjoy the new edition of *Grammar in Context!*

Sandra N. Elbaum

In memory of
Roberto Garrido Alfaro

Welcome to *Grammar in Context,*
Fifth Edition

Grammar in Context presents grammar in interesting contexts that are relevant to students' lives and then recycles the language and context throughout every activity. Learners gain knowledge and skills in both the grammar structures and topic areas.

The new fifth edition of *Grammar in Context* engages learners with updated readings, clear and manageable grammar explanations, and a new full-color design.

New To This Edition!

Full-color design makes grammar more visually contextualized and even easier to study and teach from.

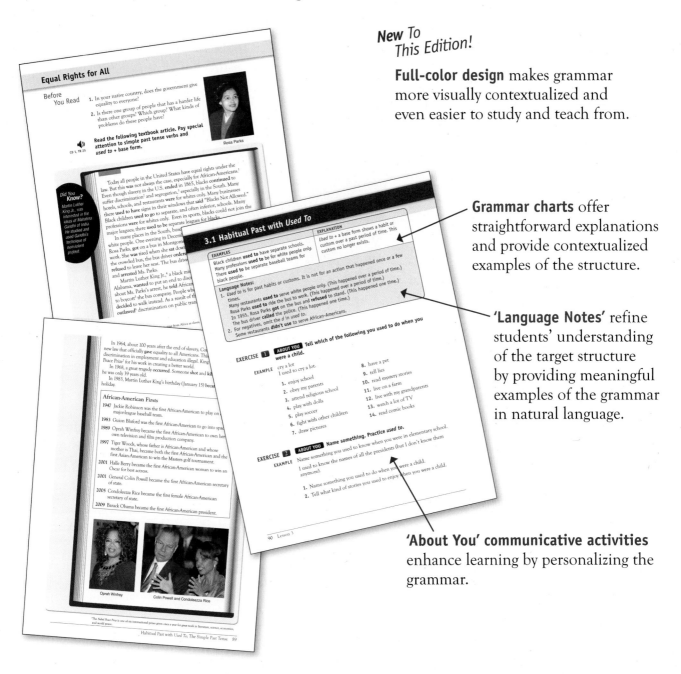

Grammar charts offer straightforward explanations and provide contextualized examples of the structure.

'Language Notes' refine students' understanding of the target structure by providing meaningful examples of the grammar in natural language.

'About You' communicative activities enhance learning by personalizing the grammar.

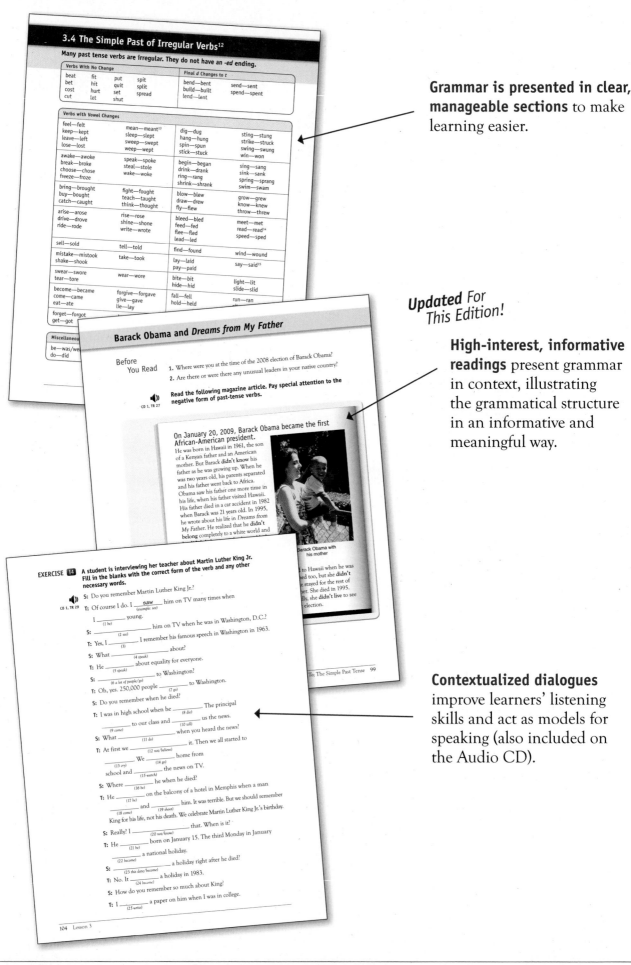

3.4 The Simple Past of Irregular Verbs[12]

Many past tense verbs are irregular. They do not have an -ed ending.

Verbs With No Change				Final d Changes to t	
beat	fit	put	spit	bend—bent	send—sent
bet	hit	quit	split	build—built	spend—spent
cost	hurt	set	spread	lend—lent	
cut	let	shut			

Verbs with Vowel Changes

feel—felt	mean—meant[13]	dig—dug	sting—stung
keep—kept	sleep—slept	hang—hung	strike—struck
leave—left	sweep—swept	spin—spun	swing—swung
lose—lost	weep—wept	stick—stuck	win—won
awake—awoke	speak—spoke	begin—began	sing—sang
break—broke	steal—stole	drink—drank	sink—sank
choose—chose	wake—woke	ring—rang	spring—sprang
freeze—froze		shrink—shrank	swim—swam
bring—brought	fight—fought	blow—blew	grow—grew
buy—bought	teach—taught	draw—drew	know—knew
catch—caught	think—thought	fly—flew	throw—threw
arise—arose	rise—rose	bleed—bled	
drive—drove	shine—shone	feed—fed	meet—met
ride—rode	write—wrote	flee—fled	read—read[14]
		lead—led	speed—sped
sell—sold	tell—told	find—found	
mistake—mistook	take—took		wind—wound
shake—shook		lay—laid	say—said[15]
		pay—paid	
swear—swore	wear—wore	bite—bit	light—lit
tear—tore		hide—hid	slide—slid
become—became	forgive—forgave	fall—fell	run—ran
come—came	give—gave	hold—held	
eat—ate	lie—lay		
forget—forgot			
get—got			

Miscellaneous

be—was/we...
do—did

EXERCISE **14**
A student is interviewing her teacher about Martin Luther King Jr.
Fill in the blanks with the correct form of the verb and any other
necessary words.

CD 1, TR 29

S: Do you remember Martin Luther King Jr.?

T: Of course I do. I ___saw___ him on TV many times when
(example: see)

I _____ young.
(1 be)

S: _____ him on TV when he was in Washington, D.C.?
(2 see)

T: Yes, I _____ I remember his famous speech in Washington in 1963.
(3)

S: What _____ about?
(4 speak)

T: He _____ about equality for everyone.
(5 speak)

S: _____ to Washington?
(6 a lot of people/go)

T: Oh, yes. 250,000 people _____ to Washington.
(7 go)

S: Do you remember when he died?

T: I was in high school when he _____. The principal
(8 die)

_____ to our class and _____ us the news.
(9 come)   (10 tell)

S: What _____ when you heard the news?
(11 do)

T: At first we _____ it. Then we all started to
(12 not/believe)

_____. We _____ home from
(13 cry)   (14 go)

school and _____ the news on TV.
(15 watch)

S: Where _____ he when he died?
(16 be)

T: He _____ on the balcony of a hotel in Memphis when a man
(17 be)

_____ and _____ him. It was terrible. But we should remember
(18 come)   (19 shoot)

King for his life, not his death. We celebrate Martin Luther King Jr.'s birthday.

S: Really? I _____ that. When is it?
(20 not/know)

T: He _____ born on January 15. The third Monday in January
(21 be)

_____ a national holiday.
(22 become)

S: _____ a holiday right after he died?
(23 this date/become)

T: No. It _____ a holiday in 1983.
(24 become)

S: How do you remember so much about King?

T: I _____ a paper on him when I was in college.
(25 write)

Barack Obama and *Dreams from My Father*

Before You Read

1. Where were you at the time of the 2008 election of Barack Obama?

2. Are there or were there any unusual leaders in your native country?

CD 1, TR 27

Read the following magazine article. Pay special attention to the negative form of past-tense verbs.

On January 20, 2009, Barack Obama became the first African-American president.
He was born in Hawaii in 1961, the son of a Kenyan father and an American mother. But Barack **didn't know** his father as he was growing up. When he was two years old, his parents separated and his father went back to Africa. Obama saw his father one more time in his life, when his father visited Hawaii. His father died in a car accident in 1982 when Barack was 21 years old. In 1995, he wrote about his life in *Dreams from My Father*. He realized that he **didn't belong** completely to a white world and

Barack Obama with his mother

... to Hawaii when he was
... ed too, but she **didn't**
... e stayed for the rest of
... er. She died in 1995.
... lly, she **didn't live** to see
... election.

... To: The Simple Past Tense   99

Grammar is presented in clear, manageable sections to make learning easier.

Updated For This Edition!

High-interest, informative readings present grammar in context, illustrating the grammatical structure in an informative and meaningful way.

Contextualized dialogues improve learners' listening skills and act as models for speaking (also included on the Audio CD).

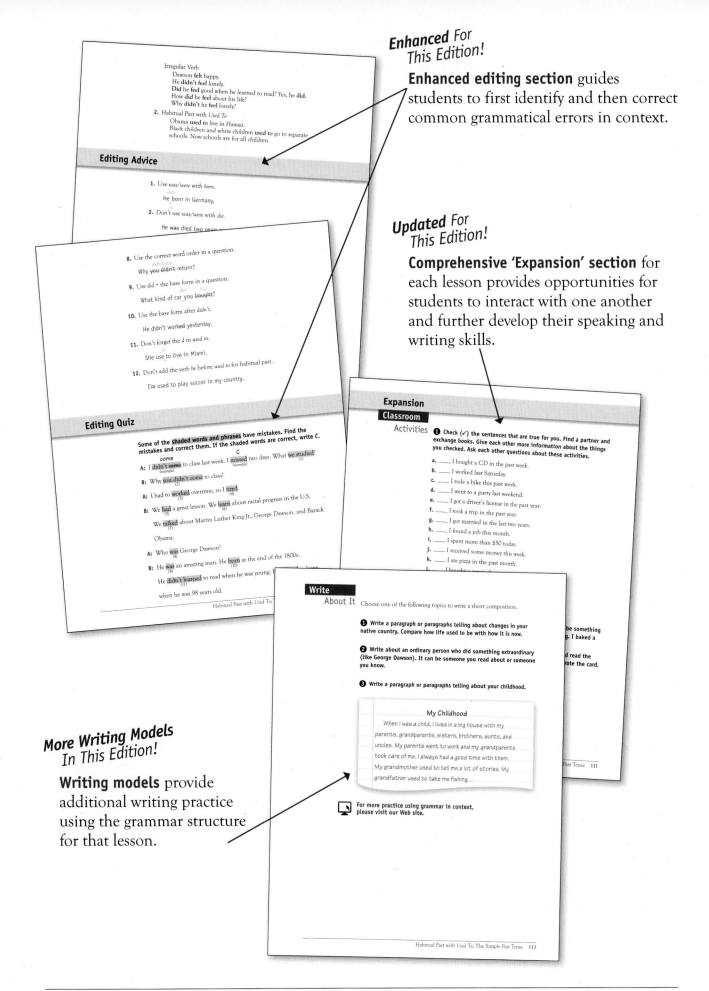

Enhanced editing section guides students to first identify and then correct common grammatical errors in context.

Irregular Verb
Dawson **felt** happy.
He **didn't feel** lonely.
Did he **feel** good when he learned to read? Yes, he **did**.
How **did** he **feel** about his life?
Why **didn't** he **feel** lonely?

2. Habitual Past with *Used To*
Obama **used to** live in Hawaii.
Black children and white children **used to** go to separate schools. Now schools are for all children.

Editing Advice

1. Use *was/were* with *born*.
   was
   He ~~born~~ in Germany.

2. Don't use *was/were* with *die*.
   He was died two years...

8. Use the correct word order in a question.
   didn't you
   Why ~~you didn't~~ return?

9. Use did + the base form in a question.
   did   buy
   What kind of car you ~~bought~~?

10. Use the base form after *didn't*.
    He didn't ~~worked~~ yesterday.

11. Don't forget the *d* in *used to*.
    She ~~use~~ to live in Miami.

12. Don't add the verb *be* before *used to* for habitual past.
    ~~I'm~~ used to play soccer in my country.

Editing Quiz

Some of the **shaded words and phrases** have mistakes. Find the mistakes and correct them. If the shaded words are correct, write *C*.

come   C
A: I ~~didn't came~~ to class last week. I ~~missed~~ two days. What ~~we studied?~~
   (example)   (example)   (1)

B: Why ~~you didn't come~~ to class?
          (2)

A: I had to ~~worked~~ overtime, so I ~~tired.~~
           (3)   (4)

B: We ~~had~~ a great lesson. We ~~learn~~ about racial progress in the U.S.
      (5)   (6)
   We ~~talked~~ about Martin Luther King Jr., George Dawson, and Barack
       (7)
   Obama.

A: Who ~~was~~ George Dawson?
        (8)

B: He ~~was~~ an amazing man. He ~~born~~ at the end of the 1800s.
      (9)   (10)
   He ~~didn't learned~~ to read when he was young. ... learn
       (11)
   when he was 98 years old.

Habitual Past with Used To;

Comprehensive 'Expansion' section for each lesson provides opportunities for students to interact with one another and further develop their speaking and writing skills.

Expansion
Classroom
Activities

❶ **Check (✓) the sentences that are true for you. Find a partner and exchange books. Give each other more information about the things you checked. Ask each other questions about these activities.**

a. ____ I bought a CD in the past week.
b. ____ I worked last Saturday.
c. ____ I rode a bike this past week.
d. ____ I went to a party last weekend.
e. ____ I got a driver's license in the past year.
f. ____ I took a trip in the past year.
g. ____ I got married in the last two years.
h. ____ I found a job this month.
i. ____ I spent more than $50 today.
j. ____ I received some money this week.
k. ____ I ate pizza in the past month.

Write
About It   Choose one of the following topics to write a short composition.

❶ **Write a paragraph or paragraphs telling about changes in your native country. Compare how life used to be with how it is now.**

❷ **Write about an ordinary person who did something extraordinary (like George Dawson). It can be someone you read about or someone you know.**

❸ **Write a paragraph or paragraphs telling about your childhood.**

My Childhood

When I was a child, I lived in a big house with my parents, grandparents, sisters, brothers, aunts, and uncles. My parents went to work and my grandparents took care of me. I always had a good time with them. My grandmother used to tell me a lot of stories. My grandfather used to take me fishing...

💻 **For more practice using grammar in context, please visit our Web site.**

Past Tense   111

Writing models provide additional writing practice using the grammar structure for that lesson.

Habitual Past with Used To; The Simple Past Tense 113

FOR THE STUDENT:

New To This Edition!

- **Online Workbook** features additional exercises that learners can access in the classroom, language lab, or at home.

- **Audio CD** includes dialogues and all readings from the student book.

- Student Web site features additional practice: http://elt.heinle.com/grammarincontext.

FOR THE TEACHER:

New To This Edition!

- **Online Lesson Planner** is perfect for busy instructors, allowing them to create and customize lesson plans for their classes, then save and share them in a range of formats.

Updated For This Edition!

- **Assessment CD-ROM with Exam*View*®** lets teachers create and customize tests and quizzes easily and includes many new contextualized test items.

- **Teacher's Edition** offers comprehensive teaching notes including suggestions for more streamlined classroom options.

- Instructor Web site includes a printable Student Book answer key.

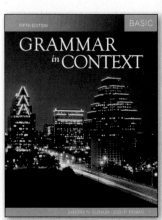 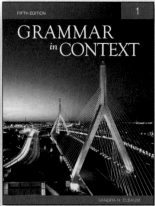 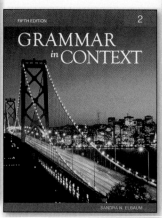 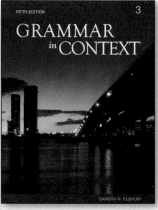

Grammar
The Simple Present Tense
Frequency Words

Context
Pets and Other Animals

Americans and Their Pets

1. Do you like animals?

2. Do you have a pet?

CD 1, TR 01

Read the following magazine article. Pay special attention to the verb *be* and other verbs in the simple present tense.

Did You Know?

The most common registered breed of dog in the United States is the Labrador retriever, as seen on page 9.

Most Americans **love** pets. About 63 percent of Americans **live** with one or more animals. About 39 percent of households **have** at least one dog. Thirty-four percent of households **own** at least one cat.

Americans **think** of their pets as part of the family. Americans **spend** approximately $5 billion a year on holiday presents for their pets. Almost half of all pet owners **talk** to their pets on occasion. Many pet owners **sleep** with their dogs or cats. Many people **travel** with their pets. (It **costs** between $25 and $150 to fly with a pet.) Some hotels **allow** guests to bring their pets.

Americans **pay** a lot of money to keep pets. They **spend** about $43.2 billion a year in vet[1] bills. There **are** schools, toys, hotels, restaurants, clothes, perfumes, and cemeteries for pets. There **are** magazines for pet owners. There **are** hundreds of Web sites for pet owners.

Pets **are** a lot of fun. They **are** affectionate[2] too. People who **are** lonely **get** a lot of love from their animals. Medical research **shows** that contact with a dog or a cat can lower a person's blood pressure.

Pets **need** a lot of attention. Before you **buy** a pet, it **is** important to answer these questions:

- **Are** you patient?
- **Are** you home a lot?
- If you **have** children, **are** they responsible?
- **Are** pets allowed where you live?
- **Do** you **have** money for medical bills for your pet?

Unfortunately, some people **don't realize** that pets **need** a lot of care. Some people **see** a cute puppy or kitten, **buy** it, and later **abandon**[3] it because they **don't want** to take care of it. It **is** important to understand that a pet **is** a long-term responsibility.

[1]*Vet* is short for *veterinarian*. This is an animal doctor.
[2]*Affectionate* means loving.
[3]*To abandon* means to leave something. When people abandon a pet, they leave it on the street.

1.1 *Be*—Forms and Uses

Forms

EXAMPLES			EXPLANATION
Subject	**Form of *Be***	**Complement**	
I	**am**	home a lot.	Use *am* with *I*.
My father	**is**	patient.	Use *is* with *he, she, it, this, that*, and singular subjects (for example, *cat*).
He	**is**	intelligent.	
She	**is**	lonely.	
The cat	**is**	happy.	
That	**is**	a friendly cat.	
We	**are**	responsible.	Use *are* with *we, you, they, these, those*, and plural subjects (*pets, cats*, etc.).
You	**are**	home a lot.	
Pets	**are**	fun.	
Those	**are**	cute kittens.	

Uses

EXAMPLES	USES
I **am** patient. The pet shop **is** located on the corner. The children **are** excited about the puppy.	With a description (adjective) **Note:** Some words that end in *-ed* are adjectives: *tired, married, worried, interested, bored, excited, crowded, located*.
This **is** a Labrador. A Labrador **is** a big dog.	With a classification or definition of the subject
My dog **is** in the yard.	With a location
My husband **is** from Guatemala.	With a place of origin
It **is** cold outside. The dog **is** cold.	With weather and physical reaction to the weather (*hot, cold, warm*)
My dog **is** three (years old).	With age
The cat **is** hungry. I **am** afraid of dogs.	With physical or emotional states: *hungry, thirsty, afraid*
There **are** toys for dogs. There **is** a dog restaurant near my house.	With *there*
It **is** ten o'clock now.	With time
It **is** warm today.	With weather
Language Note: *Be cold* means to feel a low temperature. *Have a cold* shows an illness. Please bring me my sweater. *I'm cold.* I'm sick. *I have a cold.*	

EXERCISE **1** **Fill in the blanks with the correct form of *be*.**

EXAMPLE   My dog _____is_____ very small.

1. You take care of your dog. You _____ responsible.

2. Pet ownership _____ a big responsibility.

3. My cat _____ soft.

4. Dogs _____ great pets because they _____ affectionate.

   They _____ also good protection for a house.

5. My dog _____ a member of my family.

6. Some cats _____ very affectionate. Other cats _____ very

   independent.

7. It _____ fun to own a pet.

8. Kittens and puppies _____ cute.

9. We _____ ready to get a pet.

10. Some people _____ lonely.

11. My kitten _____ very sweet.

12. The dog _____ cold.

1.2 Contractions with *Be*

A *contraction* combines two words. We can make a contraction with *be*. We put an apostrophe (') in place of the missing letter.

EXAMPLES	EXPLANATION
I am **I'm** responsible. You are **You're** patient. She is **She's** happy. He is **He's** kind. It is **It's** necessary to walk a dog. We are **We're** busy. They are **They're** cute.	We can make a contraction with the subject pronoun (*I, you, she*, etc.) and *am, is,* or *are*.
There is **There's** a cat hotel near my house. That is **That's** a friendly cat.	We can make a contraction with *there is*. We can make a contraction with *that is*.
My **grandmother's** lonely. Your **dog's** cute.	We can make a contraction with most nouns and *is*.
A fo<u>x</u> **is** a relative of a dog. A mou<u>se</u> **is** a small animal. Thi<u>s</u> **is** a cute cat.	We don't make a contraction with *is* if the noun ends in *s, se, ce, ge, ze, sh, ch,* or *x*.
Pet **products are** expensive. **Dogs are** popular pets. **There are** hotels for pets.	In writing, don't make a contraction with a plural noun and *are* or with *there are*.
The owner **is not** home now. She **isn't** home during the day. You **are not** ready for a pet. You **aren't** patient.	To make a negative with *be*, put *not* after a form of *be*. The negative contractions are *isn't* and *aren't*. There is no contraction for *am not*.

EXERCISE **2**   **Which of the sentences in Exercise 1 can use a contraction?**

EXERCISE **3**   **Fill in the first blank with the correct form of *be*. Then fill in the second blank with a negative form. Use contractions wherever possible.**

    EXAMPLE   Today's_____ my daughter's birthday. It ___isn't___ a holiday.

      1. My daughter and I _____ at the pet shop. We _____ at home.

      2. My husband _____ at work now. He _____ with me.

      3. I _____ patient. My husband _____ patient.

      4. This puppy _____ for my daughter. It _____ for my son.

      5. My daughter _____ responsible. My son _____ responsible.

                                                             (continued)

6. Dogs _____ good for protection. Cats _____ good for protection.

7. My daughter _____ excited. She _____ bored.

8. I _____ afraid of big dogs. I _____ afraid of small dogs.

9. This _____ a Chihuahua. It _____ a big dog.

EXERCISE **4** **Fill in the blanks.**

EXAMPLE My dog _'s_____ hungry. He wants to eat.

1. My cat _____ near the window.

2. My aunt _____ married. Her dog _____ her favorite
       (not)

companion.

3. In the U.S., there _____ cemeteries for pets.

4. Some cats _____ very affectionate.

5. The dog _____ thirsty. Put water in his dish.

6. This _____ a kitten. It _____ only two weeks _____.

7. Don't leave your dog in the car. _____ hot today.

8. My dog _____ cold in the winter. She needs a sweater.

9. My vet's office _____ located about two miles from my house.

10. _____ is a picture of my dog.

11. I _____ worried about my dog because she _____ sick.

12. Your son _____ responsible because he _____ only four
              (not)

years _____.

Dog Walkers

1. Do working people have problems taking care of their pets?

2. Are some animals easier to take care of than others?

CD 1, TR 02

Read the following conversation. Pay special attention to questions with the verb _be_.

A: Your dog is beautiful. What kind of a dog **is it**?

B: It's a Dalmatian.

A: How old **is he**?

B: It's a _she_. She's two years old.

A: What**'s her name**?

B: Her name is Missy.

A: **Are we** neighbors? **Are you** new in the neighborhood?

B: I don't live here. Missy isn't my dog. I'm a dog walker.

A: A dog walker? What's **that**?

B: I walk other people's dogs when they're at work or on vacation.

A: **Are you** a friend of the family?

B: No. I'm from an agency.

A: What agency **are you** from?

B: It's a professional dog-walking service.

A: **Are you** serious?

B: Of course I'm serious.

A: **Is the pay** good?

B: It's OK. But I love my job for other reasons. My "customers" are always happy to see me. Also, I'm outside all day.

A: Cool! **Are the owners** happy too?

(continued)

B: Yes, they are. When they go to work, they're worried that their dogs can be lonely or bored. Some people even leave the TV on for their pets. But when they use a dog-walking service, they are happy because their dogs are happy too.

A: **Are there** jobs at your agency?

B: Yes, there are. **Are you** interested in becoming a dog walker too?

A: Yes. It sounds like fun.

B: Here's my card. The agency's phone number is on the card.

A: Thanks!

1.3 Questions with *Be*

Compare statement word order and word order in *yes/no* questions.

STATEMENT WORD ORDER	*YES/NO* QUESTION	SHORT ANSWER	EXPLANATION
I am responsible.	**Am I** responsible with pets?	Yes, you are.	In a *yes/no* question, we put *am, is, are* before the subject.
You are a dog walker.	**Are you** a friend of the family?	No, I'm not.	
The owner is busy.	**Is the owner** at home?	No, she isn't.	
The pay is important.	**Is the pay** good?	No, it isn't.	We usually answer a *yes/no* question with a short answer. A short answer contains a pronoun (*he, it, we, they,* etc.).
The dog is a female.	**Is the dog** young?	Yes, she is.	
It is a big dog.	**Is it** a Labrador?	No, it isn't.	
We are new here.	**Are we** neighbors?	No, we aren't.	
The owners are at work.	**Are the owners** happy?	Yes, they are.	
They are out.	**Are they** at work?	Yes, they are.	
There are interesting jobs.	**Are there** jobs at your agency?	Yes, there are.	We don't use a contraction for a short *yes* answer. We usually use a contraction for a short *no* answer.
That is a cute dog.	**Is that** your dog?	No, it isn't.	
It isn't a big dog.	**Isn't it** a puppy?	No, it isn't.	

Pronunciation Note: We usually end a *yes/no* question with rising intonation. Listen to your teacher pronounce the questions above.

Compare statement word order and word order in *wh-* questions.

STATEMENT WORD ORDER	*Wh-* QUESTION	EXPLANATION
I am lost. **You are** from an agency. **That is** a nice dog. **The dog is** old. **That is** a strange pet. **Her name is** long. **You are** here. **There are** a lot of dog walkers.	Where **am I**? What agency **are you** from? What kind of dog **is that**? How old **is the dog**? What **is that**? What **is her name**? Why **are you** here? How many dog walkers **are there**?	We put *am, is,* and *are* before the subject.
The owner isn't home. The dogs **aren't bored**. **You aren't** at work.	Why **isn't the owner** at home? Why **aren't the dogs** bored? Why **aren't you** at work?	Notice the word order in negative *wh-* questions.

Language Notes:
1. Most question words can contract with *is*.
   (Exceptions: *which is; how much is*)
   Who's that?
   What's a Dalmatian?
   Where's your cat?
   Which is bigger, a collie or a Labrador?
2. Study these common questions and answers with *be*.
   What's your name? My name is Linda.
   What time is it? It's 4:32.
   What color is the dog? It's tan.
   What kind of dog is this? It's a Labrador.
   What's a Dalmatian? It's a dog.
   What's this? It's a leash.
   How are you? I'm fine.
   How's the weather? It's sunny and warm.
   How old is your daughter? She's 10 (years old).[4]
   How tall are you? I'm five feet, three inches tall (or 5'3").[5]
   Where are you from? I'm from Mexico.
   What's wrong? I'm sick.

leash

EXERCISE 5 **ABOUT YOU** Interview another student.

EXAMPLE
A: Are you interested in a pet?
B: Yes, I am.

1. Are you home a lot?
2. Are there children in your house?
3. Are they responsible?
4. Are pets allowed where you live?
5. Are you allergic to cats?

[4]It is not polite to ask an American adult about his or her age.
[5]For conversion to the metric system, see Appendix D.

EXERCISE **6** **ABOUT YOU** Interview another student.

EXAMPLE **A:** Is this class hard for you?
B: No, it isn't.

1. Are you an immigrant?
2. Is the teacher from your native country?
3. Is your country in North America?
4. Is your hometown cold at this time of year?
5. Are we from the same country?
6. Are there other students from your country in this class?
7. Is the school located near your house?

EXERCISE **7** One student reads a question. Another student answers.

1. What pets are good for children?
2. What kind of pets are popular in your native country (or with people in your native culture)?
3. What's your favorite animal in the zoo?
4. What's a popular name for dogs in your native culture?
5. When's a good time to get a pet?
6. What's a better pet—a dog or a cat?

EXERCISE **8** Fill in the blanks to complete this conversation. Use contractions wherever possible.

CD 1, TR 03

A: _____ Is this _____ your dog?
           (example)

B: Yes, it _____.
           (1)

A: He _____ beautiful.
           (2)

B: Thanks. But it's a "she."

A: _____ friendly?
     (3)

B: Yes, she _____.
         (4)

A: What kind of dog _____?
           (5)

B: She _____ a collie.
     (6)

A: What _____?
     (7)

B: Her name is Samantha.

A collie

A: _____ ?
(8)

B: She _____ three years old now.
(9)

A: _____ hard to take care of a dog?
(10)

B: Not for me. I _____ home a lot. And when
(11)

I _____ home, my brother or parents
(12 not)

_____ home.
(13)

A: I love dogs, but I _____ home very much, so that's
(14 not)

a problem.

B: Why _____ a lot?
(15)

A: Because I'm a nurse. I work eight hours a day. I want to get a dog for

my grandmother.

B: Why?

A: Because _____ lonely.
(16)

B: Why _____ lonely?
(17)

A: Because nobody _____ home all day.
(18)

We _____ all at work.
(19)

B: I think it _____ a good idea for your grandmother
(20)

to have a dog.

EXERCISE **9** **Fill in the blanks in the following cell phone conversation.**

CD 1, TR 04

A: Hello?

B: Hi. This _____ is _____ Betty.
(example)

A: Hi, Betty. How _____ ?
(1)

B: I'm fine. How _____ ?
(2)

A: I'm fine. But the cat _____ sick.
(3)

I _____ home now.
(4 not)

I _____ at the animal hospital.
(5)

B: _____ wrong?
(6)

(continued)

A: Fluffy _____ hungry or thirsty.
   (7 not)

He _____ tired all the time.
   (8)

B: _____ so hot today. Maybe the heat
   (9)

_____ the problem.
   (10)

A: I don't think so. The house _____ air-conditioned.
   (11)

B: _____?
   (12)

A: He _____ only four years _____.
   (13)   (14)

B: _____ alone?
   (15)

A: No, I'm not.

B: _____ with you?
   (16)

A: My daughter _____ with me.
   (17)

We _____ in the waiting room.
   (18)

B: Why _____ at school?
   (19)

A: She _____ on spring break now. I think
   (20)

the doctor _____ ready to see us now.
   (21)

EXERCISE 10   **Fill in the blanks in the following conversation.**

🔊

CD 1, TR 05

A: Look at the dog. What kind of dog ___**is it**___?
   (example)

B: I think it _____ a mutt.
   (1)

A: What _____ a mutt?
   (2)

B: It _____ a mixed breed dog. Look, it _____
   (3)   (4)

so friendly with those children.

A: My daughter's birthday is next week. She wants a dog. But dogs

_____ so expensive.
   (5)

B: A purebred[6] dog, like a Labrador, is expensive, but a mutt

_____ so expensive. In fact, there _____ animal shelters
   (6 not)   (7)

that can give you a dog for free or for a very low price.

A: What _____ an animal shelter?
   (8)

---

[6]A *purebred* dog is one breed only. It is not mixed with other breeds.

B: It's an organization that takes unwanted pets and tries to find homes for them.

A: But _____ healthy?
(9)

B: Yes, they are. The shelter's doctors check an animal's health before giving it to a family.

A: Why _____ so many unwanted pets?
(10)

B: There are unwanted pets because some people get a pet and then realize it _____ too much trouble to take care of it.
(11)

A: That _____ terrible.
(12)

B: Yes, it is. What about your daughter? _____ responsible?
(13)

A: Yes, she _____.
(14)

B: How old _____?
(15)

A: She _____ ten years old.
(16)

B: My son has a dog. But he _____ responsible. He says it's *his* dog,
(17 not)
but I _____ the one who feeds it and takes it out three times a day.
(18)

A: Why _____ responsible?
(19)

B: He says he _____ too busy with school and sports.
(20)
I _____ busy too. But I find time to take care of the dog.
(21)
What about you? _____ home a lot?
(22)

A: No, I _____. My work day _____ very long. And my
(23)   (24)
daughter _____ at school all day.
(25)

B: Then you should find a dog-walking service.

A: _____ expensive?
(26)

B: Yes, it _____. But _____ the only way to have a happy dog.
(27)   (28)

A: Maybe a fish would be a better pet!

Guide Dogs

1. Do you think most dogs are intelligent? Are some dogs more intelligent than others?

2. Do you ever see blind[7] people walking with dogs?

CD 1, TR 06

Read the following magazine article. Pay special attention to simple present tense verbs.

Most dogs **have** an easy life in the U.S. They **eat, play, get** attention from their owners, and **sleep**. But some dogs **work** hard. They are called guide dogs. Guide dogs **help** blind people move from place to place safely.

Guide dogs and their owners **are** a team. Guide dogs **don't lead** the owners, and their owners **don't** completely **control** the guide dogs. They **work** together. The guide dogs **don't know** where the owners **want** to go, so they **follow** the owners' instructions. The owners can't see the obstacles[8] along the way, so the dogs **make** decisions for the safety of the owners. Guide dogs **stop** at all curbs and intersections before crossing a street. They **don't see** color, so they **don't know** if the light is red or green. The owners **decide** if it **is** time to cross the street by listening to the sound of traffic. The dogs **help** the owners get on a bus or train. They **learn** to obey many verbal commands.

Most guide dogs **are** golden retrievers, Labrador retrievers, or German shepherds. These three breeds **are** very intelligent, obedient,[9] and friendly. A guide dog **needs** to work without distraction in noisy places, bad weather, crowds of people, and difficult situations. When you **see** a guide dog, it **is** important that you recognize that the dog **needs** to concentrate on its job. Don't pet or talk to the dog. Guiding **is** very complicated, and it **requires** a dog's full attention.

Guide dog training **lasts** about five months. Only about 72 percent of dogs that **enter** the training program "**graduate**." Those that **graduate bring** their owners valuable help and love. In other dog training programs, trainers **use**

food as a reward. In guide dog training, the trainer **does not use** food. He or she **uses** physical and verbal affection. This is because a guide dog sometimes **takes** the owner to a restaurant. It must **lie** patiently at the owner's feet without wanting to eat.

Guide dogs **like** to play too, but only after the work **is** finished. How **do** dogs **know** when their work is finished? When the harness **is** on, they **know** they **have to** work. When it **is** off, they can play. Like all dogs, they **love** to play.

[7]A *blind* person cannot see.
[8]An *obstacle* is something that blocks your way. An obstacle creates an unsafe situation.
[9]An *obedient* animal is one that obeys.

1.4 The Simple Present Tense—Affirmative Statements

Form
A simple present tense verb has two forms: the base form and the -s form.[10]

EXAMPLES	EXPLANATION
Subject **Base Form** **Complement** I You We **work** hard. They Guide dogs	We use the base form when the subject is *I*, *you*, *we*, *they*, or a plural noun.
Subject **-s Form** **Complement** He She It **works** hard. The dog	We use the -s form when the subject is *he*, *she*, *it*, or a singular noun.
My family **has** three cats. Everyone in the shelter **likes** animals. No one **wants** the new kittens.	We use the -s form with *family*, *everyone*, *everybody*, *no one*, *nobody*, and *nothing*.
I **have** a pet dog. My friend **has** a guide dog.	*Have* is an irregular verb. have ⟶ has

Use

EXAMPLES	USES
Dogs **give** people love. Guide dogs **help** people. Most dogs **have** an easy life. Americans **love** pets.	With general truths, to show that something is consistently true
Many pet owners **sleep** with their dogs or cats. Some pet owners **buy** presents for their pets. Owners **walk** dogs on a leash.	With customs
He **walks** his dog three times a day. He **feeds** his cat every morning and every night.	To show regular activity (a habit) or repeated action
I **come** from Bosnia. He **comes** from Pakistan.	To show place of origin

[10]For the spelling of the -s form, see Appendix A.

EXERCISE 11 **Fill in the blanks with the base form or the -s form.**

EXAMPLES   Americans ___*love*___ pets.
(love)

My son ___*loves*___ his new kitten.
(love)

1. Most dogs _____ an easy life.
(have)

2. My dog _____ all day.
(sleep)

3. Guide dogs _____ to obey many commands.
(learn)

4. A guide dog _____ safety decisions.
(make)

5. Trainers _____ with a dog for five months.
(work)

6. Most guide dogs _____ from the training program.
(graduate)

7. My girlfriend _____ her dog a present on his birthday.
(give)

8. People _____ affection from animals.
(get)

9. Everyone _____ affection.
(need)

10. It _____ a lot of money to have a pet.
(cost)

11. Some pet owners _____ to their pets on the phone.
(talk)

12. My daughter _____ a puppy for her birthday.
(want)

13. My neighbor's dog _____ all the time.
(bark)

14. Some people _____ with their dogs.
(travel)

15. Thirty-nine percent of Americans _____ at least one dog.
(have)

16. My brother _____ three dogs.
(have)

17. Dogs _____ their owners.
(protect)

18. My family _____ animals.
(love)

19. Nobody _____ the dog's age.
(know)

20. Everybody _____ that puppies and kittens are cute.
(think)

1.5 Negative Statements with the Simple Present Tense

EXAMPLES	EXPLANATION
The owner **knows** the destination. The dog **doesn't know** the destination. The dog **stops** at a curb. It **doesn't stop** because of a red light.	Use *doesn't* + the base form with *he, she, it,* or a singular noun. **Compare:** knows ⟶ doesn't **know** ⠀⠀⠀⠀⠀⠀⠀⠀stops ⟶ doesn't **stop** *Doesn't* is the contraction for *does not.*
Some trainers **use** food to reward a dog. Guide dog trainers **don't use** food. Guide dogs **work** when the harness is on. They **don't work** when the harness is off. You **have** a cat. You **don't have** a dog.	Use *don't* + the base form with *I, you, we, they,* or a plural noun. **Compare:** use ⟶ don't **use** ⠀⠀⠀⠀⠀⠀⠀⠀work ⟶ don't **work** *Don't* is the contraction for *do not.*

Usage Note: American English and British English use different grammar to form the negative of *have*.
Compare:
⠀⠀⠀American: He *doesn't have* a dog.
⠀⠀⠀⠀British: He *hasn't* a dog. OR He *hasn't got* a dog.

EXERCISE 12 ⠀⠀**Fill in the blanks with the negative form of the underlined verb.**

EXAMPLE⠀⠀A guide dog <u>needs</u> a lot of training. A pet dog ___doesn't need___ a lot of training.

1. Most dogs <u>play</u> a lot. Guide dogs _____ a lot.

2. Obedience trainers <u>use</u> food to teach dogs. Guide dog trainers _____ food.

3. A guide dog <u>works</u> hard. A pet dog _____ hard.

4. People <u>see</u> colors. Dogs _____ colors.

5. A guide dog <u>goes</u> on public transportation. A pet dog _____ on public transportation.

6. My cats <u>eat</u> special food. They _____ food from our table.

7. My cats <u>like</u> fish. They _____ chicken.

8. One cat <u>sleeps</u> on my bed. She _____ alone.

9. My landlord <u>allows</u> cats. He _____ dogs.

10. My cats <u>need</u> attention. They _____ a lot of my time.

11. We <u>have</u> cats. We _____ fish.

12. I <u>like</u> cats. My sister _____ cats.

Search and Rescue Dogs

Before You Read

1. Besides helping blind people, do you know of any other ways that dogs work?

2. Do dogs have some qualities that humans don't have?

CD 1, TR 07

Read the following conversation. Pay special attention to questions with the simple present tense.

> **A:** There's a program on TV tonight about search and rescue dogs. **Do** you **want** to watch it with me?
>
> **B:** I know about guide dogs. But I don't know anything about search and rescue dogs. What **does** "search" **mean**? What **does** "rescue" **mean**?
>
> **A:** Search means "look for." Rescue means "to help someone in a dangerous situation." These dogs are called SAR dogs.
>
> **B:** What **do** these dogs **do**?
>
> **A:** When there is a disaster, like an earthquake or a flood, they help the workers find missing people. They save people's lives.
>
> **B:** How **do** they **do** that?
>
> **A:** They have a great sense of smell. They can find things that people can't.
>
> **B:** **Do** they **need** a lot of training?
>
> **A:** I think they need at least one year of training.
>
> **B:** What kind of dogs **do** they **use** as SAR dogs?
>
> **A:** They usually use large, strong dogs. Labrador retrievers or golden retrievers are often SAR dogs. Let's watch the program together tonight.
>
> **B:** What time **does** it **begin**?
>
> **A:** At 9 P.M.
>
> **B:** **Does** your dog **want** to watch the program with us?
>
> **A:** My dog is a lazy, spoiled Chihuahua. She just wants to eat, play, and sleep.

1.6 Questions with the Simple Present Tense

Compare statements and *yes/no* questions.

Do	Subject	Verb	Complement	Short Answer	Explanation
	Guide dogs	need	training.		For *yes/no* questions with *I*, *we*, *you*, *they*, or a plural noun, use:
Do	rescue dogs	need	training?	Yes, they do.	
	You	like	dogs.		*Do* + subject + base form + complement
Do	you	like	cats?	No, I don't.	

Does	Subject	Verb	Complement	Short Answer	Explanation
	Jamie	trains	rescue dogs.		For *yes/no* questions with *he*, *she*, *it*, or a singular subject, use:
Does	Jamie	train	guide dogs?	No, she doesn't.	
	My dog	plays	a lot.		*Does* + subject + base form + complement
Does	a rescue dog	play	a lot?	No, it doesn't.	

Compare statements and *wh-* questions.

Wh- Word	do	Subject	Verb	Complement	Explanation
		Rescue dogs	need	training.	For *wh-* questions with *I*, *we*, *you*, *they*, or a plural noun, use:
How much training	do	they	need?		
		You	prefer	cats.	*Wh-* word + *do* + subject + base form + complement
Why	do	you	prefer	cats?	

Wh- Word	does	Subject	Verb	Complement	Explanation
		The program	begins	soon.	For *wh-* questions with *he*, *she*, *it*, or a singular noun, use:
What time	does	the program	begin?		
		My dog	sleeps	a lot.	*Wh-* word + *does* + subject + base form + complement
Where	does	your dog	sleep?		

Compare negative statements and questions.

Why	don't/doesn't	Subject	Verb	Complement
		I	don't like	cats.
Why	don't	you	like	cats?
		My dog	doesn't sleep	in his bed.
Why	doesn't	he	sleep	in his bed?

Language Note: Compare questions with *be* to other simple present tense questions:
   Is the dog cold? Yes, it **is**.
   Does the dog **have** a sweater? Yes, it **does**.

   Where **is** your dog?
   What kind of dog **do** you **have**?

EXERCISE 13 Fill in the blanks to complete this conversation.

CD 1, TR 08

A: Do you ___like___ animals?
   (example)

B: Yes, I _____. In fact, I love animals very much. I especially like dogs.
   (1)

A: _____ you have a dog?
   (2)

B: No, I _____.
   (3)

A: If you love dogs, why _____ a dog?
   (4 not/have)

B: Because my landlord _____ dogs.
   (5 not/permit)

A: _____ he permit cats?
   (6)

B: Yes, he _____.
   (7)

A: _____ a cat?
   (8 have)

B: Yes, I do. But I _____ to find a new home for my cat.
   (9 need)
   _____ you know anyone who wants a cat?
   (10)

A: Why _____ your cat?
   (11 not/want)

B: I'm getting married in three months, and my girlfriend
   _____ to live with cats.
   (12 not/want)

A: Why _____ to live with cats? Doesn't she
   (13 not/want)
   _____ them?
   (14 like)

B: She _____ them, but she's allergic to them. When she
   (15 like)
   _____ over, she _____ and _____.
   (16 come)   (17 sneeze)   (18 cough)
   She _____ to come over any more.
   (19 not/want)

A: That's a big problem.

EXERCISE 14 **ABOUT YOU** Part 1: Use the words below to interview a student
with a dog.

EXAMPLES your dog/big

A: Is your dog big?
B: Yes, she is.

your dog/sleep a lot (how many hours)

A: Does your dog sleep a lot?
B: Yes, she does.
A: How many hours does she sleep?
B: She sleeps about 15 hours a day.

1. how old/your dog
2. what/your dog's name
3. it/a male or a female
4. what/your dog/eat
5. how often/you/take your dog out
6. your dog/do tricks (what kind)
7. your dog/have toys (what kind)
8. your dog/friendly
9. your dog/bark a lot
10. why/you/like dogs

Part 2: Use the words below to interview a student with a cat.

1. how old/your cat
2. what/your cat's name
3. it/a male or a female
4. your cat/catch mice
5. your cat/friendly
6. your cat/sit on your lap a lot
7. your cat/have toys (what kind)
8. why/you/like cats

1.7 *Wh-* Questions with a Preposition

EXAMPLES	EXPLANATION
What does she talk **about**? She talks about her cats. What does your cat sleep **on**? She sleeps on a pillow.	In conversation, most people put the preposition at the end of the *wh-* question.
Formal: With whom does the dog sleep? **Informal: Who** does the dog sleep **with**?	Putting the preposition before a question word is very formal. When the preposition comes at the beginning, we use *whom*, not *who*.
Where do you **come from**? I come from Mexico. Where **are** you **from**? I'm from Mexico.	For place of origin, you can use *be from* or *come from*.
What time does the program begin? It begins **at** 9 P.M.	Omit *at* in a question about time.

EXERCISE 15 **ABOUT YOU** Ask a *yes/no* question using the words given. Then use the words in parentheses ( ) to ask a *wh-* question whenever possible. Another student will answer.

EXAMPLE you/eat in the cafeteria (with whom) OR (who . . . with)

A: Do you eat in the cafeteria?
B: Yes, I do.
A: Who do you eat with? OR With whom do you eat?
B: I eat with my friends.

1. you/live alone (with whom) OR (who . . . with)
2. you/go to bed early (what time)
3. your teacher/come to class on time (what time)
4. your teacher/come from this city (where . . . from)
5. you/practice English outside of class (with whom) OR (who . . . with)
6. you/think about your future (what else)
7. you/complain about English grammar (what else)
8. you/listen to the radio (what station)
9. your teacher/talk about spelling (what else)
10. you/interested in animals (what animals)
11. you/come from Mexico (where)
12. you/go to sleep before midnight (what time)

EXERCISE 16 **Circle the correct words to complete this conversation.**

CD 1, TR 09

A: We're late. Hurry. The train is ready to leave.

B: Let's go . . . (*on the train*) . . . Why (*that dog is*/(*is that dog*)) on the train?
(*example*)
(*Are/Do*) they allow dogs on trains?
(1)

A: That's not an ordinary dog. That's a guide dog.

B: What's a guide dog?

A: It's a dog that helps people with disabilities.

B: How (*do they help/they help*) people?
(2)

A: They (*help/helps*) blind people move from place to place, on foot and
(3)
by public transportation.

B: (*Are/Do*) they need special training?
(4)

A: Yes, they (*are/do*).
(5)

B: Where (*do/are*) they get their training?
(6)

A: They get their training at special schools.

B: Are they only for blind people?

A: No. Guide dogs help people with other disabilities too. There are guide dogs for the deaf[11] and for people in wheelchairs.

B: Why (*are you/you are*) such an expert on guide dogs?
(7)

A: My cousin is blind. He has a guide dog.

B: Let's play with the dog.

A: No. (*It's not/It doesn't*) good to distract a guide dog. A guide dog
(8)
(*need/needs*) to concentrate.
(9)

B: When (*are/do*) they play?
(10)

A: They (*play/plays*) when the owner (*takes/take*) off the dog's harness.
(11)   (12)

B: What (*do/does*) they eat?
(13)

A: They eat the same thing other dogs eat.

B: It's amazing what a dog can do.

1.8 Questions About Meaning, Spelling, Cost, and Time

Wh- Word	Do/ Does	Subject	Verb (Base Form)	Complement	Explanation
What	does	"kitten"	mean?		*Mean, spell, say,* and *cost* are verbs and should be in the verb position of a question. Use the base form in the question.
How	do	you	spell	"kitten"?	
How	do	you	say	"kitten" in Spanish?	
How much	does	a kitten	cost?		
How long	does	it	take	to train a dog?	We use the verb *take* with time. The subject is *it*.

[11]A *deaf* person cannot hear.

EXERCISE 17 **Fill in the blanks to complete the conversation.**

CD 1, TR 10

A: _____*Do you have*_____ a pet?
(example)

B: Yes. I have a new kitten.

A: I don't know the word "kitten." What _____?
(1)

B: Kitten means "baby cat."

A: Oh. What's his name?

B: Romeo.

A: How _____?
(2)

B: R-O-M-E-O.

A: Where _____?
(3)

B: He sleeps with me, of course. _____ any pets?
(4)

A: Yes, I do.

B: What kind of pet _____?
(5)

A: I have a bird that talks. I don't know the word in English.

How _____ "loro" in English?
(6)

B: Parrot. So you have a parrot. What _____?
(7)

A: His name is Chico.

B: How old _____?
(8)

A: He's almost 20 years old.

B: Wow! How long _____?
(9)

A: They live a long time. Some live up to 80 years.

B: Are parrots expensive? How much _____?
(10)

A: It depends on what kind you get. But they usually cost between $175 and $1,000.

B: _____ parrots affectionate?
(11)

A: Oh, yes. They're very affectionate. Chico sits on my shoulder all the time.

B: What _____?
(12)

A: He eats fruit, vegetables, rice, nuts, and seeds.

B: _____?
(13)

A: Yes. He talks a lot.

B: What _____(14)_____?

A: He says, "Good-bye," "Hello," "I love you," and many more things. He speaks Spanish and English.

B: Maybe he speaks English better than we do!

EXERCISE 18 **Fill in the blanks to complete the conversation.**

🔊
CD 1, TR 11

A: I know you love dogs. _____Do you have_____ a dog now?
(example)

B: No, I _____(1)_____. But I have two cats. I don't have time for a dog.

A: Why _____(2)_____ time for a dog?

B: Because I'm not at home very much.

A: Why _____(3)_____?

B: Because I work eight hours a day, and at night, I take classes. Dogs need a lot of attention. I _____(4)_____ have enough time right now.

A: What about your cats? _____(5)_____ need attention too?

B: Not as much as dogs. What about you? _____(6)_____ any pets?

A: I have several tropical fish.[12]

B: _____(7)_____ expensive?

A: Some of them are very expensive.

B: How much _____(8)_____?

A: Some of them cost more than $100.

B: Wow! That's a lot of money for a boring pet.

A: Fish _____(9)_____ boring. It _____(10)_____ fun to look at them. And when I go to work, they _____(11)_____ get lonely, like dogs and cats.

B: Yes, but they _____(12)_____ affectionate like dogs and cats.

---

[12]*Fish can be singular or plural. In this case, fish is plural.*

(continued)

A: They _____ make noise like dogs do, so neighbors never
    (13)
complain about fish.

B: How many fish _____?
                          (14)

A: I have about 14 or 15. My favorite is my Oranda.

B: How _____ "Oranda"?
              (15)

A: O-R-A-N-D-A. It's a kind of a goldfish. When you have time, come and
see my fish tank.

Marianne and Sparky

Before You Read

1. Do people in your native culture treat pets the same way Americans do?

2. What kinds of animals or pets do people prefer in your native culture?

CD 1, TR 12

Read the following e-mail from Elena in the U.S. to her friend Sofia in Russia. Pay special attention to frequency words.

To: sofia1980@e*mail.com

Subject: American pets

Dear Sofia,

I want to tell you about one aspect of American life that seems strange to me—how Americans treat their pets. I have a new American friend, Marianne. She lives alone, but she has a dog, Sparky. Marianne treats him like a child. She **always** carries a picture of Sparky in her wallet. She **often** buys toys for him, especially on his birthday. She **often** calls him on the telephone when she's not home and talks into the answering machine. Sparky **always** sleeps in bed with her.

When she goes to work, she uses a dog-walking service. **Twice a day**, someone comes to her house to play with Sparky and take him for a walk. She says that he gets lonely if he's home alone all day. She **always** leaves the TV on when she goes to work to keep Sparky entertained.

Once a month, she takes him to a dog groomer. The groomer gives him a bath and cuts and paints his nails. When she travels, she **usually** takes him with her, but **sometimes** she puts him in a kennel[13] or pet hotel. All of these dog services cost a lot of money. But Marianne doesn't care. Nothing is too expensive when it comes to Sparky.

There's a small beach near her house that is just for dogs and their owners. She takes Sparky there **whenever** the weather is nice so that he can play with other dogs. While the dogs play together, the dog owners talk to each other. She **always** cleans up after her dog.

In winter, she **always** puts a coat on Sparky. In fact, Sparky has about four different winter coats. **Whenever** it rains, Sparky wears his bright yellow raincoat.

Sometimes I think American dogs live better than most people in the world.

Your good friend,

Elena

1.9 Simple Present Tense with Frequency Words

EXAMPLES	EXPLANATION
Marianne **often** calls her dog on the phone. Sparky **always** sleeps in bed with her. When she travels, she **usually** takes Sparky with her.	We use the simple present tense with frequency words to show a regular activity. Frequency words are: *always, usually, often, sometimes, rarely, seldom, hardly ever,* and *never.*
Whenever the weather is nice, she takes her dog to the beach. Sparky wears a raincoat **whenever** it rains.	*Whenever* shows a regular activity. It means "any time."
Once a month, she takes her dog to a groomer. Someone comes to her house to walk the dog **twice a day**.	Expressions that show frequency are: • every day (week, month, year) • every other day (week, month, year) • once (twice, etc.) a day (week, month, year) • from time to time • once in a while
Frequency Words	always 100% usually/generally often/frequently sometimes/occasionally rarely/seldom/hardly ever never/not ever 0%

[13]A *kennel* is a place where pets are kept while their owners are away.

EXERCISE 19   **Fill in the blanks with an appropriate verb. Answers may vary.**

EXAMPLE   Marianne always ____puts____ a coat on Sparky when the weather is cold.

1. Elena sometimes _____ a letter to her friend Sofia.
2. Marianne _____ always worried about her dog.
3. The dog _____ always happy to see Marianne when she comes home.
4. Marianne often _____ toys for her dog.
5. The TV _____ always on when Marianne is at work.
6. Sparky always _____ in bed with Marianne.
7. Marianne usually _____ with her dog when she goes on vacation.

EXERCISE 20   **ABOUT YOU**   **Fill in the blanks with an appropriate frequency word.**

EXAMPLE   I ____rarely____ use a public telephone.

1. I _____ say, "How are you?" when I meet a friend.
2. I'm _____ confused about American customs.
3. I _____ smile when I pass someone I know.
4. I _____ shake hands when I get together with a friend.
5. Americans _____ ask me, "What country are you from?"
6. I _____ celebrate my birthday in a restaurant.
7. I _____ buy birthday presents for my good friends.
8. If I invite a friend to a restaurant, I _____ pay for both of us.
9. I _____ take my cell phone with me.
10. I _____ eat in fast-food restaurants.
11. I _____ leave my computer on overnight.

EXERCISE 21   **ABOUT YOU**   **Fill in the blanks with an appropriate frequency word. You may find a partner and compare your answers.**

EXAMPLE   People in my native culture ____rarely____ have cats in the house.

1. Dogs in my native culture _____ sleep with their owners.
2. Dogs in my native culture are _____ part of the family.
3. Cats in my native culture are _____ part of the family.
4. People in my native culture _____ feed pet food to cats and dogs.
5. People in my native culture _____ travel with their pets.

EXERCISE **22** In the sentences in Exercise 21, notice if the frequency word comes before or after the verb. Write *B* for *before* or *A* for *after*.

EXAMPLE   People in my native culture ____*rarely*____ have cats in the house. **B**

1.10 Position of Frequency Words and Expressions

EXAMPLES	EXPLANATION
Verb Sparky *is* **always** happy to see Marianne. **Verb** The TV *is* **always** on in the day. **Verb** Marianne *is* **rarely** home during the day.	The frequency word comes **after** the verb *be*.
Verb Marianne **often** *calls* Sparky on the phone. **Verb** She **usually** *travels* with Sparky. **Verb** She **always** *carries* a picture of Sparky.	The frequency word comes **before** other verbs.
Sometimes she puts Sparky in a kennel. **Usually** she feeds Sparky dog food. **Often** Elena writes to her friend about American customs.	*Sometimes, usually,* and *often* can come at the beginning of the sentence too. Do not put *always, never, rarely,* and *seldom* before the subject. *Wrong: Always* she carries a picture of her dog.
Once a month, she travels. She travels **once a month**. **Every week**, she goes to the beach. She goes to the beach **every week**.	A frequency expression can come at the beginning or at the end of a sentence. When it comes at the beginning of the sentence, we sometimes separate it from the sentence with a comma.

EXERCISE **23** Rewrite the sentence, adding the word in ( ).

EXAMPLE   Marianne carries a picture of Sparky. (always)

Marianne always *carries* a picture of Sparky.

1. She talks to Sparky on the telephone. (often)

_____

2. She puts Sparky in a pet hotel. (sometimes)

_____

(continued)

3. She takes her dog on vacation. (usually)

_____

4. She's with her dog. (always)

_____

5. Sparky goes out in the rain without a coat. (never)

_____

EXERCISE 24   **ABOUT YOU** Add a frequency word to each sentence to make a true statement about yourself.

EXAMPLE   I drink coffee at night.
I never drink coffee at night.

1. I talk to my neighbors.

2. I study in the public library.

3. I'm busy on Saturdays.

4. I receive e-mail from my friends.

5. I call my family in my native country.

6. I travel in the summer.

7. I speak English at home with my family.

8. I eat meat for dinner.

9. I go out of town.

10. I study in the library.

11. I eat cereal for breakfast.

12. I bring my dictionary to class.

EXERCISE 25   **ABOUT YOU** Add a verb (phrase) to make a true statement about yourself.

EXAMPLE   I/usually

I usually _drink coffee in the morning._   OR _____

I'm usually _afraid to go out at night._ _____

1. I/rarely/on Sunday

_____

2. I/usually/on the weekend

_____

3. I/hardly ever

_____

4. I/sometimes/at night

_____

5. my family/sometimes

_____

6. my family/rarely

_____

1.11 Questions with *Ever*

We use *ever* in a question when we want an answer that has a frequency word.

Do/Does	Subject	*Ever*	Verb	Complement	Short Answer
Do Does	you the teacher	**ever** **ever**	sleep bring	with your cat? her dog to school?	Yes, I **sometimes** do. No, she **never** does.

Be	Subject	*Ever*		Complement	Short Answer
Are Is	dogs Marianne	**ever** **ever**		unhappy? home during the day?	Yes, they **sometimes** are. No, she **never** is.

Language Notes:
1. In a short answer, the frequency word comes between the subject and the verb.
2. The verb after *never* is affirmative.
   Does your cat ever drink milk?
   No, she never **does.**

EXERCISE 26 **Answer the questions with a short answer and the frequency word in parentheses ( ).**

EXAMPLE Do dogs ever bark? (sometimes)
Yes, they sometimes do.

1. Does Marianne ever sleep with her dog? (always)

2. Does Marianne ever travel? (often)

3. Do fish ever make noise? (never)

4. Do birds ever make noise? (always)

5. Do parrots ever live for more than 20 years? (usually)

6. Do dogs ever live for more than 20 years? (rarely)

7. Are parrots ever affectionate? (sometimes)

8. Are cats ever lazy? (usually)

EXERCISE 27 **ABOUT YOU** Fill in the blanks with a frequency word to make a true statement about yourself. Then ask a question with *ever*. Another student will answer.

EXAMPLE   I ___rarely___ eat breakfast in a restaurant.

A: Do you ever eat breakfast in a restaurant?
B: No, I never do.

1. I _____ sleep with the light on.
2. I _____ watch TV in the morning.
3. I _____ cry during a sad movie.
4. I _____ dream in English.
5. I _____ take off my shoes when I enter my house.
6. I _____ wear a watch.
7. I _____ use cologne or perfume.
8. I _____ fall asleep with the TV on.
9. I _____ carry an MP3 player.
10. I _____ discuss politics with my friends.
11. I _____ wear sandals in warm weather.
12. I'm _____ friendly with my neighbors.

1.12 Questions with *How Often* and Answers with Frequency Expressions

EXAMPLES	EXPLANATION

How often do you take your dog out?
    I take her out **three times a day**.
 How often does Marianne travel?
    She travels **every other month**.
 How often do you take your cat to the doctor?
    I take my cat to the doctor **twice a year**.
	We use *how often* when we want to know about the frequency of an activity.

EXERCISE 28 **ABOUT YOU** Ask a question with *"How often do you* . . . ?" and the words given. Another student will answer.

EXAMPLE eat in a restaurant

A: How often do you eat in a restaurant?
B: I eat in a restaurant once a week.

1. check your e-mail
2. shop for groceries
3. exercise
4. get a haircut
5. use your dictionary

6. use public transportation
7. use the Internet
8. go to the dentist
9. watch the news on TV
10. go to the teacher's office

Summary of Lesson 1

1. Observe the simple present tense with the verb *be*.
     Your dog **is** beautiful.
     It **isn't** big.
     Is it a collie? No, it **isn't**.
     What kind of dog **is** it?

     You **are** young.
     You **aren't** ready for a dog.
     Are you responsible? Yes, I **am**.
     Why **aren't** you ready for a dog?

2. Observe the simple present tense with other verbs.

Base Form	-s Form
My friends **have** a dog.	She **likes** birds.
They **don't have** a cat.	She **doesn't like** cats.
Do they **have** a bird?	**Does** she **like** small birds?
No, they **don't**.	Yes, she **does**.
What kind of dog **do** they **have**?	Why **does** she **like** birds?
Why **don't** they **have** a cat?	Why **doesn't** she **like** cats?

3. Frequency words:

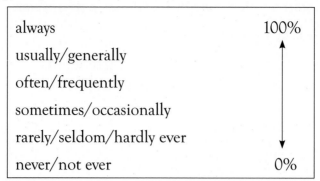

always	100%
usually/generally	
often/frequently	
sometimes/occasionally	
rarely/seldom/hardly ever	
never/not ever	0%

4. Questions with frequency words:
Does he **ever** take his dog to the park? Yes, he often does.
How often does he feed his dog? Twice a day.

Editing Advice

1. Don't use *have* with age. Don't use *years* without *old*.

My daughter ~~has~~ 10 years. (is ... old)

2. Don't use *have* with *hungry, thirsty, hot, cold,* or *afraid.*

Please open the window. I ~~have~~ hot. (am)

3. Don't forget the verb *be*. Remember that some words that end in *-ed* are adjectives, not verbs.

The college located downtown. (is)
I very tired. (am)

4. Use the correct word order in questions.

Why ~~you are~~ late? (are you)
Why ~~your sister doesn't~~ drive? (doesn't your sister)

5. Don't use *be* with another present tense verb.

I'~~m~~ come from Poland.

We'~~re~~ have a new computer.

6. Use the *-s* form when the subject is *he, she, it, everyone,* or *family.*

My father live in New York. *(s)*

Everyone know the answer. *(s)*

My family live in Egypt. *(s)*

7. Use *doesn't* when the subject is *he, she, it,* or *family.*

He ~~don't~~ *doesn't* have a car.

My family ~~don't~~ *doesn't* live here.

8. Use the base form after *does.*

He doesn't speaks English.

Where does he lives?

9. Don't forget to use *do* or *does* and the base form in the question.

Where *does* your father works?

10. Use normal question formation for *spell, mean, cost,* and *take.*

What ~~means "custom"~~ *does "custom" mean*?

How *do you* spell "responsible"?

How much ~~costs~~ *does* the newspaper *cost*?

How long *does* it takes to do the exercise?

11. Use the correct word order with frequency words.

He ~~goes sometimes~~ *sometimes goes* to the zoo.

~~Never I~~ *I never* eat in a restaurant.

I ~~never am~~ *am never* late to class.

12. Don't put a frequency phrase between the subject and the verb.

She ~~all the time~~ talks on the phone *all the time*.

Editing Quiz

Some of the shaded words and phrases have mistakes. Find the mistakes and correct them. If the shaded words are correct, write _C_.

       _C_

A: Is that your dog?
  (example)

B: Yes. His name is Buddy.

      _do_

A: How ^ you spell "Buddy"?
  (example)

B: B-U-D-D-Y. He's a therapy dog.

A: What a therapy dog does?
           _(1)_

B: He make sick people feel better. We're often go to hospitals to visit sick
     _(2)_   _(3)_

people. He's sits on their laps and they pet him.
       _(4)_   _(5)_

A: How that makes sick people feel better?
      _(6)_

B: They feel happy when they're with a nice dog. Everyone love
     _(7)_   _(8)_

Buddy—the patients, the nurses, the doctors. He's very popular.

Patients smile usually when they're with Buddy.
       _(9)_

A: How does a dog becomes a therapy dog?
      _(10)_

B: Not every dog is good for this job. First we has to answer a few
                               _(11)_

questions like these:

- Does he like people? (Buddy loves people.)
   _(12)_   _(13)_

- Does he has a calm personality? (Buddy doesn't barks.)
   _(14)_   _(15)_

- Is the dog at least one year old? (Buddy has six years.)
                        _(16)_

Then the dog needs training. And he have to pass a test.
       _(17)_   _(18)_

A: What kind of test does he have to pass?
         _(19)_

B: He has to come when I call him. He has to follow commands, like "sit"

and "stay." And a lot of other things too.

A: How much cost the training?
        _(20)_

B: It costs $10 to register the dog. Then he gets a certificate.
   _(21)_   _(22)_

A: How long it takes to train the dog?
       _(23)_

B: That depend on the dog.
     _(24)_

A: Are the dog owners make money?
(25)

B: No. We work as volunteers.
(26)

A: How often do you visit the hospital with Buddy?
(27)

B: We once a week go to the hospital. The hospital located a few blocks
(28)   (29)

from my house. Always I bathe him and brush him before we go.
(30)

If you want more information, go to www.tdi-dog.org.

A: What means TDI?
(31)

B: It means Therapy Dogs International. I have to go now. Buddy needs
(32)   (33)

water. He has thirsty.
(34)

A: How you know that?
(35)

B: His tongue is out. That's dog talk for "I thirsty."
(36)

Lesson 1 Test/Review

PART 1 Fill in the blanks with the affirmative form of the verb in parentheses ( ). Then write the negative form of the verb.

EXAMPLES Elena ___wants___ to write about strange American customs.
(want)

She ___doesn't want___ to write about the weather.

1. Marianne _____ Elena.
(know)

She _____ Sofia.

2. Marianne _____ a dog.
(have)

Elena _____ a dog.

3. Elena _____ in the U.S.
(live)

Sofia _____ in the U.S.

4. Marianne _____ American.
(be)

Elena _____ American.

(continued)

5. You _____ some American customs.
(understand)

You _____ all American customs.

6. American customs _____ strange for Elena.
(be)

American customs _____ strange for Marianne.

7. I _____ cats.
(like)

I _____ dogs.

8. Dogs _____ a lot of attention.
(need)

Cats _____ as much attention.

9. Almost everyone _____ kittens and puppies.
(love)

Most people _____ snakes.

PART 2 **Read each statement. Then write a *yes/no* question about the words in parentheses ( ). Write a short answer.**

EXAMPLE   Elena lives in the U.S. (Marianne) (yes)

Does Marianne live in the U.S.? Yes, she does.

1. Marianne has a dog. (Elena) (no)

_____

2. Elena and Marianne live in the U.S. (Sofia) (no)

_____

3. Elena has an American friend. (Sofia) (no)

_____

4. Elena often writes letters. (you/ever) [Give a true answer about yourself.]

_____

5. You like animals. (you/ever/go to the zoo) [Give a true answer about yourself.]

_____

6. American customs are strange for Elena. (for Marianne) (no)

_____

PART 3

Fill in the blanks to complete the question.

EXAMPLE Dogs like people.

Why   *do dogs like people?*

1. Marianne sometimes travels with her dog.

   How _____ with her dog?

2. Sofia doesn't understand American customs.

   Why _____ American customs?

3. Elena writes to Sofia once a week.

   How often _____ to Elena?

4. A dog-walking service costs a lot of money.

   How much _____?

5. Elena doesn't have a dog.

   Why _____ a dog?

6. Marianne carries a picture of Sparky in her wallet.

   Why _____ in her wallet?

7. Marianne walks her dog every day.

   How often _____?

8. She takes her dog to the animal hospital.

   How often _____ to the animal hospital?

9. Guide dogs need a lot of training.

   Why _____ a lot of training?

10. Rescue dogs save people's lives.

    How _____ people's lives?

11. A purebred dog costs a lot of money.

    How much _____?

PART 4 **Write a question with the words given.**

EXAMPLE What/a dog/eat

**What does a dog eat?**

1. How/spell/"kitten"

   _____

2. What/ "puppy"/mean

   _____

(continued)

3. How/say/"cat" in Spanish

_____

4. How much/cost/a parrot

_____

5. How long/take/to train a dog

_____

Expansion

Classroom Activities

❶ **Put a check (✓) to indicate which of the following customs are typical customs in the U.S. and which are typical customs in your native culture. Discuss your answers in a small group or with the entire class.**

Customs	In the U.S.	In my native culture
People walk their dogs on a leash.	✓	
Dogs have jackets and other clothes.		
Supermarkets sell a lot of pet food.		
Students wear jeans to class.		
Students write in their textbooks.		
People talk a lot about politics.		
Children watch TV a lot.		
Friends get together in coffee houses.		
People eat some foods with their hands.		
People are friendly with their neighbors.		
People say, "How are you?"		
Teenagers text a lot.		
People wear gym shoes.		
People take off their shoes when they enter a house.		
Young adults live separately from their parents.		
People usually leave a tip in a restaurant.		
Students study a foreign language.		

2 Work with a partner or in a small group. Tell if you think each animal is a good pet. Why or why not?

a. a snake

e. a turtle

b. a parakeet

f. a hamster

g. a cat

c. a rabbit

h. a dog

d. a lizard

i. a tropical fish

Talk About It

1 Do you or any of your friends or family members have a pet? Is the pet like a member of the family?

2 The following proverbs mention animals. Discuss the meaning of each proverb. Do you have a similar proverb in your native language?

a. You can't teach an old dog new tricks.

b. When the cat's away, the mice will play.

c. Man's best friend is his dog.

d. Curiosity killed the cat.

e. The dog's bark is worse than his bite.

3 Why do you think pets can improve the lives of sick or elderly people?

4 Do you think some dogs are more intelligent than others? Do you think some dogs have a better temperament than others?

Write

About It

❶ Write about differences in how people treat pets in the U.S. and in another country you know about.

❷ Write about American customs that seem strange to you. Compare these customs to how people behave in your country or native culture.

> ### A Strange American Custom
>
> There is one American custom that seems strange to me. Americans always seem so cheerful. When they meet you, they always smile. When they leave you, they often say, "Have a nice day." In my country, Ukraine, people say hello but don't usually smile...

 For more practice using grammar in context, please visit our Web site.

Grammar
The Present Continuous Tense[1]

Action and Nonaction Verbs

The Future Tense

Context
Getting Older

[1]Some textbooks refer to this tense as the *present progressive tense*.

Retirement Living

1. What observations do you make about older people in the U.S.?

2. What is the retirement age in other countries? Do older people usually have a good life?

CD 1, TR 13

As the U.S. population ages, many building developers are building homes for people over 55. Read the following conversation between a 62-year-old man, Jack (J), who is taking a tour of a retirement village, and the manager of the retirement village (M). Pay special attention to present continuous tense verbs.

J: I'm **thinking** about moving to this retirement village. Can you give me some information?

M: This is a village for people over 55 years old. The people here are retired, but most are very active. There are different types of housing: single family homes, townhouses,[2] and apartments. For those who need more help, we also have an assisted-living section. Let me give you a tour. This is our fitness center. It has state-of-the-art equipment.[3]

J: What **are** these people **doing**?

M: They'**re doing** yoga. And that group over there **is lifting** weights. Another group **is doing** aerobics. Let's move on to the game room. Those people **are playing** chess. And that group **is playing** cards. Now let me take you to the pool area. In this area, people **are swimming** laps.[4]

J: What **are** those people **doing**?

M: Those people **are taking** a water aerobics class. Let's go to the computer room now. That's the computer teacher. He'**s teaching** that group how to design Web pages. Jerry, over there, **is putting** all his family pictures

[2]A *townhouse* is one of a series of houses attached to each other in a row.
[3]*State-of-the-art* equipment is the latest equipment.
[4]Swimming *laps* means swimming from one end of the pool to the other and back again, over and over.

on his Web site. Marge, in the corner, **is designing** a Web site with her vacation pictures and stories about her interesting trips. She likes to travel all over the world. Now let's look at the dance area.

J: The band **is playing** a great song, and many of the people **are dancing**. This place is beautiful and certainly offers a lot of activities. But I don't know if it's right for me. I don't know how to dance, play chess, or design Web pages.

M: Don't worry. There are instructors here who will help you.

J: **Is** everybody **doing** something?

M: No. My wife is at home now. I think she**'s reading** or **watching** TV. Or maybe she**'s playing** with our grandchildren.

J: I notice that there are more women than men here.

M: Well, as you know, women live longer than men.

J: I'm a widower, you know. Maybe I can meet a woman here.

M: That's entirely possible. We have a singles group that meets once a week in the game room. Mary Dodge can give you information about the singles group. She**'s standing** over there. She**'s wearing** blue jeans and a red T-shirt.

J: How much does it cost to live here?

M: That depends on what kind of a house you choose. Come to my office and we'll look at the costs.

2.1 Present Continuous Tense

To form the present continuous tense, use a form of *be* (*is, am, are*) + verb *-ing*.[5]

Forms

EXAMPLES	EXPLANATION
Subj. **Be** **Verb + -*ing*** **Complement** I **am** **putting** my pictures on a Web site. Jack **is** **visiting** a retirement village. She **is** **teaching** Web design. They **are** **doing** yoga.	I → am He/She/It → is Singular Subject → is } + verb *-ing* We/You/They → are Plural Subject → are
They're playing cards. **Jack's** taking a tour of the retirement village. **He's** asking questions. The **manager's** answering his questions.	We can make a contraction with the subject pronoun and a form of *be*. Most nouns can also contract with *is*.[6]

Jack **isn't** doing yoga.
Most people **aren't** watching TV.
I'm not playing tennis.
	To form the negative, put *not* after the verb *am/is/are*.
	Negative contractions:
	  is not = isn't
	  are not = aren't
	There is no contraction for *am not*.

Jerry **is designing** a Web site *and* **putting** his family pictures on it.
They **are playing** cards *and* **laughing**.
She**'s reading** *or* **watching** TV.
	Do not repeat the *be* verb after these connectors:
	  and
	  or

Use

EXAMPLES	EXPLANATION
a. Some people **are dancing** now. b. My wife **is reading** now.	In sentences (a) and (b), we use the present continuous tense to describe an action in progress at this moment.
c. Mary Dodge **is standing** over there. d. She **is wearing** jeans. e. A man **is sitting** in front of a computer.	In sentences (c), (d), and (e), we use the present continuous tense to describe a state or condition, using the following verbs: *sit, stand, wear,* and *sleep*. We can observe these things now.

[5]For a review of the spelling of the *-ing* form of the verb, see Appendix A.
[6]See Lesson 1, page 5 for exceptions.

EXERCISE 1   **Fill in the blanks with the present continuous form of the verb in parentheses ( ). Use correct spelling.**

EXAMPLE   Jack _**'s visiting**_____ a retirement village.

(visit)

1. He _____ a tour.

(take)

2. He _____ at the different activities.

(look)

3. The manager of the village _____ him information.

(give)

4. Some people _____.

(dance)

5. Some people _____ the exercise equipment.

(use)

6. One woman _____ weights.

(lift)

7. Those people _____ chess.

(play)

8. Some people _____.

(swim)

9. Jerry _____. He _____

(not/read)   (put)

   his family pictures on his Web site.

10. The manager's wife is at home. She _____ or

(read)

   _____ TV. She _____ an

(watch)   (not/take)

   aerobics class.

11. Some people _____ anything.

(not/do)

EXERCISE 2   **Fill in the blanks with an affirmative or negative verb to make a true statement about what is happening now.**

EXAMPLES   I _**'m wearing**_____ jeans now.

(wear)

The teacher _____ **isn't writing** _____ on the blackboard now.

(write)

1. The sun _____ now.

(shine)

2. It _____ now.

(rain)

3. I _____ my answers in my book.

(write)

(continued)

4. I _____ a pencil to write this exercise.
(use)

5. We _____ this exercise together.
(do)

6. The teacher _____ the students with this exercise.
(help)

7. The teacher _____ a watch.
(wear)

8. I _____ my dictionary now.
(use)

9. We _____ possessive forms now.
(practice)

10. I _____ jeans.
(wear)

11. The teacher _____ .
(stand)

12. I _____ near the door.
(sit)

Life After Retirement

Before You Read

1. Is anyone in your family retired? How does that person keep busy?

2. At what age do you think people should retire?

CD 1, TR 14

Read the following magazine article. Pay special attention to present continuous tense verbs.

The U.S. population **is aging**. More and more Americans **are thinking** about retirement. But today, many people **are retiring** younger and healthier than ever before. People **are living** longer. But they **are not leaving** their jobs to spend their days at the beach or to babysit for their grandchildren. Most older people prefer to keep busy. Many healthy seniors **are starting** new careers. They want to explore new avenues in their lives.

Judy Pearlman is a 62-year-old retired school teacher from Chicago. After 35 years in education, she **is starting** a new career—making dolls. "Now I have time to do what I always dreamed about," she says. "I'm **having** more fun than ever before. I'm **meeting** new people, **traveling** in my new job, and **earning** money all at the same time. And I'm still **getting** my teacher pension. I'm **enjoying** every minute of it. I think this is the best time of my life."

"After 33 years as an accountant, I'm now **taking** art classes," says Charles Haskell of Cleveland. "I'm **discovering** a new talent."

Some senior citizens decide not to retire at all. Frank Babbit of Milwaukee is a carpenter. He has his own business and works 50 hours a week. And he's almost 88 years old.

Many older women **are returning** to work after raising their children. "My kids are grown and don't need me now," says Miriam Orland of San Francisco. "So I have time for myself now. I'm **taking** courses at a community college. I'm **thinking** about a career in Web design."

Some retirees **are using** their free time to volunteer. "I retired as an accountant six months ago, and now I volunteer as a math tutor in a public library near my house. I go to the library twice a week to help students who **are having** trouble with math," says Ron Meyers of Miami. "I work in a food pantry and feed the homeless three times a week," says Linda Carlson of Washington, D.C. "It gives me a lot of satisfaction."

Today healthy retirees **are exploring** many options, from relaxing to starting a new business or making a hobby into a new career. How do you see yourself as a retiree?

2.2 Using the Present Continuous for Longer Actions

EXAMPLES	EXPLANATION
Judy **is meeting** new people. She **is getting** her pension and **earning** money from her new job. She is **enjoying** her new career. My grandfather **is planning** to retire soon.	We use the present continuous tense to show a long-term action that is in progress. It may not be happening at this exact moment.
More and more retired Americans **are looking** for a second career. Some older people **are working** because of economic necessity. Americans **are living** longer. Many older women **are returning** to work after their children are grown.	We use the present continuous tense to describe a *trend*. A trend is a behavior that many people in society are doing at this time. It describes a change in behavior from an earlier time.

EXERCISE 3 Fill in the blanks with an appropriate present continuous tense verb. Answers may vary.

EXAMPLE More and more older people _____*are working*_____ these days.

1. Many people _____ at a younger age.

2. They _____ their time at the beach or babysitting for
   (not)
   their grandchildren.

3. They _____ new careers.

4. People _____ longer and healthier lives.

5. Some people _____ new talents and abilities.

6. Some older women _____ to work after raising a family.

EXERCISE 4 **ABOUT YOU** Write three sentences about being a student. Tell what is happening in your life as a student. You may share your sentences with the class.

EXAMPLES *I'm taking five courses this semester.*

I'm staying with my sister this semester.

I'm majoring in math.

You may use these verbs:

learn	*study*
stay	*live*
plan	*take courses*
major	*improve*

1. _____

2. _____

3. _____

EXERCISE 5 **ABOUT YOU** Write three sentences to tell about current changes in your life. Then find a partner and compare your sentences to your partner's.

EXAMPLES   I'm gaining weight.

I'm planning to buy a house.

My English pronunciation is improving.

You may use the following verbs:

plan	get (become)
grow	learn
gain	improve
lose	think about
start	change

1. _____

2. _____

3. _____

EXERCISE 6 Tell if these things are happening at this point in time in the U.S., in the world, or in another country you know about. Discuss your answers.

1. Older people are getting more respect than before.
2. People are living healthier lives.
3. People are living longer.
4. The world is becoming a more dangerous place.
5. The economy is getting better.
6. Medical science is advancing quickly.
7. A lot of people are losing their jobs.
8. People are working harder than before.
9. People are doing more and enjoying less.
10. The cost of a college education is going down.
11. The cost of computers is going down.
12. More and more people are using cell phones.
13. Cars are getting bigger.
14. Kids are growing up faster than before.

2.3 Questions with the Present Continuous Tense

Compare affirmative statements and questions.

Wh- Word	Be	Subject	Be	Verb + -ing	Complement	Short Answer
		Jerry	is	designing	something.	
	Is	he		designing	a house?	No, he **isn't**.
What	is	he		designing?		A Web site.
		They	are	taking	courses at college.	
	Are	they		taking	biology?	No, they **aren't**.
What courses	are	they		taking?		Computer courses.
		He	is	thinking	about a new career.	
	Is	he		thinking	about a career in computers?	No, he **isn't**.

Language Notes:
1. We can leave a preposition at the end of a question.
   What kind of career is he thinking **about**?
2. When the question is "What . . . doing?" we usually answer with a different verb.
   What are they **doing**? They're **taking** an aerobics class.
   What are those people **doing**? They're **playing** chess.

Compare negative statements and questions.

Wh- Word	Be + n't	Subject	Be + n't	Verb + -ing	Complement
		Mary	isn't	dancing.	
Why	isn't	she		dancing?	
		You	aren't	using	the computer.
Why	aren't	you		using	the computer?

EXERCISE 7 Fill in the blanks to make *yes/no* questions about the readings in this lesson.

EXAMPLE _____ Are those men playing _____ checkers?

No, they aren't. Those men are playing chess.

1. _____ this retirement home?

   Yes, I am. I'm considering it now that my wife is gone.

2. _____ a Web site? Yes, she is.

   Marge is designing a Web site with pictures of her vacations.

3. _____ pictures now? No, she

   isn't taking pictures. She's putting her pictures on her Web site.

4. _____ something? No, not
everyone is doing something. Some people are just relaxing.

5. _____ art classes? Yes,
they are. Judy and Charles love art, so they're taking a lot of classes.

6. _____ too many questions?
No, you're not. You can ask as many questions as you want.

EXERCISE 8 **Read each statement. Then write a question using the word(s) in parentheses ( ). An answer is not necessary.**

EXAMPLE   Some retirees are discovering new interests. (how)

_How are they discovering new interests?______

1. Judy is having more fun now. (why)

_____

2. Judy is traveling to many new places. (where)

_____

3. I'm starting a new career. (what kind of career)

_____

4. Some seniors are studying new things. (what)

_____

5. My father is thinking about retirement. (why)

_____

6. My mother is looking for a new career. (what kind)

_____

7. We're not planning to retire. (why)

_____

8. People are living longer nowadays. (why)

_____

9. I'm doing things that interest me. (what kinds of things)

_____

EXERCISE 9 Fill in the blanks to form *yes/no* questions about the reading on pages 44–45. Use the present continuous tense.

CD 1, TR 15

Jack (J) is talking to his neighbor Alan (A).

A: What ___are you doing___, Jack?
(example: you/do)

J: I _____ at some brochures.
(1 look)

A: What kind of brochures _____?
(2 you/look at)

J: They're from a retirement village.

A: So _____ about moving?
(3 you/think)

J: Yes. I'm thinking about moving into a retirement village.

A: Why?

J: Now that Rose is gone, I feel lonely.

A: But you have a lot of good neighbors here.

J: Most of the people here are young. My neighbors to the north are never home. Right now they _____. And my
(4 work)
neighbors across the street are never home.

A: They're older people. _____ too?
(5 work)

J: No. They _____ now. Right now
(6 travel)
they _____ a cruise[7] to Alaska.
(7 take)

A: But I'm here. I _____ my lawn, as usual. And my
(8 water)
wife is inside. She _____ on the phone, as usual.
(9 talk)

J: I'm sorry I'm complaining so much.

A: You _____. You _____ for
(10 not/complain)   (11 just/look)
something to do.

J: There's a lot to do. I just don't want to do things alone.

A: But your daughter lives with you.

J: She's in her 20s. She doesn't want to do things with her dad. Right now
she _____ a movie with her friends.
(12 watch)

A: What movie _____?
(13 they/watch)

J: Who knows? Something for young people. Her movies don't interest me.

---

[7]A *cruise* is a pleasure trip on a large passenger boat.

A: What retirement village _____ to go to?
        (14 you/plan)

J: Sun Valley Senior Village seems nice.

A: What about your daughter?

J: She _____ to move in with a friend of hers.
        (15 plan)

EXERCISE 10 **Fill in the blanks to complete the questions. Use the present continuous tense. Answers may vary.**

EXAMPLE **A:** Why ___is your sister wearing___ sunglasses? It's not sunny.

🔊
CD 1, TR 16

B: My sister's wearing sunglasses because she wants to look like a movie star.

1. **A:** What _____?

   B: I'm reading an article about older Americans.

   A: _____ the article?

   B: Oh, yes. I'm enjoying it very much.

2. **A:** Where _____ now?

   B: She's going to the park. Grandma always goes to the park on Sundays to jog.

   A: (not) _____ now?

   B: Yes, it's raining. But that doesn't matter. The park has an indoor track.

3. **A:** Martha is on her cell phone. Who _____?

   B: She's talking to her grandfather.

   A: Why _____ on her cell phone?
       Why _____ her home phone?

   B: Because her sister is using the home phone.

4. **Student:** _____?

   Teacher: Yes. Your accent is improving a lot.

   Student: How _____ with my grammar?

   Teacher: You're doing very well.

5. **Wife:** Something smells good. What _____?

   Husband: I'm cooking your favorite dinner—steak and potatoes.

   (A few minutes later)

   Wife: _____ something _____?

   Husband: Uh-oh. The steaks are burning.

(continued)

6. **A:** The kids are watching TV. What _____?

   B: They're watching cartoons.

   A: Why _____ their homework?

   B: They're not doing their homework because they don't have homework today.

7. **A:** I'm leaving.

   B: Where _____?

   A: I'm going to Grandma's house.

   B: Why _____?

   A: Because you're making too much noise. I have to study. It's quieter at Grandma's house.

8. **Dad:** I'm planning to retire next year.

   Son: You're so young. Why _____?

   Dad: First of all, I'm not so young. I'm almost 60. I'm planning to travel.

   Son: _____ alone?

   Dad: No, of course not. I _____ with Mom.

   Son: But she's still _____.

   Dad: She is now. But she's thinking about retiring too. She loves her work, but enough's enough. It's time to have fun.

Technology and the Generation Gap

Before You Read

1. Is it hard for older people to learn about new technology?

2. Do you text a lot?

CD 1, TR 17

A teenager, Marco (M), is visiting his grandmother (G). Read their conversation. Pay special attention to the present continuous tense and the simple present tense.

G: Listen, Marco, I'm **thinking** about getting a new computer. Can you help me pick one out?

M: Sure, Grandma. How about on Saturday?

G: Saturday's good. What's that sound? It **sounds** like rock music **is coming** from your pocket.

M: It's my cell phone. It's my new ring tone. I'm **receiving** a text message now.

G: **Is** it important?

M: It's a message from Dad. See?

G: It **looks** like Greek to me. What **does** it **say**?

M: He's **reminding** me to come home early. He **wants** to give me another driving lesson. I'm **learning** to drive, you know.

G: When I **have** something to say, I **use** the phone. **Don't** you ever **use** your phone anymore?

M: Of course I **do**. But I also **text** at least 20 times a day. It **saves** time. You can text me too, Grandma.

G: OK. It **looks** hard. Teach me.

M: Try it. Grandma, you'**re writing** so slowly. And you'**re using** whole words. Use abbreviations. And forget about punctuation. You **need** to write fast.

G: You know I'm an English teacher, and I **don't like** to write without punctuation.

M: Everyone **writes** without punctuation.

G: I **don't think** I can do it.

M: But you **send** e-mail.

G: That's different. I **write** slowly and **check** my spelling before I **send**.

M: You're so old-fashioned!

G: No, I'm not. **I'm** still **learning** new things. I'm **studying** photo editing at the senior center. I'm **making** a digital family album. I **love** it!

M: I'm proud of you, Grandma.

G: Thanks. Life **is** different today. But one thing **is** the same: 16-year-olds **want** to get their driver's license.

2.4 Contrasting the Simple Present and the Present Continuous

Forms

SIMPLE PRESENT TENSE	PRESENT CONTINUOUS TENSE
Grandma **uses** e-mail.	Marco **is receiving** a message.
She **doesn't use** text messages.	He **isn't receiving** a phone call.
Does she **use** the Internet?	**Is** he **receiving** a message from his friend?
Yes, she **does**.	No, he **isn't**.
When **does** she **use** the Internet?	How **is** he **receiving** a message?
Why **doesn't** she **use** text messages?	Why **isn't** he **receiving** a message from his friend?

Use

EXAMPLES	EXPLANATIONS
a. Most people **have** a computer. a. Young people **like** to send text messages. b. Grandma often **e-mails** her friends. b. Marco sometimes **visits** his grandmother. c. Many people **text** without punctuation. c. People **use** abbreviations in text messages.	Use the **simple present tense** to talk about: a. a general truth b. a habitual activity c. a custom
a. Dad **is reminding** me to put gas in the tank. a. You**'re writing** so slowly. b. Marco **is learning** to drive. b. I**'m making** a family album. c. People **are living** longer these days. c. People **are retiring** earlier these days.	Use the **present continuous tense** for: a. an action that is in progress now b. a longer action that is in progress at this general time c. recent trends in society
Compare: a. My grandparents **live** in a retirement village. b. My sister **is living** in a dorm this semester.	a. *Live* in the simple present shows a person's home. b. *Live* in the present continuous shows a temporary, short-term residence.

Compare:
 a. **What does she do (for a living)?**
     She's an English teacher.
 b. **What is she doing now?**
     She's talking to her grandson.
	Sentence (a) asks about a job or profession. It uses the simple present tense.
	
	 Sentence (b) asks about an activity now. It uses the present continuous tense.

EXERCISE 11 **Fill in the blanks with the simple present or the present continuous tense of the verb in parentheses ( ).**

1. **A:** What ___are you eating___? Is it a hamburger?
    (example: you/eat)

    B: No, it isn't. It's a veggie burger. I never _____ meat.
    (1 eat)

    Where's your lunch?

    A: I don't want to eat lunch. I _____ too much weight.
    (2 gain)

    I _____ to lose weight. I _____
    (3 try) *(4 eat)*

    only twice a day—breakfast and dinner.

    B: But you _____ a soda now.
    (5 drink)

    A: It's a diet cola.

2. **A:** What _____?
    (6 you/do)

    B: I _____ in the answers.
    (7 fill)

    A: Why _____ a pen? A pencil is better. What if
    (8 you/use)

    you make a mistake?

    B: I never _____ mistakes. My grammar is perfect!
    (9 make)

    A: That's not true. We all _____ mistakes. That's
    (10 make)

    why we're in this class.

    B: I'm just kidding. Of course I _____ mistakes all
    (11 make)

    the time.

3. **A:** What _____ for a living?
    (12 your father/do)

    B: He's a commercial artist. He _____ for a big
    (13 work)

    company downtown. But this week he's on vacation.

    A: What _____ this week?
    (14 he/do)

    B: He _____ golf with his friends.
    (15 play)

(continued)

A: Is your mom on vacation too?

B: No. She _____ a vacation every December.
(16 take)

4. A: Where _____?
(17 the teacher/go)

B: She _____ to her office.
_(18 go)_

A: She _____ heavy books. Let's help her.
(19 carry)

B: I'm late for my next class. My math teacher always

_____ on time. He _____ angry
(20 start) _(21 get)_

if someone is late.

5. A: You _____, Daniel. Wake up.
(22 sleep)

B: I'm so tired. I never _____ enough sleep.
(23 get)

A: How many hours _____ a night?
(24 you/sleep)

B: Only about 4 or 5.

A: That's not enough. You always _____ asleep in class.
(25 fall)

B: I know. But I _____ 18 credit hours this semester.
(26 take)

A: That's too much. I never _____ more than 12.
(27 take)

2.5 Action and Nonaction Verbs

Some verbs are action verbs. These verbs show physical or mental activity (*run*, *play*, *study*, *drive*, *eat*, etc.). Some verbs are nonaction verbs. These verbs describe a state, condition, or feeling, not an action.

EXAMPLES	EXPLANATION
Marco **wants** to get a driver's license. Grandma **loves** her class.	With nonaction verbs, we use the simple present tense, even when we talk about now. We do not usually use a continuous form with these verbs.
Marco is **looking** at his cell phone. He **sees** a message from his father.	*Look* is an action verb. *See* is a nonaction verb.
Grandma **is listening** to her grandson. She **hears** his ring tone.	*Listen* is an action verb. *Hear* is a nonaction verb.
Judy **is meeting** new people. She **knows** a lot of people.	*Meet* is an action verb. *Know* is a nonaction verb.
Grandma **is thinking** about getting a new computer. She **thinks** that using the phone is better than texting.	When you think *about* or *of* something, *think* is an action verb. *Think that* shows an opinion about something. It is a nonaction verb.
Grandma **is having** a good time in her photo class. She**'s having** lunch now. Grandma **has** free time now. She **has** five grandchildren. Marco **has** a cold now.	When *have* means to experience something or to eat or drink something, it is an action verb. When *have* shows possession, relationship, or illness, it is a nonaction verb.
She**'s looking** at her photo album. She**'s smelling** the coffee. I want to learn to text, but it **looks** hard. Your ring tone **sounds** loud.	When the sense-perception verbs describe an action, they are action verbs. When the sense-perception verbs describe a state, they are nonaction verbs.

Nonaction Verbs:

like	remember	see	seem
love	believe	cost	prefer
hate	think (that)	own	know
want	care (about)	have	mean
need	understand	matter	

Sense-Perception Verbs:

smell	taste	feel	look	sound

EXERCISE 12 **Fill in the blanks with the simple present or the present continuous tense of the verb in parentheses ( ).**

CD 1, TR 18

1. **A:** Grandpa volunteers his time. Twice a week he _____reads_____
   (example: read)

   for blind people.

   B: My grandmother _____ part-time in a bookstore.
   (1 work)

   She _____ books. She usually _____
   (2 love)   (3 ride)

   her bike to work. She _____ the exercise.
   (4 like)

   A: Where is she now? _____ now?
   (5 she/work)

   B: Now she's on vacation. She _____ in Florida.
   (6 sail)

2. **A:** Can I borrow your dictionary?

   B: I'm sorry. I _____ it now. Where's your dictionary?
   (7 use)

   A: I never _____ it to class. It's too heavy.
   (8 bring)

   B: _____ to use my dictionary all the time?
   (9 expect)

   You _____ an electronic dictionary. It's very light.
   (10 need)

3. **A:** What _____?
   (11 the teacher/say)

   She _____ too fast, so I _____ her now.
   (12 talk)   (13 not/understand)

   B: I don't know. I _____. I _____
   (14 not/listen)   (15 think)

   about my grandparents.

   A: I _____ you are a very good grandson.
   (16 think)

   B: Yes. I _____ about visiting them next weekend.
   (17 think)

4. **A:** What _____?
   (18 you/write)

   B: I _____ a composition about
   (19 write)

   my grandparents. I _____ them very much.
   (20 love)

A: _____ with you?
        (21 they/live)

B: No, they don't. They live in Pakistan. They

_____ us once a year.
   (22 visit)

A: _____ them e-mail?
        (23 you/ever/send)

B: Sometimes I do. But right now their computer _____.
                                                           (24 not/work)

Anyway, they _____ handwritten letters.
                   (25 prefer)

5. A: Look at that girl. Who is she?

B: She's in my math class. I _____ her pretty well.
                                 (26 know)

A: What _____?
               (27 she/wear)

B: She _____ a dress and army boots.
         (28 wear)

A: She _____ strange. _____
         (29 look)   *(30 she/always/wear)*

a dress and army boots?

B: No, not always. Sometimes she _____ sandals.
                                (31 wear)

And sometimes she _____ any shoes at all.
                   (32 not/wear)

6. A: _____ that guy over there? Who is he?
      (33 you/see)

B: That's my English teacher.

A: He _____ jeans and gym shoes. And he
      (34 wear)

_____ an earring in his ear.
   (35 have)

He _____ like a student.
    (36 look)

B: I _____. Everyone _____ he's a student.
    (37 know)   *(38 think)*

But he's a very professional teacher.

A: What level _____?
         (39 he/teach)

(continued)

B: He teaches level four. But now he _____ for
                                           (40 look)

another job because he _____ a full-time job
                              (41 not/have)

here. He _____ to work full-time.
               (42 want)

7. A: What _____ this semester?
                    (43 you/study)

B: English, math, and biology.

A: _____ well in all your courses?
           (44 you/do)

B: I _____ well in English and math. But biology
            (45 do)

is hard for me. I _____ to drop it.
                        (46 need)

I _____ the teacher very well.
     (47 not/understand)

He _____ too fast for me.
        (48 talk)

8. A: What _____ for a living?
                    (49 your mother/do)

B: She's retired now.

A: _____ old?
           (50 she/be)

B: No, she's only 58.

A: What _____ with her free time?
                 (51 she/do)

B: She does a lot of things. In fact, she _____ any
                                                  (52 not/have)

free time at all. She _____ two art courses at the
                            (53 take)

art center this semester. Right now she _____ a
                                               (54 paint)

beautiful picture of me. She also _____ at a
                                        (55 volunteer)

hospital twice a week.

A: That's wonderful. A lot of retired people _____
                                                      (56 volunteer)

these days.

EXERCISE 13 This is a phone conversation between two friends, Patty (P) and Linda (L). Fill in the blanks with the missing words. Use the simple present or the present continuous tense.

CD 1, TR 19

P: Hello?

L: Hi, Patty. This is Linda.

P: Hi, Linda. What ____are you doing____ now?
    (example: you/do)

L: Not much. _____ to meet for coffee?
    (1 you/want)

P: I can't. I _____. I _____
    (2 cook)   *(3 have)*
    dinner in the oven now, and I _____ for it to be
    (4 wait)
    finished. What _____?
    (5 you/do)

L: I _____ for a test. But I _____
    (6 study)   *(7 want)*
    to take a break now. Besides, I _____ to talk to
    (8 need)
    someone. I usually _____ to my roommate when
    (9 talk)
    I _____ a problem, but
    (10 have)
    she _____ some friends in New York now.
    (11 visit)

P: We can talk while I _____ dinner.
    (12 prepare)
    It _____ serious.
    (13 sound)

L: My parents _____ to put Grandma in a nursing home.
    (14 plan)

P: But why?

L: My mom _____ she'll receive better care there.
    (15 think)

P: I _____ that's such a good idea. In my family,
    (16 not/think)
    we _____ our parents and grandparents in a nursing
    (17 never/put)
    home. We _____ of them at home.
    (18 always/take care)

L: My mom _____ what else to do. Grandma
    (19 not/know)
    _____ all the time.
    (20 fall)

P: Maybe she _____ a cane or a walker.
    (21 need)

L: Her memory is terrible too. She _____ where she
    (22 never/remember)
    puts things.

P: I _____ my husband coming in the door, and
    (23 hear)
    dinner is almost ready. I'll call you later when we can talk more about it.

L: Thanks for listening. Talk to you later.

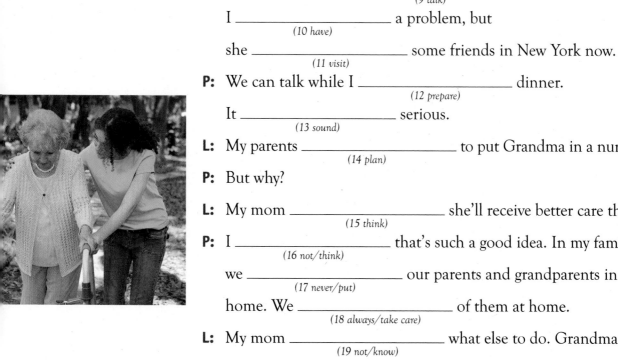

The Present Continuous Tense; Action and Nonaction Verbs; the Future Tense **65**

The Graying of America

Before
You Read

1. In your native culture, who takes care of people when they get old?

2. Do old people in your native culture get a lot of respect?

CD 1, TR 20

Read the following magazine article. Pay special attention to future tense verbs.

The overall population of the U.S. is growing slowly. In the year 2009, the American population was 303 million. By the middle of this century, it **is going to be** 404 million. Even though this is not a big growth, one group is growing very fast—the elderly (65 years old and over). By 2030, 20 percent of the American population **will be** 65 or over. Today there are three million people 85 or older. In 2050, 28 million **will be** 85 or older.

There are two reasons for this sudden rise in the number of older Americans. First, life expectancy is increasing. In 1900, when the life expectancy was 47, 1 in 25 Americans was elderly. In 2000, with a life expectancy of 79.5 years for women and 74 for men, 1 in 8 was elderly. By 2050, 1 in 5 **will be** elderly.

The second reason for this growth is the aging of the "baby boomers." In the 18 years after World War II, from 1946 to 1964, a large number of babies were born—75 million. The people born during this period, known as the baby boomers, are now middle-aged and **will** soon **be** elderly. The average age of the population is increasing as the baby boomers get older and live longer. The median age of Americans in 1970 was 28; in 2000 it was 35.3. By 2050, it **will be** 41.1.

What does this mean for America? First, there **will be** a labor shortage as the baby boomers retire. There are fewer younger people to take their place at work. For taxpayers, the aging of Americans means that they **are going to pay** more taxes as one-fifth of the population uses one-half of the resources. Also, the country **will see** an increase in the number of nursing homes and the need for people to work in them.

The housing market **will have** to respond to the needs of the baby boomers too. As their children grow up and move out, many baby boomers **will sell** their bigger houses and **move** to smaller ones. Others **will convert** extra bedrooms to offices and home gyms. Also, we **will see** more and more retirement villages for active seniors. Some seniors **will move** from the suburbs to the city. "We live in a suburb of Chicago now," says Paula Hoffman, 52, "because the schools for our teenage children are good. But when they go away to college, we **are going to move** back into the city. There's much more activity for us there."

Susan Brecht, a housing consultant in Philadelphia, Pennsylvania, says, "Baby boomers do not view retirement the way their parents and grandparents did. For starters, they're much more active. My 55 is not my mother's 55," Brecht stated. "I think there is a change in how different generations respond to the aging process. And that's what we're seeing now and **will see** in a dramatic way for the next 10 to 20 years."

It **will be** interesting to see how the baby boomers **are going to continue** to influence the future of America.

2.6 The Future Tense with *Will*

EXAMPLES	EXPLANATION
We **will move** back to the city. You **will see** a big change in the next 10 to 20 years.	We use *will* + the base form for the future tense.
I *will* **always** *help* my parents. My parents *will* **never** *go* to a nursing home.	We can put a frequency word between *will* and the main verb.
I'll be 72 in 2050. **You'll** take care of your elderly parents.	We can contract *will* with the subject pronouns. The contractions are *I'll, you'll, he'll, she'll, it'll, we'll,* and *they'll*.
The population **will not** go down. I **won't** live with my grown children.	To form the negative, put *not* after *will*. The contraction for *will not* is *won't*.

Compare affirmative statements and questions with *will*.

Wh- Word	*Will*	Subject	*Will*	Verb (Base Form)	Complement	Short Answer
		She	**will**	live	with her daughter.	
	Will	she		live	with her son?	No, she **won't**.
When	**will**	she		live	with her daughter?	Soon.

(continued)

Compare negative statements and questions with *will*.

Wh- Word	Won't	Subject	Won't	Verb (Base Form)	Complement
		They	won't	need	a large house.
Why	won't	they		need	a large house?

EXERCISE 14 Fill in the blanks with an appropriate verb in the future tense. Use *will*. Answers may vary.

EXAMPLE In the future, people _____will live_____ longer.

1. The population of old people _____.

2. There _____ more older people by 2050.

3. Where _____ you _____

    when you are old?

4. _____ your children _____

    care of you?

5. How old _____ you _____ in 2050?

6. Many baby boomers are middle-aged now. They _____

    soon _____ elderly.

EXERCISE 15 A 30-year-old woman is saying good-bye to her 60-year-old parents. They are leaving on a trip in their recreational vehicle (RV). Fill in the blanks to complete this conversation. Use the future tense with *will*. Answers may vary.

A: I'm worried about you. You _'ll be_____ gone for a long time.
                                        (example)

B: Don't worry. We _____ only _____
                           (1)   *(2)*

    gone for the summer months.

A: You _____ alone on the road.
              (3)

B: We _____ on the road all the time.
            (4)

    We _____ at campsites with lots of other
         (5)

    RVs and campers.

A: How _____ your clothes?
            (6)

B: The RV has a washing machine.

A: Where _____ your food?
              (7)

B: We'll buy food at a supermarket on the way and cook it in the RV. The RV has everything—a stove, a microwave, a dishwasher. Sometimes we _____ (8) a fire and cook on the grill. Other times we _____ (9) out in restaurants.

A: Where _____ (10) first?

B: First, we'll go to the Grand Canyon.

A: That's fabulous! _____ (11) me a postcard from there?

B: Of course we _____ (12). And we _____ (13) send you e-mail too.

A: How _____ (14) e-mail?

B: From our computer, of course. We _____ (15) it with us.

A: Where _____ (16) electricity for all these things?

B: At the campsites. There are electrical hookups.

A: You _____ (17) all the comforts of home. Why, then, are you leaving?

B: We can't see the Grand Canyon from our home.

A: _____ (18) pictures?

B: Yes, we'll take lots of pictures. We'll have our digital camera with us. There _____ (19) a lot of beautiful things to take pictures of. We _____ (20) them to you by e-mail.

A: Have a good time. I _____ (21) you.

B: We'll miss you too.

2.7 The Future Tense with *Be Going To*

EXAMPLES	EXPLANATION
People **are going to live** longer. They **are going to need** help from their children. There **are going to be** more elderly people in 50 years.	We use a form of *be* + *going to* + the base form to form the future tense.
I**'m not** going to live with my grown children. He **isn't** going to retire.	To form the negative, put *not* after *am, is,* or *are.*
We're **going to go** on a long trip in the RV. We're **going** on a long trip in the RV.	We often shorten *going to go* to *going.*
We're going to return **in** two months. I'm going to retire **in** ten years.	We use the preposition *in* with the future tense to mean *after.*

Pronunciation Notes:

1. In informal speech, *going to* before another verb often sounds like "gonna." In formal English, we don't write "gonna." Listen to your teacher's pronunciation of *going to* in the following sentences.

    Where's he going to live? (Where's he "gonna" live?)
    He's going to live in a dorm. (He's "gonna" live in a dorm.)

2. Only *going to* before another verb sounds like "gonna." We don't pronounce "gonna" before a noun.

    Where is he going?
    He's going to the bookstore.

Compare affirmative statements and questions with *be going to*.

Wh-Word	Be	Subject	Be	Going to + Verb (Base Form)	Complement	Short Answer
		They	are	**going to sell**	their house.	
	Are	they		**going to sell**	it soon?	Yes, they **are.**
Why	**are**	they		**going to sell**	it?	Because it**'s** too big.

Compare negative statements and questions with *be going to*.

Wh-Word	Be + n't	Subject	Be + n't	Going to + Verb (Base Form)	Complement
		She	**isn't**	**going to retire**	from her job.
Why	**isn't**	she		**going to retire?**	

EXERCISE 16 Fill in the blanks with an appropriate verb in the future tense. Use *be going to*. Answers may vary.

EXAMPLE _____Are_____ your children _going to take care of_ you?

1. The cost of health care _____.

2. People _____ higher taxes.

3. How old _____ your daughter _____ in 2050?

4. _____ you _____ care of your elderly parents?

5. A lot of people _____ over 100 years old in 2050.

EXERCISE 17 Two co-workers are talking. Fill in the blanks with the future using *be going to*.

CD 1, TR 22

A: I'm so excited. I _'m going to retire_____ at the end of this year.
(example: retire)

B: That's wonderful news. What _____ next?
(1 you/do)

A: I don't really know yet. I _____ new things.
(2 explore)

B: For example, what _____?
(3 you/explore)

A: I think I have a talent for art. I _____ art classes.
(4 take)

B: _____ part-time?
(5 you/work)

A: No way! I _____ exactly what I
(6 do)
want to do, when I want to do it.

B: Is your husband happy about your retirement?

A: Yes. He _____ too.
(7 retire)

B: But you're not that old.

A: I'm 58 and he's 56. Our children aren't going to
need us much anymore.

B: Why _____ you?
(8 not/need)

A: Our youngest son _____ from college in June. And
(9 graduate)
the other two are already on their own. The oldest _____
(10 get)
married next year, and the middle one has her own apartment and a job.

B: I _____ you at work.
(11 miss)

A: I _____ you too. But I _____ the boss
(12 miss)   *(13 not/miss)*
and the long hours.

Do you have questions for the teacher about this semester, next semester, or his or her life in general? Write three questions to ask the teacher about the near or distant future.

EXAMPLES   *What time are you going to leave today?*

              When are you going to give us a test?

              Are you going to retire soon?

1. _____

2. _____

3. _____

2.8 Choosing *Will* or *Be Going To*

In many cases, you can use either *will* or *be going to*. But in a few cases, one is preferred over the other.

EXAMPLES	EXPLANATION
A: When is Grandpa going to move into the retirement home? B: He**'s going to move** next summer. He needs help. I**'m going to rent** a moving truck and help him.	If the decision or plan was made before this conversation takes place, use *be going to*.
A: What are you going to do when you retire? B: I don't know. I**'ll cross** that bridge when I come to it.[8]	Speaker B is thinking about the future at the time of talking. There is no previous plan. If there is no previous plan, use *will*.
Grandma: I don't know how to send a text message. Grandson: No problem. I**'ll teach** you. Grandma: I need to buy a cell phone. What should I buy? Grandson: Don't worry. I**'ll help** you.	The grandson is making an offer to help at the time of talking. He had no previous plan. If there is an offer to help, use *will*.
Grandma: I'm lonely. Grandson: I**'ll visit** you on the weekend. Grandma: You always say that. But you never have time. Grandson: I**'ll make time.** I promise.	The grandson is making a promise. If there is a promise, use *will*.

Language Notes:
1. For predictions, facts about the future, or scheduled events, you can use either *will* or *be going to*.
   The movie **will begin** at 8 PM. = The movie **is going to begin** at 8 PM.
   Technology **will improve** in the future. = Technology **is going to improve** in the future.

2. We sometimes use the present continuous tense with a future meaning. We can do this with planned events in the near future. We do this especially with verbs of motion.
   My grandmother **is moving** into a retirement home on Friday.
   I**'m helping** her move on Friday.

[8]This is an expression that means: I'll worry about it when the time comes, not before.

EXERCISE 19 Choose *be going to* or *will* + the verb to fill in the blanks. In some cases, both are possible.

1. **A:** Where are you going?

   B: I'm going to the park this afternoon. I <u>'m going to meet</u>
   (example: meet)

   my friend and play tennis with her. I have to return some videos to

   the video store, but I don't have time.

   A: Give them to me. I _____ that way.
   (1 pass)

   I _____ them for you.
   (2 return)

2. **A:** I have to go to the airport. My sister's plane

   _____ at four o'clock this afternoon.
   (3 arrive)

   B: I _____ with you. I _____
   (4 go)   *(5 stay)*

   in the car while you go into the airport. That way, you

   _____ pay for parking.
   (6 not/have to)

3. **A:** My sister's birthday is next week.

   B: _____ her a birthday present?
   (7 you/give)

   A: Of course I _____.
   (8)

   B: What _____ her?
   (9 you/give)

   A: She loves the theater. I _____ her tickets to a play.
   (10 buy)

   B: How old _____?
   (11 be)

   A: She _____ 21 years old.
   (12 be)

4. **Teacher:** Next week we _____ our midterm test.
   (13 have)

   Student: _____ hard?
   (14 it/be)

   Teacher: Yes, but I _____ you prepare for it.
   (15 help)

(continued)

5. **Wife:** I won't have time to pick up the children this afternoon. I have

   to work late.

   Husband: Don't worry. I _____ them up.
   (16 pick)

   Wife: I won't have time to cook either.

   Husband: Just relax. I _____ dinner tonight.
   (17 prepare)

6. **Man:** I want to marry you.

   Woman: But we're only 19. We're too young.

   Man: I _____ 20 in April.
   (18 be)

   Woman: But you don't even have a job.

   Man: I _____ a job.
   (19 find)

   Woman: Let's wait a few years.

   Man: I _____ for you forever. I _____ you.
   (20 wait)   (21 always/love)

7. **A:** Do you want to watch the football game with me on Saturday?

   B: I can't. My brother _____. I _____ him.
   (22 move)   (23 help)

   A: Do you need any help?

   B: We need boxes. Do you have any?

   A: No, but I _____ for boxes. I _____
   (24 look)   (25 go)

   to the supermarket this afternoon. I _____
   (26 get)

   boxes there. I _____ them to your house.
   (27 bring)

   B: Thanks.

8. **A:** I'm so excited! I _____ a puppy.
   (28 get)

   B: That's a big responsibility. You're never home. How

   _____ care of it?
   (29 take)

   A: My cousin lives with me now. She doesn't have a job.

   She _____ me take care of the dog.
   (30 help)

B: What about your landlord? Is it OK with him?

A: I _____ him.
(31 not/tell)

B: You have to tell him. He _____ if you have a
(32 know)

dog. You _____ take the dog out
(33 have to)

three times a day. And the dog _____.
(34 bark)

2.9 Future Tense + *If* Clause[9]

Some future sentences have two clauses: a main clause and a time or *if* clause.

Time or *If* Clause (Simple Present Tense)	Main Clause (Future Tense)	Explanation
When the children **grow** up,	we **will move** back to the city.	We use the *future* only in the main clause; we use the *simple present tense* in the time/*if* clause.
If I **am** healthy,	I **will continue** to work for the rest of my life.	
Main Clause (Future Tense)	**Time or *If* Clause (Simple Present Tense)**	We can put the time/*if* clause before the main clause. Or we can put the main clause before the time/*if* clause.
He **will move** to a warm climate	as soon as he **retires**.	
My parents **are going to travel**	if they **take** an early retirement.	

Punctuation Note: If the time/*if* clause comes before the main clause, we use a comma to separate the two parts of the sentence. If the main clause comes first, we don't use a comma.

EXERCISE **20** **Connect the sentences using the word in parentheses ( ).**

EXAMPLE I will retire. I will play golf. (when)

_____**When I retire, I will play golf.**_____ OR _____**I will play golf when I retire.**_____

1. I will retire. I'm not going to live with my children. (when)

_____

2. I will be old. I will take care of myself. (when)

_____

[9]A *clause* is a group of words that has a subject and a verb. Some sentences have more than one clause.

(continued)

3. I won't be healthy. I'll live with my children. (if)

_____

4. I won't have money. I will get help from the government. (if)

_____

5. My parents will die. I'll move to another city. (after)

_____

6. I will get a pension. I won't need to depend on my children. (if)

_____

7. I'll retire. I'm going to save my money. (before)

_____

EXERCISE 21   **ABOUT YOU**   **Think about a specific time in your future (when you graduate, when you get married, when you have children, when you find a job, when you return to your native country, when you are old, etc.). Write three sentences to tell what will happen at that time. Find a partner who is close to your age. Compare your answers to your partner's answers.**

EXAMPLES   When I have children, I won't have as much free time as I do now.

When I have children, I'm going to have a lot more responsibilities.

When I have children, my parents will be very happy.

1. _____

2. _____

3. _____

EXERCISE 22   **A Korean student (K) is talking to an American (A) about getting old. Fill in the blanks with the correct form of the verb to complete this conversation. In many cases, you can use either _be going to_ or _will_.**

🔊

CD 1, TR 23

K: How's your grandfather?

A: He's OK. I __'m going to visit__ him this afternoon.
               (example: visit)

K: How's he doing?

A: He's in great health. Next week he _____
                                             _(1 go)_

to Hawaii to play golf.

K: How old is he?

A: He _____ 78 next month. Did I tell you?
(2 be)

In June, he _____ married to
(3 get)

a widow he met in the retirement home.

K: That seems so strange to me.

Why _____ that?
(4 he/do)

A: Why not? They like each other, and they want to be together.

K: What _____ when he's no longer
(5 you/do)

able to take care of himself?

A: We never think about it. He's in such great shape that we think

he _____ healthy forever. I think
(6 be)

he _____ us all.
(7 outlive)

K: But he _____ help as he gets older.
(8 probably/need)

A: We _____ that bridge when we come
(9 cross)

to it. Do you have plans for your parents as they get older?

K: They're in their 50s now. But when they _____
(10 be)

older, they _____ with me and my wife.
(11 live)

In our country, it's an honor to take care of our parents.

A: That sounds like a great custom. But I think older people should

be independent. I'm glad that Grandpa doesn't depend on us.

And when I _____ old, I _____
(12 be)   (13 take)

care of myself. I don't want to depend on anyone.

K: You _____ your mind when
(14 change)

you _____ old.
(15 be)

A: Maybe. I have to catch my bus now. Grandpa is waiting for me.

I _____ you later.
(16 see)

K: Wait. I have my car. I _____ you to your
(17 drive)

grandfather's place.

A: Thanks.

EXERCISE 23 This is a conversation between two co-workers. They are talking about retirement. Fill in the blanks with the correct form and tense of the verb in parentheses ( ).

CD 1, TR 24

A: I hear you're going to retire this year.

B: Yes. Isn't it wonderful? I __'ll be_____ 65 in September.
(example: be)

A: What _____ after you _____?
(1 you/do) *(2 retire)*

B: I'm trying to sell my house now. When I _____
(3 sell)

it, I _____ to Florida and buy a condo.
(4 move)

A: What _____ in Florida?
(5 you/do)

B: I _____ a sailboat and spend most of my time on the water.
(6 buy)

A: But a sailboat is expensive.

B: When I _____ 65, I _____ to use my
(7 be) *(8 start)*

savings. Also, I _____ a lot of money
(9 get)

when I _____ my house.
(10 sell)

What _____ when you _____?
(11 you/do) *(12 retire)*

A: I'm only 45 years old. I have another 20 years until I _____.
(13 retire)

B: Now is the time to start thinking about retirement. If you

_____ your money for the next 20 years,
(14 save)

you _____ a comfortable retirement.
(15 have)

But if you _____ about it until the time
(16 not/think)

_____, you _____
(17 come) *(18 not/have)*

enough money to live on.

A: I _____ about it when the time _____.
(19 worry) *(20 come)*

I'm too young to worry about it now.

B: If you _____ until you _____ 65 to
(21 wait) *(22 be)*

think about it, you _____ a poor old man.
(23 be)

On Monday morning when we _____ at work,
(24 be)

I _____ you to a woman who can explain the
(25 introduce)

company's savings plan to you. After you _____
(26 talk)

to her, I'm sure you _____ your mind about
(27 change)

when to worry about retirement.

Summary of Lesson 2

Use of Tense

Simple Present Tense	
General truths, facts	Many people **retire** in their sixties. Retirees **get** Social Security.
Regular activities, habits, customs	Jack **plays** golf twice a week. I **always** visit my grandparents on the weekend.
Place of origin	My grandfather **comes** from Mexico. My grandmother **comes** from Peru.
In a time clause or in an *if* clause of a future statement	When she **retires**, she will enjoy life. If Grandma **needs** help, she will live with her daughter.
With nonaction verbs	I **care** about my grandparents. Your grandfather **needs** help now. My grandfather **prefers** to live alone now.

Present Continuous Tense (with action verbs only)	
Now	We**'re comparing** verb tenses now. I**'m looking** at page 79 now.
A long-term action in progress at this general time	Judy **is earning** money by making dolls. Jack is retired now. He **is starting** a new career.
A trend in society	The population of the U.S. **is getting** older. Americans **are living** longer.
A plan in the near future	She **is retiring** next month. She **is going** on a long trip soon.
A descriptive state	Mary **is standing** over there. She **is wearing** jeans and a T-shirt.

Future Tense

	will	*be going to*
A plan		He **is going to retire** in two years.
A fact	The number of old people **will increase**.	The number of old people is **going to increase**.
A prediction	I think you **will enjoy** retirement.	I think you **are going to enjoy** retirement.
A promise	I **will** take care of you when you're old.	
An offer to help	Grandma, I'**ll carry** your grocery bags for you.	
A scheduled event	Dance instruction **will begin** at 8 PM on Saturday.	Dance instruction **is going to begin** at 8 PM on Saturday.

Editing Advice

1. Always include *be* in a present continuous tense verb.

      is

    She ˄ working now.

2. Don't use the present continuous tense with a nonaction verb.

            e

    I ~~am~~ lik~~ing~~ your new car.

3. Don't use *be* with another verb for the future.

    I will ~~be~~ go back to my native country in five years.

4. Include *be* in a future sentence that has no other verb.

          be

    He will ˄ angry.

             be

    There will ˄ a party soon.

5. Don't combine *will* and *be going to*.

    He will ~~going to~~ leave. *OR He's going to leave.*

6. Don't use the future tense after a time word or *if*.

When they ~~will~~ go home, they are going to watch TV.

am
If I ~~will be~~ late, I'll call you.

7. Use a form of *be* with *going to*.

is
He ˄ going to help me.

8. Use the correct word order in questions.

will you
When ~~you will~~ go back to your native country?

isn't she
Why ~~she isn't~~ going to buy a new car?

Editing Quiz

Some of the shaded words and phrases have mistakes. Find the mistakes and correct them. If the shaded words are correct, write *C*.

My grandfather is retired now and he's not happy. He wakes up every day

will I
and says, "What ~~I will~~ do today?" On the other hand, my grandmother
(example)

C
is very busy. My grandparents live in a retirement village and Grandma
(example)

is learning how to draw. She's also take singing lessons, and she
(1) *(2)* *(3)*

studying photography. Next month, she going to take a trip to India with
(4) *(5)*

a group of older people. When Grandma will get back from India,
(6)

she's going to make a photo slideshow of her trip.
(7)

Grandpa doesn't want to travel. He says, "What I'm going to do
(8)

in India?" I'm thinking that Grandpa is needing to find a hobby.
(9) *(10)*

Grandma always tells him, "You will happy if you find something to
(11)

do." Will I going to have a hard time like Grandpa when I will retire?
(12) *(13)*

I'll be cross that bridge when I come to it.
(14) *(15)*

Lesson 2 Test/Review

PART 1   Mary (M) is talking to her friend Sue (S) on the phone. Fill in the blanks with the correct tense and form of the words in parentheses ( ). Use the simple present, present continuous, or future tense. In some cases, more than one answer is possible.

S: Hi, Mary.

M: Hi, Sue. How are you?

S: Fine. What are you doing?

M: I **'m packing** _____ now. We _____
           (example: pack)   _(1 move)_
   next Saturday.

S: Oh, really? Why? You _____ such a lovely
                         (2 have)
   apartment now.

M: Yes, I know we do. But my father _____
                         (3 come)
   soon, so we _____ a bigger apartment.
            (4 need)

S: When _____?
          (5 come)

M: He _____ as soon as he _____
      (6 come)   _(7 get)_
   his visa. That'll probably be in about four months.

S: But your present apartment _____ an extra bedroom.
                       (8 have)

M: Yes. But my husband _____ to have an extra room
                (9 always/like)
   for an office. He usually _____ a lot of work home.
                 (10 bring)
   He _____ a place where he can work without noise.
       (11 need)

S: _____ his own apartment after he
    (12 your father/get)
   _____ a job?
    (13 find)

M: He's retired now. He _____ with us.
                 (14 live)
   He _____ to live alone.
      (15 not/like)

S: Do you need help with your packing?

M: No, thank you. Bill and I _____ home this week to
                 (16 stay)
   finish the packing. And my sister _____ me now too.
                     (17 help)

S: I _____ over next Saturday to help you move.
      (18 come)

M: We _____ professional movers on
    (19 use)
Saturday. We don't want to bother our friends.

S: It's no bother. I _____ to help.
                     (20 want)

M: Thanks. There probably _____ a few things you
                            (21 be)
can help me with on Saturday. I have to go now. I

_____ Bill. He _____ me.
    (22 hear)   (23 call)
He _____ me to help him in the basement.
     (24 want)
I _____ you back later.
    (25 call)

S: You don't have to call me back. I _____ you on
                                       (26 see)
Saturday. Bye.

PART **2**   **Fill in the blanks with the negative form of the underlined verb.**

EXAMPLE   Mary is busy. Sue _____isn't_____ busy.

1. Sue is talking to Mary. She _____ to her husband.

2. Mary is going to move to a bigger apartment. She _____
   to a house.

3. Mary's husband needs an extra room. He _____ a big
   room.

4. Sue will go to Mary's house on Saturday. She _____
   tomorrow.

5. Mary will move the small things. She _____
   the furniture.

6. Her new apartment has an extra room for her father. Her old apartment
   _____ an extra room.

7. Her father likes to live with family. He _____ to live
   alone.

PART 3 Write a *yes/no* question about the words in parentheses ( ). Then write a short answer based on the conversation in Part 1 on pages 82–83.

EXAMPLE   Mary is busy. (her husband)
          Is her husband busy? Yes, he is.

1. Mary's husband is helping her pack. (her sister)

2. Her husband works in an office. (at home)

3. Her present apartment has an extra room for an office. (for her father)

4. Professional movers will move the furniture. (her friends)

5. Mary is staying home this week. (her husband)

6. Mary's going to move. (Sue)

PART 4 Write a *wh-* question about the words in parentheses ( ). An answer is not necessary.

EXAMPLE   Mary's packing now. (why)
          Why is she packing?

1. They're going to move to a bigger apartment. (why)

2. Her husband needs an extra room. (why)

3. She doesn't need her friends to help her move. (why)

4. Her father is going to come soon. (when)

5. Bill is calling Mary now. (why)

6. They'll use professional movers. (when)

Expansion

Classroom Activities

❶ Check (✓) your predictions about the future. Form a small group and discuss your predictions with your group. Give reasons for your beliefs.

a. _____ People are going to have fewer children than they do today.

b. _____ People will live longer.

c. _____ People will have healthier lives.

d. _____ People are going to be happier.

e. _____ People will be lonelier.

f. _____ People will be more educated.

g. _____ Everyone is going to have a computer.

h. _____ There will be a cure for cancer and other serious illnesses.

i. _____ There will be a cure for the common cold.

❷ Check (✓) the activities that you plan to do soon. Form a group of between five and seven students. Ask questions about the items another student checked.

EXAMPLE
_✓_ move
When are you going to move?
Why are you moving?
Are your friends going to help you?
Are you going to rent a truck?
Where are you going to move to?

a. _____ send e-mail

b. _____ visit a friend

c. _____ invite guests to my house

d. _____ buy something new

e. _____ take a vacation

f. _____ celebrate a birthday or holiday

g. _____ go to a concert or sporting event

h. _____ transfer to another school

i. _____ move

j. _____ take the citizenship test

k. _____ start a new job

l. _____ have an out-of-town visitor

m. _____ get married

About It

① What is the attitude toward older people in your native country or culture? Do they get a lot of respect?

② Is it hard for older people to keep up with all the changes in technology?

③ How can retired people use their time? Do you know anyone who is retired? How does this person use his/her time?

Write

About It

① Write a short composition telling how you think your life will be when you are 10 years older than you are now.

Sample beginning: I'm 25 years old now. When I'm 35 years old, I think I will . . .

② Write a short composition describing the life of an old person you know—a family member, a friend, a neighbor, etc.

My Great-Uncle

My great-uncle is 85 years old now and he lives alone, but I think he's going to need help soon. He sometimes falls. Also his memory is not good. My aunt thinks she'll have to put him in a nursing home . . .

For more practice using grammar in context, please visit our Web site.

Grammar
Habitual Past with *Used To*

The Simple Past Tense

Context
Working Toward Equality

Martin Luther King Jr., 1929–1968

Equal Rights for All

Before You Read

1. In your native country, does the government give equality to everyone?

2. Is there one group of people that has a harder life than other groups? Which group? What kinds of problems do these people have?

Rosa Parks

CD 1, TR 25

Read the following textbook article. Pay special attention to simple past tense verbs and *used to* + base form.

Did You Know?

Martin Luther King Jr., was interested in the ideas of Mahatma Gandhi of India. He studied and used Gandhi's technique of nonviolent protest.

Today all people in the United States have equal rights under the law. But this **was** not always the case, especially for African-Americans.[1] Even though slavery in the U.S. **ended** in 1865, blacks **continued** to suffer discrimination[2] and segregation,[3] especially in the South. Many hotels, schools, and restaurants **were** for whites only. Many businesses there **used to have** signs in their windows that **said** "Blacks Not Allowed." Black children **used to go** to separate, and often inferior, schools. Many professions **were** for whites only. Even in sports, blacks could not join the major leagues; there **used to be** separate leagues for blacks.

In many places in the South, buses **used to reserve** the front seats for white people. One evening in December of 1955, a 42-year-old woman, Rosa Parks, **got** on a bus in Montgomery, Alabama, to go home from work. She **was** tired when she **sat** down. When some white people **got** on the crowded bus, the bus driver **ordered** Ms. Parks to stand up. Ms. Parks **refused** to leave her seat. The bus driver **called** the police, and they **came** and **arrested** Ms. Parks.

Martin Luther King Jr.,[4] a black minister living in Montgomery, Alabama, **wanted** to put an end to discrimination. When King **heard** about Ms. Parks's arrest, he **told** African-Americans in Montgomery to boycott[5] the bus company. People who **used to** ride the bus to work **decided** to walk instead. As a result of the boycott, the Supreme Court **outlawed**[6] discrimination on public transportation.

---

[1] *African-Americans*, whose ancestors came from Africa as slaves, are sometimes called "blacks." They used to be called "negroes" or "colored."

[2] *Discrimination* means giving some people unfair treatment, especially because of race, age, religion, etc.

[3] *Segregation* means separation of the races.

[4] When a father and son have the same name, the father uses *senior* (Sr.) after his name; the son puts *junior* (Jr.) after his name.

[5] To *boycott* is to refuse to do business with a company.

[6] *To outlaw* means to make an action illegal or against the law.

In 1964, about 100 years after the end of slavery, Congress **passed** a new law that officially **gave** equality to all Americans. This law **made** discrimination in employment and education illegal. King **won** the Nobel Peace Prize[7] for his work in creating a better world.

In 1968, a great tragedy **occurred**. Someone **shot** and **killed** King when he was only 39 years old.

In 1983, Martin Luther King's birthday (January 15) **became** a national holiday.

African-American Firsts

1947 Jackie Robinson was the first African-American to play on a major-league baseball team.

1983 Guion Bluford was the first African-American to go into space.

1989 Oprah Winfrey became the first African-American to own her own television and film production company.

1997 Tiger Woods, whose father is African-American and whose mother is Thai, became both the first African-American and the first Asian-American to win the Masters golf tournament.

2001 Halle Berry became the first African-American woman to win an Oscar for best actress.

2001 General Colin Powell became the first African-American secretary of state.

2005 Condoleezza Rice became the first female African-American secretary of state.

2009 Barack Obama became the first African-American president.

Oprah Winfrey

Colin Powell and Condoleezza Rice

---

[7]The *Nobel Peace Prize* is one of six prizes given once a year for great work in promoting peace. Other prizes are for literature, science, and economics.

3.1 Habitual Past with *Used To*

EXAMPLES	EXPLANATION
Black children **used to** have separate schools. Many professions **used to** be for white people only. There **used to** be separate baseball teams for black people.	*Used to* + a base form shows a habit or custom over a past period of time. This custom no longer exists.

Language Notes:

1. *Used to* is for past habits or customs. It is not for an action that happened once or a few times.

   Many restaurants **used to** serve white people only. (This happened over a period of time.)

   Rosa Parks **used to** ride the bus to work. (This happened over a period of time.)

   In 1955, Rosa Parks **got** on the bus and **refused** to stand. (This happened one time.)

   The bus driver **called** the police. (This happened one time.)

2. For negatives, omit the *d* in *used to*.

   Some restaurants **didn't use** to serve African-Americans.

EXERCISE **1** **ABOUT YOU** Tell which of the following you used to do when you were a child.

EXAMPLE   cry a lot
I used to cry a lot.

1. enjoy school
2. obey my parents
3. attend religious school
4. play with dolls
5. play soccer
6. fight with other children
7. draw pictures
8. have a pet
9. tell lies
10. read mystery stories
11. live on a farm
12. live with my grandparents
13. watch a lot of TV
14. read comic books

EXERCISE **2** **ABOUT YOU** Name something. Practice *used to*.

EXAMPLE   Name something you used to know when you were in elementary school.

I used to know the names of all the presidents (but I don't know them anymore).

1. Name something you used to do when you were a child.
2. Tell what kind of stories you used to enjoy when you were a child.

3. Name something you used to believe when you were a child.

4. Name something you used to like to eat when you were a child.

5. Tell about some things your parents, grandparents, or teachers used to tell you when you were a child.

6. Tell about some things you used to do when you were younger.

EXERCISE **3** **ABOUT YOU** **Write sentences comparing the way you used to live with the way you live now. Share your sentences with a partner or with the entire class.**

EXAMPLES I used to live with my whole family. Now I live alone.

I used to work in a restaurant. Now I'm a full-time student.

I didn't use to speak English at all. Now I speak English pretty well.

Ideas for sentences:
school   job   hobbies   apartment/house   family life   friends

1. _____

_____

2. _____

_____

3. _____

_____

EXERCISE **4** **A young man is comparing how his life used to be five years ago and how his life is now. Complete his statements. Answers may vary.**

EXAMPLE I used to _____be lazy_____. Now I work hard.

1. I used to _____. Now I save my money.

2. I used to _____. Now I'm a serious student.

3. I used to _____. Now I live alone.

4. I used to _____. Now I almost never watch TV.

5. I used to _____. Now I come home after work and study.

6. I used to _____. Now I have short hair.

7. I used to _____. Now I have a car and drive everywhere.

8. I used to _____. Now I'm on a diet and I'm losing weight.

(continued)

9. I used to _____. Now I make my own decisions.

10. I used to _____. Now I use my credit card for most of my purchases.

George Dawson—Life Is So Good

Before You Read

1. Is it necessary to know how to read in order to have a good life?

2. Is it hard for old people to learn new things?

CD 1, TR 26

Read the following magazine article. Pay special attention to the simple past tense.

George Dawson lived in three centuries—the end of the nineteenth, all through the twentieth, and the start of the twenty-first. He **was** born in 1898 in Texas, the grandson of slaves. He **was** the oldest of five children. His family **was** very poor, so George **had** to go to work to help his family. He **started** working full-time for his father when he **was** four years old. As a result, he **didn't attend** school. He **worked** at many jobs during his lifetime: he **chopped** wood, **swept** floors, **helped** build the railroad, and **cleaned** houses. For most of his adult life, he **ran** farm machinery at a dairy farm.[8]

George Dawson (1898–2001)

In his lifetime, great technological changes **occurred:** cars, television, airplanes, spaceships, and computers **came** into being. He **saw** several wars and political changes in the U.S. He **outlived**[9] four wives and two of his seven children.

He **lived** at a time when African-Americans **had** fewer opportunities than they do today. And he **lived** in the South, where there **was** a lot of discrimination against African-Americans; African-Americans **were** segregated from others, and job possibilities **were** limited. By the end of his life, he **saw** others have the opportunities that he **didn't have** when he **was** young. He **witnessed** the success of many African-Americans.

Because he **didn't know** how to read or write, he **signed** his name with an X. Then, when he **was** 98 years old, Dawson **started** attending school. He **went** to adult literacy classes in Dallas County. The teacher **asked** him, "Do you know the alphabet?" He **answered**, "No." Over the next few years,

---

[8]On a *dairy farm*, cows are used to produce milk and milk products.
[9]*To outlive* means to live longer than others.

his teacher, Carl Henry, **taught** Dawson to read and write. Dawson **said**, "Every morning I get up and I wonder what I might learn that day."

In 1998, an elementary school teacher, Richard Glaubman, **read** an article about Dawson in the newspaper. He **wanted** to meet Dawson. Together Glaubman and Dawson **wrote** a book about Dawson's life, called *Life Is So Good*. In this book, Dawson tells about what makes a person happy. Dawson **had** a close family and never **felt** lonely. He **learned** from his father to see the good things in life. His father **told** him, "We **were** born to die. You **didn't come** here to stay, and life is something to enjoy." He **taught** his children to see the richness in life. Dawson says in the book, "We make our own way. Trouble is out there, but a person can leave it alone and just do the right thing. Then, if trouble still finds you, you've done the best you can. . . . People worry too much. Life is good, just the way it is."

Excerpt from Dawson's book:
"My first day of school **was** January 4, 1996. I **was** ninety-eight years old and I'm still going. . . . I'm up by five-thirty to make my lunch, pack my books, and go over my schoolwork. Books was[10] something missing from my life for so long. . . . I **learned** to read my ABC's in two days—I **was** in a hurry. . . . Now I am a man that can read."

3.2 Past Tense of *Be*

The past tense of *be* has two forms: *was* and *were*.

EXAMPLES	EXPLANATION

Life **was** hard for George Dawson.
He **was** poor.
His grandparents **were** slaves.
	The past tense of the verb *be* has two forms: *was* and *were*.
	    I, he, she, it ⟶ was
	    we, you, they ⟶ were

There **was** discrimination in the South. There **were** many changes in the twentieth century.	After *there*, use *was* or *were* depending on the noun that follows. Use *was* with a singular noun. Use *were* with a plural noun.
Dawson's life **wasn't** easy. Education and books **weren't** available to Dawson as a child.	To make a negative statement, put *not* after *was* or *were*. The contraction for *was not* is *wasn't*. The contraction for *were not* is *weren't*.
Dawson **was born** in 1898.	Use a form of *be* with *born*.
Dawson **was** married four times. He **was** never bored.	Use *be* with adjectives that end in -ed: *crowded, tired, bored, interested, worried, married, divorced, allowed,* and *permitted*.

[10]These are Dawson's exact words. However, this sentence is not grammatically correct. The correct way is: Books *were* . . . .

(continued)

Habitual Past with *Used To*; The Simple Past Tense   **93**

Compare affirmative statements and questions.

Wh- Word	Was/Were	Subject	Was/Were	Complement	Short Answer
		Dawson	was	poor.	
	Was	he		a slave?	No, he **wasn't**.
Where	was	he		from?	

Compare negative statements and questions.

Wh- Word	Wasn't/Weren't	Subject	Wasn't/Weren't	Complement
		Dawson	wasn't	in school.
Why	**wasn't**	he		in school?
		There	weren't	many opportunities.
Why	**weren't**	there		many opportunities?

EXERCISE 5   **Fill in the blanks with an appropriate word. Some answers may vary.**

EXAMPLE   George Dawson ____was____ poor.

1. Dawson was _____ in 1898.

2. At that time, there _____ a lot of discrimination.

3. His parents _____ poor.

4. Life for most African-Americans in the South was _____.

5. Job possibilities for African-Americans _____ limited.

6. When he was _____, he learned how to read.

7. Dawson's father used to tell him, "We _____ born to die."

8. He was poor, but he wasn't _____.

EXERCISE 6   **Fill in the blanks with the correct word(s).**

EXAMPLE   Martin Luther King Jr. _____ was _____ a great American.

1. Martin Luther King Jr. _____ born in Georgia.

2. He (not) _____ born in Alabama.

3. He and his father _____ ministers.

4. There _____ discrimination on public transportation.

5. _____ discrimination in employment? Yes, there _____.

6. Rosa Parks was a citizen of Montgomery, Alabama. _____ an African-American? Yes, she was.

7. She was tired and took a seat on the bus. Why _____ tired?

8. African-Americans weren't allowed to sit down on a crowded bus in Montgomery. Why _____ allowed to sit down?

9. George Dawson wasn't able to write his name. Why _____ able to write his name?

10. George Dawson (not) _____ lonely.

11. How old _____ when he learned to read? He was 98 years old.

12. _____ slavery when Dawson was born? No, there wasn't.

3.3 The Simple Past Tense of Regular Verbs

To form the simple past tense of regular verbs, add *-ed* to the base form.[11]

EXAMPLES	EXPLANATION
Dawson **signed** his name with an X. Dawson **learned** a lot from his father. African-Americans **suffered** discrimination. Dawson **lived** to be 103 years old.	**Base Form** **Past Form** sign sign**ed** learn learn**ed** suffer suffer**ed** live live**d** If the verb ends in an *e*, add only *-d*. The past forms are the same for all persons.
Dawson **learned** *to read* and *write*. A teacher **wanted** *to meet* Dawson.	The verb after *to* does not use the past form.

[11]For a review of the spelling and pronunciation of the *-ed* past form, see Appendix A.

EXERCISE 7   Fill in the blanks with the past tense of the verb in parentheses ( ).

EXAMPLE   Dawson __learned__ to read when he was 98.
        (learn)

1. He _____ for many, many years.
      (live)

2. He _____ his name with an X.
      (sign)

3. He _____ all his wives.
      (outlive)

4. Many changes _____ during his long life.
                  (occur)

5. He _____ school when he was 98.
      (attend)

6. His teacher _____, "Do you know the alphabet?"
                (ask)

7. Dawson _____ from his father to enjoy life.
          (learn)

8. Richard Glaubman _____ to meet Dawson.
                    (want)

EXERCISE 8   Fill in the blanks with the simple past tense of the verb in parentheses ( ).

EXAMPLE   King __lived__ in the South.
        (live)

1. Slavery _____ in 1865, but discrimination _____.
           (end)   (continue)

2. King _____ equality for all people.
        (want)

3. King _____ as a minister.
        (work)

4. In many places, the law _____ whites from blacks.
                            (separate)

5. Black children _____ separate schools.
                  (attend)

6. A bus driver _____ Rosa Parks to stand up, but she _____.
                (order)   (refuse)

7. The bus driver _____ the police.
                  (call)

8. The police _____ Ms. Parks.
              (arrest)

9. King _____ a peaceful protest.
        (organize)

10. In 1964, Congress _____ the law.
                       (change)

11. In 1968, a great tragedy _____. Someone _____ King.
                              (occur)   (kill)

Black students entering
a school in Clinton,
Tennessee, in 1956

3.4 The Simple Past of Irregular Verbs[12]

Many past tense verbs are irregular. They do not have an *-ed* ending.

Verbs With No Change				Final *d* Changes to *t*	
beat	fit	put	spit	bend—bent	send—sent
bet	hit	quit	split	build—built	spend—spent
cost	hurt	set	spread	lend—lent	
cut	let	shut			

Verbs with Vowel Changes

feel—felt	mean—meant[13]	dig—dug	sting—stung
keep—kept	sleep—slept	hang—hung	strike—struck
leave—left	sweep—swept	spin—spun	swing—swung
lose—lost	weep—wept	stick—stuck	win—won
awake—awoke	speak—spoke	begin—began	sing—sang
break—broke	steal—stole	drink—drank	sink—sank
choose—chose	wake—woke	ring—rang	spring—sprang
freeze—froze		shrink—shrank	swim—swam
bring—brought	fight—fought	blow—blew	grow—grew
buy—bought	teach—taught	draw—drew	know—knew
catch—caught	think—thought	fly—flew	throw—threw
arise—arose	rise—rose	bleed—bled	meet—met
drive—drove	shine—shone	feed—fed	read—read[14]
ride—rode	write—wrote	flee—fled	speed—sped
		lead—led	
sell—sold	tell—told	find—found	wind—wound
mistake—mistook	take—took	lay—laid	say—said[15]
shake—shook		pay—paid	
swear—swore	wear—wore	bite—bit	light—lit
tear—tore		hide—hid	slide—slid
become—became	forgive—forgave	fall—fell	run—ran
come—came	give—gave	hold—held	sit—sat
eat—ate	lie—lay		see—saw
forget—forgot	shoot—shot	stand—stood	
get—got		understand—understood	

Miscellaneous Changes

be—was/were	go—went	hear—heard
do—did	have—had	make—made

[12]For an alphabetical list of irregular verbs, see Appendix M.
[13]There is a change in the vowel sound. *Meant* rhymes with *sent*.
[14]The past form of *read* is pronounced like the color *red*.
[15]*Said* rhymes with *bed*.

EXERCISE 9 **Fill in the blanks with the past tense of the verb in parentheses ( ).**

EXAMPLE Dawson ____had____ a hard life.
(have)

1. He _____ to work for his father when he was four years old.
(begin)

2. He _____ many changes in his lifetime.
(see)

3. He _____ interested in reading when he was 98.
(become)

4. He _____ to the adult literacy program in Dallas County.
(go)

5. His teacher _____ him the alphabet.
(teach)

6. Dawson _____, "I wonder what I might learn today."
(say)

7. Dawson _____ a book.
(write)

EXERCISE 10 **Fill in the blanks with the past tense of the verb in parentheses ( ).**

EXAMPLE King ____fought____ for the rights of all people.
(fight)

1. King _____ born in 1929.
(be)

2. King _____ a minister.
(become)

3. He _____ married in 1953.
(get)

4. He _____ a job in a church in Montgomery, Alabama.
(find)

5. Rosa Parks was tired and _____ down on the bus.
(sit)

6. Some white people _____ on the bus.
(get)

7. The bus driver _____ Parks to stand up.
(tell)

8. Police _____ and arrested Parks.
(come)

9. King _____ about her arrest.
(hear)

10. In 1963, he _____ a beautiful speech in Washington, D.C.
(give)

11. Many people _____ to see King in Washington in 1963.
(go)

12. King _____ an important prize for his work.
(win)

13. A man _____ King in 1968.
(shoot)

Barack Obama and *Dreams from My Father*

Before You Read

1. Where were you at the time of the 2008 election of Barack Obama?

2. Are there or were there any unusual leaders in your native country?

CD 1, TR 27

Read the following magazine article. Pay special attention to the negative form of past-tense verbs.

On January 20, 2009, Barack Obama became the first African-American president.

He was born in Hawaii in 1961, the son of a Kenyan father and an American mother. But Barack **didn't know** his father as he was growing up. When he was two years old, his parents separated and his father went back to Africa. Obama saw his father one more time in his life, when his father visited Hawaii. His father died in a car accident in 1982 when Barack was 21 years old. In 1995, he wrote about his life in *Dreams from My Father*. He realized that he **didn't belong** completely to a white world and he **didn't belong** completely to a black world. When he was young, he **didn't have** a clear racial identity.

Barack Obama with his mother

His mother married again, this time to an Indonesian man, and for a while Barack lived with her in Indonesia. But he returned to Hawaii when he was ten to live with his grandparents. His mother returned too, but she **didn't stay** for long. She went back to Indonesia, where she stayed for the rest of her life. For many years he **didn't live** with his mother. She died in 1995.

Barack Obama adored his grandmother but, sadly, she **didn't live** to see him become president. She died one day before the election.

3.5 Negative Statements

Compare affirmative and negative statements with past tense verbs.

EXAMPLES	EXPLANATION
Obama **lived** with his mother's parents. He **didn't live** with his father's parents. Obama **grew** up in Hawaii. He **didn't grow** up in Africa. Obama **knew** his mother. He **didn't know** his father well.	For the negative past tense, we use *didn't* + base form for ALL verbs (except *be*), regular and irregular. **Compare:** lived—didn't live grew—didn't grow knew—didn't know

EXERCISE 11 **Fill in the blanks with the negative form of the underlined word.**

EXAMPLE   Obama <u>spent</u> many years in Hawaii. He ____*didn't spend*____ many years in Kenya.

1. Obama <u>wrote</u> about his life. He _____ a novel.

2. He <u>was</u> born in Hawaii. He _____ born in Illinois.

3. He <u>lived</u> in the U.S. He _____ in Kenya.

4. He <u>knew</u> his mother. He _____ his father very well.

5. His mother <u>went</u> to Indonesia. His grandparents _____ to Indonesia.

6. He <u>saw</u> his grandparents a lot. He _____ his father a lot.

7. He <u>grew</u> up with his grandparents. He _____ up with his father.

8. He <u>studied</u> law. He _____ engineering.

9. He <u>became</u> a senator of Illinois. He _____ a senator of Hawaii.

10. His grandmother <u>died</u> before the election. She _____ after the election.

Questions and Answers about Barack Obama

Before
You Read

1. What facts do you know about Barack Obama?

2. What facts do you know about the president/prime minister of your native country?

CD 1, TR 28

Read the following questions and answers about Barack Obama. Pay special attention to past tense questions and answers.

Q: What did Obama do before he became president?

A: He **was** a senator from Illinois.

Q: When did he get married?

A: He **got** married in 1989.

Q: Who did he marry?

A: He **married** Michelle Robinson.

Q: Where did he meet her?

A: He **met** her at a law office.

Q. Did he work there?

A: Yes. They both **worked** there.

Q: Did he ever teach?

A: Yes. He **taught** law at the
University of Chicago.

Q: Did he live in Chicago?

A: Yes, he **did**. He also **lived** in Springfield, the capital of Illinois,
when he was a senator from Illinois.

Q: Did he win every election?

A: No, he **didn't**. In 2000, he **wanted** to be a U.S. Representative
from Illinois, but he **didn't win**.

3.6 Questions with the Simple Past Tense

Compare affirmative statements and questions.

Wh- Word	Did	Subject	Verb	Complement	Short Answer
		Obama	lived	with his grandparents.	
	Did	he	live	in New York?	No, he didn't.
Where	did	he	live?		In Hawaii.
		Obama	went	to Africa.	
	Did	he	go	to Kenya?	Yes, he did.
When	did	he	go	to Kenya?	In 1988.

Language Note: The base form is used in questions after *did*.

Compare negative statements and questions.

Wh- Word	Didn't	Subject	Didn't	Base Form	Complement
		Obama	didn't	live	with his father.
Why	didn't	Obama		live	with his father?
		His father	didn't	stay	in the U.S.
Why	didn't	he		stay	in the U.S.?

EXERCISE 12 Read each statement. Write a *yes/no* question with the words in parentheses ( ). Give a short answer.

EXAMPLE Obama lived in Hawaii. (with his grandparents) (yes)

Did he live with his grandparents? Yes, he did.

1. His grandmother died before he became president. (his mother) (yes)

_____

2. His father went to Kenya. (his mother) (no)

_____

3. Michelle Robinson became his wife. (his law partner) (no)

_____

4. He met his wife in a law office. (in Hawaii) (no)

_____

5. He lived in Hawaii. (in Indonesia) (yes)

_____

6. He lost the election for representative of Illinois. (senator of Illinois) (no)

_____

7. He taught at the University of Chicago. (law) (yes)

_____

EXERCISE 13   **Read each statement. Write a _wh-_ question about the words in parentheses ( ). Then answer the question.**

EXAMPLE   Obama went to high school. (where) (in Hawaii)

Where did he go to high school?

He went to high school in Hawaii.

1. His mother met his father. (where) (in college)

_____

_____

2. His mother went to Indonesia. (why) (to be with her husband)

_____

_____

3. Obama returned to Hawaii. (when) (in 1971)

_____

_____

4. He studied law. (where) (at Harvard University)

_____

_____

5. He wrote a book. (what kind of book) (about his life)

_____

_____

6. Obama became president. (when) (in 2009)

_____

_____

7. Obama's grandmother died. (when) (in November 2008)

_____

_____

8. Obama didn't work in Hawaii. (why) (because he lived in Illinois)

_____

_____

EXERCISE 14 **A student is interviewing her teacher about Martin Luther King Jr. Fill in the blanks with the correct form of the verb and any other necessary words.**

CD 1, TR 29

S: Do you remember Martin Luther King Jr.?

T: Of course I do. I ___**saw**___ him on TV many times when
(example: see)

I _____ young.
(1 be)

S: _____ him on TV when he was in Washington, D.C.?
(2 see)

T: Yes, I _____. I remember his famous speech in Washington in 1963.
(3)

S: What _____ about?
(4 speak)

T: He _____ about equality for everyone.
(5 speak)

S: _____ to Washington?
(6 a lot of people/go)

T: Oh, yes. 250,000 people _____ to Washington.
(7 go)

S: Do you remember when he died?

T: I was in high school when he _____. The principal
(8 die)

_____ to our class and _____ us the news.
(9 come) *(10 tell)*

S: What _____ when you heard the news?
(11 do)

T: At first we _____ it. Then we all started to
(12 not/believe)

_____. We _____ home from
(13 cry) *(14 go)*

school and _____ the news on TV.
(15 watch)

S: Where _____ he when he died?
(16 be)

T: He _____ on the balcony of a hotel in Memphis when a man
(17 be)

_____ and _____ him. It was terrible. But we should remember
(18 come) *(19 shoot)*

King for his life, not his death. We celebrate Martin Luther King Jr.'s birthday.

S: Really? I _____ that. When is it?
(20 not/know)

T: He _____ born on January 15. The third Monday in January
(21 be)

_____ a national holiday.
(22 become)

S: _____ a holiday right after he died?
(23 this date/become)

T: No. It _____ a holiday in 1983.
(24 become)

S: How do you remember so much about King?

T: I _____ a paper on him when I was in college.
(25 write)

EXERCISE `15`   **ABOUT YOU**   Check (✓) the things you did this past week. Exchange books with another student. Ask the other student about the items he or she checked.

EXAMPLE   <u>✓</u> I made a long-distance phone call.

A: I made a long-distance phone call.

B: Who(m) did you call?

A: I called my father in Mexico.

B: How long did you talk?

A: We talked for about 15 minutes.

1. _____ I made a long-distance phone call.

2. _____ I shopped for groceries.

3. _____ I met someone new.

4. _____ I got together with a friend.

5. _____ I wrote a letter.

6. _____ I bought some new clothes.

7. _____ I went to the bank.

8. _____ I read something interesting (a book, an article).

9. _____ I went to the post office.

10. _____ I did exercises.

11. _____ I received a letter.

12. _____ I went to an interesting place.

Summary of Lesson 3

1. Simple Past Tense

   Be

   Dawson **was** happy.
   He **wasn't** rich.
   Was he from a large family? Yes, he **was.**
   Where **was** he born?
   Why **wasn't** he in school?

   Regular Verb

   Dawson **lived** for 103 years.
   He **didn't live** during the time of slavery.
   Did he **live** in the North? No, he **didn't.**
   Where **did** he **live?**
   Why **didn't** he **live** in the North?

Irregular Verb

Dawson **felt** happy.

He **didn't feel** lonely.

Did he **feel** good when he learned to read? Yes, he **did.**

How **did** he **feel** about his life?

Why **didn't** he **feel** lonely?

2. Habitual Past with *Used To*

Obama **used to** live in Hawaii.

Black children and white children **used to** go to separate schools. Now schools are for all children.

Editing Advice

1. Use *was/were* with *born*.

was
He born in Germany.
^

2. Don't use *was/were* with *die*.

He ~~was~~ died two years ago.

3. Don't use a past form after *to*.

leave
I decided to ~~left~~ early.

I wanted to go home and ~~watched~~ TV.

4. Don't use *was* or *were* to form a simple past tense.

went
He ~~was go~~ home yesterday.

5. Use *there* when a new subject is introduced.

There w
~~W~~as a big earthquake in 1906.

6. Use a form of *be* before an adjective. Remember, some *-ed* words are adjectives.

were
They excited about their trip to America.
^

7. Don't use *did* with an adjective. Use *was/were*.

were
Why ~~did~~ you afraid?

8. Use the correct word order in a question.

> *didn't you*
> Why ~~you didn't~~ return?

9. Use *did* + the base form in a question.

> *did* *buy*
> What kind of car you ~~bought~~?

10. Use the base form after *didn't*.

> He didn't worke~~d~~ yesterday.

11. Don't forget the *d* in *used to*.

> *d*
> She use to live in Miami.

12. Don't add the verb *be* before *used to* for habitual past.

> I~~'m~~ used to play soccer in my country.

Editing Quiz

Some of the shaded words and phrases have mistakes. Find the mistakes and correct them. If the shaded words are correct, write *C*.

A: I didn't *come*
~~came~~ to class last week. I missed two days. What we studied?
(example)   (example)   *C* (1)

B: Why you didn't come to class?
(2)

A: I had to worked overtime, so I tired.
(3)   (4)

B: We had a great lesson. We learn about racial progress in the U.S.
(5)   (6)

We talked about Martin Luther King Jr., George Dawson, and Barack
(7)

Obama.

A: Who was George Dawson?
(8)

B: He was an amazing man. He born at the end of the 1800s.
(9)   (10)

He didn't learned to read when he was young. He started to learn
(11)   (12)

when he was 98 years old.

(continued)

A: Wow! Is he still alive?

B: No, he <u>was died</u> in 2001. And we also <u>learned</u> about Martin Luther
(13)   (14)

King's life.

A: I <u>use</u> to read about him in my country, India. King <u>was studied</u>
(15)   (16)

the ideas of our leader, Gandhi. When I was in my country,

<u>I'm used to study</u> a lot of history.
(17)

B: And <u>was</u> a story about Barack Obama in our book too.
(18)

A: I know. I <u>read</u> it at home. It made me sad.
(19)

B: Why <u>did</u> you sad?
(20)

A: Because his grandmother <u>didn't lived</u> to see him become president.
(21)

B: Yeah, that part was sad.

A: <u>Was</u> any homework?
(22)

B: Yes, <u>there was</u>. We had to <u>wrote</u> a composition about a famous person.
(23)   (24)

A: Thanks for filling me in.

Lesson 3 Test/Review

PART 1 **Write the past form of the following verbs.**

EXAMPLE draw ___*drew*___

1. eat _____
2. put _____
3. give _____
4. write _____
5. send _____
6. listen _____
7. read _____

8. take _____
9. bring _____
10. talk _____
11. know _____
12. find _____
13. stand _____
14. leave _____

15. sit _____
16. go _____
17. make _____
18. hear _____
19. feel _____
20. fall _____
21. get _____

PART 2 **Write the negative form of the underlined word.**

EXAMPLE   Rosa Parks <u>lived</u> in Alabama. She _____ didn't live _____ in Washington.

1. She <u>was</u> tired when she got out of work. She _____ sick.

2. She <u>went</u> to work by bus. She _____ to work by car.

3. The bus driver <u>told</u> African-Americans to stand. He _____ white Americans to stand.

4. Some African-Americans <u>stood</u> up. Rosa Parks _____ up.

5. The police <u>came</u> to the bus. They _____ to her house.

6. They <u>took</u> her to jail. They _____ her to her house.

7. Many people <u>had</u> the opportunity for education. George Dawson _____ the opportunity for education.

8. George Dawson <u>wrote</u> a book. He _____ it alone.

9. Barack Obama <u>spent</u> a lot of time with his grandparents. He _____ a lot of time with his father.

PART 3 **Write a question beginning with the words given. An answer is not necessary.**

EXAMPLE   Martin Luther King Jr. lived in the South.

Where _____ did he live? _____

1. King became a minister.
   Why _____

2. King was born in Georgia.
   When _____

3. Black children went to separate schools.
   Why _____

4. Some restaurants didn't permit black people to eat there.
   Why _____

(continued)

5. King was in jail many times because of his protests.

How many times _____

6. King won the Nobel Peace Prize.

When _____

7. Rosa Parks worked in Montgomery.

Where _____

8. She was tired.

Why _____

9. She went home by bus.

How many times _____

10. She didn't want to obey the law.

Why _____

11. The police took her to jail.

Why _____

12. Dawson learned to read.

When _____

13. Dawson didn't feel lonely.

Why _____

14. Obama didn't know his father very well.

Why _____

15. Obama won the election.

When _____

16. Obama's father wasn't born in the U.S.

Where _____

17. Obama wrote a book.

What _____ about?

PART 4 **Write two sentences with *used to* comparing your life ten years ago with your life today.**

1. _____

2. _____

Expansion

Classroom Activities

1 Check (✓) the sentences that are true for you. Find a partner and exchange books. Give each other more information about the things you checked. Ask each other questions about these activities.

a. _____ I bought a CD in the past week.

b. _____ I worked last Saturday.

c. _____ I rode a bike this past week.

d. _____ I went to a party last weekend.

e. _____ I got a driver's license in the past year.

f. _____ I took a trip in the past year.

g. _____ I got married in the last two years.

h. _____ I found a job this month.

i. _____ I spent more than $50 today.

j. _____ I received some money this week.

k. _____ I ate pizza in the past month.

l. _____ I bought a car in the past year.

m. _____ I came to the U.S. alone.

2 **Who did it?**

Teacher: Pass out an index card to each student.

Students: Write something you did last weekend. It can be something unusual or something ordinary. (Examples: I went fishing. I baked a pie. I did my laundry.)

Teacher: Collect the cards. Pull out one card at a time and read the sentence to the class. The students have to guess who wrote the card.

❸ Who used to do it?

Teacher: Pass out an index card to each student.

Students: Think of some things you used to be, wear, do, etc. when you were younger. Think of things that other students would not guess about you. Write two or three of these things on the card.

Teacher: Collect the cards. Pull out one card at a time and read the sentences to the class. The students have to guess who wrote the card.

EXAMPLES   I used to hate studying a foreign language.
I used to have very long hair.
I used to be a terrible student.

❹ Bring in a picture of yourself when you were younger. Describe how you were at that time and compare yourself to how you are now.

EXAMPLE   I used to play soccer all day with my friends. Now I don't have time for it.

❺ Fill in the blank. Discuss your answers in a small group or with the entire class.

Before I came to the U.S., I used to believe that _____

_____, but now I know it's not true.

❻ With a partner, write a few questions to ask George Dawson.

EXAMPLES   Why didn't you go to school?
What kinds of jobs did you have?
What was the first book you read?

Talk
About It

In a small group or with the entire class, discuss the following:

❶ Changes in daily life: Compare how life used to be when you were younger with how it is now.

❷ Fashion: Talk about different styles or fashions in the past.

EXAMPLE   In the 1960s, men used to wear their hair long.

Write About It

Choose one of the following topics to write a short composition.

❶ Write a paragraph or paragraphs telling about changes in your native country. Compare how life used to be with how it is now.

❷ Write about an ordinary person who did something extraordinary (like George Dawson). It can be someone you read about or someone you know.

❸ Write a paragraph or paragraphs telling about your childhood.

My Childhood

When I was a child, I lived in a big house with my parents, grandparents, sisters, brothers, aunts, and uncles. My parents went to work and my grandparents took care of me. I always had a good time with them. My grandmother used to tell me a lot of stories. My grandfather used to take me fishing…

 For more practice using grammar in context, please visit our Web site.

Lesson

4

Grammar
Possessive Forms

Object Pronouns

Reflexive Pronouns

Questions

Context
Weddings

A Traditional American Wedding

1. What kind of clothes do a bride and groom wear in your native culture?

2. At what age do people usually get married in your native culture?

CD 2, TR 01

Read the following magazine article. Pay special attention to object pronouns and possessive forms.

Did You Know?

- *Most American weddings (80%) take place in a church or synagogue.*
- *The average number of guests is 175.*
- *Hawaii is the favorite honeymoon destination.*
- *August is the most popular month for weddings.*
- *Money is the most desired wedding gift.*
- *About 43 percent of marriages end in separation or divorce within 15 years.*

Many young couples consider their wedding to be one of the most important days of their life. They save for **it** and often spend a year planning for **it**: finding a place, selecting a menu and cake, buying a wedding dress, ordering invitations and sending **them** to friends and relatives, selecting musicians, and much more. The bride chooses **her** maid of honor and bridesmaids, and the groom chooses **his** best man[1] and groomsmen. The bride and groom want to make this day special for themselves and for **their** guests.

When the day arrives, the groom doesn't usually see the bride before the wedding. It is considered bad luck for **him** to see **her** ahead of time. The guests wait with excitement to see **her** too. When the wedding begins, the groom and groomsmen enter first. Then the bridesmaids enter. When the bride finally enters in **her** white dress, everyone turns around to look at **her**. Sometimes guests stand up when the bride enters. Often the **bride's** father or both of **her** parents walk **her** down the aisle to the groom's side.

During the ceremony, the bride and groom take vows.[2] They promise to love and respect each other for the rest of their lives. The groom's best man holds the rings for **them** until they are ready to place **them** on each **other's** fingers. At the end of the ceremony, the groom lifts the **bride's** veil and kisses **her**.

[1]The *best man* is the man who stands beside the groom and helps him.
[2]A *vow* is a promise.

There is a party after the ceremony. People make toasts,[3] eat dinner, and dance. The bride and groom usually dance the first dance alone. Then guests join **them**.

Before the bride and groom leave the party, the bride throws **her** bouquet over **her** head, and the single women try to catch **it**. It is believed that the woman who catches **it** will be the next one to get married.

The newlyweds[4] usually take a trip, called a honeymoon, immediately after the wedding.

4.1 Possessive Forms of Nouns

We use possessive forms to show ownership or relationship.

NOUN	ENDING	EXAMPLES
Singular noun: bride groom	Add apostrophe + **s**.	The **bride's** dress is white. The **groom's** tuxedo is black.
Plural noun ending in **-s**: parents guests	Add apostrophe only.	She got married in her **parents'** house. The **guests'** coats are in the coat room.
Irregular plural noun: men women	Add apostrophe + **s**.	The **men's** suits are black. The **women's** dresses are beautiful.
Names that end in **-s**: Charles	Add apostrophe + **s**.	Do you know **Charles's** wife? **Note:** Sometimes you will see only an apostrophe when a name ends in **s**. Do you know **Charles'** wife?
Inanimate objects: the church the dress	Use "the _____ of the _____." Do not use apostrophe + **s**.	St. Peter's is **the name of the church**. **The front of the dress** has pearls.

[3]A *toast* is a wish for good luck, usually while holding a glass.
[4]For a short time after they are married, the bride and groom are called *newlyweds*.

EXERCISE 1 Fill in the blanks to make the possessive form of the noun.

EXAMPLE The bride's grandfather looks very handsome.

1. The groom _____ mother is very nice.
2. The bride _____ flowers are beautiful.
3. The bridesmaids _____ dresses are blue.
4. They invited many guests to the wedding. They didn't invite the guests _____ children.
5. The women _____ dresses are very elegant.
6. Charles _____ sister is a bridesmaid.
7. The newlyweds _____ picture is in the newspaper.
8. Do you know the children _____ names?

EXERCISE 2 Fill in the blanks with the two nouns in parentheses ( ). Put them in the correct order. Use the possessive form of one of the nouns, except with nonliving things.

EXAMPLES The ___bride's name___ is Lisa.
(name/the bride)

The ___door of the church___ is open.
(door/church)

1. The _____ came to the wedding from London.
(bride/grandmother)

2. The _____ has a red carpet.
(church/floor)

3. The _____ are very beautiful.
(windows/church)

4. The _____ is crying.
(bride/mother)

5. The _____ is Saint Paul's.
(church/name)

6. The _____ are black.
(men/tuxedos)

7. The _____ is white.
(limousine/color)

8. The _____ are pretty.
(dresses/girls)

9. Who chose the _____?
(flowers/color)

10. Some people get married in their _____.
(house/parents)

4.2 Possessive Adjectives

Possessive adjectives show ownership or relationship.

EXAMPLES	EXPLANATION
My brother is getting married. Your gift is wonderful. The groom chooses his best man. The bride chooses her bridesmaids. The restaurant has its own reception hall. Our cousins came from out of town. The wedding is the most important day of their lives.	<table><tr><td>Subject Pronouns</td><td>Possessive Adjectives</td></tr><tr><td>I</td><td>my</td></tr><tr><td>you</td><td>your</td></tr><tr><td>he</td><td>his</td></tr><tr><td>she</td><td>her</td></tr><tr><td>it</td><td>its</td></tr><tr><td>we</td><td>our</td></tr><tr><td>they</td><td>their</td></tr></table>

My sister loves her husband.
 	
My uncle lives with his daughter.
	Be careful not to confuse *his* and *her*.
	    Wrong: My sister loves *his* husband.
	    Wrong: My uncle lives with *her* daughter.

The bride's mother's dress is blue.	We can use two possessive nouns together.
My brother's wife did not attend the wedding.	We can use a possessive adjective (*my*) before a possessive noun (*brother's*).

EXERCISE **3** **Fill in the blanks with a possessive adjective.**

EXAMPLE   I love _____ my _____ parents.

1. I have one sister. _____ sister got married five years ago.

2. She loves _____ husband very much.

3. He's an accountant. He has _____ own business.

4. They have one child. _____ son's name is Jason.

5. They bought a house last year. _____ house isn't far from my house.

6. My sister and I visit _____ parents once a month. They live two hours away from us.

7. My sister said, "My car isn't working this week. Let's visit them in _____ car."

EXERCISE **4**   **Fill in the blanks with a possessive adjective.**

CD 2, TR 02

A: What are you going to wear to ___*your*___ sister's
(example)
wedding?

B: I'm going to wear _____ new blue dress.
(1)

A: Did your sister buy a new dress for her wedding?

B: No. She's going to borrow _____ best friend's dress.
(2)

A: Will the wedding be at your home?

B: Oh, no. We live in an apartment. _____ apartment
(3)
is too small. We're going to invite more than 200 guests. The wedding
is going to be at a church. Afterwards, we're going to have a dinner in a
restaurant. The restaurant has _____ own
(4)
reception hall.

A: Are the newlyweds going on a honeymoon after the wedding?

B: Yes. They have friends who have a cottage. They're going to stay at
_____ friends' cottage in the country for a week.
(5)

A: Is the groom's mother a nice woman?

B: I don't know _____ mother. I'll meet her at the
(6)
wedding for the first time.

4.3 Possessive Pronouns

We can use possessive pronouns (*mine, yours, his, hers, ours, theirs*) to show
ownership or relationship.

POSSESSIVE ADJECTIVE	POSSESSIVE PRONOUN	EXPLANATION
Her dress is white. **Their wedding** was big. We had **our wedding** in a church.	**Mine** is blue. **Ours** was small. They had **theirs** in a garden.	When we omit the noun, we use a possessive pronoun. *mine* = my dress *ours* = our wedding *theirs* = their wedding
The groom's parents look happy.	**The bride's** do too.	After the possessive form of a noun, we can omit the noun. *The bride's* = the bride's parents

Compare the three forms below.

SUBJECT PRONOUN	POSSESSIVE ADJECTIVE	POSSESSIVE PRONOUN
I	my	mine
you	your	yours
he	his	his
she	her	hers
it	its	—
we	our	ours
they	their	theirs

EXERCISE 5 **Fill in the blanks with an appropriate possessive adjective or pronoun.**

CD 2, TR 03

A: I heard your brother got married last month. How was the wedding?

Was it anything like your wedding? I remember ___**yours**___
(example)

very well.

B: My brother's wedding was very different from

_____. His was a very formal wedding
(1)

in a church last month. _____ was very
(2)

informal, in a garden.

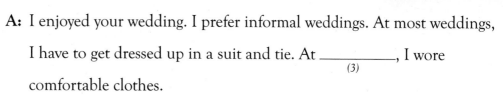

A: I enjoyed your wedding. I prefer informal weddings. At most weddings,

I have to get dressed up in a suit and tie. At _____, I wore
(3)

comfortable clothes.

B: _____ brother and _____ bride had a very different
(4) *(5)*

honeymoon too. Our honeymoon was a two-day trip. _____ was a
(6)

two-week stay in a luxury hotel in Hawaii. Their honeymoon was

expensive. _____ was very economical. We drove to Chicago and
(7)

stayed in a motel there.

A: I remember your wife made her own dress. You saved a lot of money.

B: My sister-in-law, Gina, spent a lot of money on _____ dress.
(8)

_____ cost over $1,000. My wife's was only about $100.
(9)

(continued)

A: The cost of a wedding isn't the most important thing. The most

important thing is the happiness that follows. My uncle's wedding

cost over $30,000. _____ was the most beautiful
                        (10)

wedding you can imagine. But his marriage lasted only eight months.

EXERCISE 6 Fill in the blanks with *I, I'm, me, my,* or *mine.*

1. _____ a student.

2. _____ live in an apartment near school.

3. _____ apartment is on the first floor.

4. _____ parents often visit _____.

5. They don't have a computer. They use _____.

EXERCISE 7 Fill in the blanks with *we, we're, us, our,* or *ours.*

1. _____ classroom is large.

2. _____ study English here.

3. _____ foreign students.

4. The teacher helps _____ learn English.

5. The teacher brings her book, and we bring _____.

EXERCISE 8 Fill in the blanks with *you, you're, your,* or *yours.* Pretend you are talking directly to the teacher.

1. _____ the teacher.

2. _____ come from the U.S.

3. My first language is Polish. _____ is English.

4. _____ pronunciation is very good.

5. We see _____ every day.

EXERCISE 9 Fill in the blanks with *he, he's, his,* or *him.*

1. I have a brother. _____ name is Paul.

2. _____ married.

3. _____ has four children.

4. My apartment is small. _____ is big.

5. I see _____ on the weekends.

EXERCISE 10   **Fill in the blanks with _she, she's, her,_ or _hers._**

1. I have a sister. _____ name is Marilyn.
2. I visit _____ twice a week.
3. _____ lives in a suburb.
4. _____ a teacher. _____ husband is a doctor.
5. My children go to private school. _____ go to public school.

EXERCISE 11   **Fill in the blanks with _it, it's,_ or _its._**

1. The school has a big library. _____ comfortable and clean.
2. _____ has many books and magazines.
3. _____ hours are from 8 a.m. to 8 p.m.
4. I use _____ every day.
5. _____ on the first floor.

EXERCISE 12   **Fill in the blanks with _they, they're, them, their,_ or _theirs._**

1. My parents rent _____ apartment.
2. My apartment is small, but _____ is big.
3. _____ very old now.
4. _____ live in a suburb.
5. I visit _____ on the weekends.

4.4 Questions with _Whose_

Whose + a noun asks a question about ownership.

WHOSE + NOUN	AUXILIARY VERB	SUBJECT	VERB	ANSWER
Whose dress	did	the bride	borrow?	She borrowed her sister's dress.
Whose flowers	are	those?		They're the bride's flowers.
Whose last name	will	the bride	use?	She'll use her husband's last name.

EXERCISE **13** **Write a question with *whose*. The answer is given.**

EXAMPLE <u>Whose flowers are these?</u>

They're the bride's flowers.

1. _____

   That's my father's car.

2. _____

   Those are the newlyweds' gifts.

3. _____

   She's wearing her sister's necklace.

4. _____

   I'm wearing my friend's suit.

5. _____

   I follow my parents' advice.

6. _____

   The bride borrowed her sister's dress.

4.5 Object Pronouns

We can use an object pronoun (*me, you, him, her, it, us,* or *them*) after the verb.

OBJECT NOUN	OBJECT PRONOUN	EXPLANATION
Daniel loves **Sofia**. Sofia loves **Daniel**. You met **my parents**.	He loves **her** very much. She loves **him** very much. You met **them** last night.	We can use an object pronoun to substitute for an object noun.
Do you know **the guests**? The bride and groom sent **invitations**.	Yes, we know **them**. They sent **them** last month.	We use *them* for plural people and things.
I see **the bride**. The bride is with **her father**.	Everyone is looking *at* **her**. She will dance *with* **him**.	An object pronoun can follow a preposition (*at, with, of, about, to, from, in,* etc.).

Compare subject and object pronouns.

SUBJECT	OBJECT	EXAMPLES		
		Subject	**Verb**	**Object**
I	me	You	love	me.
you	you	I	love	you.
he	him	She	loves	him.
she	her	He	loves	her.
it	it	We	love	it.
we	us	They	love	us.
they	them	We	love	them.

EXERCISE 14 **Fill in the blanks with an object pronoun in place of the underlined words.**

EXAMPLE The groom doesn't walk down the aisle with <u>the bride</u>. Her father walks with ____*her*____.

1. <u>The bride</u> doesn't enter with <u>the groom</u>. He waits for _____, and she goes to _____.

2. The groom takes <u>the ring</u>. He puts _____ on the bride's hand.

3. <u>The bride</u> wears <u>a veil</u>. The groom lifts _____ to kiss _____.

4. The bride doesn't throw <u>the bouquet</u> to all the women. She throws _____ to the single women only.

5. People make toasts to <u>the bride and groom</u>. They wish _____ health and happiness.

6. <u>The groom</u> promises to love the bride, and the bride promises to love _____.

EXERCISE 15 **Fill in the blanks with the correct subject pronoun, object pronoun, or possessive adjective.**

🔊

CD 2, TR 04

A: How was your cousin Lisa's wedding last Saturday?

B: ____*It*____ was great.
  (example)

A: How many guests were there?

B: Maybe about 200. I couldn't count _____.
  (1)

A: Wow! That's a lot. It sounds like an expensive wedding. How did they pay for _____?
  (2)

(continued)

B: Lisa and Ron worked when _____ graduated from college
(3)

and saved money for _____ wedding. _____
(4)   (5)

parents helped _____ a little, but they couldn't depend on
(6)

_____ too much. _____ parents aren't wealthy.
(7)   (8)

A: Did Lisa wear a traditional white dress?

B: Yes. In fact, _____ wore _____ mother's
(9)   (10)

wedding dress. She looked beautiful in _____.
(11)

A: Where did _____ go on their honeymoon?
(12)

B: They went to Hawaii. I was surprised—they sent _____
(13)

a postcard. They had a great time.

A: I hope _____ will be happy. The wedding and honeymoon
(14)

are important, but the marriage that follows is what really counts.

B: I agree with _____. But I'm sure they'll be happy.
(15)

She loves _____ and _____
(16)   (17)

loves _____ very much.
(18)

A: Did you take pictures?

B: Yes. Do you want to see _____? I took _____
(19)   (20)

with my new digital camera.

A: I don't have time now. Can you show _____ the pictures
(21)

tomorrow?

B: I'll e-mail _____ to _____ later this evening.
(22)   (23)

New Wedding Trends

Before You Read

1. American wedding customs are changing. Are wedding customs changing in your native culture?

2. In your native culture, what kind of vows do the bride and groom make to each other?

CD 2, TR 05

Read the following Web article. Pay special attention to direct and indirect objects after verbs.

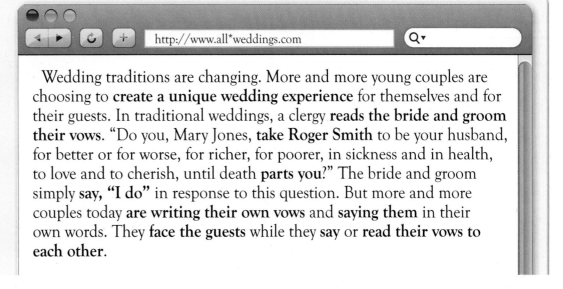

http://www.all*weddings.com

Wedding traditions are changing. More and more young couples are choosing to **create a unique wedding experience** for themselves and for their guests. In traditional weddings, a clergy **reads the bride and groom their vows**. "Do you, Mary Jones, **take Roger Smith** to be your husband, for better or for worse, for richer, for poorer, in sickness and in health, to love and to cherish, until death **parts you**?" The bride and groom simply **say, "I do"** in response to this question. But more and more couples today **are writing their own vows** and **saying them** in their own words. They **face the guests** while they **say** or **read their vows to each other**.

(continued)

Churches and synagogues are still the most popular places for a wedding. But some couples are choosing to **have a destination wedding.** They get married on the beach, on a mountain top, or other unusual place. These weddings **have fewer guests** because of the expense of traveling. Often the bride and groom **pay for the hotel rooms** of their guests. They **tell their guests the date** at least three to four months in advance. Often they **send them "save-the-date" cards** so that their guests can **make plans** to **attend the wedding.**

Another new trend in weddings is to **create a wedding** based on the couple's ethnic background. For example, in an African-American wedding, some couples want to **show respect to their ancestors**[5] by jumping over a broom, a tradition coming from the time of slavery. The jumping of the broom **symbolizes a new beginning** by sweeping away the old and welcoming the new. Some African-Americans **use colorful clothing** inspired by African costumes, rather than a white dress for the bride and a suit or tuxedo for the groom.

One thing stays the same. The newlyweds **send the guests thank–you cards** by mail to **thank them** for attending the wedding and for the gifts they gave.

[5]*Ancestors* are your grandparents, great-grandparents, great-great-grandparents, etc.

4.6 Direct and Indirect Objects

Some verbs are followed by both a direct and an indirect object. The order of the objects sometimes depends on the verb.[6] It sometimes depends on pronoun use.

EXAMPLES	EXPLANATION
Pattern A: 	Subj.	Verb	Indirect Obj.	Direct Obj.
We	gave	the couple	a wedding gift.
They	sent	us	a thank-you card.
She	read	the groom	her vows.
They	showed	me	their pictures.		With the following verbs, we follow Pattern A or Pattern B. bring read show give sell tell offer send write pay (e-)mail
Pattern B: 	Subj.	Verb	Direct Obj.	*To* Indirect Obj.
We	gave	a wedding gift	to the couple.
She	read	her vows	to the groom.		In Pattern A, we put the indirect object before the direct object. In Pattern B, we put the direct object first and then use *to* + the indirect object.
Ed gave Ann a ring. He gave **it** to Ann on her birthday. Do you have the pictures? Can you show **them** to me?	When the direct object is a pronoun, we follow Pattern B.
Direct Obj. *To* **Indirect Obj.** Please explain wedding customs to me. Please describe the wedding to us.	With the following verbs, we follow Pattern B: direct object *to* indirect object. announce mention say describe prove suggest explain report

EXERCISE 16 CD 2, TR 06 **Fill in the blanks with the words in parentheses ( ). Put them in the correct order. Add *to* if necessary. In some cases, more than one answer is possible.**

A: How was your cousin's wedding? Can you describe

_____ *it to me* _____?

(example: it/me)

B: It was beautiful. The bride read _____,

(1 a lovely poem/the groom)

and then the groom read _____ too.

(2 a poem/her)

A: Did they get married in a church?

B: No. They got married in a beautiful garden. Why didn't

you go? I thought they sent _____?

(3 an invitation/you)

[6]For a more detailed list of verbs and the order of direct and indirect objects, see Appendix I.   *(continued)*

A: They did. But I couldn't go. I wrote _____ and (4 a letter/them)

I explained _____. I had to take an important (5 them/my problem)

exam for college that day. But I sent _____. (6 a lovely present/them)

B: I'm sure they'll appreciate it. It's too bad you couldn't go.

A: I'm sure I mentioned _____ a few weeks ago. (7 you/it)

B: You probably did, but I forgot.

A: Do you have pictures from the wedding?

B: I took a lot of pictures. I'll e-mail _____ tonight. (8 you/them)

A: Thanks.

4.7 Say and Tell

Say and tell have the same meaning, but we use them differently.

EXAMPLES	EXPLANATION
Compare: a. She **said** her name. b. She **told** me her name. c. She **said** her name to me. d. They **told** the musicians to start the music.	a. We *say* something. b. We *tell* someone something. c. We *say* something to someone. d. We *tell* someone to do something.
The bride and groom **say** "I do." They **say** "thank you" to the guests.	*Say* is followed by a direct object.
They **told** the guests the wedding date. **Tell** me the bride's name.	*Tell* is followed by an indirect object and a direct object.
Tell the truth, do you love me?	We can use *tell the truth* or *tell a lie* without an indirect object.

EXERCISE 17 **Fill in the blanks with the correct form of *say* or *tell*.**

EXAMPLES The bride ___said___, "I love you."

They ___told___ me the date of the wedding.

1. You _____ me the groom's name, but I forgot it.

2. Can you _____ me where the wedding is?

3. _____ the truth, do you like the bride's dress?

4. The bride hates to _____ good-bye to her family.

5. During the ceremony, the bride and groom _____, "I do."

6. We _____ the band to play romantic music.

7. My neighbor wants to come to the wedding. I wasn't planning on inviting her, but I can't _____ no.

8. We _____ our daughter to economize on her wedding, but she _____ she wanted a fancy wedding.

Economizing on a Wedding

Before You Read

1. Does a wedding have to be expensive?

2. How can people economize on their weddings?

CD 2, TR 07

Read the following magazine article. Pay special attention to the reflexive pronouns.

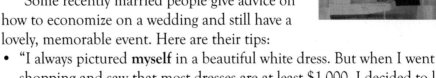

The average cost of a wedding in the U.S. today is $28,800. In days past, the bride's parents usually paid for the wedding. But as today's brides and grooms are older when they get married, they often pay for things **themselves**. There are many couples who put **themselves** in debt[7] to create a dream wedding.

Some recently married people give advice on how to economize on a wedding and still have a lovely, memorable event. Here are their tips:

- "I always pictured **myself** in a beautiful white dress. But when I went shopping and saw that most dresses are at least $1,000, I decided to look for a secondhand dress. I found something for $200, and it was lovely. When my sister got married, she made her dress **herself** and spent only $100 on fabric and lace. It isn't necessary to spend so much money on a dress. A bride is always beautiful."

- "We were going to use a professional printer for the invitations, but we decided to make the invitations **ourselves**. We designed them on the computer and added ribbons. The guests told us that they were beautiful and original."

Did You Know?

The average age of marriage is 27 for men and 25 for women.

[7]When you are *in debt*, you owe money and have to pay it back.

(continued)

- "I always wanted live music at my wedding. But when I saw the cost of musicians, I was shocked. My cousin plays piano well, so I asked her to play the piano for the wedding. And we used a DJ[8] for the dancing afterwards. We had to remind **ourselves** that the music wasn't the focus for the day—our marriage was."
- "Most couples want to get married in the summer. Ask **yourself** how important a summer wedding really is. You can cut costs by having a wedding at a less popular time. For example, a wedding in January is cheaper than a wedding in August."

According to some couples, it is not good to economize on some things:

- "Don't try to save money by sending invitations or thank-you cards through e-mail. Guests are offended. You should use postal mail."
- "We asked a friend to take pictures at our wedding but were very disappointed with the results. Our advice: Hire a professional photographer. You want to look at **yourselves** and guests for years to come."

The best way to economize is to cut the guest list and invite only your closest relatives and friends.

Although most young couples want a perfect wedding, the most important thing is to have a good marriage.

4.8 Reflexive Pronouns

We use reflexive pronouns for the object when the subject and object are the same. Compare:

The groom loves her. (object pronoun)
The bride loves herself. (reflexive pronoun)

EXAMPLES	EXPLANATION
a. I pictured **myself** in a beautiful white dress. (D.O.) b. We tell **ourselves** that money makes us happy, but it's not true. (I.O.) c. They like to look at **themselves** in their wedding photos. (O.P.)	A reflexive pronoun can be a. a direct object (D.O.) b. an indirect object (I.O.) c. the object of a preposition (O.P.)
She made the dress **all by herself**. The bride and groom made the invitations **by themselves**.	We often use a reflexive pronoun to mean alone, without help. We often add *all by* or *by* before the reflexive pronoun.
We enjoyed **ourselves** at the wedding. Help **yourself** to more cake. Make **yourself** at home.	We use reflexive pronouns in a few idiomatic expressions.

[8]A *DJ* is a disk jockey, a person who plays recorded music.

Subject	Verb	Reflexive Pronoun
I	see	myself.
You	see	yourself.
He	sees	himself.
She	sees	herself.
It	sees	itself.
We	see	ourselves.
You	see	yourselves.
They	see	themselves.

EXERCISE 18 **Frank and Sylvia are like many American couples. They have problems balancing their relationship, children, careers, families, and other responsibilities. Read each one's story and fill in the blanks with a reflexive pronoun.**

CD 2, TR 08

Sylvia's Story:

Now that I'm married, I don't have time for ___**myself**___ anymore.
(example)

We used to spend time with each other. Now that we have kids, we never

have time for _____. We both work, but Frank doesn't
(1)

help me with housework or with the kids. I have to do everything all by

_____. My husband thinks only of _____. When he wants
(2)   (3)

something, like a new digital camera or new software, he buys it.

He never buys me flowers or presents anymore. I tell _____ that
(4)

he still loves me, but sometimes I'm not so sure. Sometimes I think the

problem is his fault, but sometimes I blame _____.
(5)

Frank's Story:

Sylvia never has time for me anymore. We used to do things together.

Now I have to do everything by _____. If I want to go to a movie,
(6)

she says that she's too busy or too tired or that the kids are sick. I rarely go

to the movies, and if I do, I go by _____. It seems like all I do is
(7)

work and pay bills. Other married people seem to enjoy _____ more
(8)

than we do. She says she wants me to help her with the housework, but she

(continued)

really prefers to do everything _____ because she doesn't like
                                    (9)

the way I do things. She wants us to see a marriage counselor, but I don't

like to tell other people about my problems. I like to solve my problems

_____.
   (10)

What do you think Frank and Sylvia should do?

EXERCISE 19　**ABOUT YOU**　**Write two sentences telling about things you like to do by yourself. Write two sentences telling about things you don't like to do by yourself.**

EXAMPLES　*I like to shop by myself. I prefer to visit art museums by myself.*

I don't like to eat by myself. I don't like to go for a walk by myself.

_____

_____

_____

_____

EXERCISE 20　**Fill in the blanks with the correct pronoun or possessive form.**

Frank and Sylvia used to do a lot of things together. __**They**__ went
                                                        (example)

to movies, went out to restaurants, and took vacations together. But now

_____ are always too busy for each other. _____ have two
    (1)   (2)

children and spend most of _____ time taking care of _____.
                               (3)   (4)

Frank and Sylvia bought a house recently and spend _____ free
                                                        (5)

time taking care of _____. It's an old house and needs a lot of work.
                        (6)

When Frank and Sylvia have problems, _____ try to solve
                                          (7)

_____ by _____. But sometimes Sylvia goes to _____
    (8)   (9)   (10)

mother for advice. Frank never goes to _____ mother. He doesn't
                                            (11)

want to bother _____ with _____ problems. Frank often
                    (12)   (13)

complains that Sylvia cares more about the kids and the house than

about _____.
           (14)

Sylvia wants to go to a marriage counselor, but Frank doesn't want to

go with _____. He always says to Sylvia, "We don't need a marriage
             (15)

counselor. We can solve _____ problems by _____. You just
                              (16)   (17)

need to pay more attention to _____. If you want to see a counselor,
                                    (18)

you can go by _____. I'm not going." Sylvia feels very frustrated. She
                    (19)

thinks that the marriage isn't going to get better by _____.
                                                            (20)

Questions and Answers about an American Wedding

Before
You Read

1. Do you have any questions about American weddings?

2. How is a traditional American wedding different from a wedding
   in your native culture?

CD 2, TR 09

**Read the following questions and answers about American weddings.
Pay special attention to questions.**

Q: Who pays for the wedding?

A: In the past, the bride's parents paid for most of the wedding.
Today only about 20 percent of weddings are the responsibility of
the bride's parents. As men and women are getting married after
starting careers and earning money, more and more weddings are
becoming the responsibility of the bride and groom.

Q: What is a shower?

A: A shower is a party for
the bride (and sometimes
the groom) before the
wedding. The purpose
of the party is to give
the couple gifts that will
help them start their new
home. Typical gifts are
towels, cookware, linens,[9]
and small kitchen and
household appliances.

Q: Who hosts the shower?

A: Usually the maid of honor hosts the shower. She invites friends
and relatives of the bride and groom.

Q: When do they have the shower?

A: Usually the shower is two to six weeks before the wedding.

[9]*Linens are sheets, pillowcases, and tablecloths.*

(continued)

Possessive Forms; Object Pronouns; Reflexive Pronouns; Questions **135**

Q: How long does it take to plan a wedding?

A: Most couples plan their wedding for seven to twelve months.

Q: When do the couples send invitations?

A: They usually send the invitations about eight weeks before the wedding.

Q: When guests come in from out of town, **who pays for their hotel and transportation?**

A: The out-of-town guests pay for their own hotel. However, the groom pays for the hotel for his groomsmen and the bride pays for her bridesmaids. The guests usually pay for their own transportation.

Q: **Whom does the groom choose as his best man?**

A: Often the groom chooses his brother or best friend. However, he chooses the man he feels closest to. The groom chooses other close friends or male relatives as the groomsmen.

Q: **When do the bride and groom open their gifts?**

A: They open their gifts at home, not at the wedding.

Q: **How do the guests know what the bride and groom want as gifts?**

A: The bride and groom usually register for gifts at stores. They list the gift items they want and need for their new home, such as dishes, cookware, small appliances, and towels. When the guests go to buy a gift, they check the registry in the store. Of course, money is always a popular gift.

Q: **How do I know how much money to give?**

A: Most guests spend about $100 on a gift. People who are closer to the bride or groom often spend more. Casual friends usually spend less.

4.9 Questions about the Subject or Complement

Questions about the complement include *do, does,* or *did.* Questions about the subject do not include *do, does,* or *did.*

EXAMPLES	EXPLANATION
Who wears a white dress? The bride **does.** **Who paid** for the wedding? The parents **did.** **Whose ring has** a diamond? The bride's ring **does.**	We usually answer a subject question with a subject and an auxiliary verb.
What happened after the wedding? The bride and groom **went** on a honeymoon.	*What happened* is a subject question. We usually answer with a different verb.
a. Who **has** the prettiest dress? b. Which woman **has** the prettiest dress? c. Which women **have** the prettiest dresses? d. How many people **want** to dance? e. What **happens** at the reception?	For the simple present tense: a. Use the *-s* form after *who.* b. Use the *-s* form after *which* + singular noun. c. Use the base form after *which* + plural noun. d. Use the base form after *how many* + plural noun. e. Use the *-s* form after *what.*

Compare these statements and related questions.

Wh- Word	Do/Does/Did	Subject	Verb	Complement
What	did	The groom the bride	paid for pay for?	the rings.
		Someone Who	paid for paid for	the wedding. the wedding?
Whom	does	The groom he	chooses choose?	a best man.
		The bride Who	chooses chooses	her dress. the rings?
Why	do	Out-of-town guests they Who	stay stay stays	at a hotel. at a hotel? at a hotel?
Whose dress	did	The bride she	borrowed borrow?	a dress.
		Someone's dress Whose dress	looks looks	beautiful. beautiful?
		Something What	happened happened	next. next?

Language Note: In a question about the object, *whom* is very formal. Informally, many Americans say *who*.
Formal: *Whom* did your brother marry?
Informal: *Who* did your brother marry?

EXERCISE 21 **Read each statement. Then write a question about the words in parentheses ( ). No answer is necessary.**

EXAMPLE Someone takes the bride to the groom. (who)
<u>**Who takes the bride to the groom?**</u>

1. Someone holds the rings. (who)

   _____

2. Someone's car has a "just married" sign. (whose car)

   _____

3. Two people say, "I do." (how many people/"congratulations")

   _____

4. One woman wore a black dress. (which woman)

   _____

5. The bride pays for her white dress. (who/the bridesmaids' dresses)

   _____

EXERCISE `22`　**ABOUT YOU** Use the simple present tense of the verb in parentheses ( ) to ask a question about this class. Any student may volunteer an answer.

EXAMPLES　Who (ride) a bike to school?

A: Who rides a bike to school?

B: I do.

How many students (have) the textbook?

A: How many students have the textbook?

B: We all do.

1. Who (explain) the grammar?

2. How many students (speak) Spanish?

3. What usually (happen) after class?

4. Who (need) help with this lesson?

5. Which students (walk) to school?

6. Who (have) a digital camera?

7. Who (live) alone?

8. Whose last name (have) over ten letters?

EXERCISE `23`　**ABOUT YOU** Use the simple past tense of the verb in parentheses ( ) to ask a question. Any student may volunteer an answer.

EXAMPLE　Who (buy) a used textbook?

A: Who bought a used textbook?

B: I did.

1. Who (move) last year?

2. Who (understand) the explanation?

3. Whose family (take) a trip recently?

4. Who (bring) a dictionary to class today?

5. Who (pass) the last test?

6. Which students (come) late today?

7. Which student (arrive) first today?

8. How many students (do) today's homework?

9. How many students (study) English in elementary school?

10. How many students (bring) a cell phone to class?

EXERCISE 24 **Read each statement. Then write a question about the words in parentheses ( ). Some of the questions are about the subject. Some are not. No answer is necessary.**

EXAMPLES   The bride wears a white dress. (what/the groom)
What does the groom wear?

The bride enters last. (who/first)
Who enters first?

1. The bride throws the bouquet. (when)

   _____

2. Some women try to catch the bouquet. (which women)

   _____

3. The groom puts the ring on the bride's finger. (on which hand) OR
   (which hand . . . on)

   _____

4. The band plays music. (what kind of music)

   _____

5. Someone dances with the bride. (who)

   _____

6. Guests give presents. (what kind of presents)

   _____

7. Some people cry at the wedding. (who)

   _____

8. There's a dinner after the ceremony. (what/happen/after the dinner)

   _____

EXERCISE 25 **In the conversation below, two women are talking about their families. Fill in the blanks to complete the questions. Some of the questions are about the subject. Some are about the object. In some cases, more than one answer is possible.**

CD 2, TR 10

A: How do you have time to work, go to school, and take care of a family?

B: I don't have to do everything myself.

A: Who _____ _helps you_ _____?
          (example)

B: My husband helps me.

A: I usually cook in my house. Who _____?
                                          _(1)_

B: Sometimes my husband cooks; sometimes I cook. We take turns.

(continued)

A: I usually clean. Who _____(2)?

B: I usually clean the house.

A: How many _____(3)?

B: I have five children.

A: How many _____(4)?

B: Three children go to school. The younger ones stay home.

A: Do you send them to public school or private school?

B: One of my sons goes to private school.

A: Which _____(5)?

B: The oldest does. He's in high school now.

A: It's hard to take care of so many children. How do you find the time to go to class?

B: As I said, my husband helps me a lot. And sometimes I use a babysitter.

A: I'm looking for a sitter. Who(m) _____(6)?

B: I recommend our neighbor, Susan. She's 16 years old, and she's very good with our children.

A: Maybe she's too busy to help me. How many families

_____(7)?

B: I think she works for only one other family. I'll give you her phone number. If she's not busy, maybe she can work for you too.

A: Thanks. I could use some help.

EXERCISE 26 **Fill in the blanks with *who, whom, who's,* or *whose.***

1. _____ did you invite to the wedding?

   I invited all my friends and relatives.

2. _____ took pictures?

   My brother did. He borrowed a camera because his is broken.

3. _____ camera did he borrow?

   He borrowed my aunt's camera. She has a fantastic camera.

4. _____ your aunt?

   She's that woman over there.

Summary of Lesson 4

1. Pronouns and Possessive Forms

SUBJECT PRONOUN	OBJECT PRONOUN	POSSESSIVE ADJECTIVE	POSSESSIVE PRONOUN	REFLEXIVE PRONOUN
I	me	my	mine	myself
you	you	your	yours	yourself
he	him	his	his	himself
she	her	her	hers	herself
it	it	its	—	itself
we	us	our	ours	ourselves
you	you	your	yours	yourselves
they	them	their	theirs	themselves
who	whom	whose	whose	—

EXAMPLES

They came from Canada.
I invited **them**.
Their wedding was outdoors.
My wedding was small. **Theirs** was big.
They paid for the wedding **themselves**.

Who came from Canada?
Who(m) did you invite?
Whose wedding was outdoors?
Someone's wedding was big.
    Whose was big?

2. Possessive Form of Nouns

Singular Nouns
    the **bride's** dress
    my **father's** house
    the **child's** toy
    the **man's** hat
    Charles's wife

Plural Nouns
    the **bridesmaids'** dresses
    my **parents'** house
    the **children's** toys
    the **men's** hats

3. *Say* and *Tell*

He **said** his name.
He **told** me his name.

He **said** good-bye to his friends.
He **told** them to write often.

4. Questions about the Subject

Simple Present:
    Who has the rings?
    How many bridesmaids have a pink dress?
    Which bridesmaid has a red dress?
    Which bridesmaids have pink flowers?
    What happens after the wedding?

Simple Past:
    Who kissed the bride?
    Which man kissed the bride?
    What happened next?
    How many people came to the wedding?
    Whose mother cried?

Editing Advice

1. Don't confuse *you're* (you are) and *your* (possessive form).

~~Your~~ *You're* late.

~~You're~~ *Your* class started ten minutes ago.

2. Don't confuse *he's* (he is) and *his* (possessive form).

~~His~~ *He's* married.

~~He's~~ *His* wife is a friend of mine.

3. Don't confuse *it's* (it is) and *its* (possessive form).

This college is big. ~~Its~~ *It's* a state university.

~~It's~~ *Its* library has many books.

4. Don't confuse *his* (masculine possessor) and *her* (feminine possessor).

My sister loves ~~his~~ *her* son.

My brother loves ~~her~~ *his* daughter.

5. Don't confuse *my* and *mine*.

I don't have ~~mine~~ *my* book today.

You can borrow ~~my~~ *mine*.

6. Don't confuse *they're* and *their*.

~~They're~~ *Their* last name is Williams.

~~Their~~ *They're* from California.

7. Use the correct pronoun (subject or object).

I have a daughter. I love ~~she~~ *her* very much.

8. For a compound subject, use "another person and I." Don't use *me* in the subject position.

I
My father and ~~me~~ like to go fishing.

My father and I
~~Me and my father~~ like to go fishing.

9. For a compound object, use "another person and me." Don't use *I* in the object position.

me
My parents gave my brother and ~~I~~ a present.

10. Don't use an apostrophe to make a plural form.

guests
They invited many ~~guest's~~ to the wedding.

11. Don't use an auxiliary verb in a question about the subject.

s
Who ~~does~~ speak Spanish?

12. Don't separate *whose* from the noun.

Whose is this book?

13. Don't confuse *whose* and *who's*.

Whose
~~Who's~~ coat is that?

14. Use the correct word order for possession.

My wife's mother
~~Mother my wife~~ helps us a lot.

15. Put the apostrophe after the *s* of a plural noun that ends in *s*.

parents'
My ~~parent's~~ house is small.

16. The *s* in a possessive pronoun is not for a plural.

Theirs parents live in Canada.

17. Don't use a form of *be* with *what happened*.

What ~~was~~ happened to your new car?

18. Use the correct word order with direct and indirect objects.

the grammar to me
She explained ~~me the grammar~~.

it to him
I gave ~~him it~~.

Editing Quiz

Some of the shaded words and phrases have mistakes. Find the mistakes and correct them. If the shaded words are correct, write C.

A: I heard you got married recently. Tell me about ~~you're~~ *your* wedding. Did
(example)
you have a lot of guests? *C*
(example)

B: It was a small wedding. Sara's parents wanted a big wedding, and hers
(1)   (2)
parents offered to pay for it. But we wanted to be responsible and pay
(3)
for it ourself. We explained them the situation, and they agreed. So
(4)   (5)
we just had our immediate families: parents, grandparents, sisters,
(6)
brothers, aunts, and uncles. But grandfather Sara didn't come.
(7)

A: Why not? What was happened to he?
(8)   (9)

B: Nothing. His grandfather lives in Mexico. His very old and couldn't
(10)   (11)
travel. But her grandmother came and stayed at Sara's aunt's house.
(12)   (13)

A: Your grandparents are old too, aren't they? Did they come?
(14)

B: Yes, they did. Mine live nearby. And their in great health.
(15)   (16)

A: That's good. So you didn't spend a lot of money on your wedding?
(17)

B: No. No big ceremony, no big party. Just a small dinner at
Sara's parent's house. Aunts of Sara made a beautiful dinner. We even
(18)   (19)
saved money on the wedding dress because Sarah borrowed a dress.

A: Who's dress did she borrow?
(20)

B: She wore her mothers wedding dress. And I didn't rent a tuxedo.
(21) (22)
I wore my new blue suit. You know the tradition: "Something old,
(23)
something new, something borrowed, something blue." My suit is new
and blue. Sara's dress is old and borrowed.
(24)

A: Did you hire a photographer?

B: No. We saved money there too. Mine uncle is a photographer. He took
(25)   (26)   (27)
all the picture's and gave us them on disk. We printed they and made
(28)   (29)   (30)
an album.

A: Did you go on a honeymoon?

B: We saved money there too. Sara's uncle has a vacation home in Miami.

<u>Me and Sara</u> stayed there for a week. (<u>His</u> uncle wasn't there at the
(31) *(32)*

time.)

A: <u>Its</u> hot in Miami at this time of the year.
(33)

B: Yes, it is. But there was a swimming pool. We used <u>it</u> every day.
(34)

A: What are you going to do with all the money you saved?

B: We have to pay our college loans. We also want to buy a house and car,

so <u>we're</u> saving for <u>its</u>.
(35) *(36)*

A: <u>You're</u> a wise man! When Lisa and <u>I</u> get married after we graduate, I'd
(37) *(38)*

like to do the same thing. But I think Lisa won't agree.

B: <u>Who know</u>? Maybe she'll like the idea.
(39)

Lesson 4 Test/Review

PART 1 **Choose the correct word to complete each sentence.**

EXAMPLE Do you like __c__ neighbors?

    a. you   **b.** you're   **c.** your   **d.** yours

1. Where do your parents live? _____ live in Colombia.

    a. My   **b.** Mine   **c.** Mine's   **d.** Mines

2. _____ coat is that?

    a. Whose   **b.** Who's   **c.** Who   **d.** Whom

3. _____ went to Hawaii for our honeymoon.

    a. My wife and I   **c.** Me and my wife

    b. I and my wife   **d.** My wife and me

4. My sister's daughter is 18. _____ son is 16.

    a. His   **b.** Her   **c.** Hers   **d.** Her's

5. What's _____?

    a. the name your son   **c.** the name your son's

    b. your son's name   **d.** your the son's name

6. Look at those dogs. Do you see _____?

    a. they   **b.** its   **c.** them   **d.** it's

7. We have your phone number. Do you have _____?

    a. us   **b.** our   **c.** ours   **d.** our's

8. What is _____?

    a. that building name   **c.** the name that building

    b. the name of that building   **d.** the name's that building

9. Someone left a sweater. _____?

    a. Whose is this sweater?   **c.** Whose sweater is this?

    b. Who's is this sweater?   **d.** Who's sweater is this?

10. _____ the correct answer?

    a. Who's knows   **b.** Whom knows   **c.** Who does know   **d.** Who knows

11. They have my address, but I don't have _____.

    a. their   **b.** them   **c.** they're   **d.** theirs

12. We did it by ____.

    a. self   **b.** oneself   **c.** ourself   **d.** ourselves

13. They can help ____.

    a. theirself   **b.** theirselves   **c.** themself   **d.** themselves

14. I know ____ very well.

    a. myself   **b.** mineself   **c.** meself   **d.** self

15. My teacher speaks Spanish. My ____ teacher doesn't.

    a. husbands   **b.** husbands'   **c.** husband's   **d.** the husband's

PART 2   **Fill in the blanks with *said* or *told*.**

1. She _____, "Excuse me."

2. She _____ them to study.

3. She _____ him the truth.

4. She _____ "hello" to her neighbor.

5. She _____ them the answers.

6. She _____ us about her trip.

7. She _____ the answer out loud.

8. She _____ "good-bye."

PART 3   **Complete the question. Some of these questions ask about the subject. Some do not. The answer is underlined.**

EXAMPLES   What *does the bride wear?*

The bride wears <u>a white dress and a veil</u>.

Who *usually cries at the wedding?*

<u>The bride's mother</u> usually cries at the wedding.

1. When _____

   She throws the bouquet <u>at the end of the wedding party</u>.

2. Which women _____

   <u>The single women</u> try to catch the bouquet.

3. On which hand _____

   The groom puts the ring <u>on the bride's left hand</u>.

4. Whom _____

   The groom kisses <u>the bride</u>.

(continued)

5. Whose _____

The bride's ring has a diamond.

6. Whose _____

The bride uses her husband's last name.

7. Who _____

A professional photographer took pictures at my wedding.

8. Whose _____

I borrowed my sister's dress.

9. Whose _____, yours or your sisters?

My sister's wedding was bigger.

10. How many people _____

Over 250 people came to the wedding.

11. Who _____

The bride and groom cut the cake.

PART 4 **Fill in the blanks with a reflexive pronoun.**

EXAMPLE She likes to talk about ___herself___.

1. I made the cake all by _____.

2. The bride made her dress _____.

3. They prepared _____ financially before getting married.

4. We helped _____ to another piece of cake.

5. The groom bought _____ a new pair of shoes.

6. All of you should help _____ to more cake and coffee.

7. Did you go to the wedding by _____ or did your wife go with you?

Expansion

Classroom Activities

1 **Form a small group. The group should have people from different cultures and countries, if possible. Talk about weddings and marriages in your native cultures and countries.**

a. Who chooses a husband for a woman?

b. Who pays for the wedding?

c. What happens at the wedding?

d. What happens after the wedding?

e. Do the guests bring gifts to the wedding? What kind of gifts do they give? Where do the bride and groom open the gifts?

f. How many people attend a wedding?

g. Where do people get married?

h. Do people dance at a wedding?

i. Who takes pictures?

j. What color dress does the bride wear?

k. At what age do people usually get married?

2 **In a small group, interview one person who is married. Ask this person questions about his or her wedding.**

EXAMPLES   Where did you get married?
How many people did you invite?
How many people came?
Where did you go on your honeymoon?

3 **According to an American tradition, the bride should wear:**

Something old,
Something new,
Something borrowed,
Something blue.

Do you have any traditions regarding weddings in your native culture?

4 **Do you have a video of a wedding in your family? If so, can you bring it to class and tell the class about it? The teacher may have a video of an American wedding to show the class.**

5 Write some advice for newlyweds in each of the following categories. Discuss your sentences in a small group.

home   problem solving
children   mother-in-law
housework   money
careers   time together/time apart
family obligations

Talk

About It

1 What kind of problems do most married people have today? Do you think American married couples have the same problems as couples in other countries?

2 Do you think married couples can solve their problems by themselves? At what point should they go to a marriage counselor?

3 Do you think married people should spend most of their time together, or should they spend some time by themselves?

4 Do you think young people are realistic about marriage? How can they prepare themselves for the reality of marriage?

Write

About It

1 Write about the different ways in which a person can economize on a wedding.

2 Write about a typical wedding in your native culture, or describe your own wedding or the wedding of a family member or friend.

Weddings in China

In my country, China, weddings are different from weddings in the U.S. On the day of the wedding, the groom goes to the bride's house with his groomsmen. At the bride's house, the bride's friends play a "door game." They block the door until the men offer red packets of money . . .

 For more practice using grammar in context, please visit our Web site.

Grammar

Singular and Plural

Count and Noncount Nouns

There + Be

Quantity Words

Context

Thanksgiving, Pilgrims, and Native Americans

A Typical Thanksgiving

1. When you celebrate a holiday, what kind of food do you prepare?

2. Do you think a holiday meal is a healthy meal?

CD 2, TR 11

Read the following Web article. Pay special attention to singular and plural nouns.

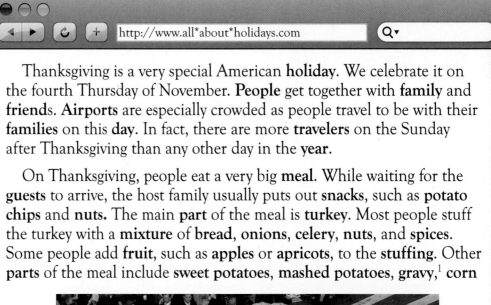

http://www.all*about*holidays.com

Thanksgiving is a very special American **holiday**. We celebrate it on the fourth Thursday of November. **People** get together with **family** and **friends**. **Airports** are especially crowded as people travel to be with their **families** on this **day**. In fact, there are more **travelers** on the Sunday after Thanksgiving than any other day in the **year**.

On Thanksgiving, people eat a very big **meal**. While waiting for the **guests** to arrive, the host family usually puts out **snacks**, such as **potato chips** and **nuts**. The main **part** of the meal is **turkey**. Most people stuff the turkey with a **mixture** of **bread**, **onions**, **celery**, **nuts**, and **spices**. Some people add **fruit**, such as **apples** or **apricots**, to the **stuffing**. Other **parts** of the meal include **sweet potatoes**, **mashed potatoes**, **gravy**,[1] **corn**

Thanksgiving Day Parade

[1]*Gravy* is a sauce made from meat drippings, flour, water, and sometimes bacon fat.

bread, and **cranberry sauce**. Then there is **dessert**. **Pumpkin pie** with whipped **cream** is a favorite dessert. The typical Thanksgiving meal contains more than 3,000 **calories** and is 45 percent **fat**. Many people talk about going on **a diet** the day after Thanksgiving.

In addition to eating a big meal, many people relax and watch TV. It is a typical **tradition** to watch professional football on Thanksgiving Day. The **men** are especially interested in football. Many **cities** also have a **parade** on Thanksgiving morning. New York City has a very big parade. **Millions** of people go to see the parade.

5.1 Noun Plurals

We use the plural to talk about more than one. Regular noun plurals add -s or -es.

REGULAR NOUN PLURALS				
Word Ending	Example Noun	Plural Addition	Plural Form	Pronunciation
Vowel	bee banana	+ s	bees bananas	/z/
ch, sh, x, s	church dish box class	+ es	churches dishes boxes classes	/əz/
Voiceless consonants	cat month	+ s	cats months	/s/
Voiced consonants	card pin	+ s	cards pins	/z/
Vowel + y	boy day	+ s	boys days	/z/
Consonant + y	lady story	y + ies	ladies stories	/z/
Vowel + o	video radio	+ s	videos radios	/z/
Consonant + o	potato hero	+ es	potatoes heroes	/z/
Exceptions: photos, pianos, solos, altos, sopranos, autos, tuxedos, and avocados				
f or fe	leaf knife	f + ves	leaves knives	/z/
Exceptions: beliefs, chiefs, roofs, cliffs, chefs, and sheriffs				

IRREGULAR NOUN PLURALS

Singular	Plural	Examples	Explanation
man woman tooth foot goose	men women teeth feet geese	The **women** cooked the dinner. The **men** washed the dishes.	Vowel change
sheep fish deer	sheep fish deer	There are two **fish** in the bowl.	No change
child mouse person	children mice people	The **children** set the table. We invited a lot of **people** to dinner.	Different word form

Language Note: The plural of *person* can also be *persons*, but *people* is more common.

EXERCISE **1** **Write the plural form of each noun. Pronounce each plural form.**

EXAMPLE   hour ___hours___

1. holiday _____
2. turkey _____
3. cranberry _____
4. potato _____
5. child _____
6. family _____
7. spice _____
8. nut _____
9. guest _____
10. man _____
11. woman _____
12. snack _____

13. apple _____
14. peach _____
15. tomato _____
16. pie _____
17. knife _____
18. deer _____
19. watch _____
20. tax _____
21. month _____
22. goose _____
23. dish _____
24. path _____

EXERCISE 2   Fill in the blanks with the plural form of the words in parentheses ( ).

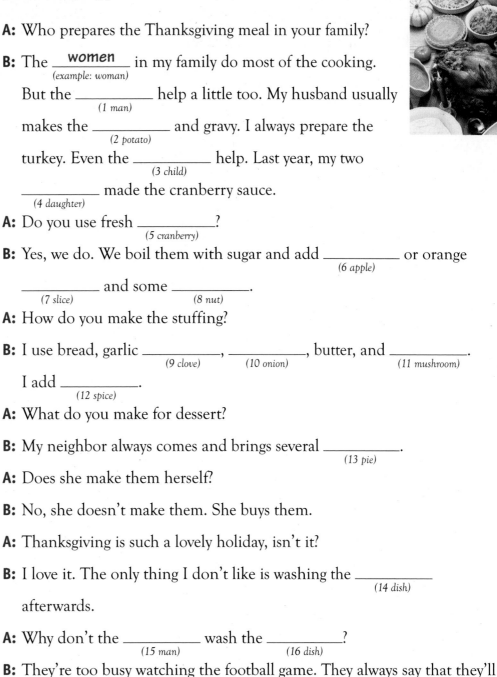

CD 2, TR 12

A: Who prepares the Thanksgiving meal in your family?

B: The ___women___ in my family do most of the cooking.
(example: woman)

   But the _____ help a little too. My husband usually
   (1 man)

   makes the _____ and gravy. I always prepare the
   (2 potato)

   turkey. Even the _____ help. Last year, my two
   (3 child)

   _____ made the cranberry sauce.
   (4 daughter)

A: Do you use fresh _____?
   (5 cranberry)

B: Yes, we do. We boil them with sugar and add _____ or orange
   (6 apple)

   _____ and some _____.
   (7 slice)   (8 nut)

A: How do you make the stuffing?

B: I use bread, garlic _____, _____, butter, and _____.
   (9 clove)   (10 onion)   (11 mushroom)

   I add _____.
   (12 spice)

A: What do you make for dessert?

B: My neighbor always comes and brings several _____.
   (13 pie)

A: Does she make them herself?

B: No, she doesn't make them. She buys them.

A: Thanksgiving is such a lovely holiday, isn't it?

B: I love it. The only thing I don't like is washing the _____
   (14 dish)

   afterwards.

A: Why don't the _____ wash the _____?
   (15 man)   (16 dish)

B: They're too busy watching the football game. They always say that they'll

   wash them later, but the _____ are in a hurry to clean up. So we
   (17 woman)

   do it ourselves.

5.2 Using the Singular and Plural for Generalizations

We can use the singular or plural to make a generalization. A generalization says something is true of all members of a group.

EXAMPLES	EXPLANATION
A football game lasts about three hours. OR **Football games** last about three hours. **A sweet potato** is nutritious. OR **Sweet potatoes** are nutritious.	To make a generalization about the subject, use the indefinite article (*a* or *an*) with a singular subject or no article with a plural subject.

EXERCISE **3** Make a generalization about the following nouns. Use the plural form. You may work with a partner.

EXAMPLE American teachers ___are very informal._____

1. American children _____
2. American colleges _____
3. Buses in this city _____
4. Elderly Americans _____
5. American cities _____
6. American doctors _____
7. American women _____
8. American men _____
9. American holidays _____
10. Football games _____

EXERCISE **4** Make a generalization about these professions. Use the singular form. You may work with a partner.

EXAMPLE A taxi driver ___has a dangerous job._____

1. A teacher _____
2. A doctor _____
3. A nurse _____
4. A garbage collector _____
5. A lawyer _____
6. A musician _____
7. A librarian _____

8. A movie star _____

9. An accountant _____

10. A newspaper reporter _____

5.3 Special Cases of Singular and Plural

EXAMPLES	EXPLANATION
a. The U.S. has more than 300 **million** people.	a. Exact numbers use the singular form.
b. **Millions** of people go shopping the day after Thanksgiving.	b. Inexact numbers use the plural form.
c. My grandfather is in his **seventies**. He was born in the **1940s**.	c. An approximate age or year uses the plural form.
One of my **neighbors** brought a pie to Thanksgiving dinner. One of the **men** helped with the dishes.	We use the plural form in the following expressions: *one of* (*the, my, his, her,* etc.).
Every **guest** brought something. We washed all the **dishes**.	We use a singular noun after *every*. We use a plural noun after *all*.
After dinner, the girl put on her **pajamas** and went to bed. We're wearing our best **clothes** today.	Some words have no singular form: *pajamas, clothes, pants, slacks, (eye)glasses, scissors.*
Let's watch the **news**. It's on after dinner. Let's not discuss **politics** during dinner. It's not a good subject.	Even though *news* and *politics* end in *-s*, they are singular.

Language Note: Do not make adjectives plural.
He made three ***wonderful*** pies.

EXERCISE 5 **Find the mistakes with the underlined words and correct them. Not every sentence has a mistake. If the sentence is correct, write C.**

EXAMPLES   Five ~~man~~ watched the football game. *(men)*

Ten <u>guests</u> came to dinner.   *C*

1. The <u>childrens</u> helped serve the dinner.

2. One of her <u>daughter</u> came from New York on Thanksgiving.

3. Ten <u>millions</u> people passed through the airports that day.

(continued)

4. <u>Millions</u> of people travel for Thanksgiving.

5. After the news <u>is</u> over, we can watch the football game.

6. His pants <u>is</u> new.

7. Five <u>women</u> prepared the dinner.

8. Every <u>guests</u> stayed to watch the game.

9. Thanksgiving is one of my favorite <u>holiday</u>.

10. <u>Hundreds</u> of people saw the parade.

11. My grandmother came for Thanksgiving. She's in her <u>eighties</u>.

12. Politics <u>is</u> not a good subject to discuss at the dinner table.

13. The boy should go to bed. His pajamas <u>are</u> on the bed.

14. Do you like <u>sweets</u> potatoes?

The Origin of Thanksgiving

Before You Read

1. What do you know about the origin of American Thanksgiving?

2. Do you have a day of thanks in your native culture?

CD 2, TR 13

Read the following textbook article. Pay special attention to count and noncount nouns.

On Thanksgiving, **Americans** come together to give thanks for all the good **things** in their **lives**. Thanksgiving officially began in 1863, when President Lincoln declared that Americans would have a **day** of thanks. What is the **origin** of this great day?

In 1620, a **group** of 120 **men, women,** and **children** left England for America on a **ship** called the Mayflower. They came to America in search of religious **freedom**. They started their new **life** in a deserted[2] Indian **village** in what is now the **state** of Massachusetts. But **half** of the **Pilgrims** did not

[2]*Deserted* means empty of people.

survive their first cold, hard **winter**. In the **spring**, two American **Indians**[3] found the **people** from England in very bad **condition**. They didn't have enough **food**, and they were in bad **health**. Squanto, an English-speaking American Indian, stayed with them for several **months** and taught them how to survive in this new **land**. He brought them deer **meat** and animal **skins**; he showed them how to grow **corn** and other **vegetables**; he showed them how to use **plants** as **medicine**; he explained how to use **fish** for **fertilizer**[4]—he taught them many **skills** for **survival** in their new land.

By the time their second **fall** arrived, the Pilgrims had enough food to get through their second winter. They were in better **health**. They decided to have a Thanksgiving **feast**[5] to celebrate their good **fortune**.

They invited Squanto and neighboring Indian **families** of the Wampanoag **tribe** to come to their **dinner**. The Pilgrims were surprised when 90 Indians showed up. The Pilgrims did not have enough food for so many people. Fortunately, the Indian **chief** sent some of his people to bring food to the **celebration**. They brought five **deer**, **fish**, **beans**, **squash**, **corn bread**, **berries**, and many wild **turkeys**. The feast lasted for three **days**. There was a short **time** of **peace** and **friendship** between the Indians and the Pilgrims.

Now on Thanksgiving, we eat some of the traditional **foods** from this **period** in American **history**.

5.4 Count and Noncount Nouns

EXAMPLES	EXPLANATION
Use one **potato** in the recipe. Use three **potatoes** in the soup.	A count noun is something we can count. It has a singular and plural form.
Corn is native to America. The Indians used a lot of **corn**.	A noncount noun is something we don't count. It has no plural form.
We used **rice** in the recipe. We use **beans** in the soup.	*Count* and *noncount* are grammatical terms, but they are not always logical. *Rice* and *beans* are both very small, but *rice* is a noncount noun and *bean* is a count noun.

[3] The native people of America are called *American Indians*, *Indians*, or *Native Americans*.
[4] We put *fertilizer* in the earth to help plants grow.
[5] A *feast* is a large dinner.

(continued)

There are several types of noncount nouns.

Group A: Nouns that have no distinct, separate parts. We look at the whole.			
milk	juice	bread	electricity
oil	yogurt	meat	lightning
water	pork	butter	thunder
coffee	poultry	paper	cholesterol
tea	soup	air	blood

Group B: Nouns that have parts that are too small or insignificant to count.		
rice	hair	sand
sugar	popcorn	corn
salt	snow	grass

Group C: Nouns that are classes or categories of things. The members of the category are not the same.	
money or cash (nickels, dimes, dollars)	mail (letters, packages, postcards, flyers)
furniture (chairs, tables, beds)	homework (compositions, exercises, readings)
clothing (sweaters, pants, dresses)	jewelry (necklaces, bracelets, rings)

Group D: Nouns that are abstractions.					
love	happiness	nutrition	patience	work	nature
truth	education	intelligence	poverty	health	help
beauty	advice	unemployment	music	fun	energy
luck/fortune	knowledge	pollution	art	information	friendship

Group E: Subjects of study.		
history	grammar	biology
chemistry	geometry	math (mathematics*)

*Note: Even though *mathematics* ends with *s*, it is not plural.

EXERCISE 6 Fill in the blanks with a noncount noun from the box below.

advice	snow	freedom✓	friendship
health	work	corn	

EXAMPLE The Pilgrims wanted to find __freedom__ in America.

1. They had poor _____ during their first winter in America.

2. The Indians gave the Pilgrims a lot of _____ about how to grow food.

3. Squanto taught them to plant _____.

4. The first winter was hard. It was cold and there was a lot of _____.

5. Learning American agriculture was hard _____ for the Pilgrims.

6. In the beginning, there was _____ between the Pilgrims and the Indians.

5.5 Nouns That Can Be Both Count or Noncount

Some nouns can be noncount or count, depending on their meaning or use.

NONCOUNT	COUNT
a. I like to spend **time** with my family on the holidays. b. My neighbors invited me to their dinner many **times**. a. Indians had **experience** with American winters. b. The first winter for the Pilgrims was **a bad experience**.	The noncount nouns in (a) and the count nouns in (b) have different meanings. In many languages, a completely different word is used.
a. **Life** in America was difficult. b. The Pilgrims had difficult **lives**. a. The Pilgrims had a lot of **trouble** their first winter. b. Do you tell your **troubles** to your friends? a. The men are watching the football game. They're making a lot of **noise**. b. There are some loud **noises** coming from the next room.	Sentences (a) show abstractions. They are noncount nouns. Sentences (b) show specific examples of these nouns. They are count nouns.
a. We put some **fruit** in the cranberry sauce. b. Oranges and lemons are citrus **fruits**. a. We prepare a lot of **food** for Thanksgiving. b. Cranberries and sweet potatoes are typical **foods** for Thanksgiving.	Sentences (a) refer to the nouns in general. They are noncount nouns. Sentences (b) refer to categories of the noun. They are count nouns.
a. We ate some **pie** for dessert. b. My friend brought three **pies** to the Thanksgiving dinner. a. We eat **turkey** on Thanksgiving. b. The Indians brought many **turkeys** to the feast.	Sentences (a) refer to a part of the whole. They are noncount nouns. Sentences (b) refer to the whole. They are count nouns. In the case of animals, the count noun usually refers to the animal rather than the food.

EXERCISE 7 Decide if the noun in parentheses ( ) is count or noncount. If it is a count noun, change it to the plural form. If it is a noncount noun, do not use the plural form.

EXAMPLE The ___Pilgrims___ wanted ___freedom___.
             (Pilgrim)   *(freedom)*

1. American Indians have a lot of respect for _____.
                                                  (nature)

   They love _____, _____, and _____.
                (tree)   *(bird)*   *(fish)*

2. Thanksgiving is a celebration of _____ and _____.
                                            (peace)   *(friendship)*

(continued)

3. On Thanksgiving, Americans eat a lot of _____ and
(food)

sometimes gain weight.

4. Americans sometimes eat _____ for dessert.
(pie)

5. Squanto gave the Pilgrims a lot of _____ about planting
(advice)

_____ and other _____. He had a lot of _____ about
(corn)   (vegetable)   (knowledge)

the land.

6. The Pilgrims didn't have any _____ with American agriculture.
(experience)

7. On the first Thanksgiving, Indians brought _____,
(meat)

_____, _____, and _____.
(bean)   (bread)   (berry)

8. The Pilgrims celebrated because they had a lot of good _____.
(fortune)

9. American Indians use _____ for _____.
(plant)   (medicine)

10. My friends went to the Southwest last summer. They

bought American Indian _____, such as _____
(jewelry)   (ring)

and _____.
(necklace)

11. Do you have a lot of _____ about American _____?
(information)   (holiday)

Before You Read

1. Do you like to cook?

2. What is a favorite recipe of yours?

CD 2, TR 14

Read the following recipe from a magazine. Pay special attention to quantities.

Turkey Stuffing[6]

¼ cup of butter or olive oil
2 cloves of garlic, minced[7]
1 cup of sliced mushrooms
1 onion, chopped
3 stalks of celery, chopped
¼ cup bacon pieces
4 cups of dry bread, cut into cubes
¼ teaspoon of salt
¼ teaspoon of pepper
¼ teaspoon of dry oregano
2 teaspoons of dry parsley
1 cup of hot chicken broth

Brown garlic[8] in butter (or olive oil). Add mushrooms and sauté[9]. Add the rest of the vegetables and cook until they begin to soften. Stir bacon pieces into mixture, then lower heat to medium and add bread cubes and seasonings.

Continue cooking for approximately 5 more minutes, stirring continuously.

Add hot chicken broth and mix well. Cover and cook over low heat for at least 30 minutes, stirring frequently.

Use as turkey stuffing and bake with turkey or place in a covered casserole dish and bake for 30 minutes in a 350–375 degree oven.

[6]Stuffing is often cooked inside the turkey.
[7]*Minced* means cut into very small pieces.
[8]Recipes often leave out articles. For example, this recipe says "brown garlic" instead of "brown the garlic."
[9]To *sauté* means to fry quickly.

5.6 Quantities with Count and Noncount Nouns

We can put a number before a count noun. We cannot put a number before a noncount noun. We use a unit of measure, which we can count—for example, two *cloves* of garlic.

BY CONTAINER	BY PORTION	BY MEASUREMENT[10]	BY SHAPE OR WHOLE PIECE	OTHER
a bottle of water	a slice (piece) of bread	an ounce of sugar	a loaf of bread	a piece of mail
a carton of milk	a piece of meat	a quart of oil	an ear of corn	a piece of furniture
a jar of pickles	a piece of cake	a pound of meat	a piece of fruit	a piece of advice
a bag of flour	a strip of bacon	a gallon of milk	a head of lettuce	a piece of information
a can of soda (pop)	a piece (sheet) of paper	a pint of cream	a candy bar	a work of art
a cup of coffee	a slice of pizza		a tube of toothpaste	a homework assignment
a glass of water	a scoop of ice cream		a bar of soap	
a bowl of soup			a clove of garlic	
			a stalk of celery	

EXERCISE 8 **Fill in the blanks with a specific quantity or unit of measure. Answers may vary.**

EXAMPLE   I drink three _____ glasses of _____ water a day.

1. I drink a _____ orange juice in the morning.

2. I'm going to buy two _____ meat to make dinner for the family.

3. _____ milk is heavy to carry.

4. She drinks two _____ coffee every morning.

5. Buy _____ bread for dinner.

6. He eats _____ fruit a day.

7. Some people carry _____ water with them.

8. I ate two _____ cake.

9. Let me give you _____ advice before you apply to colleges.

10. How many _____ gas did you buy at the gas station?

11. How many _____ garlic are you going to use in the recipe?

12. The recipe calls for ¼ _____ butter or oil.

13. The recipe calls for ¼ _____ pepper.

[10] For a list of conversions from the American system of measurement to the metric system, see Appendix D.

Taking the Land from the Native Americans

Before You Read

1. Who were the original inhabitants of your native country?

2. Are there any ethnic minorities in your native country? Do they have the respect of the majority population?

American Indian Reservations in the U.S.

CD 2, TR 15

Read the following textbook article. Pay special attention to *there* + a form of *be*.

Before the arrival of Europeans, **there were** between 10 and 16 million Native Americans in America. Today **there are** fewer than 2 million. What happened to these natives of America?

The friendship between the Indians and Europeans did not last for long. As more English people came to America, they did not need the help of the Indians, as the first group of Pilgrims did. The white people started to take the land away from the Indians. As Indians fought to keep their land, many of them were killed. Also, **there were** many deaths from diseases that Europeans brought to America. In 1830, President Andrew Jackson took the Indians' lands and sent them to live on reservations. Indian children had to learn English. Often they were punished for speaking their own language. As a result, **there are** very few Indians today who speak the language of their ancestors.

Today **there are** about 500 tribes in the U.S., each with its own traditions. **There are** about 300 reservations, but less than half of American Indians live on this land. **There is** a lot of unemployment and poverty on many reservations. As a result, many Indians move to big cities to find work. Many return to their reservations only for special celebrations such as powwows, when Indians wear their traditional clothing and dance to traditional music.

It is becoming harder and harder for Indians to keep their traditions and languages alive.

5.7 *There* + a Form of *Be*

We use *there* + a form of *be* to introduce a subject, either count or noncount, into the conversation. After the noun, we often give a time or place.

There	Be	A/An/One	Singular Subject	Complement
There	is	a	reservation	in Wyoming.
There	is	an	onion	in the recipe.
There	will be	a	football game	on TV tonight.
There	was	one	guest	for dinner.

There	Be	(Quantity Word)	Noncount Subject	Complement
There	is	a lot of	unemployment	on some reservations.
There	is	some	garlic	in the recipe for stuffing.
There	was		peace	between the Indians and the Pilgrims.

There	Be	(Quantity Word)	Plural Subject	Complement
There	are	500	Indian tribes	in the U.S.
There	were	many	deaths	from diseases after the Europeans arrived.
There	are	a lot of	calories	in a typical Thanksgiving meal.
There	are		reservations	in California.

Negative Forms

There	Be + Not + A/An	Singular Subject	Complement
There	wasn't a	problem	between the Pilgrims and Indians in 1620.

There	Be + No	Singular Subject	Complement
There	was no	problem	between the Pilgrims and Indians in 1620.

There	Be + Not + (Any)	Noncount Subject	Complement
There	isn't any	milk	in the recipe.

There	Be + No	Noncount Subject	Complement
There	is no	milk	in the recipe.

There	Be + Not + (Any)	Plural Subject	Complement
There	aren't any	reservations	in Illinois.

There	Be + No	Plural Subject	Complement
There	are no	reservations	in Illinois.

5.8 Using *There*

EXAMPLES	EXPLANATION
There's a reservation in Wyoming. **There are** reservations in California and Utah.	The contraction for *there is* = *there's*. We don't write a contraction for *there are*.
There is one onion and three celery stalks in the recipe. **There are** three celery stalks and one onion in the recipe. **There is** dessert and coffee after the dinner.	If two nouns follow *there*, use a singular verb (*is*) if the first noun is singular. Use a plural verb (*are*) if the first noun is plural.
Informal: There's a lot of reservations in California. **Formal: There are** a lot of reservations in California.	In conversation, you will sometimes hear *there's* with plural nouns.
There are over 500 tribes in the U.S. **They** each have their own traditions. There's a Navajo reservation in Arizona. **It's** very big. There's a Navajo woman in my chemistry class. **She** comes from Arizona.	After we introduce a noun with *there*, we can continue to speak of this noun with a pronoun (*they*, *it*, *she*, etc.).

Is there unemployment on some reservations?
  Yes, there is.
 	
Are there any reservations in California?
  Yes, there are.
 	
How many Navajo Indians **are there** in Arizona?
	Observe the word order in questions with *there*.

Wrong: **There's** the Grand Canyon in Arizona. *Right:* The Grand Canyon is in Arizona.	Don't use *there* to introduce a specific or unique noun.

EXERCISE **9** **Fill in the blanks with the correct form and tense of _be_.**

EXAMPLE   There ___are___ a lot of Indians in Oklahoma.

1. There _____ a lot of reservations in California.

2. There _____ more American Indians 200 years ago than there _____ today.

3. In the beginning, there _____ peace between the Indians and the Pilgrims.

4. Later, there _____ wars between the Indians and the Europeans who took their land.

5. _____ _____ enough food to eat at the first Thanksgiving? Yes, there was.

6. How many people _____ _____ at the first Thanksgiving celebration?

7. Next week there _____ _____ a test on noncount nouns.

8. How many questions _____ _____ _____ on the test?

EXERCISE **10** **Fill in the blanks with a time or place.**

EXAMPLE   There was a war __in my country from 1972 to 1975.__ _____

1. There will be a test _____

2. There's a lot of snow _____

3. There's a lot of rain _____

4. There are a lot of people _____

5. There are a lot of reservations _____

6. There was a presidential election _____

7. There are a lot of different languages _____

8. There aren't many students _____

9. There are a lot of books _____

10. There was a war _____

Navajo Code Talkers

Before You Read

1. Are some languages more complicated than others?

2. Why is a code important during wartime?

CD 2, TR 16

Read the following textbook article. Pay special attention to quantity words.

American Indian languages are very complicated. There are **many** different languages and each one has **several** dialects. **Some** languages, like Navajo, have **no** alphabet or symbols.

Philip Johnston was not an Indian but he grew up on the Navajo reservation and learned **a lot of** their language. Later, when Johnston served in World War I, he understood the importance of developing a code that the enemy could not understand. In World War II, the U.S. was at war with Japan. The Japanese were very skillful at breaking codes. In 1942, Johnston met with an American military general and explained his idea of using the Navajo language in code to send messages. Indians living on Navajo land in the southwest U.S. could speak and understand the language. **Very few** non-Navajos could speak or understand it.

The general agreed to try this idea. The U.S. Marines recruited **200** native speakers of Navajo to create a code based on their language. There were **many** military words that did not exist in the Navajo language, so the Navajo recruits had to develop words for these things. For example, the commanding general was a "war chief"; a battleship was a "whale"; a submarine was an "iron fish."

In the first **two** days of code talking, more than **800** messages were sent without **any** errors.

During and after the war, the Navajo code talkers got **little** recognition for their great help in World War II. It wasn't until 1992 that the U.S. government honored the Navajo code talkers for their help in winning major battles of the war.

5.9 Quantity Expressions—An Overview

We can use quantity expressions to talk about the quantity of count and noncount nouns.

EXAMPLES

There are about **two million** American Indians today.
There were about **200** code talkers during World War II.
Very few non-Navajos could speak the Navajo language.
Navajo code talkers got **little** recognition for their work.
The Navajo language has **no** alphabet.
The Navajo language has **several** dialects.
The Pilgrims had **very little** food during the first winter.
The American Indians had **a lot of** knowledge about the land.
The Pilgrims didn't have **much** knowledge about the land.
Many Indians died from disease after the Europeans came.
Some Indians today live on reservations.

EXERCISE 11   Fill in the blanks to complete these statements. Answers may vary.

EXAMPLE   There are 500 _____tribes_____ of American Indians in the United States.

1. Two hundred native speakers of _____ served as code talkers.

2. There is no word for "_____" in Navajo.

3. The Navajo language has no _____.

4. Before the arrival of people from Europe, there were at least _____ American Indians.

5. After the first cold winter in America, the Pilgrims didn't have much _____.

6. Many Pilgrims _____ during the first winter.

7. Some _____ helped the Pilgrims.

8. The Indians taught them many _____ to help them survive.

9. The second year in America was much better. They had a lot of _____.

10. As more Europeans came to America, many _____ lost their land.

11. Many Indians can't find work on their reservations. There is a lot of _____ on a reservation.

Native American at a Powwow

5.10 Some, Any, A, No

	EXAMPLES	EXPLANATION
Affirmative	There is **a** big reservation in the Southwest. There is **an** onion in the recipe.	Use *a* or *an* with singular count nouns.
Affirmative	I used **some** raisins in the recipe. I used **some** bread in the recipe.	Use *some* with both plural count nouns and noncount nouns.
Negative	I didn't eat **any** potatoes. I didn't eat **any** gravy.	Use *any* for negatives with both plural count nouns and noncount nouns.
Question	Did the code talkers make **any** mistakes? Did the enemy get **any** information?	Use *any* for questions with both plural count nouns and noncount nouns.
No **vs.** *any*	There isn't **any** sugar in the stuffing. There is **no** sugar in the stuffing. There aren't **any** potatoes in the soup. There are **no** potatoes in the soup.	Use *any* after a negative verb. Use *no* after an affirmative verb. *Wrong:* There *aren't no* potatoes in the soup.

Language Notes:

1. Don't use the indefinite article after *no*.
   Wrong: I have no *an* answer to your question.
   Right: I have no answer to your question.

2. You will sometimes see *any* with a singular count noun.
   Which pen should I use for the test? You can use *any* pen.

   Any, in this case, means whichever you want. It doesn't matter which pen.

EXERCISE 12 — Look at the recipe on page 163. Use *there + be +* the words given to tell about this recipe. If you use *no*, delete the article.

EXAMPLES salt
There's some salt in the recipe.

a sweet potato
There are no sweet potatoes in the recipe.

1. an onion
2. pepper
3. oil
4. raisins

5. mushrooms
6. nuts
7. carrots
8. milk

EXERCISE 13 Fill in the blanks with *some*, *any*, *a*, *an*, or *no*.

EXAMPLE A: I put ___some___ salt on the potatoes.

B: Did you put ___any___ pepper on the potatoes?

1. A: Do you know _____ American Indians?

   B: No, I don't know _____ American Indians.

2. A: Can you name _____ American Indian tribes?

   B: Yes, I can name _____ tribes.

   A: I can't name _____.

3. A: Does the Navajo language have _____ alphabet?

   B: No. It has _____ alphabet.

4. A: I'll make _____ pie.

   B: Can you cook the turkey too?

   A: Sorry, I can't. I have _____ experience cooking a turkey.

5. A: I need _____ onion.

   B: Do you need _____ carrots?

   A: Yes, I need _____ carrots too.

6. A: Do you need _____ butter for your recipe?

   B: No. I don't need _____ butter. I'm going to use oil.

7. A: Sugar is not good for you, so there's _____ sugar in this recipe.

   B: Is there any honey?

   A: No. There isn't _____ honey either.

   B: Are there _____ raisins?

   A: There are _____ raisins either.

5.11 A Lot Of, Much, Many

	EXAMPLES	EXPLANATION
Affirmative	**A lot of** American Indians served in the military. It takes **a lot of** time to develop a code.	Use *a lot of* with count and noncount nouns.
Affirmative	On Thanksgiving, we give thanks for the **many** good things in our lives. We eat **a lot of** food on Thanksgiving.	Use *many* with count nouns. Use *a lot of* with noncount nouns in affirmative statements. *Much* is rare in affirmative statements.
Negative	Today the Indians don't have **much** land. The Pilgrims didn't have **many** skills.	Use *much* with noncount nouns. Use *many* with count nouns.
Negative	Today the Indians don't have **a lot of** land. The Pilgrims didn't have **a lot of** skills.	Use *a lot of* with both count and noncount nouns.
Question	Did you eat **much** turkey? Did you eat **many** cookies?	Use *much* with noncount nouns. Use *many* with count nouns.
Question	Did you eat **a lot of** turkey? Did you eat **a lot of** cookies?	Use *a lot of* with both count and noncount nouns.
Question	**How much** experience did the code talkers have? **How many** code talkers were in the military?	Use *how much* with noncount nouns. Use *how many* with count nouns.

Language Note:
When the noun is omitted (in the following sentence, **water**), use *a lot*, not *a lot of*.
   I usually drink **a lot of** water, but I didn't drink **a lot** today.

EXERCISE 14   **Fill in the blanks with *much*, *many*, or *a lot (of)*. Avoid *much* in affirmative statements. In some cases, more than one answer is possible.**

CD 2, TR 17

A: Did you prepare ___*a lot of*___ food for Thanksgiving?
                         (example)

B: No, I didn't prepare _____.
                               (1)

A: You didn't? Why not?

B: This year I didn't invite _____ people. I just
                                  (2)

invited my immediate family.

A: How _____ people are there in your immediate family?
          (3)

B: Just seven. I bought a twelve-pound turkey. It was more than enough.

(continued)

A: I don't know how to prepare a turkey. Is it _____ work
(4)

to prepare a turkey?

B: Not really. But you have to cook it for _____ hours.
(5)

A: Did you make _____ other dishes, like sweet potatoes
(6)

and cranberry sauce?

B: No. Each person in my family made something. That way I didn't

have _____ work. But we had _____ work cleaning
(7)   (8)

up. There were _____ dirty dishes. I hate washing dishes
(9)

after a big dinner, so I'm planning to buy a dishwasher soon.

A: Does a dishwasher cost _____ money?
(10)

B: Yes, but I'd like to have one for that one day a year.

A: Maybe you should just use paper plates.

B: I know _____ people do that, but I want my dinner to look
(11)

elegant. For me, paper plates are for picnics.

5.12 *A Lot Of* vs. *Too Much/Too Many*

EXAMPLES	EXPLANATION
a. **A lot of** Navajo Indians live in the Southwest. b. My friend left the reservation because there was **too much** unemployment and she couldn't find a job. a. **A lot of** people came to dinner. We all had a great time. b. **Too many** people came to dinner. There wasn't enough food for everyone.	Sentences (a) show a large quantity. No problem is presented. *A lot of* has a neutral tone. Sentences (b) show an excessive quantity. A problem is presented or implied. A sentence with *too much/too many* can have a complaining tone.
I feel sick. I ate **too much**.	We can put *too much* at the end of a verb phrase.

Language Note: Sometimes you can use *a lot of* in place of *too much/too many*.
Too many people came to dinner. There wasn't enough food for everyone.
A lot of people came to dinner. There wasn't enough food for everyone.

EXERCISE 15   Fill in the blanks with *a lot of*, *too much*, or *too many*. In some cases, more than one answer is possible.

EXAMPLE   I love garlic. This recipe calls for __a lot of__ garlic, so it's going to be delicious.

1. I can't eat this soup. It has _____ salt.
2. A Thanksgiving dinner has about 3,000 calories. Most people eat _____ and don't feel so good afterwards.
3. You put _____ pepper in the potatoes, and they taste terrible.
4. She's going to bake a cherry pie. She needs _____ cherries.
5. I think I ate _____ pieces of pumpkin pie. Now I feel sick.
6. Before the Europeans arrived, there were _____ Indians in America.
7. There are _____ American Indian languages.
8. The Navajo code talkers gave _____ help during World War II.
9. The code talkers sent _____ messages successfully.

EXERCISE 16   Use *a lot of*, *too much*, or *too many* to fill in the blanks in the story below. In some cases, more than one answer is possible.

CD 2, TR 18

My name is Coleen Finn. I'm a Ho-chunk Indian. My tribal land is in Wisconsin. But I live in Chicago because there is __too much__ unemployment
(example)
on my tribal land, and I can't find a good job there. There are _____
(1)
opportunities in Chicago, and I found a job as a secretary in the English Department at Truman College. I like my job very much. I have
_____ responsibilities and I love the challenge.
(2)

I like Chicago, but I miss my land, where I still have _____ relatives
(3)
and friends. I often go back to visit them whenever I get tired of life in Chicago. My friends and I have _____ fun together, talking,
(4)
cooking our native food, walking in nature, and attending Indian ceremonies, such as powwows. I need to get away from Chicago once in a while to feel closer to nature. Even though there are _____ nice
(5)
things about Chicago, there are _____ cars and trucks in the big city
(6)
and there is _____ pollution. A weekend with my tribe gives me
(7)
time to relax and smell fresh air.

EXERCISE 17   **ABOUT YOU**   **Fill in the blanks after *too* with *much* or *many*. Then complete the statement.**

EXAMPLE   If I drink too ___much___ coffee, ___I won't be able to sleep tonight.___

1. If I try to memorize too _____ words, _____

_____

2. If I make too _____ mistakes on my homework, _____

_____

3. If I spend too _____ money on clothes, _____

_____

4. If I spend too _____ time with my friends, _____

_____

5.13 A Few, Several, A Little

	EXAMPLES	EXPLANATION
Count	The Navajo language has **several** dialects. She speaks **a few** languages. Put **a few** teaspoons of salt in the potato recipe.	Use *a few* or *several* with count nouns or with quantities that describe noncount nouns (*teaspoon, cup, bowl, piece*, etc.).
Noncount	He put **a little** salt in the potatoes. Please add **a little** milk to the coffee.	Use *a little* with noncount nouns.

EXERCISE 18   **Fill in the blanks with *a few*, *several*, or *a little*. In some cases, more than one answer is possible.**

EXAMPLE   We have ___a little___ information about American Indians.

1. _____ Indians came to help the Pilgrims.
2. They taught the Pilgrims _____ skills for planting.
3. The article gave us _____ information about the code talkers.
4. _____ Navajo Indians developed a code.
5. It took _____ time to develop the code.
6. The Navajos had to create _____ new words.
7. There were _____ Japanese experts at code breaking.

5.14 A Few vs. Few; A Little vs. Little

A few and **a little** have a neutral tone. **Few** and **little** (without **a**) have a negative emphasis.

EXAMPLES	EXPLANATION
a. **A few** Indians helped the Pilgrims. b. **Few** non-Navajos could speak the Navajo language. c. **Very few** young American Indians speak the language of their ancestors.	In example (a), *a few* means some or enough. *A few* has a neutral tone. In examples (b) and (c), *few* and *very few* mean not enough; almost none. We often use *very* before *few*.
a. There's **a little** food in the refrigerator. Let's make a sandwich. b. The Navajo code talkers got **little** recognition for their help in World War II. c. The Pilgrims had **very little** food the first winter.	In example (a), *a little* means some or enough. *A little* has a neutral tone. In examples (b) and (c), *little* and *very little* mean not enough; almost none. We often use *very* before *little*.

Language Note: Whether something is enough or not enough does not depend on the quantity. It depends on the perspective of the person. Is the glass half empty or half full?
☺ One person may say the glass is half full. He sees something positive about the quantity of water in the glass: The glass has *a little* water.
☹ Another person may say the glass is half empty. He sees something negative about the quantity of water in the glass: The glass has (*very*) *little* water.

EXERCISE 19 Fill in the blanks with *a little, very little, a few,* or *very few.*

EXAMPLE 1. **A:** We read about American Indians in this lesson. Did you know that Eskimos are Native Americans too?

B: Really? I know <u>very little</u> about Eskimos.
(example)
In fact, I know almost nothing.

A: They live in Alaska, Canada, and Greenland. They make their houses out of ice.

B: What do they eat? _____ plants grow
(1)
in the cold regions.

A: They use a lot of sea animals for food. They eat whale, seal, and fish.

B: I like to eat _____ fish, but I can't imagine eating it all the
(2)
time. And I really can't imagine eating whale and seal. How do you know so much about Eskimos?

(continued)

A: I saw the movie *Eskimo*. I learned _____ about Eskimos from
(3)

the movie. And I read _____ books. Do you want to borrow
(4)

my books?

B: Uh, no thanks.

2. **A:** Let's prepare the Thanksgiving dinner together. I always like to get

_____ help for the Thanksgiving holiday.
(5)

B: I don't think I'm going to be much help. You know I have

_____ experience in the kitchen.
(6)

A: Don't worry. You can be my assistant.

B: OK. What can I do?

A: I need to put _____ oil on the turkey.
(7)

B: There's _____ oil in the house. I don't think it's going to be
(8)

enough.

A: Don't worry. I have another bottle. Can you get _____ things
(9)

out of the cabinet for me?

B: Sure.

A: Get the spices. We're going to put _____ spices on the turkey.
(10)

B: What else do you need?

A: I need _____ string to tie the legs. Then the turkey will be
(11)

ready to go into the oven.

B: Is there anything else I can do?

A: Yes. I need you to go to the store and get _____ things for me.
(12)

Here's a list.

B: Shopping! That's something I can do well.

A: Why is it that _____ men cook the turkey? In fact, I almost
(13)

never see a man prepare the Thanksgiving dinner. It seems like it's

always a woman's job.

3. **A:** Do you speak another language?

B: I speak _____ Spanish. I also studied Latin in high school.
(14)

A: Who speaks Latin?

B: No one does anymore. It's dead as a spoken language. That's why

_____ high schools offer Latin classes.
(15)

A: Is it like the Navajo language?

B: No. The Navajo language is not a dead language. However, today

_____ people speak it anymore. Most American Indians speak
(16)

English.

EXERCISE 20 **ABOUT YOU** Ask a question with *"Are there . . . ?"* and the words given about another student's hometown. The other student will answer with an expression of quantity. Practice count nouns.

EXAMPLE   museums

A: Are there any museums in your hometown?

B: Yes. There are a lot of (a few, three) museums in my hometown.
OR
No. There aren't any museums in my hometown.

1. department stores   6. open markets

2. fast-food restaurants   7. hospitals

3. homeless people   8. universities

4. skyscrapers   9. American businesses

5. supermarkets   10. bridges

EXERCISE 21 **ABOUT YOU** Ask a question with *"Is there . . . ?"* and the words given about another student's native country or hometown. The other student will answer with an expression of quantity. Practice noncount nouns.

EXAMPLE   petroleum/in your native country

A: Is there much petroleum in your native country?

B: Yes. There's lot of petroleum in my native country.
OR
No. There isn't much petroleum in my native country.

In Your Native Country   **In Your Hometown**

1. petroleum   5. traffic

2. industry   6. rain

3. agriculture   7. pollution

4. tourism   8. noise

EXERCISE 22 **ABOUT YOU** Ask a student a question with *"Do you have . . . ?"* and the words given. The other student will answer. Practice both count and noncount nouns.

EXAMPLES American friends

A: Do you have any American friends?
B: Yes. I have many (OR a lot of) American friends.
OR
No. I don't have many American friends.

free time

A: Do you have a lot of free time?
B: Yes. I have some free time.
OR
No. I have very little free time.

1. problems in the U.S.

2. friends

3. relatives in New York

4. time to relax

5. brothers and sisters (siblings)

6. experience with small children

7. questions about American customs

8. trouble with English pronunciation

9. information about points of interest in this city

10. knowledge about computer programming

EXERCISE 23 **ABOUT YOU** Cross out the phrase that doesn't fit and fill in the blanks with an expression of quantity to make a true statement about another country you know about. Discuss your answers.

EXAMPLE ~~There's~~/There isn't ___much___ unemployment in ___Korea___.

1. There's/There isn't _____ opportunity to make money in _____.

2. There are/There aren't _____ divorced people in _____.

3. There are/There aren't _____ foreigners in _____.

4. There's/There isn't _____ freedom in _____.

5. There are/There aren't _____ American cars in _____.

6. There are/There aren't _____ political problems in _____.

7. There is/There isn't _____ unemployment in _____.

8. There is/There isn't _____ crime in _____.

Summary of Lesson 5

1. Study the words that are used before count and noncount nouns.

SINGULAR COUNT	PLURAL COUNT	NONCOUNT
a tomato	some tomatoes	some coffee
no tomato	no tomatoes	no coffee
	any tomatoes	any coffee
	(with questions and negatives)	
	a lot of tomatoes	a lot of coffee
	many tomatoes	much coffee *(with questions and negatives)*
	a few tomatoes	a little coffee
	several tomatoes	
	How many tomatoes?	How much coffee?

2. Sentences with *there*

Count
> **There's** an onion in the recipe.
> **There are** two carrots in the recipe.

Noncount
> **There's** some oil in the recipe.
> How much salt **is there** in the recipe?

3. *Too Much/Too Many/A Lot Of*
- *A lot of* + count or noncount noun (no problem is presented)
  > I cooked **a lot of** potatoes for Thanksgiving dinner.
  > I put **a lot of** butter on the potatoes.
- *Too much* + noncount noun (a problem is presented)
  > She doesn't qualify for financial aid because her parents make **too much** money.
- *Too many* + count noun (a problem is presented)
  > There are **too many** students in the class. The teacher doesn't have time to help everyone.

Editing Advice

1. Some plural forms are irregular and don't take -s.

   She has two childrens.

2. Use a singular noun and verb after *every*.

   s
   Every ~~children~~ need love.
   ^

3. Use the plural form of the noun after *one of*.

   s
   One of my sister is a lawyer.
   ^

4. Don't use *a* or *an* before a plural noun.

   (some)
   She bought ~~a~~ new socks.

5. Don't put *a* or *an* before a noncount noun.

   some OR *a piece of*
   I want to give you ~~an~~ advice.

6. A noncount noun is always singular.

   a lot of
   I have ~~many~~ homeworks to do.

   pieces of
   She bought three furnitures.
   ^

7. Use *there is* or *there are* to introduce a noun.

   There are
   ~~Are~~ a lot of people in China.

8. Be careful with *there* and *they're*. They sound the same.

   There
   ~~They're~~ are many problems in the world.

9. Don't use a specific noun after *there is/there are*.

   T   *is*
   ~~There's~~ the Golden Gate bridge in San Francisco.
                                         ^

10. Include *of* with a unit of measure.

    of
    He bought three tubes toothpaste.
    ^

11. Omit *of* after *a lot* when the noun is omitted.

    I have a lot of time, but my brother doesn't have a lot ~~of~~.

12. Use *a little/a few* to mean *some*. Use *little/few* to mean *not enough*.

> *(very)*
> He can't help you because he has a little time.

13. Don't use *too much* or *too many* if the quantity doesn't present a problem.

> *a lot of*
> He's a lucky man. He has ~~too many~~ friends.

14. Don't confuse *too* and *too much/many*.

> The potatoes are too ~~much~~ salty. I can't eat them.

15. Don't use a double negative.

> *any*
> He doesn't have ~~no~~ money. OR *He has no money.*

Editing Quiz

Some of the shaded words and phrases have mistakes. Find the mistakes and correct them. If the shaded words are correct, write C.

I love American Thanksgiving. Every years, the whole family comes to our
C
(example)
house for this holiday and a few other holidays. But Thanksgiving is my
(example)
favorite. There are a lot of childrens in my family and they love to see each
(1) *(2)*
other on Thanksgiving. They don't have many time to see each other the
(3)
rest of the year because of school. It's so joyful to have too many children
(4)
in the house few times a year. There's a lot of noise in the house when
(5) *(6)* *(7)*
they're here, but we don't mind.
(8)

We all bring some foods. One of my sister always makes a pumpkin pie.
(9) *(10)* *(11)*
Her husband always makes a cookies in the shape of turkeys. My other
(12)
sister makes cranberry sauce. She uses a lot of sugars and sometimes it's
(13)
too much sweet, but I never say anything. My brother doesn't like to cook,
(14)
so he brings a lot fresh fruit. My cousin brings about 10 big bottles soda.
(15) *(16)*
I prepare the sweet potatoes. My mother always makes the turkey. It takes
(17)
much time to cook a big turkey.
(18)
(continued)

We have a lot to prepare before Thanksgiving. My mother has very little
    (19)   (20)
time the week before because of her job. But I have a lot of because I don't
                                                              (21)
have no homeworks that week. So I clean the house. My father likes to
     (22)   (23)
help but he has very few experience in the kitchen, so my mother asks him
                 (24)
to do the shopping. He doesn't have much experience shopping either, so
                                        (25)
she always gives him an advice about shopping with a list. But he always
                      (26)
forgets to take the list and buys too much. Last year he bought a 50-pound
                                   (27)
bag of rice that we still haven't finished!

It's always fun to spend Thanksgiving with too many people that we love.
                                             (28)
But there's one thing I don't like: they're are always a lot of dishes to wash
    (29)   (30)   (31)
afterwards.

Lesson 5 Test/Review

PART 1 **Fill in the blanks with the singular or plural form of the word in parentheses ( ).**

EXAMPLE   The Pilgrims didn't have a lot of __experience__ with American land.
                                           (experience)

1. The Indians had many _____ with white _____ over
                        (war)   *(person)*

   their land.

2. Some _____ have a big problem with _____ and _____.
        (reservation)   *(unemployment)*   *(poverty)*

   There aren't enough _____ for everyone.
                       (job)

3. My father gave me a lot of _____. He told me that there are
                             (advice)

   more _____ in big _____ than on reservations.
        (job)   *(city)*

4. We like to visit the art museum. We like to see the _____ and
                                                        (sculpture)

   _____ by famous _____. We like all kinds of _____.
   (painting)   *(artist)*   *(art)*

5. My brother likes all kinds of _____. He has a large collection
                                 (music)

   of _____.
      (CD)

PART 2 Fill in the blanks with an appropriate measurement of quantity. In some cases, several answers are possible.

EXAMPLE   I bought a ____loaf____ of bread.

1. I drank a _____ of tea.
2. She drank a _____ of milk.
3. I usually put a _____ of sugar in my coffee.
4. There's a _____ of milk in the refrigerator.
5. I'm going to buy a _____ of furniture for my living room.
6. The teacher gave a long homework _____.
7. My father gave me an important _____ of advice.
8. I drank three _____ of water today.
9. I need a _____ of paper to write my composition.
10. We need to buy a _____ of soap.

PART 3 Read this composition by an American Indian. Circle the correct words to complete the composition.

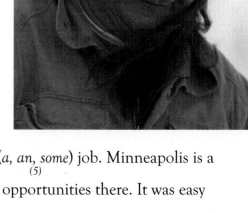

My name is Joseph Falling Snow.

I'm (an, *a*, any) Native American from
(example)
a Sioux[11] reservation in South Dakota.

I don't live in South Dakota anymore

because I couldn't find (a, any, no) job.
(1)

There's (a little, a few, very little, very few)
(2)

work on my reservation. There's

(much, a lot of, many) poverty. My uncle
(3)

gave me (a, an, some, any) good advice.
(4)

He told me to go to Minneapolis to find (a, an, some) job. Minneapolis is a
(5)

big city, so there are (much, many, any) job opportunities there. It was easy
(6)

for me to find a job as a carpenter. I had (no, not, any) trouble finding a job
(7)

because I have (a lot of, many, much) experience.
(8)

[11]Sioux is pronounced /su/.   *(continued)*

Singular and Plural; Count and Noncount Nouns; *There + Be*; Quantity Words   **185**

My native language is Lakota, but I know (*any, a few, very few*) words in
(9)
my language. Most of the people on my reservation speak English.

(*A few, Any, A little*) older people still speak Lakota, but the language is
(10)
dying out as the older people die.

(*A few, A little, Few, Little*) times a year, I go back to the reservation for
(11)
a powwow. We wear our native costumes and dance our native dances. It

gets very crowded at these times because (*much, any, a lot of*) people from
(12)
our reservation and nearby reservations attend this celebration. We have

(*much, many, a lot of*) fun.
(13)

Expansion

Classroom

Activities

❶ **Work with a partner. Imagine that you have to spend a few weeks
alone on a deserted island. You can take 15 things with you. What will
you need to survive? Give reasons for each item.**

EXAMPLE   I'll take a lot of water because I can't drink ocean water. It has salt in it.

❷ **Game: Where am I?**

Teacher: Write these words on separate index cards: *at the airport,
downtown, at the library, at a supermarket, at a department store,
on the highway, at the zoo, at church, at the beach, at home, on an
elevator, on a bus, on an airplane, at the post office,* **and** *in the school
cafeteria.*

**Students: One student picks an index card with a place name and says,
"Where am I?" Other students have to guess where he/she is by asking
questions.**

EXAMPLES   Are you indoors or outdoors?
Are there a lot of cars in this place?
Is it noisy in this place?
Are there a lot of people in this place?

❸ **Find a partner. Talk about the food you eat on a holiday or special
day. Describe the ingredients of this food.**

Read the following quotes and discuss what they mean to you.

❶ "Once I was in a big city and I saw a very large house. They told me it was a bank and that the white men place their money there to be taken care of, and that by and by they got it back with interest. We are Indians and we have no such bank. When we have plenty of money or blankets, we give them away to other chiefs and people, and by and by they return them with interest, and our hearts feel good. Our way of giving is our bank."

—Chief Maquinna, Nootka tribe

❷ "Treat the Earth well. It was not given to you by your parents; it was loaned to you by your children." (*Kenyan proverb*)

❸ "Today is a time of celebrating for you—a time of looking back to the first days of white people in America. But it is not a time of celebrating for me. It is with a heavy heart that I look back upon what happened to my people. When the Pilgrims arrived, we, the Wampanoags, welcomed them with open arms, little knowing that it was the beginning of the end. . . . Let us always remember, the Indian is and was just as human as the white people."

From a speech by a Wampanoag Indian given on Thanksgiving in 1970 in Massachusetts, at the 350th anniversary of the Pilgrims' arrival in America.

Write

About It ❶ Write about an ethnic minority in your native country or another country you know about. Where and how do these people live? Use expressions of quantity.

❷ Write a paragraph telling about the advantages or disadvantages of living in a city. You may write about pollution, job opportunities, weather, traffic, transportation, and crime. Use expressions of quantity.

Singular and Plural; Count and Noncount Nouns; *There + Be*; Quantity Words

❸ Write about a holiday in your country. How do you celebrate it?

The New Year Celebration in Vietnam

In my country, Vietnam, we celebrate the New Year (*Tet*) in a very special way. It's the most important day of the year. We follow the lunar calendar and New Year comes at the end of January or the beginning of February. It's not like the American New Year at all. We spend a lot of time preparing for this day…

 For more practice using grammar in context, please visit our Web site.

Grammar

Adjectives

Noun Modifiers

Adverbs

Too/Enough/Very/A Lot Of

Context

Health

Obesity: A National Problem

Before You Read

1. Do you ever eat at fast-food restaurants?

2. What kind of food commercials do you see on TV?

CD 2, TR 19

Read the following Web article. Pay special attention to adjectives and noun modifiers.

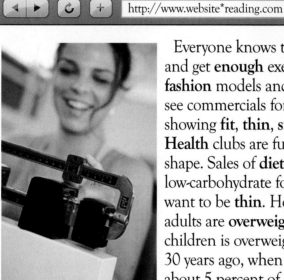

http://www.website*reading.com

Everyone knows that it's **important** to eat well and get **enough** exercise. We see **beautiful, thin fashion** models and want to look like them. We see commercials for **exercise** machines on TV showing **fit, thin, smiling** people exercising. **Health** clubs are full of people trying to get in shape. Sales of **diet** colas and low-calorie and low-carbohydrate foods indicate that Americans want to be **thin**. However, two-thirds of **American** adults are **overweight**, and one in six American children is overweight. This is a **large** increase from 30 years ago, when 50 percent of adults and only about 5 percent of children were overweight.

Approximately half of Americans are **concerned** about their weight. They spend billions of dollars on **weight-loss** products and health clubs. But weight is also becoming a **national** problem as health costs go up in response to diseases related to obesity: **heart** disease, **high blood** pressure, diabetes, arthritis, and stroke.

What is the reason for this **growing** problem? First, **today's** lifestyle does not include enough **physical** activity. When the U.S. was an **agricultural** society, farmers ate a **big, heavy** meal, but they burned off the calories by doing **hard physical** labor. **Modern** technology has removed physical activity from our **daily** lives. Seventy-five percent of all trips are less than a mile from home, but Americans drive. Only 15 percent of schoolchildren walk to school even though most of them live within one mile of school. And the **average** American child spends approximately 24 hours a week watching TV. In most physical **education** classes, kids are **active** for just three minutes.

Another reason for the **weight** problem is the American diet. The average child sees more than 10,000 **food** commercials a year. Most of these are for high-calorie foods, such as **sweetened** cereals, **sugary** soft drinks, **salty** chips, and other **snack** foods. We call these **unhealthy** foods "**junk**" food. Children and adults often prefer junk food.

Adults have **busy** lives and depend on **fast** food. The supermarkets are **filled** with **cheap, tasty** food that is **easy** to prepare and **high** in calories.

Obesity is quickly becoming the number one cause of **preventable** death.

What's Your Body Mass Index?

Body Mass Index (BMI) helps to measure if a person is overweight or not.

$$\frac{\text{weight in pounds}}{(\text{height in inches})^2} \times 703$$

Example:

$$\frac{160 \text{ lbs.}}{(69 \text{ in.})^2} \times 703 = 23.6 \text{ BMI}$$

BMI	Status
Below 18.5	Underweight
18.5–24.9	Normal
25.0–29.9	Overweight
30.0–39.9	Obese
40 and above	Extremely obese

6.1 Adjectives

An adjective describes a noun.

EXAMPLES	EXPLANATION
We ate a **big** meal. People need **physical** activity.	An adjective can come before a noun.
a. Farmers ate a **big**, **heavy** meal. a. We see **beautiful**, **thin** models. b. People used to do **hard physical** labor. b. The **average American** child watches a lot of TV.	Two adjectives can come before a noun. In examples (a), we put a comma between the two adjectives because we can reverse the order of the adjectives without changing the meaning. In examples (b), we don't use a comma because we can't reverse the order of the adjectives.
Fast food is **cheap**. Chips are **salty**. Burgers taste **delicious**. You look **healthy**.	An adjective can come after *be, seem,* and the sense-perception verbs: *look, sound, smell, taste,* or *feel.*
It is **important** to eat well. It is **easy** to gain weight if you eat junk food.	An adjective can come after impersonal expressions beginning with *it + be.*
Are you **concerned** about your weight? I'm **tired** after work. Supermarkets are **filled** with easy-to-prepare foods.	Some *-ed* words are adjectives: *tired, worried, located, crowded, married, divorced, excited, disappointed, finished, frightened, filled,* and *concerned.*
We read an **interesting** article about weight. Obesity is a **growing** problem in the U.S. **Working** parents often don't have time to prepare a good meal for their children.	Some *-ing* words are adjectives: *interesting, growing, exciting, boring,* and *working.*
She is a **thin** model. We often see **thin** models on TV.	Do not make adjectives plural.
Fast food is **very** fattening. I'm **so** tired. Some Americans are **quite** fat. People used to do **extremely** hard physical labor.	*Very, so, quite,* and *extremely* can come before adjectives.
I was **kind of** tired after work, so I just watched TV. We had a **real** delicious meal. I had a **pretty** hard day.	Conversational words that come before adjectives are: *pretty, sort of, kind of,* and *real.*
Do you want a big pizza or a small **one**? Do you prefer the purple grapes or the green **ones**?	After an adjective, we can substitute a singular noun with *one* and a plural noun with *ones.*

EXERCISE 1 **Fill in the blanks with an appropriate word. Answers may vary.**

EXAMPLE Burgers and fries are ___high___ in calories.

1. Fries are cooked in oil. They are very _____.

2. I ate a terrible meal and I got _____.

3. Do you want a large coffee or a small _____?

4. She's very _____ about her children's health because they prefer candy to fruit.

5. I didn't sleep at all last night. I'm very _____ today.

6. Have a piece of fresh apple pie. I just had a piece. It _____ good.

7. Potato chips are very _____.

8. Ice cream is _____ in calories.

9. Most Americans have _____ lives and don't make the time to eat well.

10. Obesity in the U.S. is a _____ problem. It is a much bigger problem today than it was 30 years ago.

EXERCISE 2 **Circle the correct words in italics to complete this conversation.**

CD 2, TR 20

A husband (H) and wife (W) are discussing weight.

H: We're gaining weight. We used to be (*thin* / *thins*), but when we got
(example)
(*marry* / *married*), we started to gain weight.
(1)

W: Let's go jogging after work. There's
a (*beautiful park* / *park beautiful*)
(2)
where we can go. It's (*locate* / *located*) just a
(3)
few blocks away from our apartment.

H: But after work I'm always too (*tire* / *tired*).
(4)
I just want to eat dinner and watch TV.

W: It's not good to eat a big meal so late at night. I know that's what most Americans do, but in other countries people eat a big meal during the day and (*a small one* / *a small*) at night.
(5)

H: What difference does it make?

(*continued*)

W: If we eat a big meal in the middle of the day, we have the rest of the day to burn off the calories.

H: I'm sure that's (*an idea very good / a very good idea*) but I don't have
(6)
time to eat a big meal in the middle of the day. My lunch break is
(*kind / kind of*) short.
(7)

W: We should cook more at home. We're always eating out in
(*expensive / expensives*) restaurants that have (*fatty / fattied*) foods.
(8)   (9)

H: Maybe doctors will find a pill that will make us thin with no effort.

W: You know what they say, "No pain, no gain." It takes a lot of effort to lose weight.

6.2 Noun Modifiers

EXAMPLES	EXPLANATION
Do you have an **exercise machine**? A **farm worker** gets a lot of exercise. Some people eat at **fast-food restaurants**. I joined a **health club**. **Fashion models** are very thin.	A noun can modify (describe) another noun. The second noun is more general than the first. An *exercise machine* is a machine. A *leg exercise* is an exercise.
I bought new **running** shoes. Do you ever use the **swimming** pool?	Sometimes a gerund describes a noun. It shows the purpose of the noun.
My **five-year-old** son prefers candy to fruit. **Potato** chips have a lot of grease.	The first noun is always singular. A five-**year**-old son is a son who is five **years** old. **Potato** chips are chips made from **potatoes**.
Very few **schoolchildren** walk to school. I can't read the ingredients without my **eyeglasses**.	Sometimes we write the two nouns as one word. The noun modifier and the noun become a compound word.
Do you have your **driver's** license? I can't understand the **owner's** manual for my new DVD player. **Today's** lifestyle doesn't include much physical activity.	Sometimes a possessive noun describes a noun.

Pronunciation Note: When a noun describes a noun, the first noun usually receives the greater emphasis in speaking.
   I wear my **running** shoes when I go to the **health** club and use the **exercise** machines.

EXERCISE 3 Find the noun modifiers in the reading on pages 190–191. Underline them.

EXERCISE 4 A mother (M) and son (S) are shopping at a big supermarket. Fill in the blanks by putting the nouns in parentheses ( ) in the correct order. Remember to use the singular form for the first noun.

🔊
CD 2, TR 21

S: What are we going to buy today? Just a few things?

M: No. We need a lot. Let's take a _____ shopping cart _____.
(example: cart/shopping)

S: Can I sit in the _____?
(1 child/seat)

M: You're much too big. You're a six-

_____ boy.
(2 years/old)

S: Mom, buy me that cereal. It looks good.

I saw it on a _____.
(3 commercial/TV)

M: Let's read the ingredients on the _____ first. I want to
(4 cereal/box)

see the _____ before we buy it. Let me put on my
(5 content/sugar)

_____. Oh, dear. This cereal has 20 grams of sugar.
(6 glasses/eyes)

S: But I like sugar, Mom.

M: You know it causes _____. Remember what the
(7 teeth/decay)

dentist told you?

S: But I brush my teeth once a day.

M: I want you to use your _____ after every meal, not
(8 teeth/brush)

just once a day.

S: Mom, can we buy those _____?
(9 chips/potatoes)

M: They have too much fat.

S: How about some soda?

M: You should drink more juice. How about some _____?
(10 juice/oranges)

S: I don't like juice.

M: It seems you don't like anything that's good for you. Maybe we

should shop at the _____ store next time.
(11 food/health)

S: Oh, Mom, you're no fun.

M: Let's get in the _____ and pay now.
(12 line/check-out)

Obesity: The Solution

Before You Read

1. Where and when do you eat your big meal of the day?

2. When you see commercials for food on TV, do you want to buy that food?

CD 2, TR 22

Read the following Web article. Pay special attention to adverbs.

http://website*reading.com

Millions of Americans are overweight. Health experts agree that the problem comes from a combination of things: the kind of food we eat, our lifestyle, and even technology. Experts have the following recommendations for living a healthier lifestyle:

1. Get active. Ride a bike or walk places instead of driving. Cars and other machines **greatly** reduce the need for physical activity. These machines help us move from place to place **easily** and **quickly** and work **efficiently**, but we don't use much physical energy.

2. Eat a **well**-balanced meal consisting of protein, grains, vegetables, and fruit. Unfortunately, many people often eat alone and **quickly**. Some even just eat snacks all day. Nutritionists recommend that families eat together like they used to. As they eat their big meal together **slowly**, they can discuss the events of their day and enjoy each other's company.

3. Take the soft drink and snack machines out of the schools and educate children **early** about nutrition and exercise. The typical teenager gets about 10 to 15 percent of his or her calories from soft drinks, which have no nutrition at all. Replace the food in the machines with water, juice, and healthy snacks such as raisins.

4. Be careful of the food messages you hear from advertisers that say, "Eat this. Buy that." Technology allows advertisers to send us messages **constantly** through commercials. Many of these foods are high in fat and calories. Choose natural foods, such as fruits and nuts, instead of manufactured foods.

In addition to what individuals can do, communities need to build their housing more **carefully**. In many communities in the U.S., it is hard to walk from place to place **easily** because there are no sidewalks. If we want people to get exercise in their communities, they need sidewalks and bike paths with stores and activities within walking distance.

Can you think of any other ways to solve the problem of obesity?

6.3 Adverbs of Manner

An adverb of manner tells *how* or *in what way* a person does something.

EXAMPLES	EXPLANATION
Subject **Verb Phrase** **Adverb** He does his job **efficiently.** They ate lunch **quickly.** We walk together **slowly.**	We form most adverbs of manner by putting *-ly*[1] at the end of an adjective. An adverb usually follows the verb phrase.
Cars **greatly** reduce the need for physical activity. We **constantly** see ads on TV for food.	The *-ly* adverb of manner can come before the verb. This position is more formal.
Do you eat **well**?	The adverb for *good* is *well*.
You should eat a **well**-balanced meal. We live in a **carefully** planned community.	An adverb can come before an adjective.
ADJ: He is a **hard** worker. ADV: He works **hard**. ADJ: He wants a **fast** meal. ADV: Don't eat so **fast**. ADJ: He has an **early** class. ADV: We need to educate our children **early**. ADJ: I have a **late** class. ADV: I get home **late**.	Some adjectives and adverbs have the same form: *hard, fast, early,* and *late*.
She worked **hard** to prepare a good meal, but her son **hardly** ate anything.	*Hard* and *hardly* are both adverbs, but they have completely different meanings. *She worked **hard*** means she put a lot of effort into the work. *Hard* comes after the verb phrase. *He **hardly** ate anything* means he ate almost nothing. *Hardly* comes before the verb.
He came home **late** and missed dinner. **Lately**, he doesn't have time to eat a good meal.	*Late* and *lately* are both adverbs, but they have completely different meanings. *Late* means not on time. It comes after the verb phrase. *Lately* means recently. It comes at the beginning or end of the sentence.
Compare: She is a **friendly** person. She behaves **in a friendly manner**. He is a **lively** person. He dances **in a lively way**.	Some adjectives end in *-ly*: *lovely, lonely, early, friendly, lively, ugly*. They have no adverb form. We use an adverbial phrase (*in a ___-ly way*) to describe the action.
He loses weight **very** *easily*. She cooks **extremely** *well*. He eats **so** *fast*. She exercises **real** *hard*. You eat **quite** *slowly*.	*Very, extremely, so, real,* and *quite* can come before an adverb.

[1]For the spelling of *-ly* adverbs, see Appendix C.

EXERCISE 5 Fill in the blanks with an adverb from the box below (or choose your own adverb). Several answers may be possible.

cheaply	differently	constantly	poorly
briskly ✓	regularly	quickly	well

EXAMPLE   If you walk __briskly__ every day, you can lose weight.

1. TV gives us messages _____, telling us to buy more junk food.

2. Do you eat _____ or slowly?

3. You should exercise _____ if you want to lose weight.

4. If you eat _____, you will not be healthy and strong.

5. If you eat _____, you will have no need to snack between meals.

6. In a fast-food restaurant, a family can eat _____. In another kind of restaurant, they have to spend a lot of money.

7. Some immigrants eat _____ when they come to the U.S. because they can't find food from their native countries.

EXERCISE 6   **ABOUT YOU** Write the adverb form of the word in parentheses ( ). Then check (✓) the activities that you do in this way. Make statements telling how you do these activities.

EXAMPLES   __✓__ shop __carefully__
                                  (careful)
I shop carefully. I always try to buy healthy food for my family.

_____ dance __well__
                        (good)
I don't dance well. I never learned how.

1. _____ answer every question _____
                                                    (honest)
2. _____ walk _____
                              (fast)
3. _____ cook _____
                              (good)
4. _____ talk _____
                             (constant)
5. _____ work _____
                              (hard)
6. _____ study _____
                               (hard)
7. _____ speak Spanish _____
                                          (fluent)
8. _____ type _____
                             (fast)
9. _____ exercise _____
                                  (regular)
10. _____ choose my food _____
                                             (careful)

6.4 Adjective vs. Adverb

An adjective describes a noun. An adverb describes a verb (phrase).

EXAMPLES	EXPLANATION
Jim is **serious** about good health. He takes his doctor's advice **seriously**.	*Serious* is an adjective. It describes Jim. *Seriously* is an adverb. It tells how he takes his doctor's advice.
a. Your composition looks **good**. b. The teacher is looking at it **carefully**. a. The soup tastes **delicious**. b. I tasted the soup **slowly** because it was hot.	a. Use an adjective, not an adverb, after the following verbs if you are describing the subject: *smell, sound, taste, look, seem, appear,* and *feel*. b. Use an adverb if you are telling *how* the action (the verb phrase) is done.
a. The children got **hungry**. b. They ate lunch **hungrily**.	Use an adjective, not an adverb, in expressions with *get*: *get hungry, get tired, get sick, get rich,* etc. a. *Hungry* describes the children. b. *Hungrily* describes how they ate lunch.
Her health is **absolutely** perfect. The refrigerator is **completely** empty. You should eat a **well**-balanced diet.	An adverb can come before an adjective in phrases such as these: completely right extremely important pleasantly surprised well-known perfectly clear absolutely wrong
He's sick. He doesn't feel **well** today.	For health, use *well*. In conversational English, people often use *good* for health. He's sick. He doesn't feel **good** today.
Compare: **As usual**, she cooked dinner. Her husband **usually** cooks on Saturday.	Use the adjective, not the adverb, in the expression *as usual*.

EXERCISE 7 **Fill in the blanks with the correct form of the adjective or adverb in parentheses ( ).**

Last week I was invited to a "potluck" dinner at my math teacher's

house. This is my first month in the U.S., so I didn't know what "potluck"

was. A ____good____ friend of mine told me that this is a dinner where
    (example: good)

each person brings some food. I wanted to make a _____ impression,
                                                    (1 good)

so I prepared my _____ dish from Mexico. I worked _____ hard
                    (2 favorite)   (3 extreme)

to make it look and taste _____.
                           (4 good)

Most of the people at the dinner looked at my dish _____.
                                                     (5 strange)

They didn't know what it was. They thought _____ that
                                             (6 foolish)

Mexicans just eat tacos. They tasted my food _____, thinking
                                               (7 careful)

that Mexicans make everything very hot and spicy. But I didn't. I know

that some people don't like _____ food, so I put the hot sauce
                             (8 spicy)

on the side.

A student from India brought Indian food. I was _____ to
                                                  (9 surprised)

find out how spicy Indian food is. The taste was very _____ to
                                                        (10 strange)

me, but I ate it anyway.

The party was great. I went home very _____. I had to get
                                        (11 late)

up _____ the next morning, so I _____ slept at all that night.
   (12 early)   (13 hard)

Sleep

Before You Read

1. How many hours do you sleep a night?

2. How many hours would you like to sleep a night?

CD 2, TR 23

Read the following magazine article. Pay special attention to phrases with *too, enough, a lot of*, and *very*.

Did You Know?

Albert Einstein said he needed 10 hours of sleep a night to function well.

Most people need eight hours of sleep but don't get enough. Most Americans get less than seven hours a night. Only 30 percent get **enough sleep**. When people aren't rested **enough**, there are bad results. For example, if people drive when they're **too tired**, they can cause serious accidents on the road. According to the National Transportation Administration, sleepy drivers cause 100,000 accidents each year. There are many work-related accidents too. But that's not all. If you stay awake **too long**, your mind and nervous system begin to malfunction.[2] In the long term, if you don't get **enough sleep**, you will have less resistance to infection and disease.

Are we **too busy** to get **enough sleep**? Not always. Besides job and family responsibilities, Americans have **a lot of other things** that keep them out of bed. Twenty-four-hour-a-day Internet and TV keep us awake. Supermarkets, shopping malls, and laundromats are open late.

A lot of Americans, approximately 75 percent, report having trouble sleeping a few nights per week. Maybe they have **too much stress** in their lives or don't have good sleep habits. Sleep experts have some recommendations:

- Don't nap during the day.
- Don't get **too stimulated** before going to bed. Avoid activities such as watching TV or eating before bed.
- Go to bed at the same time every night.
- Avoid caffeine after lunchtime. If you drink **too much coffee** during the day, don't expect to get a good night's sleep.
- Exercise. Physical activity is **very good** for sleep. But if you exercise **too late** in the day, it will interfere with your sleep.

A good night's sleep is **very important**, so turn off the TV, shut down the computer, and sleep well.

[2]*To malfunction* means to function, or work, poorly.

6.5 *Too* and *Enough*

Too indicates a problem. The problem is stated or implied. *Enough* means sufficient.

EXAMPLES	EXPLANATION
adjective I'm **too *tired*** to drive. **adverb** She drove **too *fast*** and got a ticket.	Put *too* **before** adjectives and adverbs.
noncount noun a. Children eat **too much *food*** that is high in calories. **count noun** b. You spend **too many *hours*** watching TV.	a. Use *too much* before a noncount noun. b. Use *too many* before a count noun.
He doesn't sleep well because he worries **too much**.	*Too much* can come at the end of the verb phrase.
adjective Five hours of sleep is not ***good* enough**. **adverb** I walked ***quickly* enough** to raise my heart rate.	Put *enough* **after** adjectives and adverbs.
noun Some children don't get **enough *exercise***. **noun** I don't have **enough *time*** to exercise.	Put *enough* **before** nouns.

Language Notes:
1. An infinitive phrase can follow a phrase with *too* and *enough*.
   He's **too young *to understand*** that candy isn't good for you.
   I don't have **enough money *to join*** a health club.

2. *Too good to be true* shows a surprised or doubtful reaction.
   I just won a million dollars. It's **too good to be true**.

EXERCISE 8   **Fill in the blanks to complete these statements. Answers may vary.**

EXAMPLES   Are Americans too ____busy____ to get a good night's sleep?

Some people don't get enough ____exercise____, so they're overweight.

1. It's hard to sleep if you exercise too _____ in the evening.

2. If you're too _____ when you drive, you can fall asleep at the wheel.

(*continued*)

3. Some people spend too much _____ on the Internet. They should shut down the computer and go to bed.

4. If you drink too much _____, it can affect your sleep.

5. People drive everywhere. They don't _____ enough.

6. When children eat too _____, they get fat.

7. Children shouldn't drink so much soda, because it contains too many _____.

8. Most Americans don't get enough _____.

9. Many people say, "I don't have enough _____ to do all the things I need to do."

10. It's never too _____ to change your bad habits.

11. His clothes don't fit him anymore because he got too _____.

EXERCISE 9 **ABOUT YOU** **Complete each statement with an infinitive.**

EXAMPLES   I'm too young _____*to retire.*_____

I'm not strong enough _____*to move a piano.*_____

1. I'm not too old _____

2. I'm too young _____

3. I don't have enough money _____

4. I don't have enough time _____

5. I don't speak English well enough _____

EXERCISE 10 **A person is complaining about the school cafeteria. Fill in the blanks with *too, too much,* or *too many.***

EXAMPLE   It's _____*too*_____ noisy, so I can't talk with my friends.

1. They serve _____ junk food there.

2. The fries have _____ grease.

3. The hamburgers have _____ calories.

4. The food is _____ expensive.

5. The tables are _____ dirty.

6. There are _____ people there, and sometimes there's no place to sit.

6.6 Too and Very and A Lot Of

EXAMPLES	EXPLANATION
a. I'm **too** tired to drive. Would you drive for a while? b. I was **very** tired, but I stayed up late and studied for my test.	Don't confuse *very* and *too*. *Too* always indicates a problem in a specific situation. The problem can be stated or implied. *Very* is a neutral word.
a. The speed limit on the highway is 55, and you're driving 40. You're driving **too** slowly. b. The speed limit on this road is 15 miles per hour. You need to drive **very** slowly. a. My brother is 14 years old. He's **too** old to get into the movie theater at half price. b. My grandmother is 85. She's **very** old, but she's in great health.	In examples (a), *too* shows a problem in a specific situation. In examples (b), *very* does not show any problem.
a. You put **too much** salt in the soup, and I can't eat it. b. She puts **a lot of** sugar in her coffee. She likes it that way. a. I ate **too many** cookies, and now I feel sick. b. She baked **a lot of** cookies for the party. Everyone enjoyed them.	Don't confuse *a lot of* and *too much/too many*. a. *Too* always indicates a problem in a specific situation. b. *A lot of* is a neutral expression.

EXERCISE 11 Fill in the blanks with *too*, *too much*, *too many*, *a lot of*, or *very*.

CD 2, TR 24

A: Your dinner was ___very___ delicious tonight.
(example)

B: I'm _____ glad you liked it.
(1)

A: Everything was great. But the soup had _____ salt.
(2)

B: Oh. I thought you liked everything.

A: I did. Other than the salt, it was good.

And I especially liked the potatoes.

B: I'm glad.

A: But you put a little _____ butter in the
(3)

potatoes. They were _____ greasy.
(4)

B: Oh.

A: But don't worry. I ate them anyway.

(continued)

B: I'm afraid the steak was burned. I left it in the oven _____ long.
                                                                    (5)

A: Well, no one's perfect. I ate it anyway.

B: What about the cake I made? Did you like that?

A: Yes. It was _____ good. The only problem was it was
                        (6)
_____ small. I was hoping to have another piece, but
      (7)
there was nothing left.

B: I thought you wanted to lose weight. You always say you're
_____ fat and need to go on a diet.
      (8)

A: Fat? I'm not fat.

B: But you can't wear your old pants anymore.

A: I'm not _____ fat. My clothes are
                    (9)
_____ small. When I washed them, the water I used
      (10)
was _____ hot and they shrank.
          (11)

B: They didn't shrink. You gained weight. You consume _____
                                                                    (12)
calories.

Summary of Lesson 6

1. Adjectives and Adverbs

ADJECTIVES	ADVERBS
We had a **quick** lunch.	We ate **quickly**.
We had a **late** dinner.	We ate **late**.
She is a **good** cook.	She cooks **well**.
She looks **serious**.	She is looking at the label **seriously**.
As usual, he drank a cup of coffee.	He **usually** drinks coffee in the morning.

2. Adjective Modifiers and Noun Modifiers

ADJECTIVE MODIFIER	NOUN MODIFIER
a **new** machine	an **exercise** machine
old shoes	**running** shoes
a **short** vacation	a **two-week** vacation
a **valid** license	a **driver's** license

3. *Very/Too/Enough/Too Much/Too Many*

He's **very** healthy.
He's **too** young to retire.
I'm relaxed **enough** to drive.
I had **enough** sleep last night.
She doesn't eat ice cream because it has **too much** fat.
She doesn't eat ice cream because it has **too many** calories.
He loves coffee, but when he drinks **too much**, he can't sleep.

Editing Advice

1. Adjectives are always singular.

I had two importants meetings last week.

2. Certain adjectives end with *-ed*.

ed
He's interest in history.

3. Put an adjective before the noun.

very intelligent girl
She is a ~~girl very intelligent~~.

4. Use *one(s)* after an adjective to take the place of a noun.

one
He has an old dictionary. She has a new.

5. Put a specific noun before a general noun.

phone call
She made a ~~call phone~~.

6. A noun modifier is always singular.

She took a three-weeks vacation.

7. An adverb describes a verb. An adjective describes a noun.

ly
The teacher speaks English fluent.

The teacher looks serious~~ly~~.

8. Don't put the *-ly* adverb between the verb and the object.

He opened carefully the envelope.

9. Adverbs of manner that don't end in *-ly* follow the verb phrase.

   He (late) came home.

10. *Too* indicates a problem. If there is no problem, use *very*.

    very
    Your father is ~~too~~ intelligent.

11. *Too much* and *too many* are followed by a noun. *Too* is followed by an adjective or adverb.

    She's too ~~much~~ old to take care of herself.

12. Put *enough* after the adjective.

    old enough
    He's ~~enough old~~ to get married.

13. Don't confuse *hard* and *hardly*.

    I'm tired. I worked hard~~ly~~ all day.

14. Don't use *too much* / *too many* when there is no problem.

    a lot of
    I love juice. Every day I drink ~~too much~~ juice.

Editing Quiz

Some of the shaded words and phrases have mistakes. Find the mistakes and correct them. If the shaded words are correct, write *C*.

             C   well

I exercise regularly and I eat very ~~good~~ most of the time. Luckily, I'm too
         (example)   *(example)*   *(1)*

healthy. I try to eat too many fresh fruits and vegetables every day. I also
                  (2)   *(3)*

eat a lot of whole grains. I rarely eat red meat. I eat fish or chicken. But I
          (4)   *(5)*

rarely eat chicken fried because it's too much greasy. Most mornings I
        (6)   *(7)*

have a glass of juice orange and cereal. For lunch, I have a small meal,
            (8)   *(9)*

usually a tuna sandwich. For dinner, I like to eat a nice meal slowly. Most
     (10)   *(11)*

of the time, I cook dinner. But on Fridays I have a three-hours biology
                                (12)

course and I late get home and I'm too much tire to cook. Then I'm not
        (13)   *(14)*   *(15)*

so carefully about what I eat. My roommate offers me his food, but he eats
  (16)

very poorly. He often eats hamburgers and greasy fries from a fast-food
    (17)   (18)
place, or he brings home a sausage pizza. He eats quickly his food. And he
                          (19)   (20)
drinks a lot of sweets colas. He thinks it's enough good, but I don't agree.
              (21)   (22)
When I eat with him, I'm not carefully about what I eat and then I don't
                            (23)
feel well the next day. I think it's important to have a diet very healthy.
     (24)   (25)
I'm going to try hardly to have a better meal on Friday nights.
                 (26)

Lesson 6 Test/Review

PART 1 **Fill in the blanks by putting the words in the correct order and making any other necessary changes.**

EXAMPLE   He ran a ___*ten-mile race*___.
                    (race/ten miles)

1. His _____ are getting old.
          (shoes/running)

2. He _____.
        (fast/ran)

3. He didn't run _____ to win the race.
                   (enough/fast)

4. He was _____ when he finished the race.
           (completely/tired)

5. He _____.
       (late/arrived home)

6. He was _____ to eat dinner.
           (too/tired)

7. He took a _____.
              (nap/two hours)

PART 2 **Fill in the blanks with the correct form, adjective or adverb, of the word in parentheses ( ).**

EXAMPLES   She has ___*clear*___ pronunciation.
                     (clear)
           She pronounces very ___*clearly*___.
                                (clear)

1. You need to find time to eat _____. Don't eat food that
                                  (good)

    is _____ for you.
        (bad)

2. Don't drive _____. It's important to arrive _____.
                 (fast)   *(safe)*

                                                    (continued)

3. I can't understand you. Could you speak more _____, please?
(slow)

4. Some people learn languages _____.
(easy)

5. Some people think that math is _____, but it's _____
(hard)   (easy)

for me.

6. As _____, we will have a test at the end of the lesson.
(usual)

7. She spoke _____, and I couldn't hear her _____.
(soft)   (good)

8. I need to learn English _____.
(quick)

9. Do you exercise _____, or are you _____?
(regular)   (lazy)

10. You seem _____ today.
(tired)

11. I'm very _____.
(busy)

12. She works very _____, but she's _____ with her job.
(hard)   (happy)

13. She is a _____ woman. She's very _____.
(lovely)   (friendly)

14. John sounds _____, but he's not angry. He just
(angry)

talks _____.
(loud)

15. You speak English _____ well. You have _____
(extreme)   (perfect)

pronunciation. Everything you say is _____ _____.
(absolute)   (clear)

Expansion

Classroom Activities

❶ **Make a list of things that you ate when you were younger that you don't eat now. Make a list of things that you eat now that you didn't eat when you were younger. Form a small group and compare your lists.**

Things I ate before that I don't eat now:	Things I eat now that I didn't eat before:

❷ **Make a list of your lifestyle changes in the past few years. Find a partner. Compare your list with your partner's list. Which of these activities affect your health?**

EXAMPLES

Things I do (or don't do) now:	Things I did (or didn't do) before:
I watch TV more often. I shop once a week.	I hardly ever watched TV before. I shopped almost every day when I lived in my country.

❸ **Bad habits: Make a list of bad habits that you or someone in your family has.**

EXAMPLES I don't get enough exercise.
My daughter talks on the phone too much.

❹ **Take something from your purse, pocket, or bag, but don't show it to anyone. Describe it. Another student will try to guess what it is.**

❺ **In some schools, students evaluate teachers. Work with a partner and write an evaluation form for teachers at this school or for another profession you are familiar with.**

EXAMPLES

	Strongly Agree	Agree	Disagree	Strongly Disagree
1. Begins class promptly. 2. Treats students with respect. 3. Explains assignments clearly.				

Talk

About It

1 In a small group or with the entire class, discuss what kind of food you usually eat. Do you think people eat healthy food in your native culture?

2 Americans often say, "You are what you eat." What do you think this means?

3 Do you get enough sleep? How much is enough for you? Do you remember your dreams?

Write

About It

1 Write a short composition comparing food in your native culture to food in the U.S.

2 Describe your eating habits.

My Eating Habits

In the U.S., I don't eat as well as I ate back home.

In the morning, I just grab a quick cup of coffee and

a piece of toast. For lunch, I usually eat fast food.

Sometimes I even eat while I'm driving. . .

 For more practice using grammar in context, please visit our Web site.

Grammar
Time Words and Time Clauses
The Past Continuous Tense[1]

Context
Immigrants and Refugees

[1]The *past continuous tense* is also called the *past progressive tense*.

Ellis Island

Before You Read

1. Who was the first member of your family to come to the U.S.?

2. Was the process of entering the U.S. difficult for your family? How was it difficult?

CD 2, TR 25

Read the following textbook article. Pay special attention to time words.

Did You **Know?**

Between 1820 and 1966, the largest number of immigrants in the U.S. came from Germany. The largest number of immigrants today come from Mexico, India, the Philippines, and China.

For many years, Ellis Island, an island in New York Harbor, was the main door through which millions of immigrants entered the United States. **From** the time it opened **in** 1892 **until** the time it closed **in** 1924, the U.S. Bureau of Immigration used Ellis Island to receive and process new arrivals. **During** this

Ellis Island today with Wall of Honor

time, 12 million foreigners passed through this door with the hope of becoming Americans. They came from Italy, Poland, Russia, Germany, China, and many other countries. Sometimes more than 10,000 people passed through the registry room in one 24-hour period. New arrivals often waited **for** many hours **while** inspectors checked to see if they met legal and medical standards. Most did not speak English, and they were tired, hungry, and confused. Two percent (250,000 people) did not meet the requirements to enter the U.S. and had to return to their countries.

After Congress passed an immigration law that limited the number and nationality of new immigrants, immigration slowed down and Ellis Island was closed as an immigration processing center. It remained abandoned **until** 1965, **when** President Lyndon Johnson decided to restore it as a monument. Restoration of Ellis Island was finished **by** 1990. Now visitors to this monument can see the building as it looked **from** 1918 **to** 1920. In addition, they can see the Wall of Honor with the names of many of those who passed through on their way to becoming American citizens.

7.1 When, Until, While

EXAMPLES	EXPLANATION
When immigration slowed down, Ellis Island was closed. **When** it reopened, visitors could see the history of immigration.	*When* means *at that time* or *starting at that time.*
Ellis Island was closed **until** 1990. Immigrants could not enter the U.S. **until** they passed an inspection.	*Until* means *before that time.*
While they waited, they were often tired, confused, and hungry. New arrivals waited **while** inspectors checked their documents. **While** they were crossing the ocean, they thought about their uncertain future.	*While* means *during that time.* We can sometimes use *when* in place of *while*: **When** they were crossing the ocean, they thought about their uncertain future.

EXERCISE **1** **Fill in the blanks with *when, while*, or *until*. In some cases, more than one answer is possible.**

EXAMPLE My grandfather came to the U.S. ___when___ he was 25 years old.

1. _____ he lived in Poland, he had a hard life.

2. _____ he left Poland, he didn't speak English at all.

3. _____ he was at Ellis Island, he had to wait for hours. He was nervous _____ he waited.

4. He was nervous _____ he got permission to enter the country. Then he felt more relaxed.

5. _____ he passed the inspection, he entered the country.

6. In Poland, he didn't study English. He didn't speak a word of English _____ he started to work in the U.S. Then he learned a little.

7. _____ he worked, he saved money to bring his wife and children to America.

8. My grandmother couldn't come to the U.S. _____ my grandfather had enough money to send for her and their children.

9. My grandfather lived in the U.S. _____ he died in 1968.

EXERCISE 2 **ABOUT YOU** Add a main clause to complete each statement.

EXAMPLE When I got to class today, _I gave the teacher my composition._

1. While I was in elementary school, _____
2. When I finished elementary school, _____
3. Until I came to this city / school, _____
4. When I arrived in the U.S., _____
5. Until I started this course, _____

EXERCISE 3 **ABOUT YOU** Finish the time expression to complete each statement.

EXAMPLE I stayed in my country until _I won the diversity lottery._

1. I found my apartment / house while _____
2. I enrolled in this English class when _____
3. I didn't understand English until _____
4. I got married / found a job / bought a car / came to this country
   (*choose one*) when _____

EXERCISE 4 **ABOUT YOU** If you are from another country, name something you never . . . until you came to the U.S.

EXAMPLE Name something you never had.
I never had a car until I came to the U.S.

1. Name something you never did.
2. Name something or someone you never heard of.
3. Name something you never saw.
4. Name something you never thought about.
5. Name something you never had.
6. Name something you never ate.
7. Name something you never knew.

7.2 When and *Whenever*

EXAMPLES	EXPLANATION
When I went to New York last year, I visited Ellis Island.	*When* means *at that time* or *after that time.*
Whenever I visit New York, I go to the theaters there.	*Whenever* means *any time* or *every time.*

EXERCISE 5 **ABOUT YOU** Add a main clause to complete each statement. Use the general present.

EXAMPLE Whenever I take a test, __I feel nervous.__

1. Whenever I feel sad or lonely, _____

2. Whenever I get angry, _____

3. Whenever I need advice, _____

4. Whenever I receive a present, _____

5. Whenever I'm on an airplane, _____

6. Whenever I'm sick, _____

7. Whenever the weather is bad, _____

8. Whenever the teacher explains the grammar, _____

_____

EXERCISE 6 **ABOUT YOU** Finish each sentence with a time clause.

EXAMPLES I feel nervous __when I take a test.__

I feel nervous __whenever I have to speak in class.__

1. I feel relaxed _____

2. I get angry _____

3. I get bored _____

4. I can't concentrate _____

5. I'm happy _____

6. I'm in a bad mood _____

7. I sometimes daydream[2] _____

8. Time passes quickly for me _____

[2]*To daydream* means to dream while you are awake. Your mind does not stay in the present moment.

7.3 Time Words

TIME WORD	EXAMPLES	EXPLANATION
on	We came to the U.S. **on** April 16, 2008. We came to the U.S. **on** a Monday.	Use *on* with a specific date or day.
in	Ellis Island closed **in** 1924. My cousins came to the U.S. **in** August.	Use *in* with a specific year or month.
in vs. after	a. My brother will come to the U.S. **in** two months. b. My brother will come to the U.S. **after** he gets his visa.	a. Use *in* to mean after a period of time. b. Use *after* with an activity. *Wrong:* My brother will come to the U.S. *after* two months.
during	a. Many immigrants came to America **during** the war. b. Ellis Island was open from 1892 to 1924. **During** that time, 12 million immigrants passed through there.	a. Use *during* with an event (*the war, the trip, the movie,* etc.). b. Use *during* with a period of time (*during that time, during the month of May, during the first week in August,* etc.).
for	**For** many years, Ellis Island was the main entrance for immigrants to America. My grandfather waited at Ellis Island **for** ten hours.	Use *for* with the quantity of years, months, weeks, days, etc. *Wrong:* They waited at Ellis Island *during* ten hours.
before vs. by	a. **Before 1990**, Ellis Island was closed. b. **By 1990**, restoration of Ellis Island was complete.	a. In the example to the left, if you use *before*, 1990 is not included. b. If you use *by*, 1990 is included.
before vs. ago	a. She got married **before** she came to the U.S. b. She got married three years **ago**.	a. Use *before* with a date, time, or event. b. Use *ago* to mean *before now*.
from . . . to till until	Ellis Island was open **from** 1892 **to** 1924. Ellis Island is open **from** 9:30 A.M. **till** 5:15 P.M. You can take a boat to Ellis Island **from** 9 A.M. **until** 4:30 P.M.	Use *from* with the starting time. Use *to, till,* or *until* with the ending time.

EXERCISE 7 Circle the correct time word to fill in the blanks.

EXAMPLE He lived with his parents (*during* /(*until*)/ *by*) he was 19 years old.

1. (*When* / *During* / *Whenever*) he was a child, he lived with his grandparents.

2. (*During* / *For* / *While*) several years, he lived with his grandparents.

3. (*For* / *While* / *During*) his childhood, he lived with his grandparents.

4. (While / Until / When) he got married, he lived with his grandparents. Then he found an apartment with his wife.

5. (While / During / Whenever) he was in elementary school, he lived with his grandparents.

6. (Whenever / While / When) he was ten years old, his grandparents gave him a bike.

7. She worked for her father (during / while / whenever) she was in college.

8. She worked for her father (for / during / while) her free time.

9. She worked for her father (during / whenever / when) she was single.

10. She worked for her father (for / during / while) three years.

11. She worked for her father full-time (while / when / during) her summer vacation.

12. She worked for her father (when / until / while) she got married. Then she quit her job to take care of her husband and children.

13. She worked for her father 12 years (before / ago / after).

14. (Until / Whenever / During) her husband needs help in his business, she helps him out.

15. She can't help you now. She's busy. She'll help you (by / after / in) an hour.

16. Please finish this exercise (by / in / until) 8:30.

17. Please finish this exercise (by / before / until) you go home. The teacher wants it today.

18. Please finish this exercise (in / after / by) ten minutes.

19. He'll retire (after / in / by) two years.

20. He'll retire (when / while / until) he's 65 years old.

21. He'll work (when / while / until) he's 65 years old. Then he'll retire.

22. I'm not going to eat dinner (when / while / until) my wife gets home. Then we'll eat together.

23. The Ellis Island Museum is open every day (for / from / by) 9:30 A.M. (at / by / till) 5:15 P.M.

24. The Ellis Island Museum is not open (in / at / on) December 25.

7.4 The Past Continuous Tense—Forms

We use the past continuous tense to show that something was in progress at a particular moment in the past.

EXAMPLES	EXPLANATION

In 2007, I **was living** in the U.S.
In 2007, my parents **were living** in Ecuador.
	To form the past continuous tense, we use *was* or *were* + verb *-ing*[3].
	    I, he, she, it → *was*
	    you, we, they → *were*

In 2007, they **were living** in California. They **weren't living** in New York. **Were** they **living** in Los Angeles? No, they **weren't**. Where **were** they **living**? Why **weren't** they **living** in Los Angeles? Who **was living** in New York?	Compare the affirmative, negative, *yes/no* question, *wh-* question, negative question, and subject question with the past continuous tense.

Terence and Charlotte—Refugees

Before You Read

1. Do you know the difference between an immigrant and a refugee?

2. Do you know anyone who is a refugee?

CD 2, TR 26

Read the following magazine article. Pay special attention to sentences with the past continuous tense.

In addition to immigrants, the U.S. takes refugees from many countries. A refugee is a person who runs away from his country because his or her life is in danger. The U.S. takes in more refugees than any other country in the world.

Terence and Charlotte and their children are refugees from Burundi, Africa. Burundi has two major tribes: the Hutus and the Tutsis. Terence is a Hutu and his wife Charlotte is a Tutsi. Terence **was working** in a hospital when he **heard** the news: Someone killed the president of Burundi. When they heard the news, violence began. Members of the Hutu tribe started killing members of the Tutsi tribe. Because the family was in danger, they ran from their country. First they ran to Congo. But their lives were in danger there. Then they ran to Zambia. While they **were living** in a Zambian refugee camp, they didn't have enough food and their children didn't go to school. Life was very hard. They applied to the UNHCR (United Nations

---

[3]To review the spelling of the *-ing* form, see Appendix A.

High Commissioner for Refugees) for permission to come to the U.S. In 2006, when they heard that they got permission, they were so happy.

When they **arrived** in Chicago, a volunteer from a refugee agency **was waiting** to meet them at the airport. She took them to their new apartment and helped them get settled. Volunteers helped them learn about life in the U.S. They helped them enroll their children in school and get medical attention. At first everything was very strange for them, but little by little life became easier. Charlotte found a job cleaning hotel rooms. Terence found a job in a factory.

When they become American citizens, they want to go back to Burundi to search for their family.

7.5 The Past Continuous Tense—with Specific Times

EXAMPLE	EXPLANATION
Terence **was working** in a hospital in 1993. Charlotte and Terence **were living** in Zambia in 2003.	We use the past continuous tense to show what was in progress at a specific moment in the past. 1993 → was working → now

EXERCISE 8 **ABOUT YOU** Tell if the following things were happening in January 2008.

EXAMPLE go to school
I was (not) going to school in January 2008.

1. work
2. go to school
3. study English
4. live in the U.S.
5. live with my parents
6. take a vacation

EXERCISE 9 **ABOUT YOU** Ask a question with *"What were you doing . . . ?"* at these times. Another student will answer.

EXAMPLE at six o'clock this morning

A: What were you doing at six o'clock this morning?

B: I was sleeping.

1. at ten o'clock last night
2. at four o'clock this morning
3. at five o'clock yesterday afternoon
4. at this time yesterday
5. at this time last year[4]

[4]*At this time last year* is very general; it does not refer to a specific hour.

7.6 The Past Continuous Tense + a *When* Clause

EXAMPLE	EXPLANATION
Terence **was working** in a hospital when he **heard** the news. They **were living** in Zambia when they **got** permission to come to the U.S.	We use the past continuous tense with the simple past to show the relationship of a longer past action to a shorter past action.

Language Notes:
1. If the main clause precedes the time clause, do not separate the two clauses with a comma.
   If the time clause precedes the main clause, separate the two clauses with a comma.
   He was working in a hospital when he heard the news. (No comma)
   When he heard the news, he was working in a hospital. (Comma)
2. To form a question with two clauses, only the verb in the main clause is in question form.
   Where **was he living** when he got the news?

EXERCISE 10 Decide which of the two verbs has the longer action (past continuous) and which has the shorter action (simple past). Fill in the blanks with the correct tense.

EXAMPLES   She _____was taking_____ a shower when the telephone
            (take)

_____rang_____.
       (ring)

When it _____started_____ to rain, I _____was walking_____
            (start)   (walk)

to school.

1. Mary _____ in a department store when she
         (shop)

_____ her purse.
   (lose)

2. I _____ my homework when my friend
      (do)

_____ over.
   (come)

3. When he _____ at the airport, his friends
           (arrive)

_____ for him.
   (wait)

4. When my neighbor _____ on the door,
                    (knock)

we _____ dinner.
   (eat)

5. She _____ dinner when the smoke alarm
   (cook)

_____ off.[5]
(go)

6. He _____ snow when he _____
   (shovel)   (lose)

his glove.

7. She _____ when the baby _____
   (sleep)   (start)

to cry.

8. When I _____ to class, the teacher
        (get)

_____ out the tests.
(pass)

9. I _____ to a friend when the baby
  (talk)

_____.
(interrupt)

Albert Einstein—Refugee from Germany

Before
You Read

1. Can you name any famous immigrants or refugees to the U.S.?

2. Did anyone from your native culture become famous in the U.S.?

CD 2, TR 27

Read the textbook article on the next page. Pay special attention to the relationship of the simple past and the past continuous tenses.

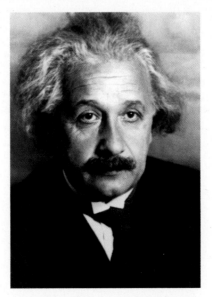

Albert Einstein, 1879–1955

[5]When an alarm *goes off*, it starts to sound.

Of the many refugees who came to the U.S., one will always be remembered throughout the world: Albert Einstein. Einstein changed our understanding of the universe.

Einstein was born in Germany in 1879 to Jewish parents. When he graduated from college in Switzerland in 1900, he was planning to become a teacher of physics and math but could not find a job in those fields. Instead, he went to work in a patent[6] office as a technical expert from 1902 to 1909. While he **was working** at this job, he **studied** and **wrote** in his spare time. In 1905, when he was only 26 years old, he published three papers that explained the basic structure of the universe. His theory of relativity explained the relationship of space and time. He returned to Germany to accept a research position at the University of Berlin. However, in 1920, while he **was lecturing** at the university, anti-Jewish groups often **interrupted** his lectures, saying they were "un-German."

In 1920, Einstein visited the United States for the first time. During his visits, he talked not only about his scientific theories, but also about world peace. While he **was visiting** the U.S. again in 1933, the Nazis **came** to power in Germany. They took his property, burned his books, and removed him from his university job. In 1933 Einstein helped establish the International Rescue Committee to assist anti-Nazi opponents of Hitler. The U.S. offered Einstein refugee status, and in 1940, he became a U.S. citizen. He received many job offers from all over the world, but he decided to accept a position at Princeton University in New Jersey. He lived and worked there until he died in 1955.

Einstein's Life	
1879	Born in Germany
1902–1909	Worked in a Swiss patent office
1905	Published his theory of relativity
1919	Scientists recognized his theory to be correct
1933	Visited the U.S.
1940	Became a U.S. citizen
1955	Died

[6]A *patent* is a document that identifies the owner of a new invention. Only the person or company who has the patent can sell the invention.

7.7 The Past Continuous Tense in a *While* Clause

EXAMPLE	EXPLANATION
While Einstein **was living** in Switzerland, he developed his theory of relativity. While Einstein **was visiting** the U.S., the Nazis took power in Germany.	Use *while* + the past continuous with the longer action.
Compare: Einstein was living in the U.S. **when** he **died**. **While** he **was living** in the U.S., he wrote many papers.	Use *when* + the simple past with the shorter action. Use *while* + the past continuous with the longer action.

Language Notes:
1. You can use *when* in place of *while* with a continuous action.
> **While** Einstein was living in Switzerland, he developed his theory.
> **When** Einstein was living in Switzerland, he developed his theory.
3. You cannot use *while* with an action that has no continuation.
> *Wrong:*   I was running *while* I fell.
> *Right:*   I was running *when* I fell.

EXERCISE **11** Decide which of the two verbs has the longer action (past continuous) and which has the shorter action (simple past). Fill in the blanks with the correct tense.

EXAMPLE It _____started_____ to rain while I _____was walking_____ to school.
   (start)   (walk)

1. While the teacher _____ on the blackboard, she
   (write)

   _____ the chalk.
   (drop)

2. He _____ his arm while he _____
   (break)   (climb)

   a tree.

3. She _____ her husband while she
   (meet)

   _____ college.
   (attend)

4. While I _____ to work, I _____ out
   (drive)   (run)

   of gas.[7]

5. While I _____ my bike, I _____ a
   (ride)   (get)

   flat tire.

[7]To *run out of* means to use something up completely.   (continued)

6. I _____ my tooth while I _____ a nut.
   (break)   (eat)

7. I _____ an old friend while I _____
   (meet)   (walk)

   in the park.

8. While he _____ dishes, he _____
   (wash)   (break)

   a plate.

EXERCISE 12 **Fill in the blanks with the simple past or the past continuous form of the verb in parentheses ( ) in the following conversations.**

Conversation 1, **between a wife (W) and husband (H)**

CD 2, TR 28

W: Look what I found today! Your favorite watch!

H: Where _____ did you find _____ it?
            (example: find)

W: In your top drawer. I _____ away your socks when
                              (1 put)

   I _____ it.
       (2 find)

H: I wonder how it got there.

W: Probably while you _____ something in that drawer,
                          (3 put)

   it _____ off your wrist.
       (4 fall)

Conversation 2, **between two students**

A: When did you come to the U.S.?

B: Two months ago.

A: Really? But you speak English so well.

B: While I _____ in a refugee camp in Kenya, I studied
                (1 live)

   English.

A: _____ to come to the U.S.?
       (2 you/plan)

B: Not really. I had no plans at all. I _____ in the
                                            (3 just/wait)

   refugee camp.

A: Are you from Kenya?

B: No. I'm from Sudan. But while I _____ in Sudan, a
                                        (4 live)

   war _____ there and I had to leave my country.
        (5 start)

A: Are you here with your family?

B: No. I'm alone. When the war _____ ,
(6 start)

I _____ far away from my family. I escaped to Kenya.
(7 live)

Conversation 3, between a granddaughter (GD) and grandmother (GM)

GD: I _____ through some old boxes when I
(1 look)

_____ this picture of you and Grandpa when you were
(2 find)

young. By the way, how _____ Grandpa?
(3 you/meet)

GM: One day I _____ in the park in my hometown
(4 walk)

when he _____ me to ask what time it was. We
(5 stop)

_____ to talk, and then he _____
(6 start)   (7 ask)

me to go out with him.

GD: Did you date for a long time?

GM: We _____ for ten months. A few months after we
(8 date)

met, his family _____ for the green card lottery in the
(9 apply)

U.S. While we _____ , they _____ a
(10 date)   (11 receive)

letter that gave them permission to immigrate to the U.S.

GD: What _____ ?
(12 happen)

GM: At first, I was worried that I'd never see your grandfather again. But he

_____ to me often and _____ me
(13 write)   (14 call)

whenever he could. About a year later, he _____ back
(15 go)

to our country to visit me. While we _____ in a
(16 eat)

beautiful restaurant, he _____ me to marry him.
(17 ask)

GD: _____ him right away?
(18 you/marry)

GM: Yes, we got married a few weeks later and then he

_____ to the U.S. But I couldn't go to the U.S. with
(19 return)

him. I _____ to wait for permission.
(20 have)

Finally, I _____ permission to come.
(21 get)

7.8 Was/Were Going To

We use *was/were going to* + the base form to describe a plan that we didn't carry out. It means the same thing as *was/were planning to*.

EXAMPLES	EXPLANATION
a. Einstein **was going to** return to Germany, but the Nazis came to power.	a. Einstein was planning to return, but didn't.
b. I **was going to** call you, but I lost your phone number.	b. I was planning to call, but didn't.

EXERCISE 13 Fill in the blanks with *was going to* + one of the verbs from the box below.

use	write ✓	go
say	call	

CD 2, TR 29

A: What did you write for your composition today?

B: I ___was going to write___ about Einstein, but I couldn't find
(example)
any information.

A: What? There's tons of [8] information. Did you go to the library?

B: I _____ to the library, but the library near my
(1)
house is closed for construction.

A: How about the college library?

B: I didn't think of it.

A: Why didn't you use the Internet? You can find plenty of information there.

B: I _____ the Internet, but my computer crashed.
(2)

A: Why didn't you call me? You're welcome to use my computer.

B: I _____ you, but I lost your phone number.
(3)

A: I'm beginning to think you didn't really want to do your homework.

B: Maybe you're right. I'm kind of lazy.

A: I _____ that, but I didn't want to hurt your feelings.
(4)

---

[8]Tons of means *a lot of.*

EXERCISE 14 Fill in the blanks to tell what prevented a plan from happening.

EXAMPLE He was going to return to his country, but _he couldn't get permission._

1. My cousin was going to come to the U.S., but _____

_____

2. He was going to work in the U.S. for only three months, but _____

_____

3. We were going to return to our country, but _____

_____

4. I was going to call my grandparents last night, but _____

_____

5. We were going to rent an apartment in this city, but _____

_____

7.9 Simple Past vs. Past Continuous with *When*

Both the simple past and the past continuous can be used in a sentence that has a *when* clause. However, the time sequence is completely different.

EXAMPLES	EXPLANATION
a. *When* Einstein graduated from college, he **tried** to get a job as a teacher.	In sentences (a), the simple past in the main clause shows what happened *after* an action.
b. *When* Einstein entered college, he **was living** in Switzerland.	
a. Einstein **came** to live in the U.S. *when* he lost his German citizenship.	In sentences (b), the past continuous in the main clause shows what was happening *at the same time* a shorter action occurred.
b. Einstein **was living** in the U.S. *when* he died.	
a. *When* Terence got permission, he **came** to the U.S.	
b. *When* Terence got permission, he **was living** in Zambia.	

EXERCISE 15 Fill in the blanks with the simple past or the past continuous of the verb in parentheses ( ).

EXAMPLES Terence _was living_ in a refugee camp when he got his visa.
           (live)

When he got to the U.S., he _needed_ to find a job.
                             (need)

1. When he _____ permission, he left Zambia.
            (get)

   He _____ in a hospital when he heard the news.
       (work)

(continued)

2. When they arrived in the U.S., volunteers _____ them.
   (help)

When they arrived in the U.S., a volunteer _____ for them at the
   (wait)

airport.

3. They _____ in the U.S. when their fourth child was born.
   (live)

When their fourth child was born, they _____ to a bigger apartment.
   (move)

4. When Charlotte learned English well enough, she _____ to
   (start)

work in a hotel.

She _____ in a hotel when her daughter was born.
   (work)

5. Terence _____ morning English classes when he found a job.
   (take)

Terence _____ to night classes when he found a job.
   (change)

6. When Einstein entered college, he _____ to become a teacher.
   (want)

When Einstein entered college, he _____ in Switzerland.
   (live)

7. Einstein _____ a resident of the U.S. when he lost his German
   (become)

citizenship.

Einstein _____ in the U.S. when he died.
   (live)

7.10 Simple Past vs. Past Continuous

EXAMPLES	EXPLANATION
While they **lived** in the refugee camp, they **studied** English. **While** Einstein **worked** at a patent office, he **studied** and **wrote**.	We can connect two past actions that happened in the same time period with *while* and use the simple past tense in both clauses.
While I **was reading** the story about Terence and Charlotte, I **was underlining** the verbs. **While** we **were doing** the last exercise, the teacher **was helping** us.	We can connect two past actions that happened in the **exact** same time period with *while* and use the past continuous tense in both clauses.
When they **got** permission, they came to the U.S. **When** they **came** to the U.S., they started to study English.	Use *when* to mean *at a specific time*. Use the simple past tense.

EXERCISE 16   **Fill in the blanks with *when* for an action at a specific time or *while* for an action that continues over time.**

EXAMPLE   ___While___ Terence was working in a factory, he practiced English with his coworkers.

1. _____ Terence left his country, he went to Congo.

2. _____ I was reading the story, I was paying attention to the verbs.

3. _____ Charlotte cleaned hotel rooms, she listened to music.

4. _____ their youngest daughter was born, Charlotte stopped working.

5. Charlotte started to work again _____ her daughter was a year old.

6. _____ Charlotte worked, her baby was in day care.

7. Terence worked in a factory _____ Charlotte worked in a hotel.

7.11 Using the *-ing* Form After Time Words

When the main clause and the time clause have the same subject, we can delete the subject of the time clause and use a present participle (verb + *-ing*) after the time word.

EXAMPLES

Einstein left high school **before he finished** his studies.

Einstein left high school **before finishing** his studies.

After Einstein left high school, he studied mathematics and physics.

After leaving high school, Einstein studied mathematics and physics.

Terence and Charlotte studied English **while they lived** in a refugee camp.

Terence and Charlotte studied English **while living** in a refugee camp.

EXERCISE **17** **Change these sentences. Use a present participle after the time word. Make any necessary changes.**

EXAMPLE
                  entering   Einstein
    After ~~Einstein entered~~ the university, ~~he~~ developed his theory.

1. Einstein passed an exam before he entered the university.
2. He left high school before he received his diploma.
3. After Einstein developed his theory of relativity, he became famous.
4. He became interested in physics after he received books on science.
5. After Einstein came to the U.S., he got a job at Princeton.
6. Before they came to the U.S., Terence and Charlotte lived in Zambia.
7. While they lived in the refugee camp, the children didn't go to school.
8. Charlotte listened to music while she cleaned hotel rooms.
9. The parents were working and going to school while they were raising a family.

Summary of Lesson 7

1. Time Words

Time Word	Examples
When	**When** immigrants came to America, they passed through Ellis Island.
While	They waited **while** inspectors checked their health.
Until	Ellis Island remained closed **until** 1990.
Before	**Before** 1920, many immigrants came to America.
After	**After** 1920, Congress limited the number of immigrants.
From . . . to, until, or till	The Ellis Island Museum is open **from** 9:30 **till** 5:15. **From** 1892 **to** 1924, Ellis Island was an immigrant processing center.
During	**During** that time, 12 million immigrants passed through Ellis Island.
For	New arrivals had to wait **for** hours.
In	**In** 1905, Einstein wrote about relativity. We will finish the test **in** an hour.
By	Restoration of Ellis Island was finished **by** 1990.
Ago	One hundred years **ago**, new arrivals passed through Ellis Island.
On	We came to the U.S. **on** Wednesday.

2. Uses of the past continuous tense:

A. To describe a past action that was in progress at a specific moment:
He **was sleeping** at six o'clock this morning.
Where **were** you **living** in December 2001?

B. With the past tense, to show the relationship of a longer past action to a shorter past action:
Terence **was living** in Zambia when he **got** permission to come to the U.S.
Einstein **was living** in New Jersey when he **died**.
While I **was reading** the story, I **had** to use my dictionary.

C. To show past intentions:
I **was going to call** you, but I lost your phone number.
She **was going to cook** dinner, but she didn't have time.

Editing Advice

1. Put the subject before the verb in all clauses.
the teacher entered
When ~~entered the teacher~~, the students stood up.

2. Use *when*, not *while*, if the action has no duration.
When
~~While~~ she spilled the milk, she started to cry.

3. Don't confuse *during* and *for*.
for
He watched TV ~~during~~ three hours.

4. Don't confuse *until* and *when*.
when
She will eat dinner ~~until~~ her husband comes home.

5. Don't confuse *before* and *ago*.
ago
They came to the U.S. three years ~~before~~.

6. After a time word, use an *-ing* form, not a base form.
finding
After ~~find~~ a job, he bought a car.

Editing Quiz

Some of the shaded words and phrases have mistakes. Find the mistakes and correct them. If the shaded words are correct, write _C_.

                                                      _C_
I left my country three years ago. But my husband didn't come with me.
                        (example)   **for**
He wanted to stay in our country ~~during~~ two more years until he
                                 (example)   _(1)_
finished college. While I got here, I started to study English right away.
               _(2)_
While I was going to school, I was work in the school library.
_(3)_   _(4)_   _(5)_

    My husband was going to get a degree in engineering when a war broke
                       _(6)_   _(7)_   _(8)_
out in our country. When started the war, he fled the country quickly
                         _(9)_
and went to a neighboring country. He was in a refugee camp during one
                                                              _(10)_
year. While he was in the camp, he started to study English. He applied
      _(11)_
for permission to come to the U.S. After wait for one year, he finally got
                                        _(12)_
permission. When he was getting here, we were so excited to see each other
            _(13)_   _(14)_
again.

    He's learning English quickly. After he learns English well enough, he's
going to enter an engineering program. I know he'll be happy until he gets
                                                          _(15)_
his engineering degree.

Lesson 7 Test/Review

PART 1 **Fill in the blanks with the simple past or the past continuous form of the verb in parentheses ( ).**

EXAMPLE He _____**was walking**_____ to his car when he ___**lost**___ his glove.
                    (walk)   _(lose)_

1. What _____ at 4 P.M. yesterday afternoon? I tried
            (you/do)

   to call you, but you weren't home.

2. She _____ to be an engineer when the war
            (study)

   _____.
      (start)

3. I _____ your necklace while I _____ for
      (find)   _(look)_

   my watch.

4. She _____ a house three years ago.
   (buy)

5. He _____ his wife while he _____ in a
   (meet)   (work)

   restaurant.

6. When my grandfather _____ to America, he
   (come)

   _____ a job in a factory.
   (find)

7. When he _____ at Ellis Island, his uncle
   (arrive)

   _____ for him.
   (wait)

8. While she _____ the computer, it _____.
   (use)   (crash)

9. He _____ dinner when the fire _____.
   (cook)   (start)

10. I _____ my car and _____
    (drive)   (listen)

    to the radio when I _____ about the plane crash.
    (hear)

PART 2 **Fill in the blanks with an appropriate time word. Choose *when,
whenever, while, until, before, after, by, ago, in, for, on, from, till, to,*
or *during*. In some cases, more than one answer is possible.**

EXAMPLE I will continue to work ___until___ I am 65 years old. Then I will retire.

1. _____ it snows, there are a lot of traffic accidents.

2. I was walking to my friend's house _____ it started to rain. I was
   glad I had my umbrella with me.

3. The teacher was watching the students _____ the test.

4. _____ I finished my homework last night, I watched the news
   on TV.

5. I got my visa _____ coming to the U.S.

6. He must stay in his country _____ he gets permission to come to
   the U.S.

7. _____ he dropped his glasses, they broke.

8. We have to finish this lesson _____ ten o'clock.

9. He found a job two months _____.

10. He found a job three weeks _____ coming to the U.S.

11. He found a job _____ April.

(continued)

12. It's 7:50. The movie will begin _____ ten minutes, at 8:00.

13. _____ the movie began, everyone became quiet.

14. _____ she was watching the sad movie, she started to cry.

15. Einstein was 61 years old _____ he became a U.S. citizen.

16. Einstein lived in the U.S. _____ 22 years.

17. I had a doctor's appointment _____ Monday.

18. I work every day _____ 9:00 A.M. _____ 5:00 P.M.

19. _____ the summer, many teenagers get jobs.

Expansion

Classroom
Activities

❶ Pick an important event in your life (*immigrating to a new country, moving to a new town, going to a new school, getting married,* etc.) and make a list of things you did before, during, and after the event. Discuss your sentences with a small group.

Event: _____

Before	
During	
After	

2 Form a small group. Turn to the person next to you and say a year or a specific time of the year. The person next to you tells what was happening in his or her life at that time.

EXAMPLES   1996

I was living with my parents.

January 2004

I was studying to be a nurse.

Talk
About It

1 Read these quotes by Einstein. Discuss their meaning.

- "Imagination is more important than knowledge."
- "The only real valuable thing is intuition."
- "A person starts to live when he can live outside himself."
- "I never think of the future. It comes soon enough."
- "Anyone who has never made a mistake has never tried anything new."
- "Science is a wonderful thing if one does not have to earn one's living at it."
- "Peace cannot be kept by force. It can only be achieved by understanding."
- "Education is what remains after one has forgotten everything he learned in school."
- "Not everything that counts can be counted, and not everything that can be counted counts." (Sign hanging in Einstein's office at Princeton)

2 Einstein is often called a genius. Can you think of any other famous people who are geniuses?

3 In a small group or with the entire class, discuss your experience of immigration. Was the process difficult? How did you feel during the process?

Write

About It **1** Write a paragraph about the changes that took place after a major historical event in your country or elsewhere in the world.

2 Write about the reasons people leave your country or the reasons you left your country.

3 Write about your arrival in the U.S.

EXAMPLE

My Arrival in the U.S.

My family and I arrived in the U.S. in September 2008.

When we arrived, our cousins were waiting for us at the airport.

They took us to their house and gave us something to eat. But

we were tired and we just wanted to sleep for a while…

 For more practice using grammar in context, please visit our Web site.

Grammar
Modals

Related Expressions

Context
Renting an Apartment

8.1 Modals and Related Expressions—An Overview

A modal adds meaning to the verb that follows it.

List of Modals	Modals are different from other verbs in several ways.
can could should will would may might must	1. The base form of a verb follows a modal.[1] You **must pay** your rent. (*Not:* You must <u>to</u> pay your rent.) He **should clean** his apartment now. (*Not:* He should clean<u>ing</u> his apartment now.) 2. Modals never have an *-s, -ed,* or *-ing* ending. He **can** rent an apartment. (*Not:* He can<u>s</u> rent an apartment.)

Related Expressions	Some verbs are like modals in meaning.
have to be able to be supposed to be permitted/allowed to	He **must** sign the lease. = He **has to** sign the lease. He **can** pay the rent. = He **is able to** pay the rent. I **must** pay my rent by the first of the month. = I'**m supposed to** pay my rent by the first of the month. You **can't** change the locks in your apartment. = You **are not permitted to** change the locks in your apartment. = You **are not allowed to** change the locks in your apartment.

An Apartment Lease

Before You Read

1. Do you live in an apartment? Do you have a lease? Did you understand the lease when you signed it?

2. What kinds of things are not allowed in your apartment?

---

[1]Do not follow a modal with an infinitive. There is one exception: *ought to*. *Ought to* means *should*.

Read the following Web article. Pay special attention to modals and related expressions.

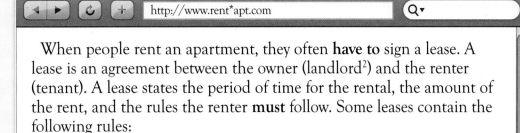

When people rent an apartment, they often **have to** sign a lease. A lease is an agreement between the owner (landlord[2]) and the renter (tenant). A lease states the period of time for the rental, the amount of the rent, and the rules the renter **must** follow. Some leases contain the following rules:

- Renters **must not** have a water bed.
- Renters **must not** have a pet.
- Renters **must not** change the locks without the owner's permission.
- Renters **must** pay a security deposit.

Many owners ask the renters to pay a security deposit in case there are damages. When the renters move out, the owners **are supposed to** return the deposit plus interest if the apartment is in good condition. If there is damage, the owners **can** use part or all of the money to repair the damage. However, they **may not** keep the renters' money for normal wear and tear (the normal use of the apartment).

Renters **do not have to** agree to all the terms of the lease. They **can** ask for changes before they sign. A pet owner, for example, **can** ask for permission to have a pet by offering to pay a higher security deposit.

There are laws that protect renters. For example, owners **must** provide heat during the winter months. In most cities, they **must** put a smoke detector in each apartment and in the halls. In addition, owners **can't** refuse to rent to a person because of sex, race, religion, nationality, or disability.

When the lease is up for renewal, owners **can** offer the renters a new lease or they **can** ask the renters to leave. The owners **are supposed to** notify the renters (usually at least 30 days in advance) if they want the renters to leave.

---

[2]A *landlord* is a man. A *landlady* is a woman.

8.2 Negatives with Modals

To form the negative of a modal, put *not* after the modal. You can make a negative contraction with some, but not all, modals.

Negatives and Negative Contractions	Examples
cannot → can't could not → couldn't should not → shouldn't will not → won't would not → wouldn't may not → (no contraction) might not → (no contraction) must not → mustn't	We **cannot** pay the rent. You **can't** have a dog in your apartment. We **will not** renew our lease. We **won't** stay here. You **may not** know legal terms. You **might not** understand the lease.
Language Note: Write *cannot* as one word.	

EXERCISE 1 Write the negative form of the underlined words. Use a contraction whenever possible.

EXAMPLE You <u>must</u> pay a security deposit. You _____*mustn't*_____ have a water bed.

1. I <u>can</u> have a cat in my apartment. I _____ have a dog.

2. You <u>should</u> read the lease carefully. You _____ sign it without reading it.

3. The landlord <u>must</u> install a smoke detector. You _____ remove it.

4. You <u>may</u> have visitors in your apartment. You _____ make a lot of noise and disturb your neighbors.

5. If you damage something, the landlord <u>can</u> keep part of your security deposit. He _____ keep your deposit without proof of damages.

6. You <u>might</u> get back all of your security deposit. If you leave your apartment in bad condition, you _____ get all of it back.

8.3 Statements and Questions with Modals

Compare affirmative statements and questions with a modal.

Wh- Word	Modal	Subject	Modal	Verb (base form)	Complement	Short Answer
		He	**can**	have	a cat in his apartment.	
	Can	he		have	a water bed?	No, he **can't.**
What	**can**	he		have	in his apartment?	
		Who	**can**	have	a dog?	

Compare negative statements and questions with a modal.

Wh- Word	Modal	Subject	Modal	Verb (base form)	Complement
		He	**shouldn't**	pay	his rent late.
Why	**shouldn't**	he		pay	his rent late?

EXERCISE 2 Read each statement. Fill in the blanks to complete the question.

EXAMPLE You should read the lease before you sign it. Why _____ should I _____ read the lease before I sign it?

1. You can't have a water bed. Why _____ a water bed?

2. We must pay a security deposit. How much _____?

3. Someone must install a smoke detector. Who _____ a smoke detector?

4. The landlord can't refuse to rent to a person because of race, religion, or nationality. Why _____ to rent to a person for these reasons?

5. Tenants shouldn't make a lot of noise in their apartments. Why _____ a lot of noise?

6. I may have a cat in my apartment. _____ have a dog in my apartment?

7. The landlord can have a key to my apartment. _____ _____ enter my apartment when I'm not home?

8.4 Must, Have To, Have Got To

The modal *must* has a very official tone. For nonofficial situations, we usually use *have to* or *have got to*.

EXAMPLES	EXPLANATION
The landlord **must** give you a smoke detector. The tenant **must** pay the rent on the first of each month.	For formal obligations, use *must*. *Must* is often used in legal contracts, such as apartment leases.
The landlord **has to** give you a smoke detector. The landlord **has got to** give you a smoke detector.	We can also use *have to* or *have got to*, for obligations.
You **must** leave the building immediately. It's on fire! You **have to** leave the building immediately. It's on fire! You**'ve got to** leave the building immediately. It's on fire!	*Must, have to,* and *have got to* express a sense of urgency. All three sentences to the left have the same meaning. *Have got to* is usually contracted: I have got to = I've got to He has got to = He's got to
Our apartment is too small. We **have to** move. Our apartment is too small. We**'ve got to** move.	Avoid using *must* for personal obligations. It sounds very official or urgent and is too strong for most situations. Use *have to* or *have got to*.
At the end of my lease last May, I **had to** move. I **had to** find a bigger apartment.	*Must* has no past form. The past of both *must* and *have to* is *had to*. *Have got to* has no past form.

Language Note: We don't usually use *have got to* for questions and negatives.
Pronunciation Note: In fast, informal speech, *have to* is often pronounced "hafta." *Has to* is often pronounced "hasta." *Got to* is often pronounced "gotta." Often *have* is omitted before "gotta." Listen to your teacher pronounce the sentences in the above chart.

EXERCISE 3 Fill in the blanks with an appropriate verb. Answers may vary.

EXAMPLE The landlord must __provide__ heat in cold weather.

1. You must _____ the lease with a pen. A pencil is not acceptable.
2. The landlord must _____ your security deposit if you leave your apartment in good condition.

3. The landlord must _____ you if he wants you to leave at the end of your lease.

4. You must _____ quiet in your apartment at night. Neighbors want to sleep.

EXERCISE 4 **ABOUT YOU** Make a list of personal obligations you have.

EXAMPLE   I have to help my parents on the weekend.

1. _____

2. _____

3. _____

EXERCISE 5 **ABOUT YOU** Make a list of things you had to do last weekend.

EXAMPLE   I had to do my laundry.

1. _____

2. _____

3. _____

EXERCISE 6 Finish these statements. Practice *have got to*. Answers will vary.

EXAMPLE   When you live in the U.S., you've got to _____learn English._____

1. When I don't know the meaning of a word, I've got to _____

_____

2. English is so important in the U.S. We've got to _____

_____

3. For this class, you've got to _____

_____

4. If you rent an apartment, you've got to _____

_____

5. If you want to drive a car, you've got to _____

_____

8.5 Obligation with *Must* or *Be Supposed To*

EXAMPLES	EXPLANATION
Landlord to tenant: "You **must** pay your rent on the first of each month." Judge to landlord: "You have no proof of damage. You **must** return the security deposit to your tenant."	*Must* has an official, formal tone. A person in a position of authority (like a landlord or judge) can use *must*.
Wording on a lease: The tenant **must not** change the locks.	Legal documents use *must*.
You**'re supposed to** put your name on your mailbox. The landlord **is supposed to** give you a copy of the lease.	Avoid using *must* if you are not in a position of authority. Use *be supposed to*.
We**'re not supposed to** have cats in my building, but my neighbor has one. The landlord **was supposed to** return my security deposit, but he didn't. I**'m supposed to** pay my rent on the first of the month, but sometimes I forget.	*Be supposed to*, not *must*, is used when reporting on a law or rule that was broken or a task that wasn't completed.

Pronunciation Note: The *d* in *supposed to* is usually not pronounced.

EXERCISE 7 **Make these sentences less formal by changing from *must* to *be supposed to*.**

EXAMPLE You must wear your seat belt.
You're supposed to wear your seat belt.

1. You must carry your driver's license with you when you drive.
2. You must stop at a red light.
3. We must put money in the parking meter during business hours.
4. Your landlord must notify you if he wants you to leave.
5. The landlord must give me a smoke detector.
6. The teacher must give a final grade at the end of the semester.
7. We must write five compositions in this course.
8. We must bring our books to class.

EXERCISE 8   **Finish these statements. Use *be supposed to* plus a verb. Answers may vary.**

EXAMPLE   I <u>'m supposed to pay my rent</u> on the first of the month.

1. Pets are not permitted in my apartment. I (not) _____ a pet.

2. The landlord _____ heat in the winter months.

3. The tenants _____ before they move out.

4. The landlord _____ a smoke detector in each apartment.

5. I _____ my rent last week, but I forgot.

6. My stove isn't working. My landlord _____ it.

7. We're going to move out next week. Our apartment is clean and in good condition. The landlord _____ our security deposit.

8. The janitor _____ the garbage every day.

9. The janitor _____ the hallway twice a week.

10. When we move furniture, we _____ the back stairs, not the front stairs.

EXERCISE 9   **ABOUT YOU**   **Write three sentences to tell what you are supposed to do for this course. You may work with a partner.**

EXAMPLE   <u>We're supposed to write three compositions this semester.</u>

1. _____

_____

2. _____

_____

3. _____

_____

8.6 *Can, May, Could,* and Alternate Expressions

EXAMPLE WITH A MODAL	ALTERNATE EXPRESSION	EXPLANATION
I **can** clean the apartment by Friday.	It **is possible** (for me) **to** clean the apartment by Friday.	Possibility
I **can't** understand the lease.	I **am not able to** understand the lease.	Ability
I **can't** have a pet in my apartment.	I **am not permitted to** have a pet. I **am not allowed to** have a pet.	Permission
The landlord **may not** keep my deposit if my apartment is clean and in good condition.	The landlord **is not permitted to** keep my deposit. The landlord **is not allowed to** keep my deposit.	Permission
I **couldn't** speak English five years ago, but I can now.	I **wasn't able to** speak English five years ago, but I can now.	Past Ability
I **could** have a dog in my last apartment, but I can't have one in my present apartment.	I **was permitted to** have a dog in my last apartment, but I can't have one in my present apartment.	Past Permission

Language Note: We use *can* in the following common expression:
    I *can't afford* a bigger apartment. I don't have enough money.
Pronunciation Note: *Can* is not usually stressed in affirmative statements. In negative statements, *can't* is stressed but it is hard to hear the final *t*. So we must pay attention to the vowel sound to hear the difference between *can* and *can't*. Listen to your teacher pronounce these sentences:
    I can gó. /kIn/
    I cán't go. /kænt/
In a short answer, we pronounce *can* as /kæn/.
    Can you help me later?
    Yes, I can. /kæn/

EXERCISE **10** Fill in the blanks with an appropriate permission word to talk about what is or isn't permitted at this school. Answers may vary.

EXAMPLES   We ___aren't allowed to___ bring food into the classroom.

We ___can___ leave the room without asking the teacher for permission.

1. We _____ eat in the classroom.
2. Students _____ talk during a test.

3. Students _____ use their dictionaries when they write compositions.

4. Students _____ write a test with a pencil.

5. Students _____ sit in any seat they want.

6. Students _____ use their textbooks during a test.

EXERCISE 11   **Complete each statement. Answers may vary.**

EXAMPLES   The landlord may not ___refuse to rent___ to a person because of his or her nationality.

The tenants may _____use_____ the washing machines in the basement.

1. The tenants may not _____ the locks without the landlord's permission.

2. Each tenant in my building has a parking space. I may not _____ in another tenant's space.

3. Students may not _____ during a test.

4. Teacher to students: "You don't need my permission to leave the room. You may _____ the room if you need to."

5. Some teachers do not allow cell phones in class. In Mr. Klein's class, you may not _____ during class.

6. My teacher says that after we finish a test, we may _____. We don't have to stay in class.

EXERCISE 12   **ABOUT YOU** **Write statements to tell what is or is not permitted in this class, in the library, at this school, or during a test. If you have any questions about what is permitted, write a question for the teacher. You may work with a partner.**

EXAMPLES   We aren't allowed to talk in the library.

May we use our textbooks during a test?

_____

_____

_____

_____

_____

ABOUT YOU Write three sentences telling about what you couldn't do in another class or school that you attended.

EXAMPLE In my school, I couldn't call a teacher by his first name, but I can do it here.

1. _____

_____

2. _____

_____

3. _____

_____

EXERCISE **14** **ABOUT YOU** If you come from another country, write three sentences telling about something that was prohibited there that you can do in the U.S.

EXAMPLE I couldn't criticize the political leaders in my country, but I can do it in the U.S.

1. _____

_____

2. _____

_____

3. _____

_____

Tenants' Rights

Before
You Read

1. What are some complaints you have about your apartment? Do you ever tell the landlord about your complaints?

2. Is your apartment warm enough in the winter and cool enough in the summer?

CD 3, TR 02

Read the following conversation. Pay special attention to *should* and *had better*.

A: My apartment is always too cold in the winter. I've got to move.

B: You don't have to move. The landlord is supposed to provide enough heat.

A: But he doesn't.

B: You **should** talk to him about this problem.

A: I did already. The first time I talked to him, he just told me I **should** put on a sweater. The second time I said, "You**'d better** give me heat, or I'm going to move."

B: You **shouldn't** get so angry. That's not the way to solve the problem. You know, there are laws about heat. You **should** get information from the city so you can know your rights.

A: How can I get information?

B: You **should** go online and get information about tenants' rights from the city's Web site. When you know exactly what the law is, you **should** present this information to your landlord.

A: And what if he doesn't want to do anything about it?

B: Then you **should** report the problem to the mayor's office.

A: I'm afraid to do that.

B: Don't be afraid. You have rights. Maybe you **should** talk to other tenants and see if you can do this together.

8.7 Should; Had Better

EXAMPLES	EXPLANATION

You **should** talk to the landlord about the problem.
You **should** get information about tenants' rights.
You **shouldn't** get so angry.
	For advice, use *should*.
	  Should = It's a good idea.
	  Shouldn't = It's a bad idea.

Compare: Your landlord **must** give you a smoke detector. You **should** check the battery in the smoke detector occasionally.	Remember, *must* is very strong and is not for advice. It is for rules and laws. For advice, use *should*.
You **had better** give me heat, or I'm going to move. We**'d better not** make so much noise, or our neighbors will complain.	For a warning, use *had better (not)*. Something bad can happen if you don't follow this advice. The contraction for *had* (in *had better*) is *'d*. I'd you'd he'd she'd we'd they'd

Pronunciation Note:
Native speakers often don't pronounce the *had* or *'d* in *had better*. You will hear people say, "**You better** be quiet; **you better** not make so much noise."

EXERCISE 15   **Give advice using *should*. Answers will vary.**

EXAMPLE   I'm going to move next week, and I hope to get my security deposit back.
Advice: <u>You should clean the apartment completely.</u>

1. I just rented an apartment, but the rent is too high for me alone.
Advice: _____

2. My upstairs neighbors make a lot of noise.
Advice: _____

3. The battery in the smoke detector is old.
Advice: _____

4. I want to paint the walls.
Advice: _____

5. The rent was due last week, but I forgot to pay it.
Advice: _____

6. My landlady doesn't provide enough heat in the winter.
Advice: _____

7. I can't understand my lease.

Advice: _____

8. I broke a window in my apartment.

Advice: _____

9. My landlord doesn't want to return my security deposit.

Advice: _____

10. The landlord is going to raise the rent by 40 percent.

Advice: _____

EXERCISE 16 **Fill in the blanks with an appropriate verb (phrase) to complete this conversation. Answers may vary.**

🔊

CD 3, TR 03

A: My mother is such a worrier.

B: What does she worry about?

A: Everything. Especially me.

B: For example?

A: Even if it's warm outside, she always says, "You'd better

_____take a sweater_____ because it might get cold later," or "You'd
       (example)

better _____ because it might rain." When I drive,
              (1)

she always tells me, "You'd better _____, or you might
                                          (2)

get a ticket." If I stay out late with my friends, she tells me, "You'd

better _____, or you won't get enough sleep." If I read
              (3)

a lot, she says, "You'd better not _____, or you'll ruin
                                          (4)

your eyesight."

B: Well, she's your mother. So naturally she worries about you.

A: But she worries about other things too.

B: Like what?

A: "You'd better _____ your shoes when you enter the
                           (5)

apartment, or the neighbors downstairs will hear us walking around.

We'd better _____, or the neighbors will complain
                    (6)

about the noise in our apartment."

B: It sounds like she's a good neighbor.

(continued)

A: That's not all. She unplugs the TV every night. She says, "I'd better _____, or the apartment will fill up with radiation."
(7)
And she doesn't want to use a cell phone. She says it has too much radiation. I think that's so silly.

B: I don't think that's silly. You'd better _____ some
(8)
articles about cell phones, because they do produce radiation.

A: I don't even use my cell phone very much. But my mother always tells me, "You'd better _____ in case I need to call you."
(9)

B: Do you live with your mother?

A: Yes, I do. I think I'd better _____ to my own
(10)
apartment, or she'll drive me crazy.

Using Craigslist.org to Find a Roommate

Before
You Read

1. Do you ever use the Internet to find an apartment?
2. How did you find your current apartment?

Read the following conversation. Pay special attention to the negative of modals and related expressions.

A: I'm looking for a new roommate. My roommate moved out last month, and I **can't** pay the rent by myself.

B: You can put an ad on Craigslist.

A: What's that?

B: It's a Web site where you can advertise. You can sell, buy, rent, find jobs, look for roommates—you can do a lot of things on Craigslist.org.

A: How much does it cost to put an ad on this site?

B: It's free. You **don't have to** pay anything. Let's go to the computer. I'll show you. . . . *[looking at the Web site]*

A: These ads all have pictures.

B: You **don't have to** include pictures, but it's a good idea. You get more responses if you include pictures.

A: This is great. Can you help me write an ad?

B: Sure. You included your phone number.

A: What's wrong with that?

B: You **shouldn't** include it. It's better if you get e-mail.

A: OK. Now let's take pictures of my apartment. I'll get my camera.

B: You'd **better not** take pictures yet. Your apartment is a mess. You need to clean it up first.

A: Oh, right.

B: You know, I just thought of something. My cousin, Lisa, needs a roommate.

A: Lisa? She has a dog. We **can't** have dogs in the apartment.

B: Are you sure? Look at your lease.

A: Here it is. It says, "Renters **may not** have a pet." Besides, Lisa's a woman. In my country, men and women **aren't supposed to** live together. My parents wouldn't like it.

B: They **don't have to** know. They don't even live in this country.

A: I'd **better not** do it. I **can't** lie to my parents.

8.8 Negatives of Modals

EXAMPLES	EXPLANATION
Renters **may not** have a pet. Renters **must not** change the locks without the owner's permission.	Prohibition in documents is often expressed with *may not* or *must not*. These modals sound very formal or official.
a. I **can't** have a dog in my apartment. a. We **can't** leave our bikes in the hallway. b. I **can't** pay the rent by myself. b. I **can't** carry my bike up the stairs. It's too heavy.	a. *Cannot*, in these examples, shows prohibition. It is less formal than *may not* or *must not*. b. *Cannot*, in these examples, shows inability.
a. You**'re not supposed to** have a dog in your apartment. b. In my country, men and women **are not supposed to** live together if they're not married.	a. *You're not supposed to* is a less formal way of showing prohibition than *you may not*. b. *Be not supposed to*, in this example, shows a custom.
You **shouldn't** include your phone number in the ad. In case of fire, you **shouldn't** use the elevator. You **shouldn't** leave your door unlocked. It's not safe.	*Shouldn't* gives advice.
a. You**'d better not** take pictures now. Your apartment is a mess. b. I**'d better not** get a female roommate. My parents wouldn't like it.	a. *Had better not* is used for a warning. b. *Had better not* can be an emotional response to a suggestion to do something wrong.
a. You **don't have to** tell your parents. b. You **don't have to** include pictures on Craigslist, but it's a good idea.	a. *Don't have to* means not necessary. b. *Don't have to* sometimes means that you have an option (include picture or not).
Compare: a. We**'re not supposed to** leave our bikes near the door, but someone always does it. b. You **shouldn't** lie to your parents. c. You **don't have to** include pictures on Craigslist. It's your choice. d. Tenants **must not** change the locks.	Sentence (a) shows that a rule is violated. Sentence (b) gives advice. Sentence (c) shows that something is not necessary. Sentence (d) shows that something is not permitted. In affirmative statements, *must* and *have to* have very similar meanings: However, in negative statements, the meaning is very different: • not have to = not necessary • must not = prohibited

EXERCISE 17 Practice using *must not* for prohibition. Use *you* in the impersonal sense. Answers will vary.

EXAMPLE   Name something you must not do.
You must not steal.

1. Name something you must not do on the bus.
2. Name something you mustn't do during a test.
3. Name something you mustn't do in the library.
4. Name something you must not do in the classroom.
5. Name something you mustn't do on an airplane.

EXERCISE 18   **ABOUT YOU** Tell if you *have to* or *don't have to* do the following. For affirmative statements, you can also use *have got to*.

EXAMPLES   work on Saturdays
I have to work on Saturdays.   OR   I've got to work on Saturdays.

wear a suit to work
I don't have to wear a suit to work.

1. speak English every day
2. use a dictionary to read the newspaper
3. pay rent on the first of the month
4. type my homework
5. work on Saturdays
6. come to school every day
7. pay my rent in cash
8. use public transportation
9. talk to the teacher after class
10. cook every day

EXERCISE 19 Ask a student who comes from another country these questions.

1. In your native country, does a citizen have to vote?
2. Do men have to serve in the military?
3. Do schoolchildren have to wear uniforms?
4. Do people have to get permission to travel?
5. Do students have to pass an exam to get their high school or university diploma?

(continued)

6. Do students have to pay for their own books?

7. Do citizens have to pay taxes?

8. Do people have to make an appointment to see a doctor?

EXERCISE 20 **Fill in the blanks with *be not supposed to* (when there is a rule) or *don't have to* (when something is not necessary).**

CD 3, TR 05

A: Would you like to see my new apartment?

B: Yes.

A: I'll take you there after class today. The teacher says we

_____**don't have to**_____ go to the lab this afternoon. We can take
    (example)

the day off today.

(*At the apartment*)

B: Why do you carry your bicycle up to the third floor? Wouldn't it be

better to leave it near the front door?

A: The landlord says we _____ leave anything near the
        (1)

door. The rule is to leave the front lobby empty. Besides, I can take

it up in the elevator. I _____ use the stairs, but
        (2)

I don't mind carrying it. My bicycle is light.

B: This is a great apartment. But it's so big. Isn't it expensive?

A: Yes, but I _____ pay the rent alone. I have a
        (3)

roommate.

B: I see you have lots of nice pictures on the walls. In my apartment,

we _____ make holes in the walls.
        (4)

A: You can't even put up pictures? If you use picture hooks, you

_____ make big holes. Why don't you ask your
        (5)

landlord if you can do it? If you can, I can give you some picture hooks.

B: Thanks. In my apartment, the landlord has so many rules. For

example, we _____ hang our laundry out the
        (6)

window. We have to use the clothes dryer in the basement.

And we _____ use electric heaters.
        (7)

A: An electric heater can sometimes cause a fire. I'm sure the apartment has heaters for each room. And in the U.S. people don't usually hang clothes to dry out the window. People use dryers.

B: There are so many different rules and customs here.

A: Don't worry. If you do something wrong, someone will tell you.

EXERCISE 21 Students (S) are asking the teacher (T) questions about the final exam. Fill in the blanks with the negative form of *have to, should, must, had better, can, may,* or *be supposed to*. In some cases, more than one answer is possible.

CD 3, TR 06

S: Do I have to sit in a specific seat for the test?

T: No, you ____*don't have to*____. You can choose any seat you want.
          (example)

S: Is it OK if I talk to another student during a test?

T: No. Absolutely not. You _____ talk to another
                                          (1)
student during a test.

S: Is it OK if I use my book?

T: Sorry. You _____ use your book.
                      (2)

S: What if I don't understand something on the test? Can I ask another student?

T: You _____ talk to another student, or I'll think
              (3)
you're getting an answer. Ask me if you have a question.

S: What happens if I'm late for the test? Will you let me in?

T: Of course I'll let you in. But you _____ come late.
                                                  (4)
You'll need a lot of time for the test.

S: Do I have to bring my own paper for the final test?

T: If you want to, you can. But you _____ bring paper.
                                                (5)
I'll give you paper if you need it.

S: Must I use a pen?

T: You can use whatever you want. You _____ use a pen.
                                                    (6)

S: Do you have any advice on test-taking?

(continued)

Modals; Related Expressions **259**

T: Yes. If you see an item that is difficult for you, go on to the next item. You _____ spend too much time on a difficult item, or you won't finish the test.

(7)

S: Can I bring coffee into the classroom?

T: The school has a rule about eating or drinking in the classroom. You _____ bring food or drinks into the classroom.

(8)

S: If I finish the test early, must I stay in the room?

T: No, you _____ stay. You can leave.

(9)

The New Neighbors

Before
You Read

1. Are people friendly with their neighbors in your community?

2. Do you know any of your neighbors now?

Read the following conversation. Pay special attention to *must*.

Lisa (L) knocks on the door of her new upstairs neighbor, Paula (P).

L: Hi. You **must be** the new neighbor. I saw the moving truck out front this morning. Let me introduce myself. My name is Lisa. I live downstairs from you.

P: Nice to meet you, Lisa. My name is Paula. We just moved in.

L: I saw the movers carrying a crib upstairs. You **must have** a baby.

P: We do. We have a 10-month-old son. He's sleeping now. Do you have any kids?

L: Yes. I have a 16-year-old-daughter and an 18-year-old son.

P: It **must be** hard to raise teenagers.

L: Believe me, it is! I **must spend** half my time worrying about where they are and what they're doing. My daughter talks on the phone all day. She **must spend** half of her waking hours on the phone with her friends. They're always whispering to each other. They **must have** some big secrets.

P: I know what you mean. My brother has a teenage daughter.

L: Listen, I don't want to take up any more of your time. You **must be** very busy. I just wanted to bring you these cookies.

P: Thanks. That's very nice of you. They're still warm. They **must be** right out of the oven.

L: They are. Maybe we can talk some other time when you're all unpacked.

8.9 *Must* for Conclusions

In Section 8.4, we studied *must* to express necessity. *Must* has another use: we use it to show a logical conclusion or deduction based on information we have or observations we make. *Must*, in this case, is for the present only, not the future.

EXAMPLES	EXPLANATION
a. The new neighbors have a crib. They **must have** a baby.	a. You see the crib, so you conclude that they have a baby.
b. Paula just moved in. She **must be** very busy.	b. You know how hard it is to move, so you conclude that she is busy.
c. The teenage girls whisper all the time. They **must have** secrets.	c. You see them whispering, so you conclude that they are telling secrets.
I didn't see Paula's husband. He **must not be** home.	For a negative deduction, use *must not*. Do not use a contraction.

EXERCISE 22   **A week later, Paula goes to Lisa's apartment and notices certain things. Use *must* + base form to show Paula's conclusions about Lisa's life. Answers may vary.**

EXAMPLE   There is a bowl of food on the kitchen floor.
<u>Lisa must have a pet.</u>

1. There are pictures of Lisa and her two children all over the house. There is no picture of a man.

   _____

2. There is a nursing certificate on the wall with Lisa's name on it.

   _____

3. There are many different kinds of coffee on a kitchen shelf.

   _____

4. There are a lot of classical music CDs.

   _____

5. In Lisa's bedroom, there's a sewing machine.

   _____

6. In the kitchen, there are a lot of cookbooks.

   _____

7. There's a piano in the living room.

   _____

8. On the bookshelf, there are a lot of books about modern art.

   _____

9. On the kitchen calendar, there's an activity filled in for almost every day of the week.

   _____

10. There are pictures of cats everywhere.

   _____

EXERCISE 23   **Two neighbors, Alma (A) and Eva (E), meet in the hallway of their building. Fill in the blanks with an appropriate verb to show deduction.**

CD 3, TR 08

A: Hi. My name's Alma. I live on the third floor. You must

_____ ***be*** _____ new in this building.
(example)

E: I am. We just moved in last week. My name's Eva.

A: I noticed your last name on the mailbox. It's Kovíc. That sounds like a Bosnian name. You must _____ from Bosnia.
(1)

E: I am. How did you know?

A: I'm from Bosnia too. Did you come directly to the U.S. from Bosnia?

E: No. I stayed in Germany for three years.

A: Then you must _____ German.
(2)

E: I can speak it pretty well, but I can't write it well.

A: Are you going to school now?

E: Yes, I'm taking English classes at Washington College.

A: What level are you in?

E: I'm in Level 5.

A: Then you must _____ my husband. He takes classes there too.
(3)
He's in Level 5 too.

E: There's only one guy with a Bosnian last name. That must _____ your husband.
(4)

A: His name is Hasan.

E: Oh, yes, I know him. I didn't know he lived in the same building. I never see him here. He must not _____ home very much.
(5)

A: He isn't. He has two jobs.

E: Do you take English classes?

A: Not anymore. I came here 15 years ago.

E: Then your English must _____ perfect.
(6)

A: I don't know if it's perfect, but it's good enough.

8.10 Will and May/Might

EXAMPLES	EXPLANATION
My lease **will** expire on April 30. We **won't** sign another lease.	For certainty about the future, use *will*. The negative contraction for *will not* is *won't*.
a. My landlord **might** raise my rent at that time. a. I **may** move. b. I don't know what "tenant" means. Let's ask the teacher. She **might** know. b. The teacher **may** have information about tenants' rights.	*May* and *might* both have about the same meaning: possibility or uncertainty. a. about the future b. about the present
He **may not** renew our lease. He **might not** renew our lease.	We don't use a contraction for *may not* and *might not*.

Compare:
a. **Maybe** I will move.
b. I **might** move.
a. **Maybe** he doesn't understand the lease.
b. He **might** not understand the lease.
a. **Maybe** the apartment is cold in winter.
  (*maybe* = adverb)
b. The apartment **may** be cold in winter.
  (*may + be* = modal + verb)
	Maybe is an adverb. It is one word. It usually comes at the beginning of the sentence and means *possibly* or *perhaps*. *May* and *might* are modals. They follow the subject and precede the verb. Sentences (a) and (b) have the same meaning.
	  Wrong: I *maybe* will move.
	  Wrong: He *maybe* doesn't understand.
	  Wrong: The apartment *maybe* is cold.

EXERCISE 24 **The following sentences contain *maybe*. Take away *maybe* and use *may* or *might* + base form.**

EXAMPLE   Maybe your neighbors will complain if your music is loud.
Your neighbors might complain if your music is loud.

1. Maybe my sister will come to live with me.

2. Maybe she will find a job in this city.

3. Maybe my landlord will raise my rent.

4. Maybe I will get a dog.

5. Maybe my landlord won't allow me to have a dog.

6. Maybe I will move next year.

7. Maybe I will buy a house soon.

8. Maybe I won't stay in this city.

9. Maybe I won't come to class tomorrow.

10. Maybe the teacher will review modals if we need more help.

EXERCISE 25 **ABOUT YOU** **Fill in the blanks with a possibility.**

EXAMPLES   If I don't pay my rent on time, <u>I might have to pay a late fee.</u>

If I make a lot of noise in my apartment, <u>the neighbors may complain.</u>

1. When my lease is up, _____

2. If I don't clean my apartment before I move out, _____

_____

3. If I don't study for the next test, _____

4. If we don't register for classes early, _____

_____

5. If I don't pass this course, _____

EXERCISE 26 **Fill in the blanks with possibilities. Answers may vary.**

EXAMPLE   **A:** I'm going to move on Saturday. I might <u>need</u> help. Can you

help me?

B: I'm not sure. I may <u>go</u> to the country with my family if the

CD 3, TR 09

weather is nice. If I stay here, I'll help you.

1. **A:** My next door neighbor's name is Terry Karson. I see her name on

the doorbell but I never see her.

B: Why do you say "her"? Your neighbor may _____ a man.

Terry is sometimes a man's name.

2. **A:** I need coins for the laundry room. Do you have any?

B: Let me look. I might _____ some. No, I don't have any. Look in

the laundry room. There might _____ a dollar-bill changer there.

3. **A:** Do you know the landlord's address?

B: No, I don't. Ask the manager. She might _____.

A: Where's the manager now?

B: I'm not sure. She might _____ in a tenant's apartment.

4. **A:** Do they allow cats in this building?

B: I'm not sure. I know they don't allow dogs, but they might

_____ cats.

(continued)

5. **A:** We'd better close the windows before going out.

   B: Why? It's a hot day today.

   A: Look how gray the sky is. It might _____.

6. **A:** Are you going to stay in this apartment for another year?

   B: I'm not sure. I may _____.

   A: Why?

   B: The landlord might _____ the rent. If the rent goes up more than 25 percent, I'll move.

7. **A:** I have so much stuff in my closet. There's not enough room for my clothes.

   B: There might _____ lockers in the basement where you can store your things.

   A: Really? I didn't know that.

   B: Let's look. I may _____ a key to the basement with me.

   A: That would be great.

   B: Hmm. I don't have one on me. Let's go to my apartment. My basement keys might _____ there.

At A Garage Sale

Before You Read

1. People often have a garage sale or yard sale or an apartment sale before they move. At this kind of sale, people sell things that they don't want or need anymore. Do you ever go to garage sales?

2. At a garage or yard sale, it is usually not necessary to pay the asking price. You may be able to bargain[3] with the seller. Can you bargain the price in other places?

---

[3]When a buyer *bargains* with the seller, the buyer makes an offer lower than the asking price and hopes that he or she and the seller will agree on a lower price.

This is a conversation at a garage sale between a seller (S) and a buyer (B). Read the conversation. Pay special attention to modals and related expressions.

S: I see you're looking at my microwave oven. **May** I answer any questions?

B: Yes. I'm interested in buying one. Does it work well?

S: It's only two years old, and it's in perfect working condition. **Would** you **like** to try it out?

B: Sure. **Could** you plug it in somewhere?

S: I have an outlet right here. **Why don't we** boil a cup of water so you can see how well it works?

(A *few minutes later*)

B: It seems to work well. **Would** you tell me why you're selling it, then?

S: We're moving next week. Our new apartment already has one.

B: How much do you want for it?[4]

S: $40.

B: **Will** you take $30?

S: **Can** you wait a minute? I'll ask my wife.

(A *few minutes later*)

S: My wife says she'll let you have it for $35.

B: OK. **May** I write you a check?

S: I'm sorry. **I'd rather** have cash.

B: **Would** you hold it for me for an hour? I can go to the ATM[5] and get cash.

S: **Could** you leave me a small deposit? Ten dollars, maybe?

B: Yes, I can.

S: Fine. I'll hold it for you.

---

[4]We ask "How much is it?" when the price is fixed. We ask "How much do you want for it?" when the price is negotiable—you can bargain for it.

[5]An *ATM* is an Automatic Teller Machine. You can use this machine to get cash from your bank account.

8.11 Using Modals and Questions for Politeness

	EXAMPLES	EXPLANATION
To ask permission	**May** **Can** } I write you a check? **Could**	*May* and *could* are considered more polite than *can* by some speakers of English.
To request that someone do something	**Can** **Could** } you plug it in? **Will** **Would**	For a request, *could* and *would* are softer than *can* and *will*.
To express want or desire	**Would** you **like** to try out the microwave oven? Yes, I **would like** to see if it works. I'**d like** to boil a cup of water.	*Would like* has the same meaning as *want*. *Would like* is softer than *want*. The contraction for *would* after a pronoun is '*d*.
To express preference	I **would rather** buy a used microwave **than** a new one. **Would** you **rather** pay with cash **or** by check? I'**d rather** pay by check.	Use *than* in statements with *would rather* to show options. Use *or* in questions. The second option can be omitted if it's obvious.
To offer a suggestion	**Why don't you** go to the ATM to get cash? **Why don't we** boil a cup of water? **Compare:** Go to the ATM. Boil a cup of water.	We can make a suggestion more polite by using a negative question.

Language Note: Modals and questions are often used to make direct statements more polite.
Compare:
   Plug it in. (very direct)
   Would you plug it in? (more polite)

EXERCISE 27 **Change each request to make it more polite. Practice *may*, *can*, and *could* + I.**

EXAMPLES   I want to use your phone.
   May I use your phone?

   I want to borrow a quarter.
   Could I borrow a quarter?

   1. I want to help you.

   2. I want to close the door.

   3. I want to leave the room.

   4. I want to write you a check.

EXERCISE 28 **Change these commands to make them more polite. Practice *can you, could you, will you,* and *would you.***

EXAMPLES Call the doctor for me.
Would you call the doctor for me?

Give me a cup of coffee.
Could you give me a cup of coffee, please?

1. Repeat the sentence.   3. Spell your name.
2. Give me your paper.   4. Tell me your phone number.

EXERCISE 29 **Make these sentences more polite by using *would like.***

EXAMPLE Do you want some help?
Would you like some help?

1. I want to ask you a question.
2. The teacher wants to speak with you.
3. Do you want to try out the oven?
4. Yes. I want to see if it works.

EXERCISE 30 **Make each suggestion more polite by putting it in the form of a negative question.**

EXAMPLES Plug it in.
Why don't you plug it in?

Let's eat now.
Why don't we eat now?

1. Take a sweater.   3. Turn left here.
2. Let's turn off the light. 4. Let's leave early.

EXERCISE 31 **ABOUT YOU Make a statement of preference using *would rather.***

EXAMPLE own a house / a condominium
I'd rather own a condominium than a house.

1. live in the U.S. / in another country
2. own a condominium / rent an apartment
3. have young neighbors / old neighbors
4. have wood floors / carpeted floors
5. live in the center of the city / in a suburb
6. drive to work / take public transportation
7. pay my rent by check / with cash
8. have nosy neighbors / noisy neighbors

EXERCISE 32 **ABOUT YOU** Ask a question of preference with the words given. Another student will answer.

EXAMPLE   eat Chinese food / Italian food

    A: Would you rather eat Chinese food or Italian food?

    B: I'd rather eat Italian food.

1. read fact / fiction

2. watch funny movies / serious movies

3. listen to classical music / popular music

4. visit Europe / Africa

5. own a large luxury car / a small sports car

6. watch a soccer game / take part in a soccer game

7. write a letter / receive a letter

8. cook / eat in a restaurant

EXERCISE 33 **This is a conversation between a seller (S) and a buyer (B) at a garage sale. Make this conversation more polite by using modals and other polite expressions in place of the underlined words. Answers may vary.**

CD 3, TR 11

             May I help you?
S: ~~What do you want?~~
          (example)

B: I'm interested in that lamp. <u>Show it to me</u>. Does it work?
                          (1)

S: I'll go and get a light bulb. <u>Wait a minute</u>.
                                  (2)

(A few minutes later)

B: <u>Plug it in</u>.
      (3)

S: You see? It works fine.

B: How much do you want for it?

S: This is one of a pair. I have another one just like it. They're $10 each.

    <u>I prefer to sell</u> them together.
         (4)

B: <u>Give them both to me for $15</u>.
            (5)

S: I'll have to ask my husband.

    (A few seconds later)

    My husband says he'll sell them to you for $17.

B: Fine. I'll take them. Will you take a check?

S: <u>I prefer to</u> have cash.
       (6)

B: I only have five dollars on me.

S: OK. I'll take a check. <u>Show me some identification</u>.
(7)

B: Here's my driver's license.

S: That's fine. Just write the check to James Kucinski.

B: <u>Spell your name for me</u>.
(8)

S: K-U-C-I-N-S-K-I.

Summary of Lesson 8

Modals

MODAL	EXAMPLE	EXPLANATION
can	I **can** stay in this apartment until March. I **can** carry my bicycle up to my apartment. You **can't** paint the walls without the landlord's permission. **Can** I borrow your pen? **Can** you turn off the light, please?	Permission Ability/Possibility Prohibition Asking permission Request
should	You **should** be friendly with your neighbors. You **shouldn't** leave the air conditioner on. It wastes electricity.	A good idea A bad idea
may	**May** I borrow your pen? You **may** leave the room. You **may not** talk during a test. I **may** move next month. The landlord **may** have an extra key.	Asking permission Giving permission Prohibition Future possibility Present possibility
might	I **might** move next month. The landlord **might** have an extra key.	Future possibility Present possibility
must	The landlord **must** install smoke detectors. You **must not** change the locks. Mary has a cat carrier. She **must** have a cat.	Rule or law: Official tone Prohibition: Official tone Conclusion/Deduction
would	**Would** you help me move?	Request
would like	I **would like** to use your phone.	Want
would rather	I **would rather** live in Florida than in Maine.	Preference
could	In my country, I **couldn't** choose my own apartment. The government gave me one. In my country, I **could** attend college for free. **Could** you help me move? **Could** I borrow your car?	Past permission Past ability Request Asking permission

Related Expressions

EXPRESSION	EXAMPLE	EXPLANATION
have to	She **has to** leave. He **had to** leave work early today.	Necessity Past necessity
have got to	She **has got to** see a doctor. I**'ve got to** move.	Necessity
not have to	You **don't have to** pay your rent with cash. You can pay by check.	No necessity
had better	You **had better** pay your rent on time, or the landlord will ask you to leave. You**'d better** get permission before changing the locks.	Warning
be supposed to	We**'re not supposed to** have a dog here. I **was supposed to** pay my rent by the fifth of the month, but I forgot.	Reporting a rule or obligation
be able to	The teacher **is able to** use modals correctly.	Ability
be permitted to be allowed to	We**'re not permitted to** park here overnight. We**'re not allowed to** park here overnight.	Permission

Editing Advice

1. After a modal, use the base form.

I must ~~to~~ study.

I can help~~ing~~ you now.

2. A modal has no ending.

He can~~s~~ cook.

3. Don't put two modals together. Change the second modal to another form.

have to
She will ~~must~~ take the test.

4. Don't forget *to* after *be permitted, be allowed, be supposed,* and *be able.*

to
We're not permitted ‸ talk during a test.

5. Don't forget *be* before *permitted to*, *allowed to*, *supposed to*, and *able to*.

     am
I not supposed to pay my rent late.
  ^

6. Use the correct word order in a question.

       should I
What ~~I should~~ do about my problem?

7. Don't use *can* for past. Use *could* + a base form.

    couldn't go
I ~~can't went~~ to the party last week.

8. Don't forget *would* before *rather*.

   'd
I rather live in Canada than in the U.S.
 ^

9. Don't forget *had* before *better*.

    'd
You better take a sweater. It's going to get cold.
   ^

10. Don't forget *have* before *got to*.

    've
It's late. I got to go.
     ^

11. Don't use *maybe* before a verb.

    may
It ~~maybe will~~ rain later.

Editing Quiz

Some of the shaded words and phrases have mistakes. Find the mistakes and correct them. If the shaded words are correct, write *C*.

    've
A: I got to move when my lease is up.
   ^*(example)*   *C*

B: Why do you have to move? You have a great apartment.
         (example)

A: I want to get a dog, but we not permitted to have dogs in my building.
                                    (1)

B: Maybe your landlord won't find out.

A: Of course he'll find out. I will have to take the dog out for a walk a
                                         (2)

few times a day.

B: How will he know? My landlord only comes once a month on the day
         (3)

we supposed to pay the rent.
     (4)

                                                                (continued)

A: My landlord lives on the first floor.

B: Oh. That's a problem. What about a cat? Cats are allow in your
 (5)
building, right? He maybe will let you have a cat.
 (6)

A: Cats are permit, but I can't be around cats.
 (7) (8)

B: Why you can't be around cats?
 (9)

A: I'm allergic to them. Anyway, I rather have a dog. Dogs are better
 (10)
companions.

B: If you want a companion, maybe you should find a roommate.
 (11)

A: I used to have a roommate, but we can't agreed on a lot of things.
 (12)
So when he moved out, I decided that I better not to have another
 (13) (14)
roommate.

Lesson 8 Test/Review

PART 1 **This is a conversation between two friends. Circle the correct expression in parentheses ( ) to complete the conversation.**

A: I'm moving on Saturday. (Could / May) you help me?
 (example)

B: I (should / would) like to help you, but I have a bad back. I went to
 (1)
my doctor last week, and she told me that I (shouldn't / don't have to)
 (2)
lift anything heavy for a while. (Can / Would) I help you any other
 (3)
way besides moving?

A: Yes. I don't have enough boxes. (Should / Would) you help me find
 (4)
some?

B: Sure. I (have to / must) go shopping this afternoon. I'll pick up some
 (5)
boxes while I'm at the supermarket.

A: Boxes can be heavy. You (would / had) better not lift them yourself.
 (6)

B: Don't worry. I'll have someone put them in my car for me.

A: Thanks. I don't have a free minute. I (couldn't go / can't went) to
 (7)
class all last week. There's so much to do.

B: I know what you mean. You (*might / must*) be tired.
(8)

A: I am. I have another favor to ask. (*Can / Would*) I borrow your van
(9)

on Saturday?

B: I (*should / have to*) work on Saturday. How about Sunday? I
(10)

(*must not / don't have to*) work on Sunday.
(11)

A: That's impossible. I (*'ve got to / should*) move out on Saturday. The
(12)

new tenants are moving in Sunday morning.

B: Let me ask my brother. He has a van too. He (*must / might*) be able
(13)

to let you use his van. He (*has to / should*) work Saturday too, but
(14)

only for half a day.

A: Thanks. I'd appreciate it if you could ask him.

B: Why are you moving? You have a great apartment.

A: We decided to move to the suburbs. It's quieter there. And I want to

have a dog. I (*shouldn't / 'm not supposed to*) have a dog in my
(15)

present apartment. But my new landlord says I (*might / may*) have
(16)

a dog.

B: I (*had / would*) rather have a cat. They're easier to take care of.
(17)

PART 2 **Fill in the blanks to complete the sentences. In some cases, more than one answer is possible.**

1. I don't like my apartment. I have such noisy neighbors. I ____can____
   (*example*)
   hear their music all the time. Sometimes I _____ study or sleep
   at night because it's so loud. I don't know why they play the music so
   loud. They _____ be deaf!

2. I take my bike upstairs because we're not _____ to leave our bikes
   in the hallway.

3. Stop! Put down that hammer. You'd _____ not make a hole
   in the wall to put up that picture, or the landlord will get angry. He
   _____ even keep your security deposit.

4. I'd _____ take public transportation _____ go to work
   by car. That's why I moved close to the train.

(*continued*)

5. Your brother lives alone. He _____ be lonely. Maybe he _____ get a roommate.

6. My lease says, "Tenants _____ not have a water bed."

7. My landlady is raising my rent. I've _____ to find a new apartment.

8. My mother's coming to visit, so I _____ to clean my apartment.

9. I can help you move on Saturday because I don't _____ to work that day.

10. Do you see that sign? It says "No Parking in Front of Building." You're not _____ to park here. Park in the back.

Expansion

Classroom

Activities

❶ A student will read one of the following problems out loud to the class, pretending that this is his or her problem. Other students will ask for more information and give advice about this problem.

EXAMPLE My mother-in-law comes to visit all the time. When she's here, she always criticizes everything we do. I told my wife that I don't want her here, but she says, "It's my mother, and I want her here." What should I do?

A: How long does she usually stay?

B: She might stay for about two weeks or longer.

C: How does she criticize you? What does she say?

B: She says I should help my wife more.

D: Well, I agree with her. You should help with housework. What other problems are you having with her?

B: My children aren't allowed to watch TV after 8.00 P.M. But my mother-in-law lets them watch TV as long as they want.

E: You'd better have a talk with her and tell her your rules.

Problem 1. My mother is 80 years old, and she lives with us. It's very hard on my family to take care of her. We'd like to put her in a nursing home, where she can get better care. Mother refuses to go. What can we do?

Problem 2. I'm sixteen years old. I want to get a part-time job after school. I want to save money to buy a car. My parents say I won't have enough time to study. But I think I can do both. How can I convince my parents?

Problem 3. I have a nice one-bedroom apartment with a beautiful view of a park and a lake. I live with my wife and one child. My friends from out of town often come to visit and want to stay at my apartment. In the last year, ten people came to visit us. I like to have visitors, but sometimes they stay for weeks. It's hard on my family with such a small apartment. What should I tell my friends when they want to visit?

Problem 4. My upstairs neighbors make noise all the time. I can't sleep at night. I have asked them three times to be quieter, and each time they said they would. But the noise still continues. What should I do?

Problem 5. My roommate brings friends home all the time. They eat pizza, drink sodas, and watch TV. When they leave, the apartment is a mess. What should I do?

❷ Work with a partner from your own country, if possible. Talk about some laws in your country that are different from laws in the U.S. Present this information to the class.

EXAMPLE   Citizens must vote in my country. In the U.S., they don't have to vote.

People are supposed to carry identification papers at all times. In the U.S., people don't have to carry identification papers.

Talk About It

❶ Compare renting an apartment here with renting an apartment in another country or city.

❷ How did you find your present apartment?

❸ What are some of the things you like about the place where you live? What are some of the things you dislike?

Write

About It

❶ Write a short composition comparing rules in an apartment in this city with rules in an apartment in your hometown or native country.

❷ Find out what a student has to do to register for the first time at this school. You may want to visit the registrar's office to interview a worker there. Write a short composition explaining to a new student the steps for admission and registration.

❸ Write about the differences between rules at this school and rules at another school you attended. Are students allowed to do things here that they can't do in another school?

Comparing School Rules

The rules and customs at this school, Harper College, and my college back home in the Philippines are different. At this school, we don't have to call our teachers "Mr." or "Ms." We can call them by their first names. In the Philippines, students must call teachers by their title, "Professor"...

 For more practice using grammar in context, please visit our Web site.

Grammar
The Present Perfect

The Present Perfect Continuous[1]

Context
The Internet

[1]The *present perfect continuous* is sometimes called the *present perfect progressive*.

9.1 The Present Perfect Tense—An Overview

We form the present perfect with *have* or *has* + the past participle.

Subject	*have*	Past Participle	Complement	Explanation
I	have	been	in the U.S. for three years.	Use *have* with *I*, *you*, *we*, *they*, and plural nouns.
You	have	used	your computer a lot.	
We	have	written	a job résumé.	
They	have	bought	a new computer.	
Computers	have	changed	the world.	
Subject	***has***	**Past Participle**	**Complement**	**Explanation**
My sister	has	gotten	her degree.	Use *has* with *he*, *she*, *it*, and singular nouns.
She	has	found	a job as a programmer.	
My father	has	helped	me.	
The computer	has	changed	a lot over the years.	
There	***has/have***	***been***	**Complement**	**Explanation**
There	has	been	a problem with my computer.	After *there*, we use *has* or *have*, depending on the noun that follows. Use *has* with a singular noun. Use *have* with a plural noun.
There	have	been	many changes with personal computers.	

Google

Before You Read

1. Do you use the Internet a lot? Why?

2. What search engine do you usually use?

CD 3, TR 12

Read the following Web article. Pay special attention to the present perfect tense.

Since its start in 1998, Google **has become** one of the most popular search engines. It **has grown** from a research project in the dormitory room of two college students to a business that now employs approximately 20,000 people.

Larry Page and Sergey Brin

Google's founders, Larry Page and Sergey Brin, met in 1995 when they were in their twenties and graduate students in computer science at Stanford University in California. They realized that Internet search was a very important field and began working together to make searching easier. Both Page and Brin left their studies at Stanford to work on their project. Interestingly, they **have** never **returned** to finish their degrees.

Brin was born in Russia, but he **has lived** in the U.S. since he was five years old. His father was a mathematician in Russia. Page, whose parents were computer experts, **has been** interested in computers since he was six years old.

When Google started in 1998, it did 10,000 searches a day. Today it does 235 million searches a day in 40 languages. It indexes[2] 1 trillion Web pages.

How is Google different from other search engines? **Have** you ever **noticed** how many ads and banners there are on other search engines? News, sports scores, stock prices, links for shopping, mortgage rates, and more fill other search engines. Brin and Page wanted a clean home page. They believed that people come to the Internet to search for specific information, not to be hit with a lot of unwanted data. The success of Google over its rivals[3] **has proved** that this is true.

Over the years, Google **has added** new features to its Web site: Google Images, where you can type in a word and get thousands of pictures; Google News, which takes you to today's news; Google Maps; and more. But one thing **hasn't changed:** the clean opening page that Google offers its users.

In 2009, Forbes.com listed Page and Brin as having net worths of $12 billion each, at 36 and 35 years old.

Did You Know?

The word "Google" started as a noun, the company's name. Today people use it as a verb: "I'm going to Google the Civil War to get more information about it."

[2]*To index* means to sort, organize, and categorize information.
[3]*Rivals* are competitors.

EXERCISE 1 Underline the present perfect tense in each sentence. Then tell if the sentence is true or false.

EXAMPLE Google has become a very popular search engine.   T

1. Google has grown over the years.
2. Sergey Brin has lived in the U.S. all his life.
3. Larry Page and Sergey Brin have known each other since they were children.
4. Larry Page has been interested in computers since he was a child.
5. Brin and Page have returned to college to finish their degrees.
6. Brin and Page have become rich.
7. The noun "Google" has become a verb.

9.2 The Past Participle

The past participle of regular verbs ends in **-ed**. The past participle is the same as the past form for regular verbs.

FORMS			EXAMPLES
Base Form	**Past Form**	**Past Participle**	I **work** every day. I **worked** yesterday. I **have worked** all week.
work improve	worked improved	worked improved	

The past participle of many irregular verbs is the same as the past form.

FORMS			EXAMPLES
Base Form	**Past Form**	**Past Participle**	We **have** a new car now. We **had** an old car, but we sold it. We **have had** our new car for two months.
have buy	had bought	had bought	

The past participle of some irregular verbs is different from the past form.

FORMS			EXAMPLES
Base Form	**Past Form**	**Past Participle**	I **write** a composition once a week. I **wrote** a composition yesterday. I **have written** five compositions this semester.
go write	went wrote	gone written	

For the following verbs, the base form, past form, and past participle are all different.

Base Form	Past Form	Past Participle
become	became	become
come	came	come
run	ran	run
blow	blew	blown
draw	drew	drawn
fly	flew	flown
grow	grew	grown
know	knew	known
throw	threw	thrown
swear	swore	sworn
tear	tore	torn
wear	wore	worn
break	broke	broken
choose	chose	chosen
freeze	froze	frozen
speak	spoke	spoken
steal	stole	stolen
begin	began	begun
drink	drank	drunk
ring	rang	rung
sing	sang	sung
sink	sank	sunk
swim	swam	swum

Base Form	Past Form	Past Participle
arise	arose	arisen
bite	bit	bitten
drive	drove	driven
ride	rode	ridden
rise	rose	risen
write	wrote	written
be	was/were	been
eat	ate	eaten
fall	fell	fallen
forgive	forgave	forgiven
give	gave	given
mistake	mistook	mistaken
see	saw	seen
shake	shook	shaken
take	took	taken
do	did	done
forget	forgot	forgotten
get	got	gotten
go	went	gone
lie	lay	lain
prove	proved	proven (or proved)
show	showed	shown (or showed)

EXERCISE 2 Write the past participle of these verbs.

EXAMPLE eat __eaten__

1. go _____
2. see _____
3. look _____
4. study _____
5. bring _____
6. take _____
7. say _____
8. be _____
9. find _____
10. leave _____

11. live _____
12. know _____
13. like _____
14. fall _____
15. feel _____
16. come _____
17. break _____
18. wear _____
19. choose _____
20. drive _____

21. write _____
22. put _____
23. begin _____
24. want _____
25. get _____
26. fly _____
27. sit _____
28. drink _____
29. grow _____
30. give _____

9.3 The Present Perfect—Contractions and Negatives

EXAMPLES	EXPLANATION
I've had a lot of experience with computers. **We've** read the story about Google. **He's** been interested in computers since he was a child. **There's** been an increase in searching over the years.	We can make a contraction with subject pronouns and *have* or *has*. I have = I've He has = He's You have = You've She has = She's We have = We've It has = It's They have = They've There has = There's
Larry's lived in the U.S. all his life. **Sergey's** been in the U.S. since he was five years old.	Most singular nouns can contract with *has*.
I **haven't** studied programming. Brin **hasn't** returned to college.	Negative contractions: *have not = haven't* *has not = hasn't*

Language Note: The **'s** in *he's, she's, it's,* and *there's* can mean *has* or *is*. The word following the contraction will tell you what the contraction means.

    He's working. = He *is* working.

    He's worked. = He **has** worked.

EXERCISE **3**   **Fill in the blanks to form the present perfect. Use a contraction.**

EXAMPLE   You <u>'ve</u> bought a new computer.

1. I _____ learned a lot about computers.

2. We _____ read the story about Google.

3. Larry _____ known Sergey since they were at Stanford University.

4. They (not) _____ known each other since they were children.

5. It _____ been easy for me to learn about computers.

6. You _____ used the Internet many times.

7. Larry and Sergey (not) _____ finished their degrees.

9.4 Adding an Adverb

Subject	has/ have	Adverb	Past Participle	Complement	Explanation
Page and Brin	**have**	never	**finished**	their degrees.	You can put an adverb between the auxiliary verb (*have/has*) and the past participle.
They	**have**	already*	**made**	a lot of money.	
They	**have**	even	**become**	billionaires.	
Larry Page	**has**	always	**been**	interested in computers.	
You	**have**	probably	**used**	a search engine.	

Language Note: *Already* frequently comes at the end of the verb phrase.
They have made a lot of money **already**.

EXERCISE **4** **Add the word in parentheses ( ) to the sentence.**

EXAMPLE   You have gotten an e-mail account. (probably)
You have probably gotten an e-mail account.

1. The teacher has given a test on Lesson 8. (already)

   _____

2. We have heard of Page and Brin. (never)

   _____

3. They have been interested in search technology. (always)

   _____

4. You have used Google. (probably)

   _____

5. Brin hasn't finished his degree. (even)

   _____

6. Brin and Page have become billionaires. (already)

   _____

9.5 The Present Perfect—Statements and Questions

Compare affirmative statements and questions.

Wh-Word	have/has	Subject	have/has	Past Participle	Complement	Short Answer
		Larry	has	lived	in the U.S. all his life.	
	Has	Sergey		lived	in the U.S. all his life?	No, he **hasn't**.
How long	has	Sergey		lived	in the U.S.?	Since 1979.

Language Note: For a short *yes* answer, we cannot make a contraction.
Has Larry lived in the U.S. all his life? Yes, he has. (Not: *he's*)

Compare negative statements and questions.

Wh-Word	haven't/hasn't	Subject	haven't/hasn't	Past Participle	Complement
		They	haven't	finished	their degrees.
Why	haven't	they		finished	their degrees?

EXERCISE 5 Change the statement to a question, using the word(s) in parentheses.

EXAMPLE Google has changed the way people search. (how)
<u>How has Google changed the way people search?</u>

1. I have used several search engines. (which ones)

_____

2. Larry and Sergey haven't finished their degrees. (why)

_____

3. They have made a lot of money. (how much)

_____

4. Sergey has been in the U.S. for many years. (how long)

_____

5. Larry and Sergey have hired many people to work for Google. (how many)

_____

6. We have used the computer lab several times this semester. (how many times)

_____

7. The memory and speed of computers have increased. (why)

_____

8. Computers have become part of our daily lives. (how)

_____

9.6 Continuation from Past to Present

We use the present perfect tense to show that an action or state started in the past and continues to the present.

```
                                    Now
Past ←——————————————————————————————|------------------------> Future
     ┌─────────────────────────────┐
     │ I have had my computer      │
     │ for two months.             │
     └─────────────────────────────┘
```

EXAMPLES	EXPLANATION
Larry Page **has been** interested in computers **for many years.** My sister **has been** a programmer **for three years.**	Use _for_ + an amount of time: _for two months, for three years, for one hour, for a long time,_ etc.
Brin's family **has been** in the U.S. **since 1979.** I **have had** my computer **since March.** Personal computers **have been** popular **since the 1980s.**	Use _since_ with the date, month, year, etc., that the action began.
Brin **has been** interested in computers since he **was** a child. I **have had** an e-mail account since I **bought** my computer.	Use _since_ with the beginning of the continuous action or state. The verb in the _since_ clause is simple past.
How long has Brin's family been in the U.S.? **How long** have you had your computer?	Use _how long_ to ask about the amount of time from the past to the present.
Larry Page has **always** lived in the U.S. He has **always** been interested in computers.	We use the present perfect with _always_ to show that an action began in the past and continues to the present.
My grandmother has **never** used a computer. Google has **never** put advertising on its opening page.	We use the present perfect with _never_ to show that something has not occurred from the past to the present.

EXERCISE 6 **Fill in the blanks with the missing words.**

EXAMPLE I've known my best friend ___since___ we were in high school.

1. My brother has been in the U.S. _____1998.

2. My mother _____ never been in the U.S.

3. How _____ have you been in the U.S.?

4. I've known the teacher since I _____ to study at this school.

5. My sister's _____ married for two years.

6. She's had the same job _____ ten years.

7. My best friend and I _____ known each other since we _____ in elementary school.

8. She' _____ been a student at this school _____ September.

9. I've had my car for three years. _____ long have you _____ your car?

10. I'm interested in computers. I' _____ _____ interested in computers since I was in high school.

11. _____ always wanted to have my own business.

EXERCISE 7 **ABOUT YOU** **Write true statements using the present perfect with the words given and *for, since, always,* or *never*. Share your sentences with the class.**

EXAMPLES know _My parents have known each other for over 40 years._

have _I've had my cell phone since March._

want _I've always wanted to learn English._

1. have _____
2. be _____
3. want _____
4. know _____

EXERCISE 8 **ABOUT YOU** **Make statements with *always*.**

EXAMPLE Name something you've always thought about.
I've always thought about my future.

1. Name something you've always enjoyed.

2. Name a person you've always liked.

3. Name something you've always wanted to do.

4. Name something you've always wanted to have.

5. Name something you've always been interested in.

EXERCISE 9 **ABOUT YOU** Make statements with *never*.

EXAMPLE Name a machine you've never used.
I've never used a fax machine.

1. Name a movie you've never seen.

2. Name a food you've never liked.

3. Name a subject you've never studied.

4. Name a city you've never visited.

5. Name a sport you've never played.

6. Name a food you've never tasted.

EXERCISE 10 **ABOUT YOU** Write four sentences telling about things you've always done (or been). Share your sentences with the class.

EXAMPLES I've always cooked the meals in my family.

I've always been lazy.

1. _____

2. _____

3. _____

4. _____

EXERCISE 11 **ABOUT YOU** Write four sentences telling about things you've never done (or been) but would like to. Share your sentences with the class.

EXAMPLES I've never studied photography, but I'd like to.

I've never acted in a play, but I'd like to.

1. _____

2. _____

3. _____

4. _____

9.7 The Simple Present vs. the Present Perfect

EXAMPLES	EXPLANATION
a. Larry Page **is** in California. b. Larry Page **has been** in California since he was in his twenties. a. He **loves** computers. b. He **has** always **loved** computers. a. Google **doesn't have** advertising on its home page. b. Google **has** never **had** advertising on its home page. a. **Do** you **work** at a computer company? Yes, I **do**. b. **Have** you always **worked** at a computer company? Yes, I **have**.	Sentences (a) refer only to the present. Sentences (b) connect the past to the present.

EXERCISE 12 Read each statement about your teacher. Then ask the teacher a question beginning with the words given. Include *always* in your question. Your teacher will answer.

EXAMPLE You're a teacher. Have you _____ always been a teacher _____?

No. I was an accountant before I became a teacher. I've only been a teacher for five years.

1. You teach English. Have you _____ _____?

2. You work at this college/school. Have you _____ _____?

3. You think about grammar. Have you _____ _____?

4. English is easy for you. Has English _____ _____?

5. Your last name is _____. Has your last name _____?

6. You're interested in languages. Have you _____ _____?

7. You live in this city. Have you _____ _____?

EXERCISE **Fill in the blanks with the missing words.**

CD 3, TR 13

Two students meet by chance in the computer lab.

A: <u>   Have   </u> you <u>   been   </u> in the U.S. for long?
  (example)   (example)

B: No, I _____.
               (1)

A: How _____ _____ you been in the U.S.?
            (2)   (3)

B: I _____ _____ here for about a year.
         (4)   (5)

A: Where do you come from?

B: Burundi.

A: Burundi? I _____ never _____ of it. Where is it?
                   (6)   (7)

B: It's a small country in Central Africa.

A: Do you have a map? Can you show me where it is?

B: Let's go on the Internet. We can do a search.

A: Did you learn to use a computer in your country?

B: No. When I came here, a volunteer at my church gave me her old

computer. Before, I didn't know anything about computers. I've

_____ a lot about computers since I came here.
    (8)

A: Oh, now I see Burundi. It's very small. It's near Congo.

B: Yes, it is.

A: Why did you come to the U.S.?

B: My country _____ _____ political problems for many years.
                   (9)   (10)
It wasn't safe to live there. My family left in 1995.

A: So you _____ _____ here since 1995?
              (11)   (12)

B: No. First we lived in a refugee camp in Zambia.

A: I _____ never _____ of Zambia either.
         (13)   (14)
Can we search for it on the Internet?

B: Here it is.

A: You speak English very well. Is English the language of Burundi?

B: No. Kirundi is the official language. Also French. I _____
                                                              (15)

_____ French since I was a small child. Where are you from?
    (16)

(continued)

The Present Perfect; The Present Perfect Continuous **291**

A: I'm from North Dakota.

B: I _____ never _____ of North Dakota. Is it in the U.S.?
(17)   (18)

A: Yes, it is. Let's search for an American map on the Internet. Here it is.

Winter in North Dakota is very cold. It's cold here too.

B: I don't know how people live in a cold climate. I _____
(19)

never _____ in a cold climate before. I _____
(20)   (21)

always _____ near the Equator.
(22)

A: Don't worry. You'll be OK. You just need warm clothes for the winter.

B: I have class now. I've got to go.

A: I _____ _____ so much about your country in such a
(23)   (24)

short time.

B: It's easy to learn things fast using a computer and a search engine.

9.8 The Present Perfect vs. the Simple Past

Do not confuse the present perfect with the simple past.

EXAMPLES	EXPLANATION
Compare: a. Sergey Brin **came** to the U.S. in 1979. b. Sergey Brin **has been** in the U.S. since 1979. a. Brin and Page **started** Google in 1998. b. Google **has been** popular since 1998.	Sentences (a) show a single action in the past. This action does not continue. Sentences (b) show the continuation of an action or state from the past to the present.
a. When **did** Brin **come** to the U.S.? b. How long **has** Brin **been** in the U.S.?	Question (a) with *when* uses the simple past tense. Question (b) with *how long* uses the present perfect tense.

EXERCISE 14 **Fill in the blanks with the simple past or the present perfect of the verb in parentheses ( ).**

🔊
CD 3, TR 14

A: Do you like to surf the Internet?

B: Of course, I do. I 've had _____ my Internet connection since 1999,
(example: have)

and I love it. A couple of months ago, I _____ a new computer
(1 buy)

with lots of memory and speed. And last month I _____
(2 change)

to a better service provider. Now I can surf much faster.

A: What kind of things do you search for?

B: Lots of things. I _____ to learn about the stock market, and with
   (3 always/want)
   the Web, I can start to learn. Last week I _____ my first investment
   (4 make)
   in the stock market.

A: Do you ever buy products online?

B: Sometimes I do. Last month, I _____ a great Web site where
   (5 find)
   I can download music for 99¢. So far
   I _____ about a hundred songs,
   (6 download)
   and I _____ several CDs. My old
   (7 make)
   computer _____ a CD burner,
   (8 not/have)
   so I'm very happy with my new one.

A: _____ your old computer?
   (9 you/sell)

B: No. It was about eight years old. I just _____ the hard drive
   (10 remove)
   and _____ the computer on top of the garbage dumpster.
   (11 leave)
   When I _____ by a few hours later, it was gone.
   (12 pass)
   Someone _____ it.
   (13 take)

A: Was your new computer expensive?

B: Yes, but I _____ a great deal online.
   (14 get)

A: I _____ my computer for three years, and it seems so old by
   (15 have)
   comparison to today's computers. But it's too expensive to buy a new
   one every year.

B: There's a joke about computers: When is a computer old?

A: I don't know. When?

B: As soon as you get it out of the box!

9.9 The Present Perfect Continuous—An Overview

We use the present perfect continuous for a continuous action that started in the past and continues to the present.

EXAMPLES	EXPLANATION
I **have been using** the Internet since 9 A.M. I **have been surfing** the Web for 2 hours. We **have been learning** a lot about computers.	A continuous action started in the past and continues to the present.

Genealogy

Before You Read

1. Do you think it's important to know your family's history? Why or why not?

2. What would you like to know about your ancestors?

CD 3, TR 15

Read the following magazine article. Pay special attention to the present perfect and the present perfect continuous tenses.

In the last 30 years, genealogy **has become** one of America's most popular hobbies. If you type *genealogy* in a search engine, you can find about 90 million hits. If you type *family history*, you will get about 50 million hits. The percentage of the U.S. population interested in family history **has been increasing** steadily. This increase probably has to do with the ease of searching on the Internet.

The number of genealogy Web sites **has been growing** accordingly as people ask themselves: Where does my family come from? How long **has** my family **been** in the U.S.? Why did they come here? How did they come here? What kind of people were they?

Genealogy is a lifelong hobby for many. The average family historian **has been doing** genealogy for 14 years, according to a 2001 study. Most family historians are over 40. Cyndi Howells, from Washington State, quit her job in 1992 and **has been working** on her family history ever since. She **has created** a Web site called Cyndi's List to help others with their search. Her Web site has over 260,000 resources. Since its start in 1992, her Web site **has had** millions of visitors. Every day it gets about 15,000 visitors. Over the years, she **has added** many new links and **deleted** old ones.

Although the Internet **has made** research easier for amateur genealogists, it is only the beginning for serious family historians. Researchers still need to go to courthouses and libraries to find public records, such as land deeds,[4] obituaries,[5] wedding notices, and tax records. Another good source of information is the U.S. Census. Early census records are not complete, but since the mid-1800s, the U.S. Census **has been keeping** detailed records of family members, their ages, occupations, and places of birth.

Are you interested in knowing more about your ancestors and their stories, their country or countries, and how you fit into the history of your family? Maybe genealogy is a good hobby for you.

9.10 The Present Perfect Continuous—Forms

Subject	*have/has*	*been*	Present Participle	Complement
I	have	been	using	the Internet for two hours.
We	have	been	reading	about search engines.
You	have	been	studying	computers.
They	have	been	living	in California.
He	has	been	writing	since 1:00 P.M.
She	has	been	surfing	the Internet all day.
It	has	been	raining	all day.

Language Note: To form the negative, put *not* between *have* or *has* and *been*.
You **have *not* been** listening.
She **has*n't* been** working hard.

[4]A *land deed* is a document that shows who the owner of the land is.
[5]*Obituaries* are death notices posted in the newspaper.

(continued)

Compare affirmative statements and questions.

Wh- Word	have/ has	Subject	have/ has	been + Verb -ing	Complement	Short Answer
		Cyndi	has	been working	on her family history.	
	Has	she		been working	on her Web site?	Yes, she has.
How long	has	she		been working	on her Web site?	Since 1992.

Compare negative statements and questions.

Wh- Word	haven't/ hasn't	Subject	haven't/ hasn't	been + Verb -ing	Complement
		They	haven't	been using	the public library.
Why	haven't	they		been using	the public library?

EXERCISE 15 Fill in the blanks with the present perfect continuous form of the verb in parentheses ( ).

EXAMPLE How long _____has_____ Cyndi _____been managing_____ a
(example: manage)

genealogy Web site?

1. Interest in genealogy _____.
(grow)

2. Cyndi _____ on her family history since 1992.
(work)

3. Cyndi _____ all over the U.S. to genealogy groups.
(lecture)

4. The number of genealogy Web sites _____.
(increase)

5. How long _____ the U.S. Census

_____ records?
(keep)

6. _____ you _____ on a family tree for
(work)

your family?

7. People _____ the Internet to do family research
(use)

since the 1990s.

8. My family _____ in the U.S. for many generations.
(not/live)

9.11 The Present Perfect Continuous—Use

We use the present perfect continuous tense to show that an action or state started in the past and continues to the present.

Past ◄——————————————————————— Now ------------------→ Future

He **has been living** in the U.S. since 1979.

EXAMPLES	EXPLANATION
Cyndi **has been working** on her family tree since 1992. Sergey Brin **has been living** in the U.S. for more than 30 years.	We use *for* and *since* to show the time spent on an activity from past to present.
He **has been living** in the U.S. since 1979. OR He **has lived** in the U.S. since 1979.	With some verbs (*live, work, study, teach,* and *wear*), we can use either the present perfect or the present perfect continuous with actions that began in the past and continue to the present. The meaning is the same.
My father *is working* on the family tree right now. He **has been working** on it since 9 A.M.	If the action is still happening, use the present perfect continuous, not the present perfect.
Google **has become** one of the most popular search engines. I **have had** my computer for three months.	We do not use the continuous form with nonaction verbs. See below for a list of nonaction verbs.
I **have** always **loved** computers. My grandmother **has** never **used** a computer.	Do not use the continuous form with *always* and *never*.

Action: I **have been thinking** *about* doing a family tree.
Nonaction: I **have** always **thought** *that* genealogy is an interesting hobby.
	Think can be an action or nonaction verb, depending on its meaning.
	    Think about = action verb
	    Think that = nonaction verb

Nonaction: Some people **have had** a lot of success in locating information. **Action:** We **have been having** a hard time locating information about our ancestors.	*Have* is usually a nonaction verb. However, *have* is an action verb in these expressions: *have experience, have a hard time, have a good time, have difficulty,* and *have trouble.*

Nonaction verbs:

like	know	see
love	believe	seem
hate	think (that)	cost
want	care (about)	own
need	understand	become
prefer	remember	have (for possession)

EXERCISE 16   **ABOUT YOU**   Write true statements using the present perfect continuous with the words given and *for* or *since*. Share your sentences with the class.

EXAMPLE   work   <u>My brother has been working as a waiter for six years.</u>

1. study English _____

2. work _____

3. live _____

4. use _____

5. study _____

EXERCISE 17   **ABOUT YOU**   Read aloud each of the following present tense questions. Another student will answer. If the answer is *yes*, add a present perfect continuous question with *"How long have you . . . ?"*

EXAMPLE   Do you play a musical instrument?

A: Do you play a musical instrument?
B: Yes. I play the piano.
A: How long have you been playing the piano?
B: I've been playing the piano since I was a child.

1. Do you drive?

2. Do you work?

3. Do you use the Internet?

4. Do you wear glasses?

5. Do you play a musical instrument?

EXERCISE 18   Ask the teacher questions with *"How long . . . ?"* and the present perfect continuous form of the verb given. The teacher will answer your questions.

EXAMPLE   speak English

A: How long have you been speaking English?
B: I've been speaking English all[6] my life.

1. teach English

2. work at this school

3. live in this city

4. use this book

5. live at your present address

---

[6]We do not use the preposition *for* before *all*.

EXERCISE 19 **Fill in the blanks in the following conversations. Answers may vary.**

EXAMPLE **A:** Do you wear glasses?

B: Yes, I ____do____.

A: How long ____have____ you ____been wearing____ glasses?

B: I _'ve been wearing_ glasses since I ____was____ in high school.

1. **A:** Are you working on your family history?

   B: Yes, I am.

   A: How long _____ you _____ on your family history?

   B: I _____ on it for about ten years.

2. **A:** Is your sister surfing the Internet?

   B: Yes, she _____.

   A: How long _____ she _____ surfing the Internet?

   B: Since she woke up this morning!

3. **A:** Does your father live in the U.S.?

   B: Yes, he _____.

   A: How long _____ he been _____ in the U.S.?

   B: He _____ in the U.S. since he _____ 25 years old.

4. **A:** Are you studying for the test now?

   B: Yes, I _____.

   A: How long _____ for the test?

   B: For _____.

5. **A:** Is your teacher teaching you the present perfect lesson?

   B: Yes, he _____.

   A: _____ long _____ you this lesson?

   B: Since _____.

(continued)

The Present Perfect; The Present Perfect Continuous   **299**

6. A: Are the students using the computers now?

   B: Yes, _____.

   A: How long _____ them?

   B: _____ they started to write their compositions.

7. A: _____ you using the Internet?

   B: Yes, I _____.

   A: How _____?

   B: _____ for two hours.

8. A: _____ your grandparents live in the U.S.?

   B: Yes, they _____.

   A: How _____ in the U.S.?

   B: Since they _____ born.

9. A: Is she studying her family history?

   B: Yes, she _____.

   A: How long _____?

   B: Since she _____.

E-Books

Before You Read

1. Do you read a lot? What kind of books do you like to read?

2. Have you ever shopped for books on the Internet?

CD 3, TR 16

Read the following conversation. Pay special attention to the present perfect tense.

A: Do you have any hobbies?

B: Yes. I love to read.

A: How many books **have** you **read** this year?

B: **I've read** about 20 books so far this year. Last month I went on vacation for two weeks and I read 10 books while I was at the beach.

A: How did you carry so many books on your vacation? They're heavy.

B: I carried only one: my e-book. **Have** you ever **heard** of e-books?

A: No, I **haven't**. What's an e-book?

B: It's an electronic device that holds a lot of books. It can hold over 1,500 books.

A: Cool! Is it expensive?

B: The electronic device is a bit expensive. Then you have to pay to download each book. But **I've spent** a lot more money on paper books.

A: How many books **have** you **downloaded**?

B: So far **I've downloaded** about 100 books.

A: Can you get every book in electronic form?

B: One popular Web site **has made** about 250,000 books available so far. But that number is growing all the time.

A: **I've never seen** how you can download a book. Let's go to my computer and you can show me.

B: We don't need a computer. It works like a cell phone. We can download a book wherever we are.

A: Wow!

9.12 The Present Perfect with Repetition from Past to Present

We use the present perfect to talk about the repetition of an action in a time period that started in the past and includes the present. There is a probability that this action will occur again.

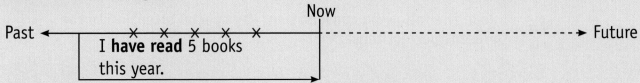

Past ← —— × — × — × — × — × —— Now - - - - - - - - - - - - - - - → Future

I **have read** 5 books this year.

EXAMPLES	EXPLANATION
a. I **have read** 20 books this year. b. He **has downloaded** over 100 books.	a. I may read more books. b. He will probably download more books.
Up to now, one Web site **has made** about 250,000 books available. I **have read** ten chapters in my book up to now.	Adding the words "so far" and "up to now" indicate that we are counting up to the present and that more is expected.
How much money **have** you **spent** on books this year? I've **spent** about $500 on books this year. How many books **have** you **bought** from a bookstore this year? I **haven't bought** any books from a bookstore **at all** this year.	We can ask a question about repetition with *how much* and *how many*. To indicate zero times, we use a negative verb + *at all*. There is a probability that this action may still happen.
Compare: a. Google **had** 10,000 searches a day in 1998. b. Google **has had** billions of searches since 1998. a. Cyndi's List **appeared** for the first time in 1996. b. Many new genealogy Web sites **have appeared** in the last fifteen years.	a. We use the simple past with a time period that is finished or closed: *1998, 50 years ago, last week,* etc. b. We use the present perfect in a time period that is open. There is a probability of more repetition.

Language Note: Do not use the continuous form for repetition.
    Right: I **have downloaded** six books this year.
    Wrong: I *have been downloading* six books this year.

EXERCISE 20 **ABOUT YOU** Ask a *yes/no* question with *so far* or *up to now* and the words given. Another student will answer.

EXAMPLE   you/come to every class

A: Have you come to every class so far?
B: Yes, I have.

OR

B: No, I haven't. I've missed three classes.

1. we / have any tests
2. this lesson / be difficult
3. the teacher / give a lot of homework
4. you / understand all the explanations
5. you / have any questions about this lesson

EXERCISE 21 **ABOUT YOU** Ask a question with *"How many . . . ?"* and the words given. Talk about this month. Another student will answer.

EXAMPLE   times / go to the post office

A: How many times have you gone to the post office this month?
B: I've gone to the post office once this month.

OR

B: I haven't gone to the post office at all this month.

1. letters / write	5. books / buy
2. times / eat in a restaurant	6. times / go to the movies
3. times / get paid	7. movies / rent
4. international calls / make	8. times / cook

EXERCISE 22 **ABOUT YOU** Write four questions to ask another student or your teacher about repetition from the past to the present. Use *how much* or *how many*. The other person will answer.

EXAMPLE   How many cities have you lived in?

How many English courses have you taken at this school?

1. _____
2. _____
3. _____
4. _____

9.13 The Simple Past vs. the Present Perfect with Repetition

We use the present perfect with repetition in a present time period. There is an expectation of more repetition. We use the simple past with repetition in a past time period. There is no possibility of any more repetition during that period.

EXAMPLES	EXPLANATION
How many hits **has** your Web site **had** today? It **has had** over 100 hits today. How many times **have** you **been** absent this semester? I'**ve been** absent twice so far.	To show that there is an expectation of more repetition, use the present perfect. In the examples on the left, *today* and *this semester* are not finished. *So far* indicates that the number given may not be final.
Last month my Web site **had** 5,000 hits. How many times **were** you absent last semester?	The number of occurrences cannot increase in a past time frame, such as *yesterday, last week, last month, last semester,* etc. Use the simple past tense.
Brin and Page **have added** new features to Google over the years. A popular Web site **has made** thousands of e-books available.	Brin and Page are still alive. They can (and probably will) add new features to Google in the years to come. This Web site continues to make e-books available.
Before she died, my grandmother **added** many details to our family tree. My grandmother **loved** to read.	Grandmother died. Therefore, all her actions are final. Nothing can be added to them.
Compare: a. I **have checked** my e-mail twice today. b. I **checked** my e-mail twice today. a. I **have downloaded** two books this month. b. I **downloaded** two books this month.	With a present time expression (such as *today, this week, this month,* etc.), you may use either the present perfect or the simple past. In sentences (a), the number may not be final. In sentences (b), the number seems final.
Compare: a. In the U.S., I **have had** two jobs. b. In my native country, I **had** five jobs. a. In the U.S., I **have lived** in three apartments so far. b. In my native country, I **lived** in two apartments.	a. To talk about your experiences in this phase of your life, you can use the present perfect tense if there is an expectation for more. b. To talk about a closed phase of your life, use the simple past tense. For example, if you do not plan to live in your native country again, use the simple past tense to talk about your experiences there.

EXERCISE 23   **ABOUT YOU**   Fill in the blanks with the simple past or the present perfect to ask a question. A student from another country will answer.

EXAMPLES   How many schools ___have you attended___ in the U.S.?
I've attended two schools in the U.S.

How many schools ___did you attend___ in your country?
I attended only one school in my country.

1. How many apartments _____ back home?

2. How many apartments _____ here?

3. How many schools _____ in your country?

4. How many schools _____ in the U.S.?

5. How many jobs _____ in the U.S.?

6. How many jobs _____ in your country?

9.14 The Present Perfect with Indefinite Past Time

We use the present perfect to refer to an action that occurred at an indefinite time in the past that still has importance to the present situation. Words that show indefinite time are: *ever, yet,* and *already.*

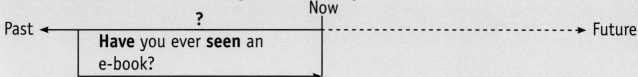

EXAMPLES	EXPLANATION
Have you **ever downloaded** a book? 　No, I **haven't.** **Have** you **ever** "Googled" your own name? 　Yes, I **have.**	A question with *ever* asks about any time between the past and the present. Put *ever* between the subject and the main verb.
Have you **finished** your book **yet**? 　No, not **yet.** **Have** Larry and Sergey **become** billionaires **yet**? 　Yes, they have. **Have** you **read** the story about genealogy **yet**? 　Yes, I **already** have.	*Yet* and *already* refer to an indefinite time in the near past. There is an expectation that an activity took place a short time ago.
The computer **has made** it possible to do many new things. E-books **have changed** the way we read books. Cyndi Howells **has created** a very useful Web site for family historians.	We can use the present perfect to talk about the past without any reference to time. The time is not important, not known, or is imprecise. Using the present perfect, rather than the simple past, shows that the past is relevant to a present situation.

EXERCISE 24 **ABOUT YOU** Answer the following questions with: *Yes, I have;* *No, I haven't;* or *No, I never have.*

EXAMPLE Have you ever studied programming? No, I never have.

1. Have you ever "Googled" your own name?
2. Have you ever researched your family history?
3. Have you ever made a family tree?
4. Have you ever used the Web to look for a person you haven't seen in a long time?
5. Have you ever added hardware to your computer?
6. Have you ever downloaded music from the Internet?
7. Have you ever used a search engine in your native language?
8. Have you ever sent photos by e-mail?
9. Have you ever received a photo by e-mail?
10. Have you ever bought something online?
11. Have you ever built a computer?

EXERCISE 25 **ABOUT YOU** Answer the questions.

EXAMPLE Have we had a test on the present perfect yet? No, not yet.

1. Have you eaten lunch yet?
2. Have we finished Lesson 8 yet?
3. Have you done today's homework yet?
4. Have we written any compositions yet?
5. Have you learned the names of all the other students yet?
6. Have you visited the teacher's office yet?
7. Have we done Exercise 22 yet?
8. Have you learned the present perfect yet?
9. Have you learned all the past participles yet?

9.15 Answering a Present Perfect Question

We can answer a present perfect question with the simple past tense when a specific time is introduced in the answer. If a specific time is not known or necessary, we answer with the present perfect.

EXAMPLES	EXPLANATION
Have you ever **used** Google? **Answer A:** Yes. I**'ve used** Google many times. **Answer B:** Yes. I **used** Google a few hours ago.	Answer A, with *many times*, shows repetition at an indefinite time. Answer B, with *a few hours ago*, shows a specific time in the past.
Have you ever **heard** of Larry Page? **Answer A:** No. I**'ve never** heard of him. **Answer B:** Yes. We **read** about him yesterday.	Answer A, with *never*, shows continuation from past to present. Answer B, with *yesterday*, shows a specific time in the past.
Have you **done** your homework yet? **Answer A:** Yes. I**'ve done** it already. **Answer B:** Yes. I **did** it this morning.	Answer A, with *already*, is indefinite. Answer B, with *this morning*, shows a specific time.
Have Brin and Page **become** rich? **Answer A:** Yes, they **have.** **Answer B:** Yes. They **became** rich before they were 30 years old.	Answer A shows no time reference. Answer B, with *before they were 30 years old*, refers to a specific time.

EXERCISE 26   **ABOUT YOU** Ask a question with *"Have you ever . . . ?"* and the present perfect tense of the verb in parentheses ( ). Another student will answer. To answer with a specific time, use the past tense. To answer with a frequency response, use the present perfect tense. You may work with a partner.

EXAMPLES   (go) to the zoo
A: Have you ever gone to the zoo?
B: Yes. I've gone there many times.

(go) to Disneyland

A: Have you ever gone to Disneyland?
B: Yes. I went there last summer.

1. (work) in a factory

2. (lose) a glove

3. (see) an e-book

4. (fall) out of bed

5. (make) a mistake in English grammar

6. (tell) a lie

7. (eat) raw[7] fish

8. (study) calculus

9. (meet) a famous person

10. (go) to an art museum

11. (download) a book

12. (break) a window

13. (buy) a book online

(continued)

[7]*Raw* means not cooked.

14. (download) music

15. (go) to Las Vegas

16. (travel) by ship

17. (be) in love

18. (write) a poem

19. (send) a text message

EXERCISE 27 **ABOUT YOU** Write five questions with *ever* to ask your teacher. Your teacher will answer.

EXAMPLES Have you ever gotten a parking ticket?

Have you ever visited Poland?

1. _____

2. _____

3. _____

4. _____

5. _____

EXERCISE 28 **ABOUT YOU** Ask a student from another country questions using the words given. The other student will answer.

EXAMPLE your country / have a woman president

A: Has your country ever had a woman president?
B: Yes, it has. We had a woman president from 1975 to 1979.

1. your country / have a civil war

2. your country's leader / visit the U.S.

3. an American president / visit your country

4. your country / have a woman president

5. you / go back to visit your country

6. there / be an earthquake in your hometown

EXERCISE 29 **ABOUT YOU** Ask a student who has recently arrived in this country if he or she has done these things yet. The other student will answer.

EXAMPLE buy a car

A: Have you bought a car yet?
B: Yes, I have. OR No, I haven't. OR I bought a car last month.

1. find a doctor

2. make any new friends

3. open a bank account

4. save any money

5. think about your future

6. write to your family

7. get a credit card

8. buy a computer

9. get a telephone

10. get a Social Security card

EXERCISE **30** Fill in the blanks with the correct tense of the verb in parentheses ( ).
Also fill in other missing words.

CD 3, TR 17

A: Your Spanish is a little different from my Spanish. Where are you from?

B: I'm from Guatemala.

A: How ___long have you been___ here?
                (example: you/be)

B: I _____ here for about six months. Where are you from?
     (1 only/be)

A: Miami. My family comes from Cuba. They

    _____ Cuba in 1962, after the revolution.
    (2 leave)

    I _____ born in the U.S. I'm starting
    (3 be)

to become interested in my family's history.

I _____ several magazine articles about
   (4 read)

genealogy so far. It's fascinating. Are you

interested in your family's history?

B: Of course I am. I _____ interested in it _____ a long time.
            (5 be)   *(6)*

    I _____ on a family tree for many years.
    (7 work)

A: When _____?
     (8 you/start)

B: I _____ when I _____ 16 years old. Over the years,
    (9 start)   *(10 be)*

    I _____ a lot of interesting information about my family.
    (11 find)

Some of my ancestors were Mayans and some were from Spain and

France. In fact, my great-great grandfather was a Spanish prince.

A: How _____ all that information?
     (12 you/find)

B: I _____ the Internet a lot. I _____ to many
    (13 use)   *(14 also/go)*

libraries to get more information.

A: _____ to Spain or France to look at records there?
   (15 you/ever/go)

B: Last summer I _____ to Spain, and I _____ a lot of
          (16 go)   *(17 find)*

information while I was there.

A: How many ancestors _____ so far?
             (18 you/find)

B: So _____ I _____ about 50, but I'm still looking.
   (19)   *(20 find)*

(continued)

A: How can I get started?

B: There's a great Web site called Cyndi's List. I'll give you the Web address, and you can get started there.

Summary of Lesson 9

1. Compare the present perfect and the simple past.

PRESENT PERFECT	SIMPLE PAST
The action of the sentence began in the past and includes the present: now past ◄———— ■ ┄┄┄┄┄► future	The action of the sentence is completely past: now past ◄—— ■ ┤┄┄┄┄► future
My father **has been** in the U.S. since 2002.	My father **came** to the U.S. in 2002.
My father **has had** his job in the U.S. for many years.	My father **was** in Canada for two years before he came to the U.S.
How long **have** you been interested in genealogy?	When **did** you **start** your family tree?
I**'ve** always **wanted** to learn more about my family's history.	When I was a child, I always **wanted** to spend time with my grandparents.

PRESENT PERFECT	SIMPLE PAST
Repetition from past to present: now past ◄—×××× ┤┄┄┄┄► future	Repetition in a past time period: now past ◄—— ×× ┤┄┄┄► future
We **have had** four tests so far.	We **had** two tests last semester.
She **has used** the Internet three times today.	She **used** the Internet three times yesterday.

PRESENT PERFECT	SIMPLE PAST
The action took place at an indefinite time between the past and the present: now past ◄—— ? ┤┄┄┄► future	The action took place at a definite time in the past: now past ◄———— × ┤┄┄┄► future
Have you ever **made** a family tree?	**Did** you **make** a family tree last month?
I**'ve done** the homework already.	I **did** the homework last night.
Have you **visited** the art museum yet?	**Did** you **visit** the art museum last month?

2. Compare the present perfect and the present perfect continuous.

PRESENT PERFECT—USE WITH:	PRESENT PERFECT CONTINUOUS—USE WITH:
A continuous action (nonaction verbs): **I have had** my car for five years.	A continuous action (action verbs): **I've been driving** a car for 20 years.
A repeated action: Cyndi's Web site **has won** several awards.	A nonstop action: The U.S. Census **has been keeping** records since the 1880s.
Question with *how many*: How many times **have** you **gone** to New York?	Question with *how long*: How long **has** he **been living** in New York?
An action that is at an indefinite time, completely in the past: Cyndi **has created** a Web site.	An action that started in the past and is still happening: Cyndi **has been working** on her family history since 1992.

Editing Advice

1. Don't confuse the *-ing* form and the past participle.

> *taking*
> She has been ~~taken~~ a test for two hours.

> *given*
> She has ~~giving~~ him a present.

2. Use the present perfect, not the simple present, to describe an action or state that started in the past and continues to the present.

> *had*
> He hasˆ a car for two years.

> *have*   *ed*
> How long ~~do~~ you workˆ in a factory?

3. Use *for*, not *since*, with the amount of time.

> *for*
> I've been studying English ~~since~~ three months.

4. Use the simple past, not the present perfect, with a specific past time.

> *came*
> He ~~has come~~ to the U.S. five months ago.

> *did*
> When ~~have~~ you come to the U.S.?

5. Use the simple past, not the present perfect, in a *since* clause.

came

He has learned a lot of English since he ~~has come~~ to the U.S.

6. Use the correct word order.

never seen

He has ~~seen never~~ a French movie.

ever gone

Have you ~~gone ever~~ to France?

7. Use the correct word order in questions.

have you

How long ~~you have~~ been a teacher?

8. Use *yet* for negative statements; use *already* for affirmative statements.

yet

I haven't eaten dinner ~~already~~.

9. Don't forget the verb *have* in the present perfect (continuous).

have

I been living in New York for two years.

10. Don't forget the *-ed* of the past participle.

ed

He's listen to that CD many times.

11. Use the present perfect, not the continuous form, with *always*, *never*, *yet*, *already*, *ever*, and *how many*.

gone

How many times have you ~~been going~~ to Paris?

visited

I've never ~~been visiting~~ Paris.

12. Don't use *time* after *how long*.

How long ~~time~~ have you had your job?

Editing Quiz

Some of the shaded words and phrases have mistakes. Find the mistakes and correct them. If the shaded words are correct, write _C_.

"How many changes ~~you have~~ *have you* made since you came *C* to the U.S.?" For our
(example)   (example)

journal, our teacher asked us to answer this question. I have come to the
(1)

U.S. two and a half years ago. Things have changing a lot for me since
(2)

I've come to the U.S. Here's a list of some of the changes:
(3)

1. Since the past two years I am studying English. I knew a little English
   (4)   (5)   (6)

   before I came here, but my English has improve a lot.
   (7)   (8)

2. Now I have a driver's permit and I'm learning how to drive. I haven't took
   (9)

   the driver's test yet because I'm not ready. I haven't practiced enough
   (10)

   already.
   (11)

3. I've been eaten a lot of different foods like hamburgers and pizza.
   (12)

   I never ate those in my country. Unfortunately, I been gaining weight.
   (13)   (14)

4. I started to work in a factory three months ago. Since I have started
   (15)   (16)   (17)

   my job, I haven't have much time for fun.
   (18)

5. I've gone to several museums in this city. But I've taken never a trip to
   (19)   (20)

   another American city. I'd like to visit New York, but I haven't saved
   (21)

   enough money yet.
   (22)

6. I've been living in three apartments so far. In my country, I lived in
   (23)   (24)

   a house with my family.

7. I've answered the following questions about a thousand times so far:
   (25)

   "Where do you come from?" and "How long time you have been in
   (26)   (27)

   the U.S.?" I'm getting tired of always answering the same question.

Lesson 9 Test/Review

PART **1** Fill in the blanks with the simple past, the present perfect, or the present perfect continuous form by using the words in parentheses ( ). In some cases, more than one answer is possible.

Conversation 1

A: ___Have___ you ever ___studied___ computer programming?
  (example: study)

B: Yes. I _____ it in college. And I _____ as a programmer
  (1 study)   *(2 work)*
  for five years. But my job is boring.

A: _____ you ever _____ about changing jobs?
  (3 think)

B: Yes. Since I _____ a child, I _____ to be an
  (4 be)   *(5 always/want)*
  actor. When I was in college, I _____ in a few plays, but
  (6 be)
  since I _____, I _____ time to act.
  (7 graduate)   *(8 not/have)*

Conversation 2

A: How long _____ in the U.S.?
  (1 you/be)

B: For about two years.

A: _____ a lot since you _____ to the U.S.?
  (2 your life/change)   *(3 come)*

B: Oh, yes. Before I _____ here, I _____ with my family.
  (4 come)   *(5 live)*
  Since I came here, I _____ alone.
  (6 live)

A: _____ in the same apartment in this city?
  (7 always/live)

B: No. I _____ three times so far. And I plan to move again at
  (8 move)
  the end of the year.

A: Do you plan to have a roommate?

B: Yes, but I _____ one yet.
  (9 not/find)

PART 2 **Fill in the blanks with the simple present, the simple past, the present perfect, or the present perfect continuous form of the verb in parentheses ( ). In some cases, more than one answer is possible.**

Paragraph 1

I _____ the Internet every day. I _____ it for many years.
(1 use)   (2 use)

I _____ to use it when I _____ interested in genealogy.
(3 start)   (4 become)

I _____ on my family tree for three years. Last month,
(5 work)

I _____ information about my father's ancestors. My grandfather
(6 find)

_____ with us now and likes to tell us about his past. He _____
(7 live)   (8 be)

born in Italy, but he _____ here when he was very young, so he
(9 come)

_____ here most of his life. He doesn't remember much about Italy.
(10 live)

I _____ any information about my mother's ancestors yet.
(11 not/find)

Paragraph 2

I _____ to the U.S. when a war _____ out in my country.
(1 come)   (2 break)

I _____ in the U.S. for five years. At first, everything
(3 live)

_____ very hard for me. I _____ any English when
(4 be)   (5 not/know)

I _____. But I _____ English for the past five years,
(6 arrive)   (7 study)

and now I _____ it pretty well. I _____ my college
(8 speak)   (9 not/start)

education yet, but I plan to next semester.

Expansion

Activities

1 **Form a group of between four and six students. Find out who in your group has done each of these things. Write that person's name in the blank.**

a. _____ has made a family tree.

b. _____ has found a good job.

c. _____ has been on a ship.

d. _____ has never eaten Mexican food.

e. _____ hasn't done today's homework yet.

f. _____ has never seen a French movie.

g. _____ has taken a trip to Canada.

h. _____ has acted in a play.

i. _____ has gone swimming in the Pacific Ocean.

j. _____ has flown in a helicopter.

k. _____ has served in the military.

l. _____ has worked in a hotel.

m. _____ has never studied chemistry.

n. _____ has taken the TOEFL[8] test.

o. _____ has just gotten a "green card."

p. _____ has downloaded music from the Internet.

2 **Draw your family tree for the past three generations, if you can. Form a small group and tell the others in your group a little about your family.**

Talk

About It

1 **Why do you think so many people are interested in genealogy? What is valuable about finding your family's history?**

2 **What are the advantages of an e-book over a paper book? What are the disadvantages?**

3 **Do you think people spend too much time surfing the Internet?**

[8]The *TOEFL*™ is the Test of English as a Foreign Language. Many U.S. colleges and universities require foreign students to take this test.

Write
About It

❶ Write about new technology that you've started using recently. How has that made your life different?

❷ Write a composition about one of the following:

How your life has changed since (*choose one*):

- **a.** you came to the U.S.
- **b.** you got married
- **c.** you had a baby
- **d.** you graduated from high school
- **e.** you started to study here

Changes in My Life

My life has changed a lot since I started college. When I was in high school, I didn't have many responsibilities. Since I started college, I've had to work and study at the same time. When I was in high school, I used to hang out with my friends. Now that I'm in college, I haven't had much time for my friends . . .

 For more practice using grammar in context, please visit our Web site.

Grammar
Gerunds

Infinitives

Context
Finding a Job

10.1 Gerunds—An Overview

To form a gerund, we use the *-ing* form of a verb (*finding, learning, eating, running*). A *gerund phrase* is a gerund + a noun phrase (*finding a job, learning English*). A gerund (phrase) can appear in several positions in a sentence.

EXAMPLES	EXPLANATION
a. **Finding** a job is hard. b. I don't enjoy **talking** about myself. c. I thought about **changing** my career. d. I got help **by talking** with my counselor. e. I like to **go shopping**.	a. The gerund is the subject. b. The gerund is the object. c. The gerund is the object of the preposition. d. The gerund is part of an adverbial phrase. e. The gerund is in many expressions with *go*.
Not having a job is frustrating. You can impress the boss by **not being** late.	We can put *not* in front of a gerund to make it negative.

Finding a Job

Before You Read

1. Have you ever had a job interview in this city?

2. What is your profession or job? What profession or job do you plan to have in the future?

CD 3, TR 18

Read the following Web article. Pay special attention to gerunds.

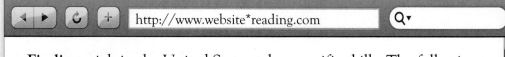
http://www.website*reading.com

Did You Know?

According to the Bureau of Labor Statistics, computer scientists and dental hygienists are among the fastest growing occupations. Between 2006 and 2016, these careers are expected to grow 37% and 30%, respectively.

    Finding a job in the United States takes specific skills. The following advice will help you find a job.

- Write a good résumé. Describe your accomplishments.[1] Avoid **including** unnecessary information. Your résumé should be one page, if possible.
- Find out about available jobs. One way is by **looking** in the newspaper or on the Internet. Another way is by **networking**. **Networking** means **exchanging** information with anyone you know—family, friends, neighbors, classmates, former coworkers, professional groups—who might know of a job. These people might also be able to give you insider information about a company, such as who is in charge and what it is like to work at their company. According to an article in

[1]*Accomplishments* are the unusual good things you have done, such as awards you have won or projects you have successfully managed.

the *Wall Street Journal*, 94 percent of people who succeed in **finding** a job say that **networking** was a big help.

- Practice the interview. The more prepared you are, the more relaxed you will feel. If you are worried about **saying** or **doing** the wrong thing, practice will help.
- Learn something about the company. You can find information by **going** to the company's Web site. **Getting** information takes time, but it pays off.

You can get help in these skills—**writing** a résumé, **networking**, **preparing** for an interview, **researching** a company—by **seeing** a career counselor. Most high schools and colleges have one who can help you get started.

Finding a job is one of the most difficult jobs. Some people send out hundreds of résumés and go on dozens of interviews before **finding** a job. And it isn't something you do just once or twice in your lifetime. For most Americans, **changing** jobs many times in a lifetime is not uncommon.

Tips For Getting a Job

Preparation:

1. Learn about the organization and have a specific job or jobs in mind.
2. Review your résumé.
3. Practice an interview with a friend or relative.
4. Arrive at least 15 minutes before the scheduled time of your interview.

Personal appearance:

1. Be well-groomed[2] and dress appropriately.
2. Do not chew gum.

The interview:

1. Relax and answer each question concisely.
2. Use good manners. Shake hands and smile when you meet someone.
3. Be enthusiastic. Tell the interviewer why you are a good candidate for the job.
4. Ask questions about the position and the organization.
5. Thank the interviewer when you leave and in writing as a follow-up.

Information to bring to an interview:

1. Social Security card.
2. Government-issued identification (driver's license).
3. Résumé or application. Include information about your education, training, and previous employment.
4. References. Employers typically require three references. Get permission before using anyone as a reference. Make sure that each will give you a good reference. Avoid using relatives as references.

[2]When you are *well-groomed*, your appearance is neat and clean.

10.2 Gerund as Subject

EXAMPLES	EXPLANATION
Gerund Phrase **Finding a good job** takes time. **Writing a résumé** isn't easy. **Not preparing** for an interview could have a bad result.	We can use a gerund or gerund phrase as the subject of the sentence.
Exchanging ideas with friends **is** helpful. **Visiting** company Web sites **takes** time.	A gerund subject takes a singular verb.

EXERCISE 1 The following things are important before a job interview. Make a sentence with each one, using a gerund phrase as the subject.

EXAMPLE get a good night's sleep

Getting a good night's sleep will help you feel rested and alert for

an interview.

1. take a bath or shower

   _____

2. select serious-looking clothes

   _____

3. prepare a résumé

   _____

4. check your résumé carefully

   _____

5. get information about the company

   _____

6. prepare answers to possible questions

   _____

EXERCISE 2 Complete each statement with a gerund (phrase) as the subject.

EXAMPLE _____ *Learning a foreign language* _____ takes a long time.

1. _____ is one of the most difficult jobs.

2. _____ is one of the best ways to find a job.

3. _____ is not permitted in this classroom.

(*continued*)

4. _____ is difficult for a foreign student.

5. _____ takes a long time.

6. _____ is not polite.

EXERCISE **3** **ABOUT YOU** In preparing for an interview, it is good to think about the following questions. Answer these questions. Use a gerund in some of your answers, but do *not* try to use a gerund in every answer. It won't work. Give a lot of thought to your answers and compare them with your classmates' answers.

EXAMPLES What are your strengths?
Working with others; learning quickly; thinking fast in difficult situations

What are your strong and weak subjects in school?
I'm strong in math. I'm weak in history.

1. What are your strengths?

_____

2. What are some of your weaknesses?

_____

3. List your accomplishments and achievements. (They can be achievements in jobs, sports, school, etc.)

_____

4. What are your interests?

_____

5. What are your short-term goals?

_____

6. What are your long-term goals?

_____

7. What are some things you like? Think about personalities, tasks, environments, types of work, and structure.

_____

8. What are some things you dislike? Think about personalities, tasks, environments, types of work, and structure.

_____

9. Why should we hire you?

_____

EXERCISE **4** Write a list of personal behaviors during an interview that would hurt your chances of getting a job. You may work with a partner or in a small group.

EXAMPLES   *Chewing gum during the interview looks bad.*

   Not looking directly at the interviewer can hurt your chances.

1. _____

2. _____

3. _____

4. _____

5. _____

10.3 Gerund after Verb

Some verbs are commonly followed by a gerund (phrase). The gerund (phrase) is the object of the verb.

EXAMPLES	EXPLANATION
Have you **considered going** to a job counselor? Do you **appreciate getting** advice? You can **discuss improving** your skills. You should **practice answering** interview questions. If you don't find a job immediately, **keep trying**.	The verbs below can be followed by a gerund: admit discuss mind put off appreciate dislike miss quit avoid enjoy permit recommend can't help finish postpone risk consider keep practice suggest
I have many hobbies: I like to **go fishing** in the summer. I **go skiing** in the winter. I like indoor sports too. I **go bowling** once a month.	*Go* + gerund is used in many idiomatic expressions. go boating go jogging go bowling go sailing go camping go shopping go dancing go sightseeing go fishing go skating go hiking go skiing go hunting go swimming
a. I don't **mind wearing** a suit to work. b. Don't **put off writing** your résumé. Do it now. c. I have an interview tomorrow morning. I **can't help feeling** nervous.	a. *I mind* means that something bothers me. *I don't mind* means that something is OK with me; it doesn't bother me. b. *Put off* means postpone. c. *Can't help* means to have no control over something.

EXERCISE 5 **ABOUT YOU** Fill in the blanks with an appropriate gerund (or noun) to complete these statements. Share your answers with the class.

EXAMPLE   I don't mind ___shopping for food___, but I do[3] mind ___cooking it___.

1. I usually enjoy _____ during the summer.

2. I don't enjoy _____.

3. I don't mind _____, but I do mind _____.

4. I appreciate _____ from my friends.

5. I need to practice _____ if I want to improve.

6. I often put off _____.

7. I need to keep _____ if I want to be successful.

8. I should avoid _____ if I want to improve my health.

9. I miss _____ from my hometown.

EXERCISE 6 **ABOUT YOU** Make a list of suggestions and recommendations for a tourist who is about to visit your hometown. Read your list to a partner, a small group, or the entire class.

EXAMPLES   I recommend taking warm clothes for the winter.

You should avoid drinking tap water.

1. I recommend:

_____

_____

_____

2. You should avoid:

_____

_____

_____

EXERCISE 7 **ABOUT YOU** Tell if you like or don't like the following activities. Explain why.

EXAMPLES   go hunting
I don't like to go hunting because I don't like to kill animals.

go bowling
I like to go bowling because I think it's a fun activity.

1. go fishing	3. go jogging	5. go hunting
2. go camping	4. go swimming	6. go shopping

---

[3]*Do makes the verb more emphatic. In this sentence, it shows contrast with *don't mind*.

10.4 Gerund after Preposition[4]

A gerund can follow a preposition. It is important to choose the correct preposition after a verb or adjective.

PREPOSITION COMBINATIONS		COMMON COMBINATIONS	EXAMPLES
Verb + Preposition	verb + *about*	care about complain about dream about forget about talk about think about worry about	I **care about doing** well in an interview. My sister **dreams about becoming** a doctor.
	verb + *to*	adjust to look forward to object to	I **look forward to getting** a job and **saving** money.
	verb + *on*	depend on insist on plan on	I **plan on going** to a career counselor.
	verb + *in*	believe in succeed in	My father **succeeded in finding** a good job.
Adjective + Preposition	adjective + *of*	afraid of capable of guilty of proud of tired of	I'm **afraid of losing** my job.
	adjective + *about*	concerned about excited about upset about worried about sad about	He is **upset about not getting** the job.
	adjective + *for*	responsible for famous for grateful to . . . for	Who is **responsible for hiring** in this company?
	adjective + *at*	good at successful at	I'm not very **good at writing** a résumé.
	adjective + *to*	accustomed to used to	I'm not **accustomed to talking** about my strengths.
	adjective + *in*	interested in successful in	Are you **interested in getting** a better job?

(continued)

[4]For a list of verbs and adjectives followed by a preposition, see Appendix H.

Language Notes:

1. *Plan, afraid,* and *proud* can be followed by an infinitive too.
   I plan **on seeing** a counselor. / I plan **to see** a counselor.
   I'm afraid **of losing** my job. / I'm afraid **to lose** my job.
   He's proud **of being** a college graduate. / He's proud **to be** a college graduate.
2. Notice that in some expressions, *to* is a preposition followed by a gerund, not part of an infinitive.

Compare:

   I need **to write** a résumé. (infinitive)
   I'm not accustomed **to writing** a résumé. (*to* + gerund)

EXERCISE 8   **ABOUT YOU** Complete the questions with a gerund (phrase). Then ask another student these questions.

EXAMPLE   Are you lazy about _doing your homework?_ _____

1. Do you ever worry about _____
2. Do you plan on _____
3. Do you ever think about _____
4. When you get tired of _____, what do you do?
5. Are you interested in _____

EXERCISE 9   **ABOUT YOU** Fill in the blanks with a preposition and a gerund (phrase) to make a true statement.

EXAMPLE   I plan _on going back to Haiti soon._ _____

1. I'm afraid _____
2. I'm not afraid _____
3. I'm interested _____
4. I'm not interested _____
5. I want to succeed _____
6. I'm not very good _____
7. I'm accustomed _____
8. I'm not accustomed _____
9. I plan _____
10. I don't care _____

EXERCISE **10**   **ABOUT YOU** Fill in the blanks with a gerund or noun phrase to complete each statement. Compare your experiences in the U.S. with your experiences in your native country. You may share your answers with a small group or with the entire class.

EXAMPLES   In the U.S., I'm afraid of _walking alone at night._

In my native country, I was afraid of _not being able to get a good education._

1. In the U.S., I'm interested in _____
   In my native country, I was interested in _____
   _____

2. In the U.S., I worry about _____
   In my native country, I worried about _____
   _____

3. In the U.S., I dream about _____
   In my native country, I dreamed about _____
   _____

4. In the U.S., I look forward to _____
   In my native country, I looked forward to _____
   _____

5. In the U.S., people often complain about _____
   In my native country, people often complain about _____
   _____

6. In the U.S., families often talk about _____
   In my native country, families often talk about _____
   _____

7. American students are accustomed to _____
   Students in my native country are accustomed to _____
   _____

10.5 Gerund in Adverbial Phrase

EXAMPLES	EXPLANATION
You should practice interview questions **before going** on an interview. I found my job **by looking** in the newspaper. She took the test **without studying**.	We can use a gerund in an adverbial phrase that begins with a preposition: *before, by, after, without,* etc.

EXERCISE 11   **Fill in the blanks to complete the sentences. Practice using gerunds.**

EXAMPLE   The best way to improve your vocabulary is by _____ reading. _____

1. One way to find a job is by _____
2. It is very difficult to find a job without _____
   _____
3. The best way to improve your pronunciation is by _____
   _____
4. The best way to quit a bad habit is by _____
5. One way to find an apartment is by _____
6. I can't speak English without _____
7. It's impossible to get a driver's license without _____
   _____
8. You should read the instructions for a test before _____
   _____

EXERCISE 12   **Fill in the blanks in the conversation below with the gerund form. Where you see two blanks, use a preposition before the gerund. Answers may vary.**

CD 3, TR 19

A: I need to find a job. I've had ten interviews, but so far no job.

B: Have you thought ___about___ ___going___ to a job counselor?
                                (example)   (example)

A: No. Where can I find one?

B: Our school office has a counseling department. I suggest
_____ an appointment with a counselor.
         (1)

A: What can a job counselor do for me?

B: Do you know anything about interviewing skills?

A: No.

B: Well, with the job counselor, you can talk _____ (2)

_____ a good impression during an interview.
(3)

You can practice _____ questions that the interviewer
(4)

might ask you.

A: Really? How does the counselor know what questions the interviewer

will ask me?

B: Many interviewers ask the same general questions. For example, the

interviewer might ask you, "Do you enjoy _____
(5)

with computers?" Or she might ask you, "Do you mind

_____ overtime and on weekends?" Or "Are you
(6)

good _____ _____ with other people?"
(7)   (8)

A: I dislike _____ about myself.
(9)

B: That's what you have to do in the U.S.

A: What else can the counselor help me with?

B: If your skills are low, you can talk _____
(10)

_____ your skills. If you don't know much about
(11)

computers, for example, she can recommend _____
(12)

more classes.

A: It feels like I'm never going to find a job. I'm tired _____
(13)

_____ and not finding anything.
(14)

B: If you keep _____, you will succeed _____
(15)   (16)

_____ a job. I'm sure. But it takes time and patience.
(17)

10.6 Infinitives—An Overview

To form an infinitive, we use *to* + the base form of a verb (*to find, to help, to run, to be*).

EXAMPLES	EXPLANATION
I want **to find** a job.	An infinitive is used after certain verbs.
I want you **to help** me.	An object can be added before an infinitive.
I'm happy **to help** you.	An infinitive can follow certain adjectives.
It's important **to write** a good résumé.	An infinitive follows certain expressions with *it*.
He went to a counselor **to get** advice.	An infinitive is used to show purpose.

Tips[5] on Writing a Résumé

Before
You Read

1. Have you ever written a résumé? What is the hardest part about writing a résumé?

2. Do people in your native country have to write a résumé?

CD 3, TR 20

Read the following Web article. Pay special attention to infinitives.

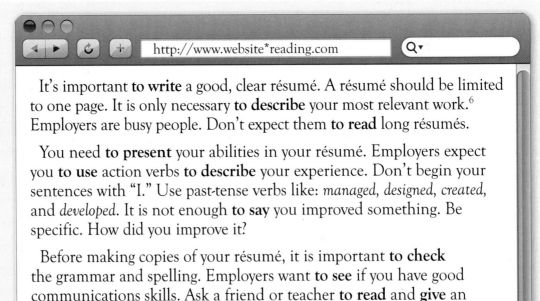

http://www.website*reading.com

It's important **to write** a good, clear résumé. A résumé should be limited to one page. It is only necessary **to describe** your most relevant work.[6] Employers are busy people. Don't expect them **to read** long résumés.

You need **to present** your abilities in your résumé. Employers expect you **to use** action verbs **to describe** your experience. Don't begin your sentences with "I." Use past-tense verbs like: *managed, designed, created,* and *developed.* It is not enough **to say** you improved something. Be specific. How did you improve it?

Before making copies of your résumé, it is important **to check** the grammar and spelling. Employers want **to see** if you have good communications skills. Ask a friend or teacher **to read** and **give** an opinion about your résumé.

[5]A *tip* is a small piece of advice.
[6]*Relevant work* is work that is related to this particular job opening.

It isn't necessary **to include** references. If the employer wants you **to provide** references, he or she will ask you **to do** so during or after the interview.

Don't include personal information such as marital status, age, race, family information, or hobbies.

Be honest in your résumé. Employers can check your information. No one wants **to hire** a liar.

TINA WHITE

1234 Anderson Avenue
West City, MA 01766
tina.white@e*mail.com
617-123-1234

EXPERIENCE

COMPUTER SALES MANAGER
Acme Computer Services, Inc., Concord, MA
March 2003–Present

- Managed computer services department, overseeing 20 sales representatives throughout New England.
- Exceeded annual sales goal by 20 percent in 2008.
- Created online customer database, enabling representatives and company to track and retain customers and improve service.
- Developed new training program and materials for all company sales representatives.

OFFICE MANAGER
West Marketing Services, West City, MA
June 1999–March 2003

- Implemented new system for improving accounting records and reports.
- Managed, trained, and oversaw five customer service representatives.
- Grew sales contracts for support services by 200 percent in first two years.

EDUCATION AND TRAINING

Northeastern Community College, Salem, MA
   Associates Degree Major: Accounting
Institute of Management, Boston, MA
   Certificate of Completion. Course: Sales Management

COMPUTER SKILLS

   Proficient in use of MS Windows, PowerPoint, Excel, Access, Outlook, Mac OS X, and several accounting and database systems.

10.7 Infinitive as Subject

An infinitive can be the subject of a sentence. We begin the sentence with *it* and delay the infinitive subject.

EXAMPLES	EXPLANATION
It is important **to write** a good résumé. It isn't necessary **to include** all your experience.	We can use an infinitive after these adjectives: dangerous good necessary difficult hard possible easy important sad expensive impossible wrong
It takes time **to prepare** for an interview. It takes patience **to find** a job. It costs money **to use** a résumé service.	We can use an infinitive after certain nouns. time patience money fun a pleasure experience
It is necessary **for the manager to choose** the best candidate for the job. It isn't easy **for me to talk** about myself. It was hard **for her to leave** her last job.	Include *for* + noun or object pronoun to make a statement that is true of a specific person.
Compare Infinitive and Gerund Subjects: It's important **to arrive** on time. **Arriving** on time is important.	There is no difference in meaning between an infinitive subject and a gerund subject.

EXERCISE **13** **Fill in the blanks with an appropriate infinitive to give information about résumés and interviews. Answers may vary.**

EXAMPLE It is necessary _____*to have*_____ a Social Security card.

1. It isn't necessary _____ all your previous experience. Choose only the most relevant experience.

2. It's important _____ your spelling and grammar before sending a résumé.

3. It is a good idea _____ interview questions before going on an interview.

4. It is important _____ your best when you go on an interview, so choose your clothes carefully.

5. It isn't necessary _____ references on a résumé. You can simply write, "References available upon request."

6. It's important _____ your past work experience in detail, using words like *managed, designed, supervised,* and *built.*

7. It takes time _____ a good résumé.

EXERCISE `14` **Complete each statement with an infinitive phrase. You can add an object, if you like.**

EXAMPLES   It's easy ___to shop in an American supermarket.___

It's necessary ___for me to pay my rent by the fifth of the month.___

1. It's important _____

2. It's impossible _____

3. It's possible _____

4. It's necessary _____

5. It's dangerous _____

6. It isn't good _____

7. It's expensive _____

8. It's hard _____

EXERCISE `15`   **ABOUT YOU Tell if it's important or not important for you to do the following.**

EXAMPLE   own a house
It's (not) important for me to own a house.

1. get a college degree
2. find an interesting job
3. have a car
4. speak English well
5. read and write English well

6. study American history
7. become an American citizen
8. own a computer
9. have a cell phone
10. make a lot of money

EXERCISE `16`   **Write a sentence with each pair of words below. You may read your sentences to the class.**

EXAMPLE   hard / the teacher

___It's hard for the teacher to pronounce the names of some students.___

1. important / us (the students)

_____

2. difficult / Americans

_____

(continued)

3. easy / the teacher

_____

4. necessary / children

_____

5. difficult / a woman

_____

6. difficult / a man

_____

EXERCISE 17 Write a list of things that a foreign student or immigrant should know about life in the U.S. Use gerunds or infinitives as subjects. You may work with a partner.

EXAMPLES It is possible for some students to get financial aid. _____

Learning English is going to take longer than you expected. _____

1. _____

2. _____

3. _____

4. _____

5. _____

6. _____

10.8 Infinitive after Adjective

Some adjectives can be followed by an infinitive.

EXAMPLES	EXPLANATION
I would be **happy to help** you with your résumé. Are you **prepared to make** copies of your résumé?	Adjectives often followed by an infinitive are: afraid happy prepared ready glad lucky proud sad

Complete this conversation with appropriate infinitives. Answers may vary.

CD 3, TR 21

A: I have my first interview tomorrow. I'm afraid _____to go_____
(example)
alone. Would you go with me?

B: I'd be happy _____ with you and wait in the
(1)
car. But nobody can go with you on an interview.
You have to do it alone. It sounds like you're not
ready _____ a job interview. You should see
(2)
a job counselor and get some practice before you
have an interview. I was lucky _____ a great job counselor.
(3)
She prepared me well.

A: I don't have time to make an appointment with a job counselor
before tomorrow. Maybe you can help me.

B: I'd be happy _____ you. Do you have some time this afternoon?
(4)
We can go over some basic questions.

A: Thanks. I'm glad _____ you as my friend.
(5)

B: That's what friends are for.

EXERCISE **19**   **ABOUT YOU**   **Fill in the blanks.**

EXAMPLE   I'm lucky _____to be in the U.S._____

1. I was lucky _____
2. I'm proud _____
3. I'm sometimes afraid _____
4. I'm not afraid _____
5. In the U.S., I'm afraid _____
6. Are we ready _____
7. I'm not prepared _____

10.9 Infinitive after Verb

Some verbs are commonly followed by an infinitive (phrase).

EXAMPLES	EXPLANATION
I need **to find** a new job. I decided **to quit** my old job. I prefer **to work** outdoors. I want **to make** more money.	We can use an infinitive after the following verbs: agree decide like promise ask expect love remember attempt forget need start begin hope plan try continue learn prefer want

Pronunciation Note: The *to* in infinitives is often pronounced "ta" or, after a *d* sound, "da." *Want to* is often pronounced "wanna." Listen to your teacher pronounce the sentences in the above box.

EXERCISE 20 **ABOUT YOU** Ask a question with the words given in the present tense. Another student will answer.

EXAMPLE like / work in an office

A: Do you like to work in an office?
B: Yes, I do. OR No, I don't.

1. plan / look for a job

2. expect / make a lot of money at your next job

3. like / work with computers

4. prefer / work the second shift

5. need / see a job counselor

6. hope / become rich some day

7. like / work with people

8. try / keep up with changes in technology

9. want / learn another language

EXERCISE 21 **ABOUT YOU** Write a sentence about yourself using the words given, in any tense. You may share your sentences with the class.

EXAMPLES like / eat
I like to eat Chinese food.

try / find
I'm trying to find a job.

1. like / read

2. not like / eat

3. want / visit

4. decide / go

5. try / learn

6. begin / study

EXERCISE 22 **ABOUT YOU** Check (✓) the activities that you like to do. Tell the class why you like or don't like this activity.

1. _____ stay home on the weekends   8. _____ go to museums
2. _____ eat in a restaurant   9. _____ dance
3. _____ get up early   10. _____ write letters
4. _____ talk on the phone   11. _____ play chess
5. _____ surf the Internet   12. _____ watch sports on TV
6. _____ go to the library   13. _____ read
7. _____ swim   14. _____ go shopping

10.10 Gerund or Infinitive after Verb

Some verbs can be followed by either a gerund or an infinitive with almost no difference in meaning.

EXAMPLES	EXPLANATION
I started **looking** for a job a month ago. I started **to look** for a job a month ago. He continued **working** until he was 65 years old. He continued **to work** until he was 65 years old.	The verbs below can be followed by either a gerund or an infinitive with almost no difference in meaning: attempt deserve prefer begin hate start can't stand[7] like try continue love

Language Notes:
1. The meaning of *try* + infinitive is a little different from the meaning of *try* + gerund. *Try* + infinitive means to make an effort.
   I'll **try to improve** my résumé.
   You should **try to relax** during the interview.
2. *Try* + gerund means to use a different technique when one technique doesn't produce the result you want.
   I wanted to reach you yesterday, but I couldn't. I **tried calling** your home phone, but I got your answering machine. I **tried calling** your cell phone, but it was turned off. I **tried e-mailing** you, but you didn't check your e-mail.

EXERCISE 23 **ABOUT YOU** Complete each statement using either a gerund (phrase) or an infinitive (phrase). Practice both ways.

EXAMPLES I started _to learn English four years ago_.
(learn)

I started _studying French when I was in high school_.
(study)

1. I started _____ to this school in _____.
   (come)

2. I began _____ English _____.
   (study)

3. I like _____ on TV.
   (watch)

4. I like _____.
   (live)

5. I hate _____.
   (wear)

6. I love _____.
   (eat)

---

[7]*Can't stand* means hate or can't tolerate. I *can't stand* waiting in a long line.

10.11 Object before Infinitive

We can use a noun or object pronoun (*me, you, him, her, it, us,* and *them*) before an infinitive.

EXAMPLES	EXPLANATION
Don't **expect an employer to read** a long résumé. I **want you to look** at my résumé. My boss **wants me to work** overtime. I **expected him to give** me a raise.	We often use an object between the following verbs and an infinitive: advise invite want allow need would like ask permit expect tell
He helped me **find** a job. He helped me *to find* a job.	*Help* can be followed by either an object + base form or an object + infinitive.

EXERCISE 24 **Fill in the blanks with pronouns and infinitives to complete the conversation below.**

CD 3, TR 22

A: I want to quit my job.

B: Why?

A: I don't like my supervisor. He expects ___me___ ___to work___
(example) (example: work)
at night and on weekends.

B: But you get extra pay for that, don't you?

A: No. I asked _____ _____ me a raise, but he said the
(1)   (2 give)
company can't afford it.

B: Is that the only problem?

A: No. My coworkers and I like to go out for lunch. But he doesn't

want _____ _____ out. He expects _____ _____
(3)   (4 go)   (5)   (6 eat)
in the company cafeteria. He says that if we go out, we might not get

back on time.

B: That's awful. He should permit _____ _____ wherever you
(7)   (8 eat)
want to.

A: That's what I think. I also have a problem with my manager.

She never gives anyone a compliment. When I do a good

job, I expect _____ _____ something nice.
(9)   (10 say)
But she only says something when we make a mistake. *(continued)*

B: It's important to get positive feedback too.

A: Do you know of any jobs in your company? I'd like

_____ _____ your boss if he
　　(11)　　　(12 ask)

needs anyone.

B: I don't think there are any job openings in my company. My boss

has two sons in their twenties. He wants _____
　　　　　　　　　　　　　　　　　　　　(13)

_____ for him on Saturdays. But they're so
(14 work)

lazy. The boss allows _____ _____
　　　　　　　　　　　(15)　　　(16 come)

late and _____ early. He would never permit
　　　　(17 leave)

_____ _____ that. We have to be
　(18)　　　(19 do)

on time exactly, or he'll take away some of our pay.

A: Maybe I should just stay at my job. I guess no job is perfect.

EXERCISE 25 **Tell if the teacher wants or doesn't want the students to do the following.**

EXAMPLES do the homework
The teacher wants us to do the homework.

use the textbook during a test
The teacher doesn't want us to use the textbook during a test.

1. talk to another student during a test
2. study before a test
3. copy another student's homework in class
4. learn English
5. speak our native languages in class
6. improve our pronunciation
7. talk about our native countries in class
8. sit in rows

EXERCISE 26 **ABOUT YOU** Tell if you expect or don't expect the teacher to do the following.

EXAMPLES give homework
I expect him/her to give homework.

give me private lessons
I don't expect him/her to give me private lessons.

1. correct the homework
2. give tests
3. speak my native language
4. help me after class
5. come to class on time

6. pass all the students
7. know a lot about my native country
8. answer my questions in class
9. teach us American history
10. pronounce my name correctly

EXERCISE 27 **ABOUT YOU** Write sentences to tell what one member of your family wants (or doesn't want) from another member of your family.

EXAMPLES My father doesn't want my brother to watch so much TV.

My brother wants me to help him with his math homework.

1. _____
2. _____
3. _____
4. _____

10.12 Infinitive to Show Purpose

We use the infinitive to show purpose.

EXAMPLES	EXPLANATION
You can use the Internet **in order to find** job information. I need a car **in order to get** to work. I'm saving my money **in order to buy** a car.	*In order to* + verb shows purpose.
You can use the Internet **to find** job information. I need a car **to get** to work. I'm saving my money **to buy** a car.	*To* is the short form of *in order to*.

EXERCISE 28 Fill in the blanks with an infinitive to show purpose. Answers will vary.

EXAMPLE   I bought the Sunday newspaper ___to look for a job___.

1. I called the company _____ an appointment.

2. She wants to work overtime _____.

3. You should use the Internet _____ jobs.

4. You can use a résumé writing service _____ your résumé.

5. My interview is in a distant suburb. I need a car _____ the interview.

6. Use express mail _____ packages faster.

7. In the U.S., you need experience _____ a job, and you need a job _____ experience.

8. I need two phone lines. I need one _____ on the phone with my friends and relatives. I need the other one _____ business calls.

9. I'm sending an envelope that has a lot of papers in it. I need extra stamps _____ this envelope.

10. You should go to the college admissions office _____ _____ a copy of your transcripts.

11. After an interview, you can call the employer _____ _____ that you're very interested in the position.

Rita's Story

Before You Read

1. What are some differences between the American workplace and the workplace in other countries?

2. In your native culture, is it a sign of respect or disrespect to look at someone directly?

Read the following journal entry. Pay special attention to *used to*, *be used to*, and *get used to*.

August 23

I've been in the U.S. for two years. I **used to** study British English in India, so I had a hard time **getting used to** the American pronunciation. But little by little, I started to **get used to** it. Now I understand Americans well, and they understand me.

I **used to** be an elementary school teacher in India. But for the past two years in the U.S., I've been working in a hotel cleaning rooms. I have to work the second shift. I'**m not used to** working nights. I don't like it because I don't see my children very much. When I get home from work, they're asleep. My husband is home in the evening and cooks for them. In India, I **used to** do all the cooking, but now he has to help with household duties. He didn't like it at first, but now he'**s used to** it.

When I started looking for a job, I had to **get used to** a lot of new things. For example, I had to learn to talk about my abilities in an interview. In India, it is considered impolite to say how wonderful you are. But my job counselor told me that I had to **get used to** it because that's what Americans do. Another thing I'**m not used to** is wearing American clothes. In India, I **used to** wear traditional Indian clothes to work. But now I wear a uniform to work. I don't like to dress like this. I prefer traditional Indian clothes, but my job requires a uniform. There's one thing I can't **get used to**: everyone here calls each other by their first names. It's our native custom to use a term of respect with people we don't know.

It has been hard to **get used to** so many new things, but little by little, I'm doing it.

10.13 *Used To* vs. *Be Used To*

Used to + base form is different from *be used to* + gerund.

EXAMPLES	EXPLANATION
Rita **used to be** an elementary school teacher. Now she cleans hotel rooms.	*Used to* + base form tells about a past habit or custom. This activity has been discontinued.
She **used to wear** traditional Indian clothes. Now she wears a uniform to work.	
She **used to cook** dinner for her family in India. Now her husband cooks dinner.	
Her husband **didn't use to cook** in India.	The negative is *didn't use to* + base form. (Remove the *d* at the end.)
I'**m used to working** in the day, not at night.	*Be used to* + gerund or noun means *be accustomed to*. Something is a person's custom and is therefore not difficult to do.
Women in India **are used to wearing** traditional clothes.	
People who studied British English **aren't used to the American pronunciation.**	The negative is *be* + *not* + *used to* + gerund or noun. (Do not remove the *d* of **used to**.)
If you immigrate to the U.S., you have to **get used to many new things.**	*Get used to* + gerund or noun means *become accustomed to*.
Children from another country usually **get used to living** in the U.S. easily. But it takes their parents a long time to **get used to a new life.**	
I **can't get used to** the cold winters here.	For the negative, we usually say *can't get used to*.
She **can't get used to** calling people by their first names.	

Pronunciation Note: We don't pronounce the *d* in *used to*.

EXERCISE 29 **ABOUT YOU** Write four sentences comparing your former behaviors to your behaviors or customs now.

EXAMPLES   I used to live with my family. Now I live with a roommate.

I used to worry a lot. Now I take it easy most of the time.

1. _____

2. _____

3. _____

4. _____

EXERCISE 30 **ABOUT YOU** Write sentences comparing the way you used to live in your country or in another city and the way you live now. Read your sentences to the class.

EXAMPLE   I used to go everywhere by bus. Now I have a car.

1. _____

2. _____

3. _____

4. _____

EXERCISE 31 A student wrote about things that are new for her in an American classroom. Fill in the blanks with a gerund.

EXAMPLE   I'm not used to ___taking___ multiple-choice tests. In my native country, we have essay tests.

1. I'm not used to _____ at small desks. In my native country, we sit at large tables.

2. I'm not used to _____ the teacher by his/her first name. In my country, we say "Professor."

3. I'm not used to _____ in a textbook. In my native country, we don't write in the books because we borrow them from the school.

4. I'm not used to _____ jeans to class. In my native country, students wear a uniform.

5. I'm not used to _____ and studying at the same time. Students in my native country don't work. Their parents support them.

6. I'm not used to _____ a lot of money to attend college. In my native country, college is free.

7. I'm not used to _____ when a teacher asks me a question. In my native country, students stand to answer a question.

EXERCISE 32 **ABOUT YOU** Name four things that you had to get used to in the U.S. or in a new town or school. (These things were strange for you when you arrived.)

EXAMPLES   I had to get used to ___living in a small apartment.___

I had to get used to ___American pronunciation.___

1. I had to get used to _____
2. I had to get used to _____
3. I had to get used to _____
4. I had to get used to _____

EXERCISE 33 **ABOUT YOU** Answer each question with a complete sentence. Practice *be used to* + gerund or noun.

EXAMPLES   What are you used to drinking in the morning?
I'm used to drinking coffee in the morning.
What kind of food are you used to? I'm used to Mexican food.

1. What kind of work are you used to?
2. What kind of relationship are you used to having with coworkers?
3. What kind of food are you used to (eating)?
4. What kind of weather are you used to?
5. What time are you used to getting up?
6. What kinds of clothes are you used to wearing to work or class?
7. What kinds of things are you used to doing every day?
8. What kinds of classroom behaviors are you used to?
9. What kinds of things are you used to doing alone?

EXERCISE 34 Circle the correct words to complete this conversation.

🔊

CD 3, TR 24

A: How's your new job?

B: I don't like it at all. I have to work the night shift. I can't get used to

(*sleep* / *sleeping*) during the day.
(example)

A: I know. That's hard. I used to (*work* / *working*) the night shift, and I
(1)

hated it. That's why I quit.

B: But the night shift pays more money.

A: I know it does, but I was never home for my children. Now my kids speak more English than Spanish. They used to (*speaking / speak*) Spanish well, but now they mix Spanish and English. They play with their American friends all day or watch TV.

B: My kids are the same way. But (*I'm / I*) used to it. It doesn't bother me.

A: I can't (*get / be*) used to it. My parents came to live with us, and they don't speak much English. So they can't communicate with their grandchildren anymore.

B: My parents used to (*living / live*) with us too. But they went back to Mexico. They didn't like the winters here. They couldn't get (*use / used*) to the cold weather.

A: Do you think Americans are (*used to / use to*) cold weather?

B: I'm not sure. My coworker was born in the U.S., but she says she hates winter. She (*is used to / used to*) live in Texas, but now she lives here in Minnesota.

A: Why did she move here if she hates the cold weather?

B: The company where she used to (*work / working*) closed down and she had to find another job. Her cousin helped her find a job here.

A: Before I came to the U.S., I thought everything here would be perfect. I didn't (*use / used*) to (*think / thinking*) about the problems. But I guess life in every country has its problems.

Summary of Lesson 10

Gerunds

EXAMPLES	EXPLANATION
Working all day is hard.	As the subject of the sentence
I don't enjoy **working** as a taxi driver.	After certain verbs
I go shopping after work.	In many idiomatic expressions with *go*
I'm worried about **finding** a job.	After prepositions
She found a job by **looking** in the newspaper.	In adverbial phrases

Infinitives

EXAMPLES	EXPLANATION
I need **to find** a new job.	After certain verbs
My boss wants me **to work** overtime.	After an object
I'm ready **to quit**.	After certain adjectives
It's important **to have** some free time. It's impossible for me **to work** 80 hours a week.	After certain impersonal expressions beginning with *it*
I work (in order) **to support** my family.	To show purpose

Gerund or Infinitive—No Difference in Meaning

GERUND	INFINITIVE
I like **working** with computers. I began **working** three months ago.	I like **to work** with computers. I began **to work** three months ago.
Writing a good résumé is important.	It's important **to write** a good résumé.

Gerund or Infinitive—Difference in Meaning

INFINITIVE (PAST HABIT)	GERUND (CUSTOM)
Rita **used to be** a teacher in India. Now she works in a hotel.	She **isn't used to working** the night shift. It's hard for her.
Rita **used to wear** traditional Indian clothes to work. Now she wears a uniform.	Rita studied British English. She had to **get used to hearing** the American pronunciation.

Editing Advice

1. Use a gerund after a preposition.

   He read the whole book without ~~use~~ *using* a dictionary.

2. Use the correct preposition.

   She insisted ~~in~~ *on* driving me home.

3. Use a gerund after certain verbs.

   I enjoy ~~to~~ walk*ing* in the park.

   He went ~~to~~ shop*ping* after work.

4. Use an infinitive after certain verbs.

   I decided *to* buy a new car.

5. Use a gerund, not a base form, as a subject.

   ~~Find~~ *Finding* a good job is important.

6. Don't forget to include *it* for a delayed infinitive subject.

   ~~Is~~ *It's* important to find a good job.

7. Don't use the past form after *to*.

   I decided to ~~bought~~ *buy* a new car.

8. After *want, expect, need, advise,* and *ask,* use an object pronoun, not a subject pronoun, before the infinitive. Don't use *that* as a connector.

   He wants ~~that I~~ *me to* drive.

   The teacher expects ~~we~~ *us to* do the homework.

9. Use *for,* not *to,* when introducing an object after impersonal expressions beginning with *it.* Use the object pronoun after *for.*

   It's important ~~to~~ *for* me to find a job.

   It's necessary for ~~he~~ *him* to be on time.

10. Use *to* + base form, not *for*, to show purpose.

                              to

I called the company ~~for~~ make an appointment.

11. Don't put *be* before *used to* for the habitual past.

     I

~~I'm~~ used to live in Germany. Now I live in the U.S.

12. Don't use the *-ing* form after *used to* for the habitual past.

                have

We used to ~~having~~ a dog, but he died.

13. Don't forget the *d* in *used to*.

           d

I use to live with my parents. Now I live alone.

Editing Quiz

Some of the shaded words and phrases have mistakes. Find the mistakes and correct them. If the shaded words are correct, write *C*.

               to   *C*

I'm planning be a nurse. I'd love to be a doctor, but I don't want be in
   (example)   (example)   (1)

school for so many years. My mother is a doctor and she wanted I study
                                                  (2)

medicine too. I know that you're never too old to learn something new,
                                       (3)

but I'm 35 years old and start something new at my age is not easy. Study
                        (4)   (5)

to become a doctor takes too long. It would take me eight years become
                                                   (6)

a doctor. I went to my college counselor to get advice. My counselor
                                     (7)

recommended entering a nursing program instead. She advised me take
            (8)   (9)

biology and chemistry this semester as well as English and math. It's hard

to me to take so many courses, but I have no choice.
(10)

In my country, I'm used to work in a nursing home. I enjoyed to help
                       (11)   (12)

older people, but I didn't make enough money. When I decided to came
                                                   (13)

to the U.S., I had to think about my future. People say that is not hard
                                                 (14)

to find a job as a nurse in the U.S. It's important for me to be in a profession
(15)   (16)

where I can help people. And I can do that more quickly by going into a
                                                  (17)

nursing program.

Lesson 10 Test/Review

PART 1 **Fill in the blanks in the conversation below. Use a gerund or an infinitive. In some cases, either the gerund or the infinitive is possible. Answers may vary.**

A: Hi, Molly. I haven't seen you in ages. What's going on in your life?

B: I've made many changes. First, I quit ___**working**___ in a factory.
(example)

I disliked _____ the same thing every day. And I wasn't
_(1)_

used to _____ on my feet all day. My boss often wanted me
_(2)_

_____ overtime on Saturdays. I need _____ with my
_(3)_ _(4)_

children on Saturdays. Sometimes they want me _____
_(5)_

them to the zoo or to the museum. And I need _____ them
_(6)_

with their homework too.

A: So what do you plan on _____ ?
_(7)_

B: I've started _____ to college _____ some general courses.
_(8)_ _(9)_

A: What career are you planning?

B: I'm not sure. I'm interested in _____ with children. Maybe I'll
_(10)_

become a teacher's aide. I've also thought about _____ in a day-
_(11)_

care center. I care about _____ people.
_(12)_

A: Yes, it's wonderful _____ other people, especially children. It's
_(13)_

important _____ a job that you like. So you're starting a whole
_(14)_

new career.

B: It's not new, really. Before I came to the U.S., I used _____
_(15)_

a kindergarten teacher in my country. But my English wasn't

so good when I came here, so I found a job in a factory. I look

forward to _____ to my former profession or doing
_(16)_

something similar.

A: How did you learn English so fast?

(continued)

B: By _____ with people at work, by _____ TV, and by
        (17)   (18)

_____ the newspaper. It hasn't been easy for me _____
    (19)   (20)

American English. I studied British English in my country, but

here I have to get used to _____ things like "gonna" and
                                    (21)

"wanna." At first I didn't understand Americans, but now I'm

used to their pronunciation. I've had to make a lot of changes.

A: You should be proud of _____ so many changes in your life
                                      (22)

so quickly.

B: I am.

A: Let's get together some time and talk some more.

B: I'd love to. I love to dance. Maybe we can go _____ together
                                                              (23)

sometime.

A: That would be great. And I love _____. Maybe we can go
                                              (24)

shopping together sometime.

PART **2** **Fill in the blanks with the correct preposition. If no preposition is necessary, write X in the blank.**

EXAMPLES   I believe ____in____ doing my best.

Not ____X____ knowing English well makes it hard to find a job.

1. She dreams _____ becoming an engineer.

2. Are you good _____ working with people?

3. I'm not worried _____ finding a job.

4. When he's not working, he likes to go _____ fishing.

5. You can prepare for an interview _____ practicing with a friend.

6. A nurse is responsible _____ improving a patient's health.

7. Do you mind _____ working in a restaurant?

8. She went to a job counselor _____ get advice.

9. It's important _____ him to finish college.

10. I want you _____ help me write a résumé.

Expansion

Classroom
Activities

❶ If you have a job, write a list of five things you enjoy and don't enjoy about your job. If you don't have a job, you can write about what you enjoy and don't enjoy about this school or class. Share your answers with the class.

❷ Compare the work environment in the U.S. to the work environment in another country. Discuss your answers in a small group or with the entire class. (If you have no experience with American jobs, ask an American to fill in his/her opinions about the U.S.)

	The U.S.	Another Country
1. Coworkers are friendly with each other at the job.		
2. Coworkers get together after work to socialize.		
3. Arriving on time for the job is very important.		
4. The boss is friendly with the employees.		
5. The employees are very serious about their jobs.		
6. The employees use the telephone for personal use.		
7. Everyone wears formal clothes.		
8. Employees get long lunch breaks.		
9. Employees get long vacations.		
10. Employees call the company if they are sick and can't work on a particular day.		
11. Employees are paid in cash.		
12. Employees often take work home.		

❸ Find a partner. Pretend that one of you is the manager of a company and the other one is looking for a job in that company. First decide what kind of company it is. Then write the manager's questions and the applicant's answers. Perform your interview in front of the class.

About It

1 Talk about your experiences in looking for a job in the U.S.

2 Talk about the environment where you work.

3 Talk about some professions that interest you.

4 Talk about some professions that you think are terrible.

Write

About It

1 Write your résumé and a cover letter.

2 Write about a job you wouldn't want to have. Tell why.

3 Write about a profession you would like to have. Tell why.

4 Write about your current job or a job you had in the past. Tell what you like(d) or don't (didn't) like about this job.

My Last Job

I used to work as a server in a restaurant. I hated this job for several reasons. First, my boss expected me to be on my feet all day even when the restaurant was empty. Also, I didn't like the customers. I always tried to be nice to them, but some of them weren't nice to me . . .

 For more practice using grammar in context, please visit our Web site.

Grammar
Adjective Clauses

Context
**Making Connections—
Old Friends and New**

11.1 Adjective Clauses—An Overview

An adjective is a word that describes a noun. An adjective clause is a group of words (with a subject and a verb) that describes a noun. Compare adjectives (ADJ) and adjective clauses (AC) below.

EXAMPLES	EXPLANATION
ADJ: Do you know your **new** neighbors? **AC:** Do you know the people **who live next door to you**?	An adjective (ADJ) precedes a noun.
ADJ: This is an **interesting** book. **AC:** This is a book **that has pictures of the high school graduates.**	An adjective clause (AC) follows a noun.
ADJ: I attended an **old** high school. **AC:** The high school **that I attended** was built in 1920.	Relative pronouns, such as *who* and *that*, introduce an adjective clause.

Finding Old Friends

Before You Read

1. Do you keep in touch with old friends from your previous schools?

2. Have you ever thought about contacting someone you haven't seen in years?

CD 4, TR 01

Read the following magazine article. Pay special attention to adjective clauses.

Americans move numerous times during their lives. As a result, they often lose touch with old friends. Usually, during their twenties and thirties, people are too busy building their careers and starting their families to think much about the past. But as people get older, they often start to wonder about the best friend **they had in high school**, the soldier **with whom they served in the military**, the person **who lived next door** when they were growing up, or their high school sweetheart. Many people want to connect with the past.

Before the Internet, finding a lost love or an old friend required searching through old phone books in libraries in different cities, hard work, and a lot of luck. It was especially hard to find married women **who changed their names**.

Now with the Internet, old friends can sometimes find each other in seconds. Several Web sites have emerged to meet people's growing desire to make connections with former classmates. There are Web sites **that list the students in high schools and colleges in the U.S.** People **who went to high school in the U.S.** can list themselves according to the school **they attended** and the year **they graduated**. A man might go to these Web sites looking for the guys **he played football with** or a long-lost friend—and find the name of a first love **whom he hasn't seen in years**.

One Web site, Classmates.com, claims that more than 40 million Americans have listed themselves on their site. Married women **who have changed their names** list themselves by their maiden names so that others can recognize them easily.

High School Yearbook

Another way **that people make connections with old classmates** is through reunions. Some high school graduating classes meet every ten years. They usually have dinner, remember the time **when they were young**, and exchange information about what they are doing today. They sometimes bring their high school yearbooks, **which have pictures of the graduates and other school memories**.

Some classes have their reunions in the schools **where they first met**. Others have their reunions in a nice restaurant. There are Web sites **that specialize in helping people find their former classmates and plan reunions**.

In America's highly mobile society, it takes some effort to connect with old friends. Looking back at fond memories, renewing old friendships, making new friends, and even starting a new romance with an old love can be the reward for a little work on the Internet.

Tell if the statement is true or false based on the reading on pages 358–359. Write *T* or *F*.

EXAMPLE   People who attend reunions meet their old classmates.   T

1. A yearbook is a book that has the diplomas of the graduates.
2. Classmates.com is a Web site that has lists of students from various high schools in the U.S.
3. Americans move a lot and often lose touch with the friends that they had in high school.
4. Women who get married list their maiden names on Classmates.com.
5. People who graduate from high school have to attend their reunions.
6. There are several Web sites that help people make connections with old friends.

EXERCISE 2   Underline the adjective clauses in the sentences in Exercise 1.

EXAMPLE   People who attend reunions meet their old classmates.

11.2 Relative Pronoun as Subject

The relative pronouns *who*, *that*, and *which* can be the subject of the adjective clause. Use *who* or *that* for people. Use *that* or *which* for things.

Subject I found a Web site. *The Web site* lists people by high school. I found a Web site **that** lists people by high school.   **which**

Women . . . . often change their last names.
  Subject
      Women get married.
 	
      who
Women **that** get married often change their last names.

Language Notes:
1. *That* is considered more correct than *which*.
2. A present tense verb in the adjective clause must agree in number with its subject.
    A woman who **gets** married usually changes her name.
    Women who **get** married usually change their names.

EXERCISE 3 Fill in the blanks with *who* for people and *that* for objects + the correct form of the verb in parentheses ( ).

EXAMPLE A yearbook has photos _____*that show*_____ the activities of the high school.
(show)

1. He has a yearbook _____ pictures of all his classmates.
(have)

2. People _____ to a reunion exchange information
(go)
about their lives.

3. Classmates.com is a Web site _____ people make
(help)
connections with old friends.

4. There are Web sites _____ in helping people
(specialize)
plan a reunion.

5. People _____ a reunion contact former classmates.
(plan)

EXERCISE 4 Fill in the blanks with *who* or *that* + the correct form of the verb in parentheses ( ). Then complete the statement. Answers will vary.

EXAMPLE People _____*who work*_____ hard _*are often successful.*_
(work)

1. People _____ regularly _____
(exercise)

2. A person _____ a cell phone while
(use)
driving _____

3. Students _____ absent a lot _____
(be)

4. Schools _____ computers _____
(not/have)

5. A computer _____ more than five years old
(be)
_____

6. People _____ digital cameras _____
(have)

7. Colleges _____ evening classes _____
(have)

8. A college _____ a day-care center _____
(have)

9. Students _____ a job _____
(have)

EXERCISE 5 Complete each statement with an adjective clause. Answers will vary.

EXAMPLE I know some women ___who OR that don't want to get married___.

1. People _____ can make a lot of friends.

2. Men _____ have a busy social life.

3. I like people _____.

4. I don't like people _____.

5. Students like a teacher _____.

6. People _____ are very fortunate.

7. People _____ aren't usually successful.

8. Parents _____ are good.

9. A college _____ is good for foreign students.

10. People _____ have a hard life.

11.3 Relative Pronoun as Object

The relative pronouns *who(m)*, *that*, and *which* can be the object of the adjective clause.

Object
She attended *the high school*.

The high school . . . ↓ . . . . is in New York City.
                    which
The high school **that** she attended is in New York City.
                    Ø

Object
I knew *a friend* in high school.

A friend . . . ↓ . . . . sent me an e-mail.
          who(m)
A friend **that** I knew in high school sent me an e-mail.
          Ø

Language Notes:
1. The relative pronoun is usually omitted in conversation when it is the object of the adjective clause.
   The high school she attended is in New York City.
2. *Whom* is considered more correct or more formal than *who* when used as the object of the adjective clause. However, as seen in the above note, the relative pronoun is usually omitted altogether in conversation.
   Formal: A friend *whom* I knew in high school sent me an e-mail.
   Informal: A friend I knew in high school sent me an e-mail.

EXERCISE 6 **In each sentence below, underline the adjective clause.**

EXAMPLE I've lost touch with some of the friends <u>I had in high school</u>.

1. The high school I attended is in another city.

2. The teachers I had in high school are all old now.

3. We didn't have to buy the textbooks we used in high school.

4. She married a man she met in college.

5. The friends I've made in this country don't know much about my country.

EXERCISE 7 **A mother (M) is talking to her teenage daughter (D). Fill in the blanks to complete the conversation. Answers may vary.**

CD 4, TR 02

M: I'd like to contact an old friend
I ___had___ in high school.
(example)
I wish I could find her. I'll never

forget the good times _____ in
(1)
high school. When we graduated, we said we'd

always stay in touch. But then we went to different colleges.

D: Didn't you keep in touch by e-mail?

M: When I was in college, e-mail didn't exist. At first we wrote letters. But

little by little we wrote less and less until, eventually, we stopped writing.

D: Do you still have the letters she _____ ?
(2)

M: Yes, I do. They're in a box in the basement.

D: Why don't you write to the address on the letters?

M: That wouldn't work. The address she _____
(3)

on the letters was of the college town where she lived. I don't know

what happened to her after she left college.

D: Have you tried calling her parents?

M: The phone number _____ is now disconnected.
(4)
Maybe her parents have died.

D: Have you looked on Classmates.com?

M: What's that?

(continued)

D: It's a Web site that _____ lists of people. The lists are
(5)

categorized by the high school you _____ and the
(6)

dates you _____ there.
(7)

M: Is everyone in my high school class on the list?

D: Unfortunately, no. Only the people _____ add their
(8)

names are on the list.

M: But my friend probably got married. I don't know the name of the

man _____ married.
(9)

D: That's not a problem. You can search for her by her maiden name.

M: Will this Web site give me her address and phone number?

D: No. But for a fee, you can send her an e-mail through the Web site. Then

if she wants to contact you, she can give you her personal information.

M: She'll probably think I'm crazy for contacting her almost 25 years later.

D: I'm sure she'll be happy to receive communication from a good friend

_____ hasn't seen in years. When I graduate
(10)

from high school, I'm never going to lose contact with the

friends _____ made. We'll always stay in touch.
(11)

M: That's what you think. But as time passes and your lives become more

complicated, you may lose touch.

D: But today we have e-mail.

M: Well, e-mail is a help. Even so, the direction you _____
(12)

in life is different from the direction your friends choose.

EXERCISE **8** **Fill in the blanks with appropriate words to complete the conversation. Answers may vary.**

CD 4, TR 03

A: I'm lonely. I have a lot of friends in my native country, but I don't

have enough friends here. The friends ___I have there___ send me
(example)

e-mail all the time, but that's not enough. I need to make new friends here.

B: Haven't you met any people here?

A: Of course. But the people _____ here don't have my
(1)

interests.

B: What are you interested in?

A: I like reading, meditating, going for quiet walks. Americans seem to like parties, TV, sports, movies, going to restaurants.

B: You're never going to meet people with the interests

_____. Your interests don't include other people.
(2)

You should find some interests _____ other people, like
(3)

tennis or dancing, to mention just a few.

A: The activities _____ cost money, and I don't have a lot
(4)

of money.

B: There are many parks in this city _____ free tennis courts.
(5)

If you like to dance, I know of a park district near here

_____ free dance classes. In fact, there are a lot of
(6)

things _____ or very low cost in this city. I can give you a
(7)

list of free activities, if you want.

A: Thanks. I'd love to have the list. Thanks for all the suggestions

_____.
(8)

B: I'd be happy to give you more, but I don't have time now. Tomorrow

I'll e-mail you a list of activities from the parks in this city. I'm sure

you'll find something _____ on that list.
(9)

A: Thanks.

EXERCISE 9   **We often give a definition with an adjective clause. Work with a partner to give a definition of the following words by using an adjective clause.**

EXAMPLES   twins
Twins are brothers or sisters who are born at the same time.

an answering machine
An answering machine is a device that takes phone messages.

1. a babysitter   **5.** a fax machine

2. an immigrant   **6.** a dictionary

3. an adjective   **7.** a computer mouse

4. a verb   **8.** a coupon

11.4 *Where* and *When*

EXAMPLES	EXPLANATION
Some classmates have their reunion in the school **where they first met.** There are Web sites **where you can find lists of high schools and their students.** She attended the University of Washington, **where she met her best friend.**	*Where* means "in that place." *Where* cannot be omitted.
Do you remember the time **(when) you were in high school**? High school was a time **(when) I had many good friends and few responsibilities.** In 1998, **when I graduated from high school**, my best friend's family moved to another state.	*When* means "at that time." *When* can sometimes be omitted.

Punctuation Notes:

1. An adjective clause is sometimes separated from the sentence with a comma. This is true when the person or thing in the main clause is unique.

Compare:

I visited a Web site **where** I found the names of my classmates. (No comma)

I visited Classmates.com, **where** I found the names of my classmates. (Comma: Classmates.com is a unique Web site.)

I remember the year **when** I graduated from high school. (No comma)

In 1998, **when** she graduated from high school, she got married. (Comma: 1998 is a unique year.)

2. Only *when* without a comma can be omitted.

I remember the year I graduated from high school.

EXERCISE 10 **This is a conversation between a son (S) and his dad (D). Fill in the blanks with *where* or *when* to complete this conversation.**

CD 4, TR 04

S: How did you meet Mom? Do you remember the place ___**where**___ *(example)* you met?

D: We met in high school. I'll never forget the day _____ *(1)* I met your mother. She was such a pretty girl.

S: Did you go to the same school?

D: Yes. We were in a typing class together. She was sitting at the typewriter next to mine.

S: Dad, what's a typewriter?

D: There was a time _____ we didn't have computers. We had
(2)

to type our papers on typewriters.

S: Did you start dating right away?

D: No. We were friends. There was a time _____ people were
(3)

friends before they started dating. There was a soda shop near

school _____ we used to meet.
(4)

S: What's a soda shop, Dad?

D: It's a store _____ you could buy milk shakes, sodas, and
(5)

hamburgers. We used to sit there after school drinking one soda with

two straws.

S: That doesn't seem too romantic to me.

D: But it was.

S: So did you get married as soon as you graduated from high school?

D: No. I graduated from high school at a time _____ there was
(6)

a war going on in this country. Mom went to college and I went into the

army. We wrote letters during that time. When I got out of the army, I

started college. So we got married about seven years after we met.

11.5 Formal vs. Informal

EXAMPLES	EXPLANATION
Informal: I lost touch with the friends I went to high school **with**. **Formal:** I lost touch with the friends **with whom** I went to high school.	Informally, most native speakers put the preposition at the end of the adjective clause. The relative pronoun is usually omitted.
Informal: I saved the yearbook my friends wrote **in**. **Formal:** I saved the yearbook **in which** my friends wrote.	In very formal English, the preposition comes before the relative pronoun, and only *whom* and *which* may be used. *Who* and *that* are not used directly after a preposition.

   EXAMPLE   What is the name of the high school you graduated from?
                  What is the name of the high school from which you graduated?

1. He found his friend that he served in the military with.

_____

2. I can't find the friend I was looking for.

_____

3. The high school she graduated from was torn down.

_____

4. Do you remember the teacher I was talking about?

_____

5. In high school, the activities I was interested in were baseball and band.

_____

Social Networking in the Twenty-First Century

Before You Read

1. Where or how do you meet new people?

2. Do you use social networking Web sites? Which ones?

CD 4, TR 05

Read the following magazine article. Pay special attention to adjective clauses beginning with *whose*.

The method of social networking has changed in the twenty-first century, thanks to the Internet. Mark Zuckerman,  the creator of one popular site, Facebook, started his network in 2004, when he was a student at Harvard University. He realized that students, **whose** lives are very busy, wanted to be able to find out about their friends' thoughts and activities. By 2007, Facebook had 70 million users. Other social networking sites, like Friendster and MySpace, also became popular all over the world.

When asked, "Why did you join this site?", here is how some people responded:

- I'm interested in politics, and it's a good way to find people **whose** interests are the same as mine.

- I can share photos with my friends and make comments on their photos.
- I can see what friends we have in common.
- I can hear about events from my friends.
- I can share my favorite links with my friends.

Who are the members of these social networking sites? At first, they were mostly teenagers and college students. Soon parents **whose** kids were hooked on social networking started joining too.

Another way to bring together people **whose** interests are the same is through a Web site called Meetup.com. Unlike online social networking, **whose** members learn about each other's activities on a Web site, Meetup members get notices about events online but actually get together in coffeehouses, restaurants, parks, etc. A big city like New York has over 4,000 Meetup groups per week, ranging from chess players to book lovers, bicyclists, and French speakers.

The Internet brings people together in creative ways.

11.6 *Whose* + Noun

***Whose* is the possessive form of *who*. It substitutes for *his*, *her*, *its*, *their*, or the possessive form of the noun.**

I want to meet people.
Their interests are the same as mine.
I want to meet people **whose** interests are the same as mine.
Students .... like to communicate with their friends online.
Their lives are busy.
Students **whose** lives are busy like to communicate with their friends online.

Language Note: Use *who* to substitute for a person. Use *whose* for possession or relationship.

Compare:

    I want to meet people **who** are interested in sports.

    I want to meet people **whose** interests are the same as mine.

Punctuation Note: An adjective clause is sometimes separated from the sentence with a comma. This is true when the person or thing in the main clause is unique.

    I go to a meetup whose members are interested in sports.

    Facebook, whose members pay nothing, is a popular social networking site.

    (Facebook is unique.)

EXERCISE 12 Fill in the blanks with one of the words from the box below.

EXAMPLE Do you want to meet people whose __interests__ are the same as yours?

| schoolwork | kids | friends |
| photos | interests ✔ | members |

1. Students whose _____ keeps them busy want a way to know about their friends.

2. Meetup.com, whose _____ get together, is a good way to meet people with similar interests.

3. Parents whose _____ use Facebook are starting to become interested in it too.

4. I like to see the profiles of friends whose _____ are on the site. If they don't post their pictures, I'm not interested.

5. People whose _____ are on Facebook often get an invitation to join.

EXERCISE 13 **ABOUT YOU** Fill in the blanks.

EXAMPLE I would like to own a car that __has enough room for my large family.__

1. My mother is/was a woman who _____

2. My city is a place where _____

3. My childhood was a time when _____

4. My favorite kind of book is one that _____

5. A great teacher is a person who _____

6. I have a friend whose _____

7. I have a computer that _____

8. I like to shop at a time when _____

9. I don't like people who _____

EXERCISE 14 Some people were asked what kind of friends they'd like to meet. Fill in the blanks with a response, using the words in parentheses ( ).

EXAMPLE I'd like to meet people __whose values are the same as mine.__

(Their values are the same as mine.)

1. I'd like to find a friend _____

(I can trust him.)

2. I don't want to be with students _____

(They don't take school seriously.)

3. I want to meet people _____

(They like to play soccer.)

4. I joined a French meetup _____

(Its members speak French very well.)

5. We meet in a coffee shop _____

(It isn't crowded in the morning.)

6. I go to a book club meetup _____

(It meets near my house.)

7. My math group is a club _____

(I found it on Meetup.com.)

EXERCISE 15   **Fill in the blanks with appropriate words to complete the conversation. Answers may vary.**

CD 4, TR 06

A: I'm getting married in two months.

B: Congratulations. Are you marrying the woman _____**you met**_____

                                              (example)

    at Mark's party last year?

A: Oh, no. I broke up with that woman a long time ago. I'm going to

    marry a woman _____ online about ten months ago.
                               (1)

B: What's your fiancée's name? Do I know her?

A: Sarah Liston.

B: I know someone whose _____ is Liston.
                             (2)

    I wonder if they're from the same family.

A: I doubt it. Sarah comes from Canada.

B: Where are you going to live after you get married? Here or in Canada?

A: We're going to live here. Sarah's just finishing college and doesn't

    have a job yet. This is the place _____ I have a good job,
                                     (3)

    so we decided to live here.

B: Where are you going to get married?

(continued)

Adjective Clauses   **371**

A: At my parents' friends' house. They have a very big house and garden. The wedding's going to be in the garden.

B: My wife and I made plans to get married outside too, but we had to change our plans because it rained that day.

A: That's OK. The woman _____ is more important
(4)
than the place _____ we get married. And the
(5)
life _____ together is more important than the
(6)
wedding day.

B: You're right about that!

EXERCISE 16 **Use the words in parentheses ( ) to form an adjective clause. Then read the sentences and tell if you agree or disagree. Give your reasons.**

EXAMPLE A good friend is a person _____**(whom) I can trust**_____.
(I can trust her.)

1. A good friend is a person _____ almost every day.
(I see him.)

2. A good friend is a person _____.
(She would lend me money.)

3. A good friend is a person _____.
(He knows everything about me.)

4. A person _____ cannot be my friend.
(He has different political opinions.)

5. A person _____ cannot be my good friend.
(She doesn't speak my native language.)

6. A person _____ cannot be my good friend.
(His religious beliefs are different from mine.)

7. A person _____ cannot be a good friend.
(She lives far away.)

8. It's important to have friends _____.
(Their interests are the same as mine.)

9. This school is a place _____.
(I can make many new friends easily at this school.)

10. Childhood is the only time in one's life _____

_____.
(It is easy to make friends at this time.)

Summary of Lesson 11

Adjective Clauses

1. Pronoun as Subject

   She has a friend **who lives in Alaska**.
   The man **that arrived late** took a seat in the back.

2. Pronoun as Object

   I have some friends **(who/whom/that) I met online**.
   The book **(which/that) I'm reading** is very exciting.

3. Pronoun as Object of Preposition

   Formal: The person **about whom I'm talking** is my cousin.
   Informal: The person **(who) I'm talking about** is my cousin.

   Formal: The club **of which I am a member** meets at the
              community center.
   Informal: The club **(that) I am a member of** meets at the
              community center.

4. *Whose* + Noun

   I have a friend **whose brother lives in Japan**.
   The students **whose last names begin with A or B** can register on
   Friday afternoon.

5. *Where*

   He moved to New Jersey, **where he found a job**.
   The apartment building **where he lives** has a lot of immigrant families.

6. *When*

   She came to the U.S. at a time **when she was young enough to learn
   English easily**.
   She came to the U.S. in 1995, **when there was a war going on in her
   country**.

Editing Advice

1. Use *who*, *that*, or *which* to introduce an adjective clause. Don't use *what*.

   I know a woman ~~what~~ *who* has ten cats.

2. If the relative pronoun is the subject, don't omit it.

   I know a man *who* has visited every state in the U.S.

3. Use *whose* to substitute for a possessive form.

> *whose*
> I live next door to a couple ~~their~~ children make a lot of noise.

4. If the relative pronoun is used as the object, don't put an object after the verb of the adjective clause.

> I had to pay for the library book that I lost ~~it~~.

5. Don't use *which* for people.

> *who*
> The man ~~which~~ bought my car paid me by check.

6. Use subject-verb agreement in all clauses.

> *s*
> I have a friend who live in Madrid.

> People who talks too much bother me.

7. Don't use an adjective clause when a simple adjective is enough.

> *I don't like long movies.*
> ~~I don't like movies that are long.~~

8. Put a noun before an adjective clause.

> *A student who*
> ~~Who~~ needs help should ask the teacher.

9. Use *where*, not *that*, to mean "in a place."

> *where*
> The store ~~that~~ I buy my textbooks is having a sale this week.

10. Use *whom* and *which*, not *who* and *that*, if the preposition precedes the relative pronoun.

> *which*
> She would never want to go back to the country from ~~that~~ she came.

> *whom*
> I don't know the person about ~~who~~ you are talking.

11. Use the correct word order in an adjective clause (subject before verb).

> *my father caught*
> The fish that ~~caught my father~~ was very big.

12. Don't confuse *whose* (possessive form) and *who's* (who is).

> *who's*
> A woman ~~whose~~ in my math class is helping me study for the test.

Editing Quiz

Some of the shaded words and phrases have mistakes. Find the mistakes and correct them. If the shaded words are correct, write *C*.

  I would like to find one of the friends ~~that~~ *C* I had in college. I found a Web site

where

~~that~~ I can look for old friends. My friend, whose name is Linda Gast,
(example)   *(1)*

got married shortly after we graduated. The man which she married is Bart
               (2)

Reed. I tried using the names "Linda Gast" and "Linda Reed" but I had no

luck. I found a woman with who she shared a room in college, and she
         (3)

gave me a phone number. The phone number that gave me her roommate
             (4)   *(5)*

is not in service anymore. I called a man what used to be her neighbor, but
             (6)

he said that she moved away a long time ago. The last reunion that I
                 (7)

attended it was four years ago, but she wasn't there. The people were our
    (8)   *(9)*

friends in high school didn't know anything about her. I looked in the

phone book and found some people their name is the same as hers, but
           (10)

they weren't the right people. I went back to the high school that we were
                (11)

students, but they had no information about her. Because of the Internet,

now is a time when it's easier than ever to find people. But my search, which
     (12)   *(13)*

have taken me almost five years, has produced no result. Recently I met
(14)

someone whose a friend of her brother, and he told me that Linda's now
   (15)

living in South America. He's going to try to find Linda's current address.

Looking for Linda is a job that is hard, but I'm determined to find her.
        (16)

Who tries hard enough usually succeeds.
(17)

Lesson 11 Test/Review

PART **1** Fill in the blanks with *who, whom, that, which, whose, where, when* or Ø. In some cases, more than one answer is possible.

1. I'm still friends with the people _____ I met in elementary school.

2. Childhood is the time _____ it's easiest to make friends.

3. The elementary school _____ I attended is in Poland.

4. I'm still in contact with some of the teachers _____ I admired a lot.

5. There are some teachers _____ names I've forgotten.

6. The university is the place _____ my father met my mother.

7. Now I use social networking sites _____ allow me to exchange information with my friends.

8. I don't know if they're real friends. For me, a friend is a person _____ I can really trust.

PART **2** Fill in the blanks to complete the adjective clause. Answers may vary.

EXAMPLE **A:** You lost a glove. Is this yours?

B: No. The glove _____(that) I lost_____ is brown.

1. **A:** My neighbor's children make a lot of noise.

   B: That's too bad. I don't like to have neighbors _____
   _____ .

2. **A:** I have a new cat. Do you want to see him?

   B: What happened to the other cat _____?

   A: She died last month.

3. **A:** Do you speak French?

   B: Yes, I do. Why?

   A: The teacher is looking for a student _____ to help her translate a letter.

4. **A:** Did you meet your boyfriend on an Internet dating site?

   B: No. I didn't like any of the guys _____ on the Internet.

5. A: Does your last name begin with A?

    B: Yes, it does. Why?

    A: Registration is by alphabetical order. Students _____

    _____ can register after 2 P.M. today.

6. A: Did you go to your last high school reunion?

    B: No. I was out of town on the day _____.

    A: Do you usually go to your reunions?

    B: Yes. I love to keep in touch with the people _____.

7. A: Are you planning to marry Charles?

    B: No. He lives with his mother. I want to marry a man _____

    _____ lives far away.

Expansion

Classroom Activities

❶ Write a short definition or description of an object or a person. Read your definition to a small group. The others will try to guess what it is. Continue to add to your definition until someone guesses it.

EXAMPLE   It's an animal that lives in the water.
Is it a fish?
No, it isn't. It's an animal that needs to come up for air.
Is it a dolphin?
Yes, it is.

❷ Write a word from your native language that has no English translation. It might be the name of a food or a traditional costume. Define the word. Read your definition to a small group or to a partner.

EXAMPLE   A *sari* is a typical Indian dress for women. It is made of a cloth that a woman wraps around her. She wraps one end around her waist. She puts the other end over her shoulder.

❸ Bring to class something typical from your country. Demonstrate how to use it.

EXAMPLE   a samovar
This is a pot that we use in Russia to make tea.

Talk
About It

1 Do you think the Internet is a good way to network with friends? Why or why not?

2 How do people in your native culture usually make new friends?

3 What kind of person is a good friend?

4 In your native culture, do people usually keep in touch with the friends they made in school?

5 Are there class reunions in your native country?

Write
About It

1 Write a short composition describing your best friend from your school days.

2 Write a short composition describing the different ways to make new friends.

3 If you use a social networking Web site, write about your experience with it.

Social Networking

Since I started to do social networking online, I've been able to exchange a lot of information with my friends. I always read the short posts that they put on their page every day. Because we're so busy, we often can't find any time when we can get together . . .

 For more practice using grammar in context, please visit our Web site.

Grammar
Superlatives

Comparatives

Context
Sports and Athletes

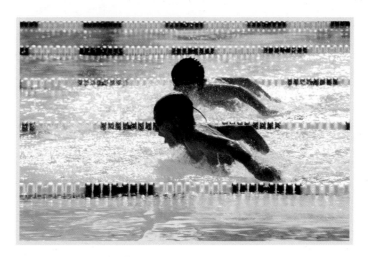

12.1 Superlatives and Comparatives—An Overview

EXAMPLES	EXPLANATION
Baseball and football are **the most popular** sports in the U.S. Jack is **the tallest player** on the basketball team.	We use the superlative form to point out the number one item or items in a group of three or more.
Baseball is **more popular than** soccer in the U.S. Basketball players are **taller than** baseball players.	We use the comparative form to compare two items or groups of items.
He is **as tall as** a basketball player. Soccer is not **as popular as** baseball in the U.S. Soccer players are not **the same height as** basketball players.	We can show equality or inequality of two items or groups of items.

Golf and Tiger Woods

Before
You Read

1. Do you like sports? Which are your favorites?

2. Who are your favorite athletes?

CD 4, TR 07

Read the following Web article. Pay special attention to superlative forms.

http://tigerwoods*golf.com

Golf is the only sport where the player with **the lowest** score wins. The player who puts the ball in the hole with **the fewest** tries (strokes)  is the winner. Golf originally comes from Scotland, where you can still find **the earliest** golf course. Until the beginning of the twentieth century, golf was mainly popular in Scotland and England. Golf is not **the most popular sport** in the U.S., but in recent years the U.S. has produced **the greatest** quantity of leading professional golfers. One of **the most remarkable** players is Tiger Woods.

Tiger Woods was born in 1975 in California. Before he could walk or talk, he loved to watch his father play golf. At age two, he began to play golf with his father—and soon became a better golfer than his father. When Woods was in high school in California, he became **the youngest** person in the U.S. to win the Junior Amateur Championship. At age 19, he became **the youngest** winner of the U.S. Amateur Championship. In 1996, at the age of 21, he became a professional golfer.

Today Woods is one of **the most successful** golfers of all time. He is the only person to be named *Sports Illustrated*'s Sportsman of the Year more than once (in 1996 and 2000).

In 2007, he was **the highest**-paid professional athlete, earning approximately $122 million from winnings and endorsements.[1]

Woods's father died in 2006. Woods wrote on his Web site at the time, "My dad was my **best** friend and **greatest** role model, and I will miss him."

12.2 The Superlative Form

We use the superlative form to point out the number one item of a group of three or more.

EXAMPLES	EXPLANATION

Woods was **the youngest** winner.
He worked **the hardest**.
	Form:
	    short adjective + -est
	    short adverb + -est

Golf is not **the most popular** sport in the U.S.
Woods learned golf **the most effortlessly** of anyone in his family.
	Form:
	    the most + longer adjective
	    the most + -ly adverb

Woods is **one of the most successful** golfer**s**. He is **one of the most remarkable** athlete**s**.	We often say "one of the" before a superlative form. The noun that follows is plural.
In golf, the winner uses **the least** number of strokes. Woods said, "My dad was my **best** friend."	Some superlatives are irregular. See Section 12.3 for more information about irregular forms.
Woods is one of the best golfers **of all time**. Soccer is the most popular sport **in the world**.	We often put a prepositional phrase after a superlative phrase: *in the world, of all time, in the U.S.,* etc.
Woods is one of the best golfers **who has ever lived**. Who is the best athlete **you have ever seen**?	An adjective clause with *ever* and the present perfect tense often completes a superlative statement.
Language Note: Use *the* before a superlative form. Omit *the* if there is a possessive form before the superlative form. Woods is one of **the best** golfers. His father was **his best** friend. (not *his the* best friend)	

[1]When a famous person makes an *endorsement*, he says that he likes a certain product. He gets paid for saying this.

Tell if the statement is true (*T*) or false (*F*). Underline the superlative forms.

EXAMPLE The <u>oldest</u> golf course is in the U.S.   F

  1. In golf, the player with the lowest score wins.

  2. Golf is the most popular sport in the U.S.

  3. Tiger Woods is one of the best golfers.

  4. Tiger's father was his best friend.

  5. Tiger's father was one of the best golfers in the world.

  6. Tiger Woods is one of the richest athletes.

12.3 Comparative and Superlative Forms of Adjectives and Adverbs

	SIMPLE	COMPARATIVE	SUPERLATIVE
One-syllable adjectives and adverbs*	tall fast	taller faster	the tallest the fastest
Two-syllable adjectives that end in *y*	easy happy	easier happier	the easiest the happiest
Other two-syllable adjectives	frequent active	more frequent more active	the most frequent the most active
Some two-syllable adjectives have two forms.**	simple common	simpler more simple commoner more common	the simplest the most simple the commonest the most common
Adjectives with three or more syllables	important difficult	more important more difficult	the most important the most difficult
-ly adverbs	quickly brightly	more quickly more brightly	the most quickly the most brightly
Irregular adjectives and adverbs	good/well bad/badly far little a lot	better worse farther less more	the best the worst the farthest the least the most

Language Notes:

1.*Exceptions to one-syllable adjectives:

  bored   more bored   the most bored
  tired   more tired   the most tired

2.**Other two-syllable adjectives that have two forms:
  handsome, quiet, gentle, narrow, clever, friendly, angry, polite, stupid

Spelling Rules for Short Adjectives and Adverbs

RULE	SIMPLE	COMPARATIVE	SUPERLATIVE
Add -er and -est to short adjectives and adverbs.	tall fast	taller faster	tallest fastest
For adjectives that end in e, add -r and -st.	nice late	nicer later	nicest latest
For adjectives that end in y, change y to i and add -er and -est.	easy happy	easier happier	easiest happiest
For words ending in consonant-vowel-consonant, double the final consonant, then add -er and -est. **Exception:** Do not double final w. new—newer—newest	big sad	bigger sadder	biggest saddest

EXERCISE 2   **Give the comparative and superlative forms of each word.**

EXAMPLES   fat   _fatter_   _the fattest_

important   _more important_   _the most important_

1. interesting   _____   _____

2. young   _____   _____

3. beautiful   _____   _____

4. good   _____   _____

5. responsible   _____   _____

6. thin   _____   _____

7. carefully   _____   _____

8. pretty   _____   _____

9. bad   _____   _____

10. famous   _____   _____

11. lucky   _____   _____

12. simple   _____   _____

13. high   _____   _____

14. delicious   _____   _____

15. far   _____   _____

16. foolishly   _____   _____

EXERCISE **3** **Write the superlative form of the word in parentheses ( ).**

EXAMPLE Football is one of __the most dangerous__ sports.
(dangerous)

1. Michael Phelps is _____ swimmer in the world.
(fast)

2. Training for the Olympics is one of _____ things
(difficult)
for an athlete.

3. Soccer is _____ sport in the world.
(popular)

4. Sumo wrestlers are _____ athletes.
(fat)

5. Michael Jordan was _____ basketball player in the
(good)
world.

6. Swimming and gymnastics are _____ events during
(watched)
the Summer Olympics.

7. Yao Ming is one of _____ basketball players
(tall)
in the world.

8. _____ name for soccer in the world is "football."
(common)

9. Running a marathon was one of _____ things
(hard)
I've ever done.

10. In your opinion, what is _____ sport?
(interesting)

Yao Ming

EXERCISE **4** **ABOUT YOU** **Write a superlative sentence giving your opinion about each of the following items. You may find a partner and compare your answers to your partner's answers.**

EXAMPLES big problem in the world today
I think the biggest problem in the world today is hunger.

big problem in the U.S. today
I think crime is one of the biggest problems in the U.S. today.

1. good way to make friends

_____

2. quick way to learn a language

_____

3. good thing about life in the U.S.

_____

4. bad thing about life in the U.S.

_____

5. big problem in (*choose a country*)

_____

EXERCISE 5 **ABOUT YOU** Write superlative sentences about your experience with the words given. Use the present perfect form + *ever* after the superlative.

EXAMPLE big / city / visit
London is the biggest city I have ever visited. _____

1. tall / building / visit

_____

2. beautiful / actress / see

_____

3. difficult / subject / study

_____

4. far / distance / travel

_____

5. bad / food / eat

_____

6. good / vacation / have

_____

7. good / athlete / see

_____

8. hard / job / have

_____

9. interesting / sporting event / see

_____

EXERCISE 6　**ABOUT YOU**　Fill in the blanks.

EXAMPLE　<u>Swimming across a lake alone at night</u>

was one of the most dangerous things I've ever done.

1. _____

is one of the most foolish things I've ever done.

2. _____

is one of the hardest decisions I've ever made.

3. _____

is one of the most dangerous things I've ever done.

12.4 Superlatives and Word Order

EXAMPLES	EXPLANATION
Superlative　　　Noun Adjective　　　Phrase Who is **the best American golfer**? Superlative Adjective　　　Noun What is **the most popular sport** in the world? Superlative　Noun In golf, the winner scores **the fewest points**.	A superlative adjective comes **before** a noun or noun phrase.
Football is **the most popular sport** in the U.S. OR **The most popular sport** in the U.S. is football.	When the verb *be* connects a noun to a superlative adjective + noun, there are two possible word orders.
Superlative Verb　　　Adverb Interest in soccer **is growing the most quickly** in the U.S. Verb　　　Superlative Phrase　　　Adverb I **watch soccer the most frequently**.	We put superlative adverbs **after** the verb or verb phrase.
Verb Superlative Tiger Woods **plays the best**. Verb Phrase　Superlative Fans **love Tiger Woods the most**.	We put *the most, the least, the best,* and *the worst* **after** a verb (phrase).

EXERCISE 7 **ABOUT YOU** Name the person who is the superlative in your family in each of the following categories.

EXAMPLE   works hard
My mother works the hardest in my family.

1. drives well
2. lives far from me
3. speaks English confidently
4. spends a lot of money
5. is well dressed
6. watches a lot of TV

7. worries a lot
8. lives well
9. works hard
10. is athletic
11. is a big sports fan
12. is learning English quickly

Americans' Attitude Toward Soccer

Before You Read

1. Are you interested in soccer? If so, what is your favorite team?

2. Should children learn to play a sport in school? Why or why not?

CD 4, TR 08

Read the following magazine article. Pay special attention to comparisons.

Soccer is by far the most popular sport in the world. Almost every country has a professional league. In many countries, top international soccer players are **as** well-known **as** rock stars or actors. However, in 1994, when the World Cup soccer competition was held in the U.S., there was not a lot of interest in soccer among Americans. Many people said that soccer was boring.

Recently, Americans' attitude toward soccer has been changing. In 1999, when the Women's World Cup was played in the U.S., there was **more** interest than ever before. Little by little, soccer is becoming **more popular** in the U.S. The number of children playing soccer is growing. In fact, soccer is growing **faster** than any other sport. For elementary school children, soccer is now the number two sport after basketball. **More** kids play soccer than baseball. Many coaches believe that soccer is **easier** to play than baseball or basketball, and that there aren't **as many** injuries **as** with sports such as hockey or football.

Interest in professional soccer in the U.S. is still much **lower** than in other countries. The number of Americans who watch professional basketball, football, or hockey is still much **higher** than the number who watch Major League Soccer. However, **the more** parents show interest in their children's soccer teams, **the more** they will become interested in professional soccer.

12.5 Comparatives

We use the comparative form to compare two items.

EXAMPLES	EXPLANATION

Soccer players are **shorter than** basketball players.
Interest in soccer is growing **faster than** interest in any other sport.
	Form:
	  short adjective + *-er* + *than*
	  short adverb + *-er* + *than*

Basketball is **more popular than** soccer in the U.S.
Interest in soccer is growing **more quickly than** interest in hockey.
	Form:
	  more + longer adjective + *than*
	  more + *-ly* adverb + *than*

My brother plays soccer **better than** I do. He can kick the ball **farther than** I can.	Some comparative forms are irregular. See 12.3 for more information about irregular forms.
Basketball is popular in the U.S., but football is **more popular**. Michael Jordan is tall, but Yao Ming is **taller**.	Omit *than* if the second item of comparison is not included.
Interest in soccer is *much* **lower** in the U.S. than in other countries. I like soccer *a little* **better** than I like baseball.	*Much* or *a little* can come before a comparative form.
Formal: You are taller than **I am**. **Informal:** You are taller than **me**. **Formal:** I can play soccer better than **he can**. **Informal:** I can play soccer better than **him**.	When a pronoun follows *than*, the correct form is the subject pronoun (*he, she, I,* etc.). Usually an auxiliary verb follows (*is, do, did, can,* etc.). Informally, many Americans use the object pronoun (*him, her, me,* etc.) after *than*. An auxiliary verb does not follow.
The more they practice, **the better** they play. **The older** you are, **the harder** it is to learn a new sport.	We can use two comparisons in one sentence to show cause and result.

EXERCISE **8**   Circle the correct word to complete each statement.

EXAMPLE   In the U.S., soccer is (*more /* (*less*)) popular than basketball.

1. Football players have (*more / fewer*) injuries than soccer players.

2. In the U.S., soccer is growing (*faster / slower*) than any other sport.

3. In 1999, there was (*more / less*) interest in soccer than in 1994.

4. Professional soccer is (*more / less*) popular in the U.S. than in other countries.

5. In the U.S., soccer players are (*more / less*) famous than movie stars.

EXERCISE **9** **Fill in the blanks with the comparative form of the word in parentheses ( ). Include *than* when necessary.**

EXAMPLE In the U.S., basketball is __more popular than__ soccer.
(*popular*)

1. Tall people are often _____ basketball players
(*good*)

_____ short people.

2. Golf is a _____ sport than soccer.
(*slow*)

3. Which do you think is _____, skiing or surfing?
(*difficult*)

4. A soccer ball is _____ a tennis ball.
(*large*)

5. Children learn sports _____ adults.
(*easily*)

6. People who exercise a lot are in _____ shape
(*good*)

_____ people who don't.

7. Do you think soccer is _____ football?
(*interesting*)

8. Do you think soccer is _____ baseball?
(*exciting*)

EXERCISE **10** **Compare adults to children. Talk in general terms. You may discuss your answers.**

EXAMPLE tall
Adults are taller than children.

1. polite
2. friendly
3. formal
4. playful

5. responsible
6. serious
7. curious
8. happy

EXERCISE 11 **ABOUT YOU** Compare the U.S. and your native country (or a place you know well). Explain your response.

EXAMPLES   cars
Cars are cheaper in the U.S. Most people in my native country can't afford a car.

education
Education is better in my native country. Everyone must finish high school.

1. rent
2. housing
3. cars

4. education
5. medical care
6. food

7. gasoline
8. the government
9. clothes (or fashions)

12.6 Comparatives and Word Order

EXAMPLES	EXPLANATION
Comparative **Be Adjective** Football **is more popular** than soccer in the U.S. **Linking Comparative** **Verb Adjective** Football **looks more dangerous** than soccer.	Put the comparative adjective after the verb *be* or other linking verbs: *seem, feel, look, sound*, etc.
Verb Comparative **Phrase Adverb** Woods **played golf more successfully** than his father. **Comparative** **Verb Adverb** Soccer **is growing faster** than any other sport.	Put the comparative adverb **after** the verb (phrase).
Comparative Noun There is **less interest** in hockey than there is in golf. **Comparative Noun** Soccer players have **fewer injuries** than football players.	We can put *more, less, fewer, better*, and *worse* **before** a noun.
Verb **Phrase Comparative** My sister **likes soccer more** than I do. **Verb** **Phrase Comparative** I **play soccer worse** than my sister does.	You can put *more, less, better, worse*, and other comparative forms **after** a verb (phrase).

EXERCISE 12 **Find the mistakes with word order and correct them. Not every sentence has a mistake. If the sentence is correct, write C.**

EXAMPLES A football team has players ⁀more than a baseball team.

A golf ball is smaller than a tennis ball. *C*

1. A basketball player is taller than a gymnast.
2. A baseball game has action less than a soccer game.
3. Football players use more padding than soccer players.
4. Tiger Woods more remarkably plays golf than most other players.
5. I more like baseball than basketball.
6. Team A won more games than Team B.
7. Team A better played than Team B.

EXERCISE 13 **ABOUT YOU** **Compare yourself to another person, or compare two people you know using these verb phrases.**

EXAMPLE drive well
I drive better than my brother.

1. dress stylishly   4. speak English well   7. have freedom
2. work hard   5. worry a little   8. have an easy life
3. spend a lot   6. live comfortably   9. exercise a lot

EXERCISE 14 **ABOUT YOU** **Compare this school to another school you attended. Use *better*, *worse*, *more*, *less*, or *fewer* before the noun.**

EXAMPLE classroom / space
This classroom has more space than a classroom in my native country.

1. class / students   4. library / books
2. school / courses   5. school / facilities[2]
3. teachers / experience   6. school / teachers

EXERCISE 15 **Fill in the blanks with the comparative or superlative form of the word in parentheses ( ). Include *than* or *the* when necessary.**

EXAMPLES In the U.S., baseball is ___more popular than___ soccer.
(popular)

Baseball is one of ___the most popular___ sports in the U.S.
(popular)

1. A tennis ball is _____ a baseball.
(soft)

[2]*Facilities* are things we use, such as a swimming pool, cafeteria, library, exercise room, or student union.

(continued)

2. An athlete who wins the gold medal is _____ athlete
(good)

in his or her sport.

3. Who is _____ basketball player in the world?
(tall)

4. I am _____ in baseball _____ in
(interested)

basketball.

5. In my opinion, soccer is _____ sport.
(exciting)

6. Weightlifters are _____ than golfers.
(muscular)

7. Golf is a _____ sport _____ soccer.
(slow)

8. A basketball team has _____ players
(few)

_____ a baseball team.

9. Even though January is _____ month of the year,
(cold)

football players play during this month.

10. My friend and I both jog. I run _____ than my friend.
(far)

11. Who's a _____ soccer player—you or your brother?
(good)

An Amazing Athlete

Before You Read

1. Can people with disabilities do well in sports?

2. Why do people want to climb the tallest mountain in the world?

🔊
CD 4, TR 09

Read the following magazine article. Pay special attention to comparisons.

Erik Weihenmayer is as tough as any mountain climber. In 2001 he made his way to the top of the highest mountain in the world—Mount Everest—at the age of 33. But Erik is **different from** other mountain climbers in one important way—he is completely blind. He is the first sightless person to reach the top of the tallest mountain.

Erik was an athletic child who lost his vision in his early teens. At first he refused to use a cane or learn Braille, insisting he could do **as well as** any teenager. But he finally came to accept his disability. He couldn't play **the same** sports **as** he used to. He would never be able to play basketball or catch a football again. But then he discovered wrestling, a sport where sight was not **as important as** feel and touch. Then, at 16, he discovered rock climbing, which **was like** wrestling in some ways; a wrestler and a rock climber get information through touch. Rock climbing led to mountain climbing, the greatest challenge of his life.

Teammates climbing with Erik say that he isn't **different from** a sighted mountaineer. He has **as much training as** the others. He is **as strong as** the rest. The major difference is he is not **as thin as** most climbers. But his strong upper body, flexibility, mental toughness, and ability to tolerate physical pain make him a perfect climber. The only accommodation for Erik's blindness is to place bells on the jackets of his teammates so that he can follow them easily.

Climbing Mount Everest was a challenge for every climber on Erik's team. The reaction to the mountain air for Erik was **the same as** it was for his teammates: lack of oxygen causes the heart to beat slower than usual, and the brain does not function **as clearly as** normal. In some ways, Erik had an advantage over his teammates: as they got near the top, the vision of all climbers was restricted. So at a certain altitude, all his teammates **were like** Erik—nearly blind.

To climb Mount Everest is an achievement for any athlete. Erik Weihenmayer showed that his disability wasn't **as important as** his ability.

12.7 As . . . As

EXAMPLES	EXPLANATION
Erik is **as strong as** his teammates. At high altitudes, the brain doesn't function **as clearly as** normal. Erik can climb mountains **as well as** sighted climbers.	We can show that two things are equal or unequal in some way by using: *(not) as* + adjective/adverb + *as*.
Erik is not **as thin as** most climbers. Skiing is not **as difficult as** mountain climbing.	When we make a comparison of unequal items, we put the lesser item first.
Baseball is popular in the U.S. Soccer is not **as popular.**	Omit the second *as* if the second item of comparison is omitted.

(continued)

> **Usage Note:** A very common expression is *as soon as possible*. Some people say *A.S.A.P.* for short.
>
> I'd like to see you *as soon as possible*.
> I'd like to see you *A.S.A.P.*

EXERCISE 16 **Tell if the statement is true or false. Write *T* for true and *F* for false.**

EXAMPLE In wrestling, the sense of sight is as important as the sense of touch. **F**

1. Rock climbing is not as dangerous as mountain climbing.
2. At high altitudes, you can't think as clearly as you can at lower altitudes.
3. Erik was not as strong as his teammates.
4. When Erik became blind, he wanted to do as well as any other teenager.
5. Erik could not go as far as his teammates on Mount Everest.
6. Erik was as prepared for the climb as his teammates.

EXERCISE 17 **ABOUT YOU** **Compare yourself to another person. (Or compare two people you know.) Use the following adjectives and *as . . . as*. You may add a comparative statement if there is inequality.**

EXAMPLES thin
I'm not as thin as my sister. (She's thinner than I am.)

smart
My mother is as smart as my father.

1. old	4. patient	7. religious	10. talkative
2. educated	5. lazy	8. friendly	11. athletic
3. intelligent	6. tall	9. strong	12. interested in sports

EXERCISE 18 **ABOUT YOU** **Use the following phrases to compare yourself to the teacher.**

EXAMPLE speak Spanish well
The teacher doesn't speak Spanish as well as I do. (I speak Spanish better.)

1. arrive at class promptly
2. work hard in class
3. understand American customs well
4. speak quietly
5. speak English fluently

6. understand a foreigner's problems well

7. write neatly

8. speak fast

12.8 As Many/Much . . . As

EXAMPLES	EXPLANATION
Soccer players don't have **as many injuries as** football players. Erik had **as much training as** his teammates.	We can show that two things are equal or not equal in quantity by using: (not) as many + count noun + as OR (not) as much + noncount noun + as.
I don't play soccer **as much as** I used to. She doesn't like sports **as much as** her husband does.	We can use as much as after a verb phrase.

EXERCISE 19 **ABOUT YOU** *PART A:* **Fill in the blanks.**

EXAMPLE   I drive about _____30_____ miles a week.
(number)

1. I'm _____ tall.
(feet/inches OR centimeters)

2. The highest level of education that I have completed is

_____.
(high school, bachelor's degree, master's degree, doctorate)

3. I work _____ hours a week.
(number)

4. I study _____ hours a day.
(number)

5. I exercise _____ days a week.
(number)

6. I'm taking _____ courses now.
(number)

7. I have _____ siblings.[3]
(number)

8. I live _____ miles from this school.
(number)

---

[3]*Siblings* are a person's brothers and sisters.

(continued)

PART B: **Find a partner and compare your answers to your partner's answers. Write statements with the words given and *(not) as . . . as* or *(not) as much / many as.***

EXAMPLE   drive ___I don't drive as much as Lisa._____

1. tall _____
2. have education _____
3. work _____
4. study _____
5. exercise frequently _____
6. take courses _____
7. have siblings _____
8. live far from school _____

EXERCISE **20** **Compare yourself to another person, or compare two people you know. Use *as many as* or *as much as*.**

EXAMPLE   show emotion
My mom doesn't show as much emotion as my grandmother. (My grandmother shows more emotion than my mom.)

1. earn
2. spend money
3. talk
4. gossip
5. like to go shopping
6. have responsibilities
7. have freedom
8. have free time

EXERCISE **21** **Compare this school and another school you attended. Use *as many as*.**

EXAMPLE   classrooms
This school doesn't have as many classrooms as King College. (King College has more classrooms.)

1. teachers
2. classrooms
3. floors (or stories)
4. English courses
5. exams
6. students

EXERCISE **22** **Make a comparison between this city and another city you know well using the categories below.**

EXAMPLE   public transportation ___The buses are cleaner in Boston than in this city.___

OR   _The buses in this city are not as crowded as the buses in Boston._

1. traffic _____

2. people _____

3. gardens and parks _____

4. public transportation _____

5. museums _____

6. universities _____

7. houses _____

8. buildings _____

9. stores or shopping _____

12.9 *The Same . . . As*

EXAMPLES	EXPLANATION
Pattern A: Erik had **the same ability as** his teammates. A soccer ball isn't **the same shape as** a football.	We can show that two things are equal or not equal in some way by using: *(not) the same* + noun + *as*.
Pattern B: Erik and his teammates had **the same ability.** A soccer ball and a football aren't **the same shape.**	Omit *as* in Pattern B.
Language Note: We can make statements of equality or inequality with many nouns, such as *size, shape, color, value, religion,* or *nationality*.	

EXERCISE 23 Make statements with *the same . . . as* using the words given.

EXAMPLE   a golf ball / a tennis ball (size)
   A golf ball isn't the same size as a tennis ball.

1. a soccer ball / a volleyball (shape)

_____

2. a soccer player / a basketball player (height)

_____

3. an amateur athlete / a professional athlete (ability)

_____

4. a soccer player / a football player (weight)

_____

5. team A's uniforms / team B's uniforms (color)

_____

EXERCISE 24 Talk about two relatives or friends of yours. Compare them using the words given.

EXAMPLE   age
My mother and my father aren't the same age.
OR
My mother isn't the same age as my father. (My father is older than my mother.)

1. age   3. weight   5. religion
2. height   4. nationality   6. (have) level of education

EXERCISE 25 **ABOUT YOU** Work with a partner. Make a true affirmative or negative statement about you and your partner with the words given.

EXAMPLES   the same nationality
I'm not the same nationality as Alex. I'm Colombian, and he's Russian.

the same color shoes
Martina's shoes are the same color as my shoes. They're brown.

1. the same hair color   4. (like) the same sports
2. the same eye color   5. (have) the same level of English
3. (speak) the same language   6. the same nationality

12.10 Equality with Nouns or Adjectives

For equality or inequality with nouns, use *(not) the same . . . as.* For equality or inequality with adjectives and adverbs, use *(not) as . . . as* or the comparative form.

NOUN	ADJECTIVE	EXAMPLES
height	tall, short	A soccer player is not **the same height as** a basketball player.
		A soccer player is not **as tall as** a basketball player.
		A soccer player is **shorter**.
age	old, young	He's not **the same age as** his wife.
		He's not **as old as** his wife.
		His wife is **older**.

NOUN	ADJECTIVE	EXAMPLES
weight	heavy, light	The wrestler in blue is not **the same weight as** the wrestler in red. The wrestler in blue is not **as heavy as** the wrestler in red. The wrestler in blue is **lighter**.
length	long, short	This shelf is not **the same length as** that shelf. This shelf is not **as long as** that shelf. This shelf is **shorter**.
price	expensive, cheap	This car is not **the same price as** that car. This car is not **as expensive as** that car. This car is **cheaper**.
size	big, small	Those shoes are not **the same size as** these shoes. Those shoes are not **as big as** these shoes. Those shoes are **smaller**.

EXERCISE 26 **Change the following sentences to use** *as . . . as* **and then the comparative form. Answers may vary.**

EXAMPLE   Lesson 11 isn't the same length as Lesson 12.

Lesson 11 is _____ not as long as Lesson 12. Lesson 11 is shorter. _____

1. I'm not the same height as my brother.

   My brother is _____

2. You're not the same age as your husband.

   You're _____

3. I'm not the same height as a basketball player.

   A basketball player is _____

4. My left foot isn't the same size as my right foot.

   My right foot is _____

5. My brother isn't the same weight as I am.

   My brother is _____

Football and Soccer

1. Which do you like better, football or soccer?

2. How are soccer players different from football players?

CD 4, TR 10

Read the following Web article. Pay special attention to similarities and differences.

http://www.all*sports.com

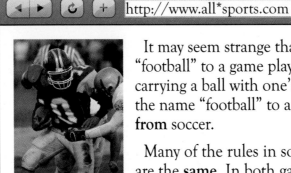

It may seem strange that Americans give the name "football" to a game played mostly by throwing and carrying a ball with one's hands. But Americans give the name "football" to a sport that is very **different from** soccer.

Many of the rules in soccer and American football are the **same**. In both games, there are 11 players on each side, and a team scores its points by getting the ball past the goal of the other team. The playing fields for both teams are also very much **alike**.

When the action begins, the two games look very **different**. In addition to using their feet, soccer players are allowed to hit the ball with their heads. In football, the only person allowed to touch the ball with his feet is a special player known as the kicker. Also, in football, tackling the player who has the ball is not only allowed but encouraged, whereas tackling any player in soccer will get the tackler thrown out of the game.

Football players and soccer players don't **dress alike** or even **look alike** in many ways. Since blocking and tackling are a big part of American football, the players are often very large and muscular and wear heavy padding and helmets. Soccer players, on the other hand, are usually thinner and wear shorts and polo shirts. This gives them more freedom of movement to show off the fancy footwork that makes soccer such a popular game around the world.

While both games are very **different**, both have a large number of fans that enjoy the exciting action.

12.11 Similarity with *Like* and *Alike*

We can show that two things are similar (or not) with *like* and *alike*.

EXAMPLES	EXPLANATION
Pattern A: A soccer player **looks like** a rugby player. A soccer player doesn't **dress like** a football player.	**Pattern A:** Noun 1 + verb + *like* + Noun 2
Pattern B: A soccer player and a rugby player **look alike**. A soccer player and a football player don't **dress alike**.	**Pattern B:** Noun 1 and Noun 2 + verb + *alike*
Language Note: We often use the sense perception verbs (*look, sound, smell, taste, feel,* and *seem*) with *like* and *alike*. We can also use other verbs with *like*: *act like, sing like, dress like,* etc.	

Rugby

Soccer

Football

EXERCISE 27 **Make a statement with the words given. Use *like* or *alike*.**

EXAMPLE   taste / decaf[4] / regular coffee
Decaf tastes like regular coffee (to me).
OR
Decaf and regular coffee taste alike (to me).

1. taste / diet cola / regular cola

2. taste / 2% milk / whole milk

3. look / an American classroom / a classroom in another country

---

[4]*Decaf* coffee doesn't contain caffeine.

(*continued*)

4. sound / Asian music / American music

5. feel / polyester / silk

6. smell / cologne / perfume

7. look / salt / sugar

8. taste / salt / sugar

9. act / American teachers / teachers in other countries

10. dress / American teenagers / teenagers in other countries

EXERCISE 28 Fill in the blanks. Practice using *like* and *alike*. In some cases, more than one answer is possible.

EXAMPLE Players on the same team dress _____alike_____.

1. Identical twins _____ alike.

2. Americans and people from England don't sound _____. They have different accents.

3. My daughter is only 15 years old, but she _____ an adult. She's very responsible and hardworking.

4. My son is only 16 years old, but he _____ an adult. He's tall and has a beard.

5. Teenagers often wear the same clothing as their friends. They like to _____.

6. Soccer players don't look _____ football players at all.

7. Do you think I'll ever _____ an American, or will I always have an accent?

8. In some schools, children wear a uniform. They _____ alike.

9. My children learned English very quickly. Now they sound _____ Americans. They have no accent at all.

10. Dogs don't _____ cats at all. Dogs are very friendly. Cats are more distant.

12.12 Be Like

We can show that two things are similar (or not) in internal characteristics with *be like* and *be alike*.

EXAMPLES	EXPLANATION
Pattern A: For Erik, mountain climbing **is like** wrestling in some ways. Touch is more important than sight. Erik **was like** his teammates in many ways—strong, well trained, mentally tough, and able to tolerate pain.	**Pattern A:** Noun 1 + *be like* + Noun 2
Pattern B: For Erik, wrestling and mountain climbing **are alike** in some ways. Erik and his teammates **were alike** in many ways.	**Pattern B:** Noun 1 and Noun 2 + *be alike*
Compare: a. Erik **looks like** an athlete. He's tall and strong. b. Erik **is like** his teammates. He has a lot of experience and training.	a. Use *look like* to describe an outward appearance. b. Use *be like* to describe an internal characteristic.

EXERCISE 29 **ABOUT YOU** Work with a student from another country. Ask a question with the words given. Use *be like*. The other student will answer.

EXAMPLE   families in the U.S. / families in your native country

> **A:** Are families in the U.S. like families in your native country?
> **B:** No, they aren't. Families in my native country are very big. Family members live close to each other.

1. an English class in the U.S. / an English class in your native country
2. your house (or apartment) in the U.S. / your house (or apartment) in your native country
3. the weather in this city / the weather in your hometown
4. food in your country / American food
5. women's clothes in your native country / women's clothes in the U.S.
6. a college in your native country / a college in the U.S.
7. American teachers / teachers in your native country
8. American athletes / athletes in your native country

12.13 Same or Different

We show that two things are the same (or not) by using *the same as*. We show that two things are different by using *different from*.

EXAMPLES	EXPLANATION
Pattern A: Football is **not the same as** soccer. Football is **different from** soccer.	**Pattern A:** Noun 1 is *(not) the same as* Noun 2. Noun 1 is *different from* Noun 2.
Pattern B: Football and soccer are **not the same**. Football and soccer are **different**.	**Pattern B:** Noun 1 and Noun 2 are *(not) the same*. Noun 1 and Noun 2 are *different*.
Language Note: You will hear some Americans say *different <u>than</u>*.	

EXERCISE 30   **Tell if the two items are the same or different.**

EXAMPLES   boxing, wrestling
Boxing and wrestling are different.

fall, autumn
Fall is the same as autumn.

1. Michael Jordan, Michael Phelps

2. a century, one hundred years

3. rock climbing, mountain climbing

4. a kilometer, 1,000 meters

5. L.A., Los Angeles

6. a mile, a kilometer

7. football, rugby

8. football rules, soccer rules

EXERCISE 31   **Fill in the blanks in the following conversation.**

CD 4, TR 11

A: I heard that you have a twin brother.

B: Yes, I do.

A: Do you and your brother look _____ alike _____?
                                       (example)

B: No. He _____ look _____ me at all.
                    (1)   *(2)*

A: But you're twins.

B: We're fraternal twins. That's different _____ identical
                                                      (3)

   twins, who have the _____ genetic code. We're just
                             (4)

   brothers who were born at _____ time. We're not
                                 (5)

   even the same _____. I'm much taller than he is.
                      (6)

A: But you're _____ in many ways, aren't you?
(7)

B: No. We're completely _____. I'm athletic and I'm on
(8)

the high school football team, but David hates sports. He's a much

_____ student than I am. He's much more
(9)

_____ our mother, who loves to read and learn
(10)

new things, and I _____ our father, who's athletic
(11)

and loves to build things.

A: What about your character?

B: I'm outgoing and he's very shy. Also we don't dress _____
(12)

at all. He likes to wear neat, conservative clothes, but I prefer torn jeans

and T-shirts.

A: From your description, it _____ like you're not even
(13)

from the same family.

B: We have one thing in common. We were both interested in

_____ girl at school. We both asked her out, but she
(14)

didn't want to go out with either one of us!

EXERCISE 32 **This is a conversation between two women. Fill in the blanks with an appropriate word to complete the comparisons.**

CD 4, TR 12

A: In the winter months, my husband doesn't pay as ____**much**____
(example)

attention to me _____ he does to his football games.
(1)

B: Many women have the same problem _____ you do.
(2)

These women are called "football widows" because they lose their

husbands during football season.

A: I feel _____ a widow.
(3)

My husband is in front of the TV all day

on the weekends. In addition to the

football games, there are pre-game shows.

These shows last _____ long as the game itself.
(4)

(continued)

B: I know what you mean. He's no different _____ my
(5)

husband. During football season, my husband is _____
(6)

interested in watching TV _____ he is in me. He looks
(7)

_____ a robot sitting in front of the TV. When I
(8)

complain, he tells me to sit down and join him.

A: It sounds _____ all men act _____
(9)(10)

during football season.

B: To tell the truth, I don't like football at all.

A: I don't either. I think soccer is much _____ interesting
(11)

than football.

B: Soccer is very different _____ football. I think the
(12)

action is _____ exciting. And it's more fun to watch
(13)

the footwork of the soccer players. Football players look

_____ big monsters with their helmets and padded
(14)

shoulders. They don't look handsome at all.

A: Soccer is not _____ popular in the U.S.
(15)

_____ it is in other countries. I wonder why.
(16)

B: What's your favorite team?

A: I like the Chicago Fire.

B: In my opinion they're not _____ good as the Los
(17)

Angeles Galaxy. But to tell the truth, I'm not very interested in sports

at all. When our husbands start watching football next season, let's do

our favorite sport: shopping. We can spend _____
(18)

time shopping as they spend in front of the TV.

A: I was just thinking the same thing! You and I think

_____. We're football widows, but our husbands can be
(19)

"shopping widowers."

Summary of Lesson 12

1. Simple, Comparative, and Superlative Forms

SHORT WORDS

Jacob is **tall**.
Mark is **taller than** Jacob.
Bart is **the tallest** member of the basketball team.

LONG WORDS

Golf is **popular** in the U.S.
Baseball is **more popular than** golf.
Soccer is **the most popular** game in the world.

2. Other Kinds of Comparisons

She looks **as young as** her daughter.
She speaks English **as fluently as** her husband.
She is **the same age as** her husband.
She and her husband are **the same age**.
She works **as many hours as** her husband.
She doesn't have **as much time as** her husband.
She works **as much as** her husband.

3. Comparisons with *Like*

She**'s like** her mother. (She and her mother **are alike**.) They're both
athletic.
She **looks like** her sister. (She and her sister **look alike**.) They're
identical twins.
Lemons **don't taste like** limes. (They don't taste **alike**.)
Western music doesn't **sound like** Asian music. (They don't **sound
alike**.)

4. Comparisons with *Same* and *Different*

Football is **different from** soccer.
My uniform is **the same as** my teammates' uniforms.

Editing Advice

1. Don't use *more* and *-er* together.

He is ~~more~~ older than his teacher.

2. Use *than* before the second item of comparison.

than
He is younger ~~that~~ his wife.

3. Use *the* before a superlative form.

     the
  The Nile is ˄ longest river in the world.

4. Use a plural noun in the phrase "one of the [superlative] [nouns]."

           cities
  Chicago is one of the biggest ~~city~~ in the U.S.

5. Use the correct word order.

    talks more
  She ~~more talks~~ than her husband.

     more time
  I have ~~time more~~ than you.

6. Use *be like* for inward similarity. Use *look like* for an outward similarity.

    s
  He ~~is~~ look ˄ like his brother. They both have blue eyes and dark hair.

  He is ~~look~~ like his sister. They are both talented musicians.

7. Use the correct negative for *be like, look like, sound like, feel like,* etc.

    don't
  ~~I'm not~~ look like my father.

    does
  He ~~is~~ not act like a professional athlete.

Editing Quiz

Some of the shaded words and phrases have mistakes. Find the mistakes and correct them. If the shaded words are correct, write *C*.

              s
  Soccer is one of my favorite sport. In fact, it is probably
    C   *(example)*   ˄

the most popular sport in the world. I know Americans prefer football,
 (example)

but for me soccer is much more interesting that football. In fact, I think
        (1)   *(2)*

soccer is the more exciting sport in the world. There are some good
      (3)

American teams, but they aren't as good as some of the European
            (4)

teams. I think Italy has one of the best team. In South America, Brazil
           (5) *(6)*

has a very good team.
     (7)

The name "football" is confusing. "Football" is sounds like you use only
                                              (8)
your feet, but football players carry the ball. A football and a soccer ball don't

look alike at all. A soccer ball is round, but a football isn't. The game of
(9)
football isn't look like the game of soccer at all. These sports are
               (10)
completely different. The players are different too. Soccer players are not

the same big as football players. There is just one similarity: a soccer team
(11)
has the same number of players than a football team.
    (12)   (13)
    I love to watch soccer, but I like to play it even more. When I lived in

my country I played more better because I more practiced. I played every
                      (14)   (15)
weekend. But here I don't have as much time than before. I watch it on
                                 (16)   (17)
TV but it isn't as much fun as playing it.
            (18)

Lesson 12 Test/Review

PART 1 **Fill in the blanks with the comparative or superlative form of the
word in parentheses ( ). Include *than* or *the* when necessary.**

1. Soccer is _____ sport in the world.
              (popular)

2. In the U.S., football is _____ soccer.
                            (popular)

3. Erik Weihenmayer is one of _____ athletes in the world.
                              (interesting)

4. Weihenmayer is _____ other mountain climbers.
                  (heavy)

5. He found climbing _____ wrestling.
                     (exciting)

6. Climbing Mount Everest is _____ climbing any
                            (difficult)
   other mountain.

7. Mount Everest is _____ mountain in the world.
                    (tall)

8. Tiger Woods played golf _____ his father.
                          (good)

9. In golf, the player who has _____ scores wins.
                               (low)

10. In the 2008 Olympics, Michael Phelps swam _____.
                                              (fast)

PART 2   Fill in the blanks.

EXAMPLE   A tangerine is _____*the same*_____ color _____*as*_____
an orange.

1. She's 35 years old. Her husband is 35 years old. She and her husband
   are _____ age.

2. She earns $30,000 a year. Her husband earns $35,000. She doesn't
   earn as _____ her husband.

3. The little girl _____ like her mother. They both have
   brown eyes and curly black hair.

4. My name is Sophia Weiss. My teacher's name is Judy Weiss. We have
   _____ last name.

5. Chinese food is different _____ American food.

6. A dime isn't the same _____ a nickel. A dime is
   smaller.

7. She is as tall as her husband. They are the same _____.

8. A grapefruit doesn't _____ like an orange. An orange
   is sweeter.

9. She _____ like her husband in many ways. They're
   both intelligent and hardworking. They both like sports.

10. **A:** Are you like your mother?

    B: Oh, no. We're not _____ at all! We're completely
    different.

11. Please finish this test _____ possible.

12. *Borrow* and *lend* don't have _____ meaning. *Borrow*
    means take. *Lend* means give.

13. My two sisters look _____. In fact, some people think
    they're twins.

Expansion

❶ **Work with a partner. Find some differences between the two of you. Then write five sentences that compare you and your partner. Share your answers in a small group or with the whole class.**

EXAMPLES I'm taller than Alex.
Alex is taking more classes than I am.

❷ **Form a small group (about 3–5 people) with students from different native countries, if possible. Make comparisons about your native countries. Include a superlative statement. (If all the students in your class are from the same native country, compare cities in your native country.)**

EXAMPLES Cuba is closer to the U.S. than Peru is.
China has the largest population.
Cuba doesn't have as many resources as China.

❸ **Work with a partner. Choose one of the categories below, and compare two examples from this category. Use any type of comparative method. Write four sentences. Share your answers with the class.**

a. countries	**f.** animals
b. cars	**g.** types of transportation
c. restaurants	**h.** schools
d. teachers	**i.** sports
e. cities	**j.** athletes

EXAMPLE animals

A dog is different from a cat in many ways.

A dog can't jump as high as a cat.

A dog is a better pet than a cat, in my opinion.

A cat is not as friendly as a dog.

4 Compare the U.S. to another country you know. Tell if the statement is true in the U.S. or in the other country. Form a small group and explain your answers to the others in the group.

	Country _____	The U.S.
People have more free time.		
People have more political freedom.		
Families are smaller.		
Children are more polite.		
Teenagers have more freedom.		
People are friendlier.		
The government is more stable.		
Health care is better.		
There is more crime.		
There are more poor people.		
People are generally happier.		
People are more open about their problems.		
Friendship is more important.		
Women have more freedom.		
Schools are better.		
Job opportunities are better.		
Athletes make more money.		
Children have more fun.		
People dress more stylishly.		
Families are closer.		
People are healthier.		

5 Look at the list of jobs below. Use the superlative form to name a job that matches each description. You may discuss your answers in a small group or with the entire class.

EXAMPLE   interesting
In my opinion, a psychologist has the most interesting job.

coach   referee
psychologist   letter carrier
computer programmer   athlete
high school teacher   actress
factory worker   photojournalist
doctor   firefighter
police officer   politician
engineer   nurse

(*you may add other professions*)

a. interesting _____

b. dangerous _____

c. easy _____

d. tiring _____

e. dirty _____

f. boring _____

g. exciting _____

h. important _____

i. challenging _____

j. difficult _____

Talk About It

1 Do athletes in other countries make a lot of money?

2 Do children in most countries participate in sports? Which sports?

3 Why do you think soccer isn't as popular in the U.S. as it is in other countries?

4 Do you watch the Olympic Games? What's your favorite sport to watch?

About It

Write a short composition comparing one of the sets of items below:

- two stores where you shop for groceries
- watching a movie at home and at a movie theater
- you and your parents
- football and soccer (or any two sports)
- life in the U.S. (in general) and life in your native country
- schools (including teachers, students, classes, etc.) in the U.S. and schools in your native country
- American families and families in your native country
- clothing styles in the U.S. and in your native country

Clothing Styles

People dress differently in my country, Lithuania. Styles are much more formal than in the U.S. People usually wear dressy clothes and shoes to work. Here people wear very informal clothes. It's more important for Americans to be comfortable than to be fashionable . . .

For more practice using grammar in context, please visit our Web site.

Grammar
Passive Voice and Active Voice

Context
The Law

	EXAMPLES			EXPLANATION
Active	**Subject** The thief The police	**Active Verb** **stole** **arrested**	**Object** the bicycle. the thief.	The **active voice** focuses on the person who performs the action. The subject is active.
Passive	**Subject** The bicycle The thief	**Passive Verb** **was stolen** **was arrested**	***By* Phrase** *by* the thief. *by* the police.	The **passive voice** focuses on the receiver or the result of the action. The subject is passive. The person who does the action is in the *by* phrase.
Passive	**Subject** The thief The bicycle	**Passive Verb** **was taken** **will be returned**	**Complement** to jail. tomorrow.	Many passive sentences do not contain a *by* phrase.

Jury Duty

Before You Read

1. Have you ever been to court?

2. Have you ever seen a courtroom in a movie or TV show?

CD 4, TR 13

Read the following magazine article. Pay special attention to the passive voice.

All Americans **are protected** by the Constitution. No one person can decide if a person is guilty of a crime. Every citizen has the right to a trial by jury. When a person **is charged** with a crime, he **is considered** innocent until the jury decides he is guilty.

Most American citizens **are chosen** for jury duty at some time in their lives. How **are** jurors **chosen**? The court gets the names of citizens from lists of taxpayers, licensed drivers, and voters. Many people **are called** to the courthouse for the selection of a jury. From this large number, 12 people **are chosen**. The lawyers and the judge ask each person questions to see if the person is going to be fair. If the person has made any judgment about the case before hearing the facts presented in the trial, he **is not selected**. If the juror doesn't understand enough English, he **is not selected**. The court needs jurors who can understand the facts and be open-minded. When the final jury selection **is made**, the jurors must raise their right hands and promise to be fair in deciding the case.

Sometimes a trial goes on for several days or more. Jurors **are** not **permitted** to talk with family members and friends about the case. In some cases, jurors **are** not **permitted** to go home until the case is over. They stay in a hotel and **are** not **permitted** to watch TV or read newspapers that give information about the case.

After the jurors hear the case, they have to make a decision. They go to a separate room and talk about what they heard and saw in the courtroom. When they are finished discussing the case, they take a vote.

Jurors **are paid** for their work. They receive a small amount of money per day. Employers must give a worker permission to be on a jury. Being on a jury **is considered** a very serious job.

13.2 The Passive Voice

EXAMPLES			EXPLANATION
	Be	**Past Participle**	The passive voice uses a form of *be* (any tense) + the past participle.
The jurors	**are**	**chosen** from lists.	
My sister	**was**	**selected** to be on a jury.	
The jurors	**will be**	**paid** for jury duty.	
Compare Active (A) and Passive (P): (A) Ms. Smith **paid** her employees at the end of the week. (P) Ms. Smith **was paid** for being a juror.			The verb in active voice (A) shows that the subject (Ms. Smith) performed the action of the verb. The verb in passive voice (P) shows that the subject (Ms. Smith) did not perform the action of the verb.
I was helped **by the lawyer.** My sister was helped **by him** too.			When a performer is included after a passive verb, use *by* + noun or object pronoun.

EXERCISE **1** Read the following sentences. Decide if the underlined verb is active (*A*) or passive (*P*).

EXAMPLES   I received a letter from the court.   **A**

I was told to go to court on May 10.   **P**

1. The jury voted at the end of the trial.
2. The jurors received $20 a day.
3. Some jurors were told to go home.
4. Not every juror will be needed.
5. Twelve people were selected for the jury.
6. The judge told the jurors about their responsibilities.
7. My sister has been selected for jury duty three times.
8. You will be paid for jury duty.
9. A juror must be at least 18 years old and an American citizen.
10. The judge and the lawyers ask a lot of questions.

13.3 The Passive Voice—Form and Uses

Form: The passive voice can be used with different tenses and with modals. The tense of the sentence is shown by the verb *be*. Use the past participle with every tense.

TENSE	ACTIVE	PASSIVE (*BE* + PAST PARTICIPLE)
Simple Present	They **take** a vote.	A vote **is taken**.
Simple Past	They **took** a vote.	A vote **was taken**.
Future	They **will take** a vote. They **are going to take** a vote.	A vote **will be taken**. A vote **is going to be taken**.
Present Perfect	They **have taken** a vote.	A vote **has been taken**.
Modal	They **must take** a vote.	A vote **must be taken**.

Language Notes:
1. An adverb can be placed between the auxiliary verb and the main verb.
   The jurors **are** *always* **paid**.
   Noncitizens **are** *never* **selected** for jury duty.
2. If two verbs in the passive voice are connected with *and*, do not repeat *be*.
   The jurors **are taken** to a room and **shown** a film about the court system.

Uses: The passive voice is used more frequently without a performer than with a performer.

EXAMPLES	EXPLANATION
English **is spoken** in the U.S. Independence Day **is celebrated** in July.	The passive voice is used when the action is done by people in general.
The jurors **are given** a lunch break. The jurors **will be paid** at the end of the day. Jurors **are** not **permitted** to talk with family members about the case.	The passive voice is used when the actual person who performs the action is of little or no importance.
a. The criminal **was arrested**. b. The students **will be given** a test on the passive voice.	The passive voice is used when it is obvious who performed the action. In (a), it is obvious that the police arrested the criminal. In (b), it is obvious that the teacher will give a test.
Active: The lawyers **presented** the case yesterday. **Passive:** The case **was presented** in two hours. **Active:** The judge and the lawyers **choose** jurors. **Passive:** People who don't understand English **are not chosen**.	The passive voice is used to shift the emphasis from the performer to the receiver of the action.

EXERCISE 2 **Change to the passive voice. (Do not include a *by* phrase.)**

ACTIVE   PASSIVE

EXAMPLE   They chose him.   _____He was chosen._____

1. They will choose him.   _____
2. They always choose you.   _____
3. They can't choose them.   _____
4. They have never chosen us.   _____
5. They didn't choose me.   _____
6. They shouldn't choose her.   _____

EXERCISE 3 Fill in the blanks with the passive voice of the verb in parentheses ( ). Use the present tense.

EXAMPLE Jurors ___are chosen___ from lists.
(choose)

1. Only people over 18 years old _____ for jury duty.
(select)

2. Questionnaires[1] _____ to American citizens.
(send)

3. The questionnaire _____ out and
(fill)

_____.
(return)

4. Many people _____ to the courthouse.
(call)

5. Not everyone _____.
(choose)

6. The jurors _____ a lot of questions.
(ask)

7. Jurors _____ to discuss the case with outsiders.
(not/permit)

8. Jurors _____ a paycheck at the end of the day for
(give)

their work.

EXERCISE 4 Fill in the blanks with the passive voice of the verb in parentheses ( ). Use the past tense.

EXAMPLE I ___was sent___ a letter.
(send)

1. I _____ to go to the courthouse on Fifth Street.
(tell)

2. My name _____.
(call)

3. I _____ a form to fill out.
(give)

4. A video about jury duty _____ on a large TV.
(show)

5. The jurors _____ to the third floor of the building.
(take)

6. I _____ a lot of questions by the lawyers.
(ask)

7. I _____.
(not/choose)

8. I _____ home before noon.
(send)

[1]A *questionnaire* is a list of questions about a topic.

EXERCISE 5 Fill in the blanks with the passive voice of the verb in parentheses ( ). Use the present perfect tense.

EXAMPLE The jurors ___have been given___ a lot of information.
                              (give)

1. Many articles _____ about the courts.
                        (write)

2. Many movies _____ about the courts.
                        (make)

3. Many people _____ for jury duty.
                       (choose)

4. Your name _____ for jury duty.
                     (select)

5. The jurors _____ for their work.
                    (pay)

6. The check _____ at the door.
                    (leave)

7. The money _____ in an envelope.
                    (put)

EXERCISE 6 The people called to jury duty are getting instructions about what to expect. Fill in the blanks with the passive voice of the verb in parentheses ( ). Use the future tense.

EXAMPLE You ___will be taken___ to a courtroom.
                        (take)

1. You _____ to stand up when the judge enters the room.
            (tell)

2. Each of you _____ a lot of questions.
                     (ask)

3. The lawyers _____.
                     (introduce)

4. Information about the case _____ to you.
                                        (give)

5. You _____ to eat in the courtroom.
        (not/allow)

6. Twelve of you _____.
                       (select)

7. If you do not speak and understand English well, you

   _____.
         (not/pick)

8. Besides the 12 jurors, two alternates[2] _____.
                                                    (choose)

9. The rest of you _____ home.
                         (send)

10. All of you _____.
                    (pay)

[2]An *alternate* takes the place of a juror who cannot serve for some reason (such as illness).

EXERCISE 7 **Fill in the blanks with the passive voice of the underlined verbs. Use the same tense.**

EXAMPLE   The jury <u>took</u> a vote. The vote _____ _was taken_ _____ after three hours.

1. The lawyers <u>asked</u> a lot of questions. The questions

   _____ in order to find facts.

2. The court <u>will pay</u> us. We _____ $20 a day.

3. They <u>told</u> us to wait. We _____ to wait on the second

   floor.

4. They <u>gave</u> us instructions. We _____ information

   about the law.

5. People <u>pay</u> for the services of a lawyer. Lawyers _____

   a lot of money for their services.

6. You <u>should use</u> a pen to fill out the form. A pen

   _____ for all legal documents.

7. They <u>showed</u> us a film about the court system. We

   _____ the film before we went to the courtroom.

13.4 Negatives and Questions with the Passive Voice

Compare affirmative statements to negative statements and questions with the passive voice.

SIMPLE PAST	PRESENT PERFECT
The jurors **were paid**.	I **have been chosen** for jury duty several times.
They **weren't paid** a lot.	I **haven't been chosen** this year.
Were they **paid** in cash?	**Have** you ever **been chosen**?
No, they **weren't**.	No, I **haven't**.
How much **were** they **paid**?	How many times **have** you **been chosen**?
Why **weren't** they **paid** in cash?	Why **haven't** you **been chosen**?
Who **was paid** first?	Which people **have been chosen**?

Language Note: Never use *do*, *does*, or *did* with the passive voice.
   Wrong: The juror **didn't** paid.

EXERCISE 8 **Fill in the blanks with the negative form of the underlined verbs. Use the same tense as the underlined verbs.**

EXAMPLE I <u>was selected</u> for jury duty last year. I ___wasn't selected___ this year.

1. The jurors <u>are paid</u>. They _____ a lot of money.

2. Twelve people <u>were chosen</u>. People who don't speak English well _____.

3. Jurors <u>are allowed</u> to talk with other jurors about the case. They _____ to talk to friends and family about the case.

4. We <u>were told</u> to keep an open mind. We _____ how to vote.

5. We <u>have been given</u> instructions. We _____ our checks yet.

EXERCISE 9 **Change the statements to questions using the words in parentheses ( ).**

EXAMPLE The jurors are paid. (how much)
How much are the jurors paid? _____

1. Some people aren't selected. (why)
_____

2. The jurors are given a lunch break. (when)
_____

3. I wasn't chosen for the jury. (why)
_____

4. You were given information about the case. (what kind of information)
_____

5. A film will be shown. (when)
_____

6. Several jurors have been sent home. (which jurors)
_____

7. The jurors should be paid more money. (why)
_____

8. We were told to go to the courtroom. (when)
_____

9. The jury has been instructed by the judge. (why)

Unusual Lawsuits

Before
You Read

1. Are drivers permitted to use cell phones in the area where you live?

2. Have you read about any unusual court cases in the newspaper or heard about any on TV?

CD 4, TR 14

Read the following magazine article. Pay special attention to the active and passive voice.

When a person **is injured** or **harmed**, it is the court's job to determine who is at fault. Most of these cases never **make** the news. But a few of them **appear** in the newspapers and on the evening news because they are so unusual.

In 1992, a fast-food restaurant **was sued** by a 79-year-old woman in New Mexico who **spilled** hot coffee on herself while driving. She **suffered** third-degree burns on her body. At first the woman **asked** for $11,000 to cover her medical expenses. When the restaurant **refused**, the case **went** to court and the woman **was awarded** nearly $3 million.

In 2002, a group of teenagers **sued** several fast-food chains for serving food that **made** them fat. The case **was thrown** out of court. According to Congressman Ric Keller, Americans **have to** "get away from this new culture where people always **try** to play the victim and **blame** others for their problems." Mr. Keller, who is overweight and **eats** at fast-food chains once every two weeks, **said** that suing "the food industry **is** not **going to make** a single individual any skinnier. It **will** only **make** the trial attorneys' bank accounts fatter."

In June 2004, an Indiana woman **sued** a cell phone company for causing an auto accident in which she **was involved**. The court **decided** that the manufacturer of a cell phone **cannot be held** responsible for an auto accident involving a driver using its product. In March 2000, a teenage girl in Virginia **was struck** and **killed** by a driver conducting business on a cell phone. The girl's family **sued** the driver's employer for $30 million for wrongful death. They **said** that it was the company's fault because employees **are expected** to conduct business while driving. The family **lost** its case.

We **are protected** by the law. But as individuals, we **need** to take personal responsibility and not blame others for our mistakes. The court system **is designed** to protect us; it is up to us to make sure that trials **remain** serious.

13.5 Choosing Active Voice or Passive Voice

EXAMPLES	EXPLANATION
(A) A driver using a cell phone **caused** the accident. (P) The accident **was caused** by a driver using a cell phone. (A) A driver **struck** and **killed** a teenager. (P) A teenager **was struck** and **killed** by a driver.	When the sentence has a specific performer, we can use either the active (A) or passive (P) voice. The active voice puts more emphasis on the person who performs the action. The passive voice puts more emphasis on the action or the result. The performer is mentioned in a *by* phrase (*by the driver, by a woman, by the court*). The active voice is more common than the passive voice when there is a specific performer.
(P) The obesity case **was thrown** out of court. (P) The manufacturer of a cell phone **cannot be held** responsible for a car accident. (P) Some employees **are expected** to conduct business while driving.	When there is no specific performer or the performer is obvious, the passive voice is usually used.
(P) It **was found** that 80 percent of accidents are the result of driver distraction. (P) It **is believed** that cell phone use distracts drivers.	Often the passive voice is used after *it* when talking about findings, discoveries, or general beliefs.
(A) The woman **went** to court. (A) The accident **happened** in Virginia. (A) Unusual court cases **appear** in the newspaper. (A) The teenager **died**.	Some verbs have no object. We cannot make these verbs passive. Some verbs with no object are: happen go fall become live sleep come look die seem work complain be remain arrive stay appear rain run sound grow depend laugh leave (a place)
(A) **She** sued **them**. (P) **They** were sued by **her**. (A) **He** helps **us**. (P) **We** are helped by **him**.	Notice the difference in pronouns in an active sentence and a passive sentence. After *by*, the object pronoun is used.

Language Note: Even though ***have*** and ***want*** are followed by an object, these verbs are not usually used in the passive voice.

    He **has** a cell phone. (*Not:* A cell phone is had by him.)
    She **wants** a new car. (*Not:* A new car is wanted by her.)

EXERCISE 10 Change these sentences from active to passive voice. Mention the performer in a *by* phrase. Use the same tense as the underlined verbs.

EXAMPLE An Indiana woman <u>sued</u> a cell phone company.
A cell phone company was sued by an Indiana woman.

1. Employees <u>use</u> cell phones.

   _____

2. A driver <u>hit</u> a pedestrian.

   _____

3. The court <u>threw out</u> the case.

   _____

4. Distracted drivers <u>cause</u> accidents.

   _____

5. Congress <u>makes</u> the laws.

   _____

6. <u>Should</u> the government <u>control</u> cell phone use?

   _____

7. The president <u>signs</u> new laws.

   _____

8. The court <u>has decided</u> the case.

   _____

9. The judge <u>will make</u> a decision.

   _____

10. Fast-food restaurants <u>sell</u> hamburgers and fries.

   _____

EXERCISE 11 The following sentences would be better in passive voice without a performer. Change them to passive voice. Use the same tense as the underlined verbs.

EXAMPLE They <u>paid</u> me for jury duty.
I was paid for jury duty.

1. They <u>sent</u> me a questionnaire.

   _____

2. They <u>have taken</u> us to a separate room.

   _____

3. They <u>told</u> us not to discuss the case.

_____

4. They <u>will choose</u> 12 people.

_____

5. <u>Has</u> someone <u>selected</u> your name?

_____

6. They <u>didn't permit</u> us to read any newspapers.

_____

7. They <u>will not select</u> him again for jury duty.

_____

8. <u>Will</u> they <u>pay</u> you?

_____

9. They <u>don't allow</u> us to eat in the courtroom.

_____

10. Someone <u>has called</u> my name.

_____

EXERCISE **12** **The following sentences would be better in active voice. Change them to active voice. Use the same tense as the underlined verbs.**

EXAMPLE Fast food <u>is eaten</u> by Mr. Keller.
Mr. Keller eats fast food.

1. A cell phone <u>was had</u> by the driver.

_____

2. Hot coffee <u>was spilled</u> by the driver.

_____

3. <u>Is</u> a cell phone <u>used</u> by you?

_____

4. The car <u>has been driven</u> by me.

_____

5. A lot of money <u>is made</u> by lawyers.

_____

6. An earpiece <u>should be used</u> by drivers with cell phones.

_____

7. Business <u>is conducted</u> by me from my car.

_____

8. The news <u>is watched</u> by us every night.

_____

9. Fast food <u>is eaten</u> by a lot of teenagers.

_____

10. The accident <u>will be reported</u> by them.

_____

EXERCISE **13** **Fill in the blanks with the active or passive voice of the verb in parentheses ( ). Use the tense or modal given.**

CD 4, TR 15

In more than 50 countries, laws ___**have been passed**___ that prohibit
(example: present perfect: *pass*)

drivers from using cell phones. In a few countries, such as Japan, both

hand-held and hands-free cell phone use _____.
(1 present: *ban*)

In the U.S., the law _____ on the place where you
(2 present: *depend*)

_____. In New York, for example, the use of
(3 present: *live*)

hand-held cell phones while driving _____, but
(4 present: *prohibit*)

the use of hands-free units _____. A driver who
(5 present: *permit*)

_____ this law can be fined $100 for a first offense,
(6 present: *not/obey*)

$200 for a second, and $500 after that. More and more states

_____ to become tougher on drivers who use
(7 present perfect: *start*)

cell phones.

Texting while driving _____ an even greater problem.
(8 present perfect: *become*)

Drivers _____ to look away from the road in order to text.
(9 present: *need*)

The risk of causing an accident while texting is 15 times higher than it is while

using a cell phone. In New York, drivers who text _____
(10 future: *punish*)

with a fine of up to $150. In Utah, drivers who text and cause a serious

accident _____ to jail for up to 15 years.
(11 can/send)

But the problem of driver distraction is not only a result of cell phones

and texting. According to one study conducted, it was found that 80 percent

of accidents _____ by drivers who are not paying attention.
(12 present: *cause*)

This study _____ that drivers _____ by
(13 past: *determine*) (14 present: *distract*)

many things: eating, putting on makeup, reading, reaching for things, and changing stations on the radio. It is clear that all drivers

_____ to give driving their full attention.
(15 present: need)

EXERCISE 14 **Fill in the blanks with the passive or active voice of the verb in parentheses ( ), using the past tense.**

🔊
CD 4, TR 16

A: Why weren't you at work last week? Were you sick?

B: No. I ___ was chosen ___ to be on a jury.
(example: choose)

A: How was it?

B: It was very interesting. A man _____
(1 arrest)

for fighting with a police officer.

A: Oh. How was the jury selection process?

B: The jury selection was interesting too. But it took

half a day to choose 12 people.

A: Why?

B: The judge and lawyers _____ more than 50 people.
(2 interview)

A: Why so many people?

B: Well, several people _____ the judge's questions.
(3 not/understand)

They _____ English very well. And a
(4 not/speak)

woman _____ the judge that she was very sick.
(5 tell)

The judge _____ her permission to leave. I don't
(6 give)

know why the other people _____.
(7 not/choose)

A: What kind of questions _____ by the
(8 you/ask)

judge and lawyers?

B: First the lawyers _____ to see if we could be fair.
(9 want)

Some jurors _____ that they had a bad experience
(10 say)

with a police officer. Those jurors _____.
(11 not/select)

A: Why not?

B: Because the judge probably thought they couldn't be fair in this case.

A: How long did the trial last?

B: Only two days.

(continued)

A: _____ about the case with your family when
     (12 you/talk)

you _____ home the first night?
     (13 go)

B: Oh, no. We _____ not to talk to anyone about the
     (14 tell)

case. When it was over, I _____ my wife and kids
     (15 tell)

about it.

A: How long did it take the jurors to make a decision?

B: About two hours. One of the jurors _____
     (16 not/agree)

with the other 11 jurors. We _____ about the
     (17 talk)

evidence until she changed her mind.

A: _____ you for the days you missed work?
     (18 your boss/pay)

B: Of course. He had to pay me. That's the law.

A: Now that you've done it once, you won't have to do it again. Right?

B: That's not true. This was the second time I _____.
     (19 choose)

Summary of Lesson 13

Active and Passive Voice—Forms

ACTIVE	PASSIVE
He **drove** the car.	The car **was driven** by him.
He **didn't drive** the car.	The car **wasn't driven** by him.
He **will drive** the car.	The car **will be driven** by him.
He **has driven** the car.	The car **has been driven** by him.
He often **drives** the car.	The car **is** often **driven** by him.
He **should drive** the car.	The car **should be driven** by him.
Did he **drive** the car?	**Was** the car **driven** by him?
When **did** he **drive** the car?	When **was** the car **driven** by him?
Which car **did** he **drive**?	Which car **was driven** by him?

The Active Voice—Use

EXAMPLES	EXPLANATION
I **bought** a new cell phone. He **eats** fast food. We **will drive** the car.	In most cases, the active voice is used when there is a choice between active and passive.
The accident **happened** last month. She **went** to court.	When there is no object, the active voice must be used. There is no choice.

The Passive Voice—Use	
EXAMPLES	**EXPLANATION**
I **was chosen** for jury duty. My cell phone **was made** in Japan.	Use the passive voice when the performer is not known or is not important.
The criminal **was taken** to jail. Some employees **are expected** to conduct business while driving.	Use the passive voice when the performer is obvious.
Cell phones **are used** all over the world. Jury duty **is considered** a responsibility of every citizen.	Use the passive voice when the performer is everybody or people in general.
The court paid me. I **was paid** at the end of the day. The coffee was very hot. The coffee **was bought** at a fast-food restaurant.	Use the passive voice when the emphasis is shifted from the performer to the receiver of the action.
It **was discovered** that many accidents are the result of driver distraction. It **is believed** that a person can get a fair trial in the U.S.	Use the passive voice with *it* when talking about findings, discoveries, or beliefs.
Accidents **are caused** by distracted drivers. A fast-food company **was sued** by a woman in New Mexico.	Use the passive voice when the emphasis is on the receiver of the action more than on the performer. (In this case, the performer is included in a *by* phrase.)

Editing Advice

1. Never use *do*, *does*, or *did* with the passive voice.

   wasn't found
   The money ~~didn't find~~.

   were
   Where ~~did~~ the jurors taken?

2. Don't use the passive voice with *happen*, *die*, *become*, *sleep*, *work*, *live*, *fall*, *seem*, or other verbs with no object.

   My grandfather ~~was~~ died four years ago.

3. Don't confuse the *-ing* form with the past participle.

   taken
   The criminal was ~~taking~~ to jail.

4. Don't forget the *-ed* ending for a regular past participle.

ed

My cousin was select to be on a jury.

5. Don't forget to use *be* with a passive sentence.

were

The books found on the floor by the janitor.

6. Use the correct word order with adverbs.

I was told (never) about the problem.

Editing Quiz

Some of the shaded words and phrases have mistakes. Find the mistakes and correct them. If the shaded words are correct, write C.

C

A: You didn't come to class all last week. What was happened? Were you sick?
(example) *(example)*

B: No. I had jury duty.
(1)

A: But you're not a citizen, are you?

B: Yes, I am. I was become a citizen six months ago. Last month, I received a
(2) *(3)*

letter in the mail telling me I had to report for duty.

A: Did you selected for a jury? You're still an ESL student!
(4) *(5)*

B: Yes. I was selected. My English is far from perfect, but I was ask a lot of
(6) *(7)*

questions by the judge and I answered them without a problem. Anyway,
(8)

I was surprised that I chosen.
(9)

A: Was it an interesting case?

B: Not really. It was about a traffic accident. A man hit a woman's car and
(10)

he left the scene of the accident. Her car was badly damage.
(11) *(12)*

A: Did the woman injured?
(13)

B: She had back pain and had to go for physical therapy.

A: How did the driver caught?
      (14)   (15)

B: The woman saw his license plate and wrote down the number.
                  (16)   (17)

A: Then what was happened?
                    (18)

B: She called the police and they caught him. He was taking to the police
                                         (19)   (20)

station. He was driven without a license. Also, he was talking on a cell
            (21)   (22)

phone while he was driving. It's not permitted to do that in this city.
                  (23)

A: I didn't know that. I was told never about that rule.
                              (24)

B: Well, now you know!

Lesson 13 Test/Review

PART 1 Change sentences from active to passive voice. Do not mention the performer. (The performer is in parentheses.) Use the same tense as the underlined verb.

EXAMPLE (Someone) took my dictionary.
My dictionary was taken. _____

1. (People) speak English in the U.S.

_____

2. (You) can use a dictionary during the test.

_____

3. (The police) took the criminal to jail.

_____

4. (People) have seen the president on TV many times.

_____

5. (Someone) will take you to the courtroom.

_____

6. (Someone) has broken the mirror into small pieces.

_____

(continued)

7. (People) <u>expect</u> you to learn English in the U.S.

_____

8. (They) <u>don't allow</u> cameras in the courtroom.

_____

PART 2 **Change the sentences from passive to active voice. Use the same tense as the underlined verb.**

EXAMPLE You <u>were told</u> by me to bring your books.
I told you to bring your books. _____

1. You <u>have been told</u> by the teacher to write a composition.

_____

2. Your phone bill <u>must be paid</u>.

_____

3. You <u>are not allowed</u> by the teacher to use your books during a test.

_____

4. The tests <u>will be returned</u> by the teacher.

_____

5. When <u>are</u> wedding gifts <u>opened</u> by the bride and groom?

_____

6. Your missing car <u>was not found</u> by the police.

_____

PART 3 **Fill in the blanks with the passive or active form of the verb in parentheses ( ). Use an appropriate tense or the modal given.**

EXAMPLES The tests ___**will be returned**___ tomorrow.
      (will/return)

The teacher ___**will return**___ the tests.
      (will/return)

1. My neighbor had a heart attack and _____ to the
      (take)

hospital in an ambulance yesterday.

2. I _____ my neighbor in the hospital tomorrow.
      (will/visit)

3. I _____ the movie _Star Wars_ five times.
      (see)

4. This movie _____ by millions of people.
(see)

5. I _____ a lot of friends.
(have)

6. I _____ many times by my friends.
(help)

7. Ten people _____ in the fire last night.
(die)

8. Five people _____ by the fire department in
(rescue)

yesterday's fire.

9. Her husband _____ home from work at 6 P.M.
(come)

every day.

10. He _____ home by his coworker last night.
(drive)

11. The answer to your question _____ by anyone.
(not/know)

12. Even the teacher _____ the answer to your question.
(not/know)

Expansion

Classroom

Activities **❶ Form a small group and talk about the legal system in another country. Use the chart below to get ideas.**

Country: _____

	Yes	No
People are treated fairly in court.		
Citizens are selected to be on a jury.		
People are represented by lawyers in court.		
Lawyers make a lot of money.		
Famous trials are shown on TV.		
Punishment is severe for certain crimes.		
The death penalty is used in some cases.		
The laws are fair.		

❷ Form two groups. One group will make a presentation telling why cell phone use should be permitted in cars. One group will make a presentation telling why cell phone use should *not* be permitted in cars.

Talk

About It

❶ Would you like to be on a jury? Why or why not?

❷ In a small group, discuss your impressions of the American legal system from what you've seen on TV, from what you've read, or from your own experience.

❸ Do you think drivers who talk on cell phones or text while driving cause accidents?

❹ What laws should be changed in the U.S.? What laws should be added?

Write

About It

❶ Write about an experience you have had with the court system in the U.S. or your native country.

❷ Write about a famous court case that you know of. Do you agree with the decision of the jury?

A Famous Court Case

I read about an interesting court case involving the governor of Illinois, George Ryan. He was convicted in 2006 of corruption while in office. He illegally gave out driver's licenses to unqualified truck drivers. A family was killed by one of these drivers...

 For more practice using grammar in context, please visit our Web site.

Grammar
Articles

Other/Another

Indefinite Pronouns

Context
Money

14.1 Articles—An Overview

Articles precede nouns and tell whether a noun is definite or indefinite.

EXAMPLES	EXPLANATION
Do you have **a credit card**? I bought **an old house**.	The indefinite articles are *a* and *an*.
It's a holiday today. **The banks** are closed. There are many poor people in **the world**.	The definite article is *the*.
Money is important for everyone. **Teenagers** like to spend money.	Sometimes a noun is used without an article.

Kids and Money

Before You Read

1. Do you think parents should give money to their children? At what age?

2. Do you think teenagers should work while they're in high school?

CD 4, TR 17

Read the following magazine article. Pay special attention to nouns and the articles that precede them. (Some nouns have no article.)

Kids in the U.S. like to spend **money**. In 2009, the average 17-year-old spent more than $100 a week. Much of today's **advertising** is directed at **kids.** When you go into **a store**, you often hear **toddlers**,[1] who are

[1]A *toddler* is a child between the ages of one and three.

just learning to talk, saying to their **parents**, "Buy me **a toy**. Buy me **some candy**." Some **kids** feel **gratitude** when they receive **a dollar** or **a toy** from **a grandparent**. But some **kids** feel **a sense** of **entitlement**[2]. Even during **the** hard economic **times** of the early 1990s, **sales** of **soft drinks, designer jeans, fast food, sneakers, gum,** and **dolls** remained high. **One factor** in parents' **generosity** is **guilt**. As **parents** become busier in their **jobs**, they often feel guilty about not spending **time** with their **kids**. Often they deal with their **guilt** by giving their **kids money** and **gifts**.

To help **children** understand **the value** of **money**, **parents** often give their **children an allowance**. **The** child's **spending** is limited to **the money** he or she receives each week. How much should **parents** give **a child** as **an allowance**? Some **parents** give **the child a dollar** for each year of his or her age. **A five-year-old** would get five dollars. A fifteen-year-old would get fifteen dollars. Some **parents** pay their **kids** extra for **chores**, such as taking out **the garbage** or shoveling **snow**. Other **parents** believe **kids** should do **chores** as part of their family **responsibilities**.

When is **the right time** to start talking to **kids** about **money**? According to Nathan Dungan, a financial **expert**, **the** right **time** is as soon as **kids** can say, "I want." By **the time** they start **school**, they must know there are **limits**.

14.2 The Indefinite Article—Classifying or Identifying the Subject

EXAMPLES	EXPLANATION
A doll is **a toy**. A toddler is **a small child**. A penny is **a one-cent coin**. "Inflation" is **an economic term**.	After the verb *be*, we use the indefinite articles *a* or *an* + singular count noun to define or classify the subject of the sentence. Singular subject + *is* + *a(n)* + (adjective) + noun
Guilt is **an emotion**. Generosity is **a good quality**.	We can classify a noncount subject: Noncount subject + *is* + *a(n)* + (adjective) + noun
Jeans are **popular clothes**. Teenagers are **young adults**. Chores are **everyday jobs**.	When we classify or define a plural subject, we don't use an article. Plural subject + *are* + (adjective) + noun

Language Note: We can also use *be* in the past tense to give a definition.
   The Depression **was** a difficult time in American history.
   Abraham Lincoln **was** an American president.

---

[2]A sense of *entitlement* is a feeling that you have the right to receive something.

EXERCISE **1** **Define the following words. Answers may vary.**

EXAMPLE A toddler ___is a small child.___

1. A teenager _____
2. A quarter _____
3. A dime _____
4. A credit card _____
5. A wallet _____
6. Gold _____
7. Silver and gold _____

EXERCISE **2** **Tell who these people are or were by classifying them. These people were mentioned in previous lessons in this book. Answers will vary.**

EXAMPLE Martin Luther King, Jr. ___was an African-American leader.___

1. Albert Einstein _____
2. Tiger Woods _____
3. Erik Weihenmayer _____
4. Barack Obama _____
5. George Dawson _____
6. Navajos _____

14.3 The Indefinite Article—Introducing a Noun

EXAMPLES	EXPLANATION
She has **a son**. Her son has **a job**. Her son has **a checking account**.	Use *a* or *an* to introduce a singular noun.
He has (**some**) toys. He doesn't have (**any**) video games. Does he have (**any**) CDs?	Use *some* and *any* to introduce a plural noun. *Some* and *any* can be omitted.
He has (**some**) money. He doesn't have (**any**) cash. Does he have (**any**) time?	Use *some* and *any* to introduce a noncount noun. *Some* and *any* can be omitted.

Language Notes:
1. *Some* is used in affirmative statements.
2. *Any* is used in negative statements.
3. Both *some* and *any* can be used in questions.

EXERCISE 3 Fill in the blanks with the correct word: *a, an, some,* or *any.*

EXAMPLE There are ___*some*___ symbols on the back of a credit card.

1. Do you have _____ account with the bank?
2. Do you have _____ money in your savings account?
3. I have _____ twenty-dollar bill in my pocket.
4. I have _____ quarters in my pocket.
5. I have _____ money with me.
6. Do you have _____ credit cards?
7. I don't have _____ change.
8. Buy me _____ toy.
9. Buy me _____ candy.
10. I need _____ dollar.
11. Many teenagers want to have _____ job.
12. Does your little brother get _____ allowance?

EXERCISE 4 A mother (M) and a son (S) are talking. Fill in the blanks with *a, an, some,* or *any.*

CD 4, TR 18

S: I want to get ___*a*___ job.
  (example)

M: But you're only 16 years old.

S: I'm old enough to work. I need to

make _____ money.
  (1)

M: But we give you _____ allowance each
  (2)

week. Isn't that enough money for you?

S: You only give me $15 a week. That's not even enough to buy

_____ CD or take _____ girl to _____ movie.
  (3)   (4)   (5)

M: If you work, what are you going to do about school? You won't have

_____ time to study. Do you know how hard it is to
  (6)

work and do well in school?

S: Of course, I do. You know I'm _____ good student.
                                      (7)

I'm sure I won't have _____ problems working part-time.
                           (8)

M: Well, I'm worried about your grades falling. Maybe we should raise

your allowance. That way you won't have to work. *(continued)*

S: I want to have my own money. I want to buy _____ new clothes. (9)

And I'm going to save money to buy _____ car someday. (10)

M: Why do you want a car? You have _____ bike. (11)

S: Bikes are great for exercise, but if my job is far away, I'll need a car for transportation.

M: So, you need _____ job to buy _____ car, and you need (12) (13)

_____ car to get to work. (14)

S: Yes. You know, a lot of my friends work, and they're good students.

M: Well, let me think about it.

S: Mom, I'm not _____ baby anymore. I need _____ job. (15) (16)

14.4 The Definite Article

We use *the* to talk about a specific person or thing or a unique person or thing.

EXAMPLES	EXPLANATION
The book talks about kids and money. **The author** wants to teach kids to be responsible with money.	The sentences to the left refer to a specific object or person that is present. There is no other book or author present, so the listener knows which noun is referred to.
Many kids in **the world** are poor. **The first** chapter talks about small children. **The back** of the book has information about the author. When is **the right** time to talk to kids about money?	Sometimes there is only one of something. There is only one world, only one first chapter, only one back of a book. We use *the* with the following words: *first, second, next, last, only, same,* and *right.*
Where's **the** teacher? I have a question about **the** homework.	When students in the same class talk about **the** teacher, **the** textbook, **the** homework, **the** board, they are talking about a specific one that they share.
Did you read **the article about money**? Children often spend **the money they get from their grandparents**.	The sentences to the left refer to a specific noun that is defined in the phrase or clause after the noun: *the article **about money**; the money **they get from their grandparents**.*

EXAMPLES	EXPLANATION
I'm going to **the** store after work. Do you need anything? **The** bank is closed. I'll go tomorrow. You should make an appointment with **the** doctor.	We often use *the* with certain familiar places and people when we refer to the one that we usually use: 　the bank　the beach　　the bus 　the zoo　　the post office　the train 　the park　the doctor　　the movies 　the store
a. I saw **a child** in the supermarket with her mother. b. **The child** kept saying, "Buy me this, buy me that." a. The mother bought **some toys**. b. She paid for **the toys** with her credit card. a. The teenager saved **some money**. b. She used **the money** to buy new clothes.	a. A singular noun is first introduced with *a* or *an*. A plural noun or noncount noun is first introduced with *some*. b. When referring to the same noun again, the definite article *the* is used.
My grandparents gave me lots of presents. **Kim's kids** have lots of toys.	Don't use the definite article with a possessive form. 　*Wrong:* My the grandparents 　*Wrong:* Kim's the kids

EXERCISE 5 Fill in the blanks with *the, a, an, any,* or *some*.

CD 4, TR 19

Conversation 1: **between two friends**

A: Where are you going?

B: To _____the_____ bank. I want to

　　　(example)

deposit _____ check.

　　　　　(1)

A: _____ bank is probably closed

　(2)

now.

B: No problem. I have _____ ATM card. There's _____

　　　　　　　　　(3)　　　　　　　　*(4)*

ATM on _____ corner of Wilson and Sheridan.

　　　(5)

A: I'll go with you. I want to get _____ cash.

　　　　　　　　　　　　　(6)

(*Later, at the ATM*)

B: Oh, no. _____ ATM is out of order.

　　　(7)

A: Don't worry. There's _____ ATM in _____ supermarket

　　　　　　　　(8)　　　　*(9)*

near my house.

(*continued*)

Articles; *Other/Another*; Indefinite Pronouns　**443**

Conversation 2: between two students (A and B) at the same school

A: Is there _____ cafeteria at this school?

(1)

B: Yes, there is. It's on _____ first floor of this building.

(2)

A: I want to buy _____ cup of coffee.

(3)

B: You don't have to go to _____ cafeteria. There's _____

(4) (5)
coffee machine on this floor.

A: I only have a one-dollar bill. Do you have _____ change?

(6)

B: There's _____ dollar-bill changer next to _____

(7) (8)
coffee machine.

Conversation 3: between two students in the same class

A: Where's _____ teacher? It's already 7:00.

(1)

B: Maybe she's absent today.

A: I'll go to _____ English office and ask if anyone knows where

(2)
she is.

B: That's _____ good idea.

(3)

(A *few minutes later*)

A: I talked to _____ secretary in _____ English office. She said

(4) (5)
that _____ teacher just called. She's going to be about 15 minutes

(6)
late. She had _____ problem with her car.

(7)

14.5 Making Generalizations

When we make a generalization, we say that something is true of ALL members of a group.

EXAMPLES	EXPLANATION
a. **Children** like to copy their friends. b. **A child** likes to copy his or her friends. a. **Video games** are expensive. b. **A video game** is expensive.	There are two ways to make a generalization about a countable subject: a. Use no article + plural noun. OR b. Use *a* or *an* + singular noun.
Money doesn't buy happiness. **Love** is more important than money. **Honesty** is a good quality.	To make a generalization about a noncount subject, don't use an article.
a. Children like **toys**. a. People like to use **credit cards**. b. Everyone needs **money**. b. No one has enough **time**.	Don't use an article to make a generalization about the object of the sentence. a. Use the plural form for count nouns. b. Noncount nouns are always singular.

Language Note: Do not use *some* or *any* with generalizations.
Compare:
    I need **some money** to buy a new bike.
    Everyone needs **money**.

EXERCISE **6** Decide if the statement is general (true of all examples of the subject), or specific (true of the pictures on these pages or of specific objects that everyone in the class can agree on). Fill in the blanks with *a, an, the,* or *Ø* (for no article).

EXAMPLES   _____Ø_____ ~~C~~children like _____Ø_____ toys.

_____The_____ toys are broken.

1. _____ American teenager likes to have a job.

2. _____ teenager is shoveling snow to make money.

3. _____ teenagers like _____ cars.

4. _____ jeans are popular.

5. _____ jeans are torn.

6. _____ money is important for everyone.

7. _____ money on the table is mine.

8. Do you like _____ kids?

9. _____ American kids like to spend money.

(continued)

10. _____ child is saying to her mother, "I want."

11. Do you like to use _____ credit cards?

12. _____ credit card and the wallet are mine.

13. _____ textbooks at American colleges aren't free.

14. _____ textbook on the table costs $39.99.

15. Where did you buy _____ textbooks for your courses?

EXERCISE 7 **ABOUT YOU** Tell if you like the following or not. For count nouns (C), use the plural form. For noncount nouns (NC), use the singular form.

EXAMPLES coffee (NC)   apple (C)
I like coffee.   I don't like apples.

1. tea (NC)   **4.** potato chip (C)   **7.** cookie (C)

2. corn (NC)   **5.** milk (NC)   **8.** pizza (NC)

3. peach (C)   **6.** orange (C)   **9.** potato (C)

EXERCISE 8 Fill in the blanks with *the, a, an, some, any,* or *Ø* (for no article). In some cases, more than one answer is possible.

CD 4, TR 20

A: Where are you going?

B: I'm going to ___**the**___ post office. I need to buy _____ stamps.
        (example)   *(1)*

A: I'll go with you. I want to mail _____ package to my parents.
                                    (2)

B: What's in _____ package?
            (3)

A: _____ shirts for my father, _____ coat for my sister,
    (4)   *(5)*

and _____ money for my mother.
     (6)

B: You should never send _____ money by mail.
                  (7)

A: I know. My mother never received _____ money that I sent in my
                             (8)

last letter. But what can I do? I don't have _____ checking account.
                                  (9)

B: You can buy _____ money order at _____ bank.
        (10)   *(11)*

A: How much does it cost?

B: Well, if you have _____ account in _____ bank, it's
             (12)   *(13)*

usually free. If not, you'll probably have to pay a fee.

A: What about _____ currency exchange on Wright Street? Do
            (14)

they sell _____ money orders?
     (15)

B: Yes.

A: Why don't we go there? We can save _____ time. It's on
(16)

_____ same street as _____ post office.
(17)   (18)

EXERCISE 9 **Two women are talking. Fill in the blanks with *the, a, an, some*, or Ø (for no article). Answers may vary.**

CD 4, TR 21

A: I bought my daughter _____*a*_____ new doll for her birthday. She's
(example)

been asking me to buy it for her for two months. But she played with

_____ doll for about three days and then lost interest.
(1)

B: That's how _____ kids are. They don't understand
(2)

_____ value of money.
(3)

A: You're right. They think that _____ money grows
(4)

on _____ trees.
(5)

B: I suppose it's our fault. We have to set _____ good example. We
(6)

buy a lot of things we don't really need. We use _____ credit
(7)

cards instead of _____ cash and worry about paying the bill later.
(8)

A: I suppose you're right. Last month we bought _____ new
(9)

flat-screen TV. We were at the store looking for a DVD player when we

saw it. It's so much nicer than our old TV, so we decided to get it and

put our _____ old TV in _____ basement. I suppose
(10)   (11)

we didn't really need it.

B: Last weekend my husband bought _____ new CD
(12)

player. And he bought _____ new CDs. I asked him what
(13)

was wrong with our old CD player, and he said that it played only

two CDs at a time. _____ new CD player has room for ten CDs.
(14)

A: Well, when we complain about our kids, we should realize that they

are imitating us.

B: We need to make _____ changes in our own behavior. I'm
(15)

going to start _____ budget tonight. I'm going to start saving
(16)

_____ money each month.
(17)

A: Me too.

14.6 General or Specific with Quantity Words

If we put *of the* after a quantity word (*all, most, some,* etc.), we are referring to something specific. Without *of the*, the noun is general.

EXAMPLES	EXPLANATION
General: **All** children like toys. **Most** American homes have a television. **Many** teenagers have jobs. **Some** people are very rich. **Very few** people are billionaires.	We use *all, most, many, some, (a) few,* and *(a) little* before general nouns.

Specific:
All (of) the students in this class have a textbook.
Most of the students in my art class have talent.
Many of the topics in this book are about life in America.
Some of the people in my building come from Haiti.
Very few of the students in this class are American citizens.
Very little of the time spent in this class is used for reading.
None of the classrooms at this school has a telephone.
	We use *all of the, most of the, many of the, some of the, (a) few of the, (a) little of the,* and *none of the* before specific nouns.
	After *all, of* is often omitted.
	    All the students in this class have a textbook.
	After *none of the* + plural noun, a singular verb is correct. However, you will often hear a plural verb used.
	    None of the classrooms **have** a telephone.

Language Note: Remember there is a difference between *a few* and *(very) few, a little,* and *(very) little.* When we omit *a,* the emphasis is on the negative. We are saying the quantity is not enough. (See Lesson 5, Section 5.14 for more information.)
    Few people wanted to have a party. The party was canceled.
    A few people came to the meeting. We discussed our plans.

EXERCISE **10** **Fill in the blanks with *all, most, some,* or *(very) few* to make a general statement about Americans. Discuss your answers.**

EXAMPLE   __Most__ Americans have a car.

1. _____ Americans have educational opportunities.

2. _____ Americans have a TV.

3. _____ American families have more than eight children.

4. _____ Americans know where my native country is.

5. _____ Americans shake hands when they meet.

6. _____ Americans use credit cards.

7. _____ Americans are natives of America.

8. _____ American citizens can vote.

9. _____ Americans speak my native language.

10. _____ Americans are unfriendly to me.

EXERCISE 11 **ABOUT YOU** Fill in the blanks with a quantity word to make a true statement about specific nouns. If you use *none*, change the verb to the singular form.

EXAMPLES   _____*All of the*_____ students in this class want to learn English.

_____*None of the students*_____ in this class come̷s̷ from Australia.

1. _____ students in this class speak Spanish.

2. _____ students brought their books to class today.

3. _____ students are absent today.

4. _____ students want to learn English.

5. _____ students have jobs.

6. _____ students are married.

7. _____ students are going to return to their native countries.

8. _____ lessons in this book end with a review.

9. _____ pages in this book have pictures.

10. _____ tests in this class are hard.

Bills, Bills, Bills

Before You Read

1. How many bills a month do you get?

2. How do you pay your bills? By check? By credit card? Online?

CD 4, TR 22

Read the following conversation. Pay special attention to *other* and *another*.

(continued)

A: Last month I went to the doctor, and she sent me to get an X-ray. I got a bill and paid it, but then I got **another one**. Can you help me figure this out?

B: Let's see. Well, one bill is from the doctor. **The other one** is from the X-ray lab.

A: This is crazy. Why don't they send just one bill?

B: That's how it is in the U.S.

A: And look how high the bill is. I had one test and it cost over $600.

B: Do you have insurance?

A: Yes.

B: Wait for your insurance to pay. After your insurance pays, they'll send you **another** bill that shows the amount you have to pay.

A: There are two phone numbers. Which one should I call?

B: The first number is for telephone service. **The other** number is a fax number.

A: How do I pay? Can I send cash?

B: Never send cash by mail. There are two methods of payment: One method is by check. **The other** is by credit card.

A: I hate paying bills. Every month I get a gas bill, a cell phone bill, an electricity bill, a cable bill, and **others**. This is so confusing.

B: Some people pay by check. But **others** set up direct payment. Call the electric company and all **the others** to see if you can do a direct debit[3]. That way you don't have to think about bills every month.

---

[3]A *direct debit* means the money goes straight from your checking account to pay the bill.

14.7 *Another* and *Other*

The use of *other* and *another* depends on whether a noun is singular or plural, definite or indefinite.

The other + a singular noun is definite. It means the only one remaining.

There are two numbers.   x   ⓧ

One number is the phone number.

The other number is the fax number.

The other + a plural noun is definite. It means all the remaining ones.

                         x   (x x x x x)

Call the electric company.

Call all **the other** companies.

Another + a singular noun is indefinite. It means one of several.

                         x   x x ⓧ x x

One bill is from the electric company.

Another bill is from the gas company.

Other + a plural noun is indefinite. It means some, but not all, of the remaining ones.

                         x   x (x x) x x

Some people pay by check.

Other people pay by credit.

DR. MARY THOMPSON, M.D.
20 BAKER ST. PHOENIX, AZ 85003
PH: (602) 555-1215 FAX: (602) 555-1213
CONSULTATION BY APPOINTMENT

DATE: _____3/14/10_____

Morgan Sweet
20 Maple Rd.
Phoenix, AZ 85003

FOR PROFESSIONAL SERVICES

office visit	$40.00
blood test	$150.00
radiology	$410.00
TOTAL DUE:	$600.00
PAYMENT RECEIVED:	

14.8 More About *Another* and *Other*

EXAMPLES	EXPLANATION
One number is the phone number. The other **one** is the fax number. Call the electric company. Call the other **ones** too.	We can use the pronouns *one* or *ones* in place of the noun. For plurals, put the **s** on *one*, not on *other*. *Wrong:* the other<u>s</u> ones
Some people pay by check. **Others** pay by credit card.	When the plural noun or pronoun (*ones*) is omitted, change *other* to *others*.
I have two bank accounts. One is for savings. **My other** account is for checking.	*The* is omitted when we use a possessive form. *Wrong:* My *the* other account is for checking.
I'm busy paying bills now. Can we talk **another** time? Can we talk **any other** time? Can we talk **some other** time?	After *some* or *any*, *another* is changed to *other*. *Wrong:* Can you come *any* another time?
After your insurance pays, your doctor will send you **another** bill. I received one doctor bill. Then I received **another** one.	*Another* is sometimes used to mean a different one, or one more.

EXERCISE 12 Fill in the blanks with *the other, another, the others, others,* or *other.*

EXAMPLE I have a question about my doctor bill. I have ___another___ one about my light bill.

1. I have one more bill to pay this month. I paid all _____ bills.

2. I received one bill for the X-ray. Then I received _____ one.

3. The doctor gave me two tests. One test was an X-ray. _____ one was a blood test.

4. One side of the credit card has a name and number. _____ side has a place to sign your name.

5. If I use the ATM at my bank, I don't have to pay a fee. If I use it at any _____ bank, I have to pay a fee.

6. The bank is going to close now. Please come back some _____ time.

7. *Money* is a noncount noun. _____ ones are *love*, *freedom*, and *time*.

8. Some kids get an allowance for doing nothing. _____ have to do chores to get an allowance. But not all kids get an allowance.

9. The child gets presents from his grandparents. One grandparent died, but _____ three are alive.

10. The child has a lot of toys, but he wants _____ one.

EXERCISE 13 A grandson (GS) and grandfather (GF) are talking. Fill in the blanks with *the other, another, the others,* or *other.*

CD 4, TR 23

GS: I want to buy ___another___ pair of sneakers.
(example)

GF: What?! You already have about six pairs of sneakers. In fact, I bought you a new pair last month for your birthday.

GS: The new pair is fine, but _____ five are too small
(1)
for me. You know I'm growing very fast, so I threw them away.

GF: Why did you throw them away? _____ boys
(2)
in your neighborhood could use them.

GS: They wouldn't like them. They're out of style.

GF: You kids are so wasteful today. What's wrong with the sneakers I bought you last month? If they fit you, why do you need _____ pair?
(3)

GS: Everybody in my class at school has red sneakers with the laces tied backward. The sneakers you gave me are not in style anymore.

GF: Do you always have to have what all _____ kids in
(4)
school have? Can't you think for yourself?

GS: Didn't you ask your parents for stuff when you were in junior high?

GF: My parents were poor, and my two brothers and I worked to help them. When we couldn't wear our clothes anymore because we outgrew them, we gave them to _____ families nearby.
(5)
And our neighbors gave us the things that their children outgrew. One neighbor had two sons. One son was a year older than me. _____ one was two years younger. So we
(6)
were constantly passing clothes back and forth.

GS: What about style? When clothes went out of style, didn't you throw them out?

(continued)

GF: No. We never threw things out. Styles were not as important to us then. We didn't waste our parents' money thinking of styles. In fact, my oldest brother worked in a factory and gave all his salary to our parents. My _____ brother and I helped our father in his
(7)
business. My dad didn't give us a salary or an allowance. It was our duty to help him.

GS: You don't understand how important it is to look like all
_____ kids.
(8)

GF: I guess I don't. I'm old-fashioned. Every generation has
_____ way of looking at things.
(9)

The High Cost of a College Education

Before You Read

1. Have you received any financial aid to take this course?
2. Do you know how much it costs to get a college degree in the U.S.?

CD 4, TR 24

Read the following conversation between a son (S) and a dad (D) and the Web article that follows. Pay attention to *one*, *some*, *any* (indefinite pronouns), and *it* and *them* (definite pronouns).

S: I decided not to go to college, Dad.

D: What? Do you know how important a college education is?

S: College is expensive. Besides, if I don't go to college now, I can start making money immediately. As soon as I earn **some,** I'd like to buy a car. Besides, my friends aren't going to college.

D: I'm not concerned about **them**. I'm interested in you and your future. I was just reading an article in a magazine about how much more money a college graduate earns than a high school graduate. Here's the article. Look at **it**. It says, "According to U.S. Census Bureau statistics, people with a bachelor's degree earn nearly twice as much as those with only a high school diploma. Over a lifetime, the gap in earning potential between a high school diploma and a B.A. (or higher) is more than $1,000,000."

S: Wow. I never realized that I could earn much more with a college degree than without **one**. But look here. The article also says, "In the 2008–2009 school year, the average tuition at a four-year private college was $25,143, and at a four-year public college, it was $6,585." How can you afford to send me to college?

D: I didn't just start to think about your college education today. I started to think about **it** when you were born. We saved money each month to buy a house, and we bought **one**. And we saved **some** each month for your college tuition.

S: That's great, Dad.

D: I also want you to apply for financial aid. There are grants, loans, and scholarships you should also look into. Your grades are good. I think you should apply for a scholarship.

S: I'll need to get an application.

D: I already thought of that. I brought **one** home today. Let's fill **it** out together.

S: Dad, if a college degree is so important to you, why didn't you get **one**?

D: When I was your age, we didn't live in the U.S. We were very poor and had to help our parents. You have a lot of opportunities for grants and scholarships, but we didn't have **any** when I was young.

S: Thanks for thinking about this from the day I was born.

Did You Know?

Almost two-thirds of full-time students receive some form of financial aid: grants, loans, and scholarships.

Grants and Scholarships

Grants and scholarships provide aid that does not have to be repaid. However, **some** require that recipients maintain good grades or take certain courses.

Loans

Loans are another type of financial aid and are available to both students and parents. Like a car loan or a mortgage for a house, an education loan must eventually be repaid. Often, payments do not begin until the student finishes school. The interest rate on education loans is commonly lower than for other types of loans.

Amount You Would Need to Save to Have $10,000 Available When Your Child Begins College (Assuming a 5 percent interest rate.)					
			Amount Available When Child Begins College		
If you start saving when your child is	Number of years of saving	Approximate monthly savings	Principal	Interest earned	Total savings
Newborn	18	$29	$6,197	$3,803	$10,000
Age 4	14	41	6,935	3,065	10,000
Age 8	10	64	7,736	2,264	10,000
Age 12	6	119	8,601	1,399	10,000
Age 16	2	397	9,531	469	10,000

Source of chart: http://www.ed.gov/pubs/Prepare/pt4.html

14.9 Definite and Indefinite Pronouns

EXAMPLES	EXPLANATION
I've always thought about *your education*. I started to think about **it** when you were born. I received *two college applications*. I have to fill **them** out. The father wants *his son* to go to college. The father is going to help **him**.	We use definite pronouns *him*, *her*, *them*, and *it* to refer to definite count nouns.
A college degree is important. It's hard to make a lot of money without **one**. I don't have *a scholarship*. I hope I can get **one**.	We use the indefinite pronoun *one* to refer to an indefinite singular count noun.
a. The father knew it was important to save *money*. He saved **some** every month. b. I received *five brochures* for colleges. Did you receive **any**? c. You have a lot of *opportunities* today. When I was your age, we didn't have **any**.	We use *some* (for affirmative statements) and *any* (for negative statements and questions) to refer to an indefinite noncount noun (a) or an indefinite plural count noun (b) and (c).

Language Note: We often use *any* and *some* before *more*.
   Dad, I don't have enough money. I need **some more**.
   Son, I'm not going to give you **any more**.

EXERCISE 14 **A mother (M) is talking to her teenage daughter (D) about art school. Fill in the blanks with *one* or *it*.**

CD 4, TR 25

M: I have some information about the state university. Do you want to

   look at _____**it**_____ with me?
   (example)

D: I don't know, Mom. I don't know if I'm ready to go to college when I

   graduate.

M: Why not? We've been planning for _____
   (1)

   since the day you were born.

D: College is not for everyone. I want to be an artist.

M: You can go to college and major in art. I checked out information about

   the art curriculum at the state university. It seems to have a very

   good program. Do you want to see information about _____?
   (2)

D: I'm not really interested in college. To be an artist, I don't need a

   college degree.

(continued)

M: But it's good to have _____ anyway.
(3)

D: I don't know why. In college, I'll have to study general courses, too, like math and biology. You know I hate math. I'm not good at _____.
(4)

M: Well, maybe we should look at art schools. There's one downtown. Do you want to visit _____?
(5)

D: Yes, I'd like to. We can probably find information about _____
(6)
on the Web too.

(*Looking at the art school's Web site*)

D: This school sounds great. Let's call and ask for an application.

M: I think you can get _____ online. Oh, yes, here it is.
(7)

D: Let's print a copy of _____.
(8)

M: You can fill _____ out online and submit _____
(9)   (10)
electronically.

EXERCISE 15   **ABOUT YOU** Answer each question. Substitute the underlined words with an indefinite pronoun (*one, some, any*) or a definite pronoun (*it, them*).

EXAMPLES   Do you have <u>a pen</u> with you?
Yes, I have one.

Are you using <u>your pen</u> now?
No. I'm not using it now.

1. Does this school have <u>a library</u>?
2. How often do you use <u>the library</u>?
3. Do you have <u>a dictionary</u>?
4. When do you use <u>your dictionary</u>?
5. Did you buy <u>any textbooks</u> this semester?
6. How much did you pay for <u>your textbooks</u>?
7. Did the teacher give <u>any homework</u> last week?
8. Where did you do <u>the homework</u>?
9. Do you have any <u>American neighbors</u>?
10. Do you know <u>your neighbors</u>?
11. Does this school have <u>a cafeteria</u>?

12. Do you use <u>the cafeteria</u>?

13. Did you receive <u>any mail</u> today?

14. What time does your letter carrier deliver <u>your mail</u>?

EXERCISE 16 **This is a conversation between a teenage girl (A) and her mother (B). Fill in the blanks with *one*, *some*, *any*, *it*, *them*, *a*, *an*, *the*, or Ø (for no article).**

CD 4, TR 26

A: Can I have 15 dollars?

B: What for?

A: I have to buy _____*a*_____ poster of my favorite singer.
(example)

B: I gave you _____ money last week. What did you do
(1)

with _____?
(2)

A: I spent _____ on a CD.
(3)

B: No, you can't have _____ more money until next
(4)

week. Besides, why do you need a poster? You already

have _____ in your room.
(5)

A: I took _____ down. I don't even like that singer anymore.
(6)

B: What happened to all _____ money Grandpa gave you for
(7)

your birthday?

A: I don't have _____ more money. I spent _____.
(8)   (9)

B: You have to learn that _____ money doesn't grow on trees.
(10)

If you want me to give you _____, you'll have to work for it.
(11)

You can start by cleaning your room.

A: But I cleaned _____ two weeks ago.
(12)

B: That was two weeks ago. It's dirty again.

A: I don't have _____ time. I have to meet my friends.
(13)

B: You can't go out. You need to do your homework.

A: I don't have _____. Please let me have 15 dollars.
(14)

B: When I was your age, I had _____ job.
(15)

(continued)

A: I wanted to get a job last summer, but I couldn't find _____.
(16)

B: You didn't try hard enough. When I worked, I gave my parents

half of _____ money I earned. You kids today have
(17)

_____ easy life.
(18)

A: Why do _____ parents always say that to _____ kids?
(19) (20)

B: Because it's true. It's time you learn that _____ life is hard.
(21)

A: I bet Grandpa said that to you when you were _____ child.
(22)

B: And I bet you'll say it to your kids when you're _____ adult.
(23)

Summary of Lesson 14

1. Articles

INDEFINITE

	Count–Singular	Count–Plural	Noncount
General	*A/An* **A child** likes toys.	Ø Article **Children** like toys. I love **children**.	Ø Article **Money** can't buy happiness. Everyone needs **money**.
Indefinite	*A/An* I bought **a toy**.	*Some/Any* I bought **some toys**. I didn't buy **any games**.	*Some/Any* I spent **some money**. I didn't buy **any candy**.
Classification	*A/An* A toddler is **a young child**.	Ø Article Teenagers are **young adults**.	_____

DEFINITE

	Count–Singular	Count–Plural	Noncount
Specific	**The toy** on the floor is for the baby. **The teacher** is explaining the grammar.	**The toys** on the table are for you. **The students** are listening to the teacher.	**The money** on the table is mine. **The information** about definite articles is helpful.
Unique	**The Internet** is a great tool.	**The Hawaiian Islands** are beautiful.	_____

2. Other/Another

	Definite	Indefinite
Singular	the other book my other book the other one the other	another book some/any other book another one another
Plural	the other books my other books the other ones the others	other books some/any other books other ones others

3. Indefinite Pronouns—Use *one/some/any* to substitute for indefinite nouns.

I need a quarter. Do you have **one**?
I need some pennies. You have **some**.
I don't have any change. Do you have **any**?

Editing Advice

1. Use *the* after a quantity word when the noun is definite.

    the
Most of students in my class are from Romania.

2. Be careful with *most* and *almost*.

    Most of
Almost my teachers are very patient.

3. Use a plural count noun after a quantity expression.

    s
A few of my friend live in Canada.

4. *Another* is always singular.

    Other
Some teachers are strict. Another teachers are easy.

5. Use an indefinite pronoun to substitute for an indefinite noun.

    one
I need to borrow a pen. I didn't bring it today.

6. *A* and *an* are always singular.

She has a beautiful eyes.

7. Use *a* or *an* for a definition or a classification of a singular count noun.

a

The Statue of Liberty is ∧ monument.

Editing Quiz

Some of the shaded words and phrases have mistakes. Find the mistakes and correct them. If the shaded words are correct, write *C*.

C

I'm a teenager and I know this: ~~the~~ teenagers think about
(example)   (example)

the money. They want money to buy a new jeans or sneakers. Or they
(1)   (2)   (3)

want money to go out with their friends. They might want to go to the
(4)

restaurant or to a movie. Almost my friends try to get a job in the summer
(5)   (6)

to make some money. At the beginning of every summer, my friends always
(7)

say, "I need a job. Do you know where I can find it?"
(8)   (9)

One of my friend found a summer job at Bender's. Bender's is
(10)

big bookstore. Another friend found a job at a summer camp. But I have
(11)   (12)

the other way to make money. I prefer to work in my neighborhood.
(13)

Most of people in my neighborhood are working or elderly. I ask my
(14)

neighbors if they have a work for me. Some neighbors pay me to take care
(15)

of the lawn in front of their house. Another neighbors pay me to clean
(16)   (17)

their garage. In the winter, I shovel sidewalks in front of their houses. I like
(18)

these jobs. I love a music and I listen to my favorite music while I work.
(19)

What do I do with the money I get from my jobs? I buy songs on
(20)

Internet. I used to buy CDs, but I only liked a few songs. Some of songs
(21)   (22)

on the CDs were great but I never listened to anothers. Now I can download
(23)

the songs I like and not pay for all the other songs on a CD. This helps me
(24)   (25)

save money. I have an old MP3 player I got from my grandfather for my

twelfth birthday, but I want to buy other one. The new ones are smaller
(26)   (27)

and hold more songs. If I keep working hard, I know I'll be able to buy all the
(28)

things I want.

Lesson 14 Test/Review

PART **1** Fill in the blanks with *the, a, an, some, any,* or Ø (for no article). In some cases, more than one answer is possible.

A: Do you want to come to my house tonight? I rented ___**some**___

(example)

movies. We can make _____ popcorn and watch

(1)

_____ movies together.

(2)

B: Thanks, but I'm going to _____ party. Do you want to

(3)

go with me?

A: Where's it going to be?

B: It's going to be at Michael's apartment.

A: Who's going to be at _____ party?

(4)

B: Most of _____ students in my English class will be there. Each

(5)

student is going to bring _____ food.

(6)

A: In the U.S. _____ life is strange. In my country, _____

(7) *(8)*

people don't have to bring _____ food to a party.

(9)

B: That's the way it is in my country, too. But we're in _____

(10)

U.S. now. I'm going to bake _____ cake. You can make

(11)

_____ special dish from your country.

(12)

A: You know I'm _____ terrible cook.

(13)

B: Don't worry. You can buy something. My friend Max is going

to buy _____ crackers and cheese. Why don't you bring

(14)

_____ salami or roast beef?

(15)

A: But I don't eat _____ meat. I'm _____ vegetarian.

(16) *(17)*

B: Well, you can bring _____ bowl of fruit.

(18)

A: That's _____ good idea. What time does _____

(19) *(20)*

party start?

B: At 8 P.M.

(continued)

A: I have to take my brother to _____ airport at 6:30. I don't know
        (21)

if I'll be back on time.

B: You don't have to arrive at 8:00 exactly. I'll give you _____
                                                              (22)

address, and you can arrive any time you want.

PART 2 Fill in the blanks with *other*, *others*, *another*, or *the other*.

A: I don't like my apartment.

B: Why not?

A: It's very small. It has only two closets. One is big, but _____ **the other** _____
                                                                 (example)

is very small.

B: That's not very serious. Is that the only problem? Are there

_____ problems?
        (1)

A: There are many _____.
                          (2)

B: Such as?

A: Well, the landlord doesn't provide enough heat in the winter.

B: Hmm. That's a real problem. Did you complain to him?

A: I did, but he says that all _____ tenants are happy.
                                    (3)

B: Why don't you look for _____ apartment?
                              (4)

A: I have two roommates. One wants to move, but _____
                                                    (5)

likes it here.

B: Well, if one wants to stay and _____ two want to move,
                                       (6)

why don't you move and look for _____ roommate?
                                 (7)

PART 3 Fill in the blanks with *one*, *some*, *any*, *it*, or *them*.

EXAMPLE I have a computer, but my roommate doesn't have _____ **one** _____.

1. Do you want to use my bicycle? I won't need _____ this
   afternoon.

2. I rented a movie. We can watch _____ tonight.

3. My English teacher gives some homework every day, but she doesn't
   give _____ on the weekends.

4. My class has a lot of Mexican students. Does your class have
   _____?

5. I wrote two compositions last week, but I got bad grades because
   I wrote _____ very quickly.

6. I don't have any problems with English, but my roommate
   has _____.

7. I can't remember the teacher's name. Do you remember _____?

8. You won't need any paper for the test, but you'll need _____ for
   the composition.

9. I went to the library to find some books in my language, but I couldn't
   find _____.

Expansion

Classroom
Activities

Fill in the blanks with *all*, *most*, *some*, *a few*, or *very few* to make a general statement about your native country or another country you know well. Find a partner from a different country, if possible, and compare your answers.

a. _____ banks are safe places to put your money.

b. _____ doctors make a lot of money.

c. _____ teenagers work.

d. _____ children work.

e. _____ teachers are rich.

f. _____ government officials are rich.

g. _____ children get an allowance.

h. _____ people work on Saturdays.

i. _____ businesses are closed on Sundays.

j. _____ families own a car.

k. _____ women work outside the home.

l. _____ people have a college education.

m. _____ people have servants.

n. _____ married couples have their own apartment.

o. _____ old people live with their grown children.

p. _____ people speak English.

q. _____ children study English in school.

Talk

About It

❶ The following sayings and proverbs are about money. Discuss the meaning of each one. Do you have a similar saying in your native language?

- All that glitters isn't gold.
- Money is the root of all evil.
- Friendship and money don't mix.
- Another day, another dollar.
- Money talks.

❷ Discuss ways to save money. Discuss difficulties in saving money.

❸ Discuss this saying: The difference between men and boys is the price of their toys.

Write

About It

❶ Do you think kids should get an allowance from their parents? How much? Does it depend on the child's age? Should the child have to work for the money? Write a few paragraphs explaining your point of view.

❷ Write a short composition giving advice to teenagers on how to earn and save money.

> ### How Teenagers Can Make Money
>
> Teenagers often want to make some money. One way to make money is by taking a job in the summer. Teenagers can work at fast-food restaurants or summer camps, or by doing gardening work for their neighbors. Another way to make money . . .

 For more practice using grammar in context, please visit our Web site.

Appendices

Spelling and Pronunciation of Verbs

Spelling of the *-s* Form of Verbs

Rule	Base Form	-s Form
Add *-s* to most verbs to make the *-s* form.	hope eat	hopes eats
When the base form ends in *ss*, *zz*, *sh*, *ch*, or *x*, add *-es* and pronounce an extra syllable, /əz/.	miss buzz wash catch fix	misses buzzes washes catches fixes
When the base form ends in a consonant + *y*, change the *y* to *i* and add *-es*.	carry worry	carries worries
When the base form ends in a vowel + *y*, do not change the *y*.	pay obey	pays obeys
Add *-es* to *go* and *do*.	go do	goes does

Three Pronunciations of the *-s* Form		
We pronounce /s/ if the verb ends in these voiceless sounds: /p t k f/.	hope—hopes eat—eats	pick—picks laugh—laughs
We pronounce /z/ if the verb ends in most voiced sounds.	live—lives grab—grabs read—reads	run—runs sing—sings borrow—borrows
When the base form ends in *ss*, *zz*, *sh*, *ch*, *x*, *se*, *ge*, or *ce*, we pronounce an extra syllable, /əz/.	miss—misses buzz—buzzes wash—washes watch—watches	fix—fixes use—uses change—changes dance—dances
These verbs have a change in the vowel sound.	do/**du**/—does/**dʌz**/	say/**sei**/—says/**sez**/

Spelling of the *-ing* Form of Verbs

Rule	Base Form	*-ing* Form
Add *-ing* to most verbs. **Note:** Do not remove the *y* for the *-ing* form.	eat go study carry	eating going studying carrying
For a one-syllable verb that ends in a consonant + vowel + consonant (CVC), double the final consonant and add *-ing*.	p l a n | | | C V C s t o p | | | C V C s i t | | | C V C g r a b | | | C V C	planning stopping sitting grabbing
Do not double the final *w*, *x*, or *y*.	show mix stay	showing mixing staying
For a two-syllable word that ends in CVC, double the final consonant only if the last syllable is stressed.	refér admít begín rebél	referring admitting beginning rebelling
When the last syllable of a multi-syllable word is not stressed, do not double the final consonant.	lísten ópen óffer límit devélop	listening opening offering limiting developing
If the word ends in a consonant + *e*, drop the *e* before adding *-ing*.	live take write arrive	living taking writing arriving

Spelling of the Past Tense of Regular Verbs

Rule	Base Form	-ed Form	AP3
Add -ed to the base form to make the past tense of most regular verbs.	start kick	started kicked	
When the base form ends in e, add -d only.	die live	died lived	
When the base form ends in a consonant + y, change the y to i and add -ed.	carry worry	carried worried	
When the base form ends in a vowel + y, do not change the y.	destroy stay	destroyed stayed	
For a one-syllable word that ends in a consonant + vowel + consonant (CVC), double the final consonant and add -ed.	s t o p | | | C V C p l u g | | | C V C	stopped plugged	
Do not double the final w or x.	sew fix	sewed fixed	
For a two-syllable word that ends in CVC, double the final consonant only if the last syllable is stressed.	occúr permít	occurred permitted	
When the last syllable of a multi-syllable word is not stressed, do not double the final consonant.	ópen háppen devélop	opened happened developed	

Pronunciation of Past Forms that End in -ed

The past tense with -ed has three pronunciations.			
We pronounce a /**t**/ if the base form ends in these voiceless sounds: /**p, k, f, s, š, č**/.	jump—jumped cook—cooked	cough—coughed kiss—kissed	wash—washed watch—watched
We pronounce a /**d**/ if the base form ends in most voiced sounds.	rub—rubbed drag—dragged love—loved bathe—bathed use—used	charge—charged glue—glued massage—massaged name—named learn—learned	bang—banged call—called fear—feared free—freed stay—stayed
We pronounce an extra syllable /**ə d**/ if the base form ends in a /**t**/ or /**d**/ sound.	wait—waited hate—hated	want—wanted add—added	need—needed decide—decided

Appendix B

Irregular Noun Plurals

Singular	Plural	Explanation
man woman tooth foot goose	men women teeth feet geese	Vowel change (**Note:** The first vowel in *women* is pronounced /I/.)
sheep fish deer	sheep fish deer	No change
child person mouse	children people (OR persons) mice	Different word form
	(eye)glasses belongings clothes goods groceries jeans pajamas pants/slacks scissors shorts	No singular form
alumnus cactus radius stimulus syllabus	alumni cacti (OR cactuses) radii stimuli syllabi (OR syllabuses)	*us → i*
analysis crisis hypothesis oasis parenthesis thesis	analyses crises hypotheses oases parentheses theses	*is → es*
appendix index	appendices (OR appendixes) indices (OR indexes)	*ix → ices* OR *→ ixes* *ex → ices* OR *→ exes*

Singular	Plural	Explanation
bacterium	bacteria	*um → a*
curriculum	curricula	
datum	data	
medium	media	
memorandum	memoranda	
criterion	criteria	*ion → a*
phenomenon	phenomena	*on → a*
alga	algae	*a → ae*
formula	formulae (OR formulas)	
vertebra	vertebrae	

Appendix C

Spelling Rules for Adverbs Ending in *-ly*

Adjective Ending	Examples	Adverb Ending	Adverb
Most endings	careful quiet serious	Add *-ly.*	carefully quietly seriously
y	easy happy lucky	Change *y* to *i* and add *-ly.*	easily happily luckily
e	nice free	Keep the *e* and add *-ly.**	nicely freely
consonant + *le*	simple comfortable double	Drop the *e* and add *-ly.*	simply comfortably doubly
ic	basic enthusiastic	Add *-ally.***	basically enthusiastically

Exceptions:
   *true—truly
   **public—publicly

Appendix D

Metric Conversion Chart

Length

When You Know	Symbol	Multiply by	To Find	Symbol
inches	in	2.54	centimeters	cm
feet	ft	30.5	centimeters	cm
feet	ft	0.3	meters	m
yards	yd	0.91	meters	m
miles	mi	1.6	kilometers	km
Metric:				
centimeters	cm	0.39	inches	in
centimeters	cm	0.03	feet	ft
meters	m	3.28	feet	ft
meters	m	1.09	yards	yd
kilometers	km	0.62	miles	mi

Note:
12 inches = 1 foot
3 feet / 36 inches = 1 yard

Area

When You Know	Symbol	Multiply by	To Find	Symbol
square inches	in²	6.5	square centimeters	cm²
square feet	ft²	0.09	square meters	m²
square yards	yd²	0.8	square meters	m²
square miles	mi²	2.6	square kilometers	km²
Metric:				
square centimeters	cm²	0.16	square inches	in²
square meters	m²	10.76	square feet	ft²
square meters	m²	1.2	square yards	yd²
square kilometers	km²	0.39	square miles	mi²

Weight (Mass)

When You Know	Symbol	Multiply by	To Find	Symbol
ounces	oz	28.35	grams	g
pounds	lb	0.45	kilograms	kg
Metric:				
grams	g	0.04	ounces	oz
kilograms	kg	2.2	pounds	lb
Note: 1 pound = 16 ounces				

Volume

When You Know	Symbol	Multiply by	To Find	Symbol
fluid ounces	fl oz	30.0	milliliters	mL
pints	pt	0.47	liters	L
quarts	qt	0.95	liters	L
gallons	gal	3.8	liters	L
Metric:				
milliliters	mL	0.03	fluid ounces	fl oz
liters	L	2.11	pints	pt
liters	L	1.05	quarts	qt
liters	L	0.26	gallons	gal

Temperature

When You Know	Symbol	Do this	To Find	Symbol
degrees Fahrenheit	°F	Subtract 32, then multiply by $\frac{5}{9}$	degrees Celsius	°C
Metric:				
degrees Celsius	°C	Multiply by $\frac{9}{5}$, then add 32	degrees Fahrenheit	°F

(continued)

Sample temperatures

Fahrenheit	Celsius
0	– 18
10	–12
20	–7
32	0
40	4
50	10
60	16
70	21
80	27
90	32
100	38
212	100

Appendix E

The Verb *GET*

Get has many meanings. Here is a list of the most common ones:

- get something = receive
  I got a letter from my father.

- get + (to) place = arrive
  I got home at six. What time do you get to school?

- get + object + infinitive = persuade
  She got him to wash the dishes.

- get + past participle = become

get acquainted	get worried	get hurt	get engaged
get lost	get bored	get married	get accustomed to
get confused	get divorced	get used to	get scared
get tired	get dressed		

  They got married in 1989.

- get + adjective = become

get hungry	get sleepy	get rich	get dark	get nervous
get angry	get well	get old	get upset	get fat

  It gets dark at 6:30.

- get an illness = catch
  While she was traveling, she got malaria.

- get a joke or an idea = understand
  Everybody except Tom laughed at the joke. He didn't get it.
  The boss explained the project to us, but I didn't get it.

- get ahead = advance
  He works very hard because he wants to get ahead in his job.

- get along (well) (with someone) = have a good relationship
  She doesn't get along with her mother-in-law.
  Do you and your roommate get along well?

- get around to something = find the time to do something
  I wanted to write my brother a letter yesterday, but I didn't get around to it.

- get away = escape
  The police chased the thief, but he got away.

- get away with something = escape punishment
  He cheated on his taxes and got away with it.

- get back = return
  He got back from his vacation last Saturday.

- get back at someone = get revenge
  My brother wants to get back at me for stealing his girlfriend.

- get back to someone = communicate with someone at a later time
  The boss can't talk to you today. Can she get back to you tomorrow?

- get by = have just enough but nothing more
  On her salary, she's just getting by. She can't afford a car or a vacation.

- get in trouble = be caught and punished for doing something wrong
  They got in trouble for cheating on the test.

- get in(to) = enter a car
  She got in the car and drove away quickly.

- get out (of) = leave a car
  When the taxi arrived at the theater, everyone got out.

- get on = seat yourself on a bicycle, motorcycle, horse
  She got on the motorcycle and left.

- get on = enter a train, bus, airplane
  She got on the bus and took a seat in the back.

- get off = leave a bicycle, motorcycle, horse, train, bus, airplane
  They will get off the train at the next stop.

- get out of something = escape responsibility
  My boss wants me to help him on Saturday, but I'm going to try to get out of it.

(continued)

- get over something = recover from an illness or disappointment
  She has the flu this week. I hope she gets over it soon.

- get rid of someone or something = free oneself of someone or something undesirable
  My apartment has roaches, and I can't get rid of them.

- get through (to someone) = communicate, often by telephone
  I tried to call my mother many times, but her line was busy. I couldn't get through.

- get through (with something) = finish
  I can meet you after I get through with my homework.

- get together = meet with another person
  I'd like to see you again. When can we get together?

- get up = arise from bed
  He woke up at six o'clock, but he didn't get up until 6:30.

Appendix F

MAKE and DO

Some expressions use *make*. Others use *do*.

Make	Do
make a date/an appointment	do (the) homework
make a plan	do an exercise
make a decision	do the cleaning, laundry, dishes, washing, etc.
make a telephone call	do the shopping
make a meal (breakfast, lunch, dinner)	do one's best
make a mistake	do a favor
make an effort	do the right/wrong thing
make an improvement	do a job
make a promise	do business
make money	What do you do for a living? (asks about a job)
make noise	How do you do? (said when you
make the bed	meet someone for the first time)

Prepositions of Time

- **in** the morning: He takes a shower *in* the morning.
- **in** the afternoon: He takes a shower *in* the afternoon.
- **in** the evening: He takes a shower *in* the evening.
- **at** night: He takes a shower *at* night.
- **in** the summer, fall, winter, spring: He takes classes *in* the summer.
- **on** that/this day: May 4 is my birthday. I became a citizen *on* that day.
- **on** the weekend: He studies *on* the weekend.
- **on** a specific day: His birthday is *on* March 5.
- **in** a month: His birthday is *in* March.
- **in** a year: He was born *in* 1978.
- **in** a century: People didn't use cars *in* the 19th century.
- **on** a day: I don't have class *on* Monday.
- **at** a specific time: My class begins *at* 12:30.
- **from** a time **to** (OR **till** OR **until**) another time: My class is *from* 12:30 *to* (OR *till* OR *until*) 3:30.
- **in** a number of hours, days, weeks, months, years: She will graduate *in* three weeks. (This means "after" three weeks.)
- **for** a number of hours, days, weeks, months, years: She was in Mexico *for* three weeks. (This means during the period of three weeks.)
- **by** a time: Please finish your test *by* six o'clock. (This means "no later than" six o'clock.)
- **until** a time: I lived with my parents *until* I came to the U.S. (This means "all the time before.")
- **during** the movie, class, meeting: He slept *during* the meeting.
- **about/around** six o'clock: The movie will begin *about* six o'clock. People will arrive *around* 5:45.
- **in** the past/future: *In* the past, she never exercised.
- **at** present: *At* present, the days are getting longer.
- **in** the beginning/end: *In* the beginning, she didn't understand the teacher at all.
- **at** the beginning/end of something: The semester begins *at* the beginning of September. My birthday is *at* the end of June.
- **before/after** a time: You should finish the job *before* Friday. The library will be closed *after* six o'clock.
- **before/after** an action takes place: Turn off the lights *before* you leave. Wash the dishes *after* you finish dinner.

Verbs and Adjectives Followed by a Preposition

Many verbs and adjectives are followed by a preposition.

accuse someone of	(be) familiar with	(be) prepared for/to
(be) accustomed to	(be) famous for	prevent (someone) from
adjust to	feel like	prohibit (someone) from
(be) afraid of	(be) fond of	protect (someone) from
agree with	forget about	(be) proud of
(be) amazed at/by	forgive someone for	recover from
(be) angry about	(be) glad about	(be) related to
(be) angry at/with	(be) good at	rely on/upon
apologize for	(be) grateful to someone for	(be) responsible for
approve of	(be) guilty of	(be) sad about
argue about	(be) happy about	(be) satisfied with
argue with	hear about	(be) scared of
(be) ashamed of	hear of	(be) sick of
(be) aware of	hope for	(be) sorry about
believe in	(be) incapable of	(be) sorry for
blame someone for	insist on/upon	speak about
(be) bored with/by	(be) interested in	speak to/with
(be) capable of	(be) involved in	succeed in
care about	(be) jealous of	(be) sure of/about
care for	(be) known for	(be) surprised at
compare to/with	(be) lazy about	take care of
complain about	listen to	talk about
(be) concerned about	look at	talk to/with
concentrate on	look for	thank (someone) for
consist of	look forward to	(be) thankful (to someone) for
count on	(be) mad about	think about/of
deal with	(be) mad at	(be) tired of
decide on	(be) made from/of	(be) upset about
depend on/upon	(be) married to	(be) upset with
(be) different from	object to	(be) used to
disapprove of	(be) opposed to	wait for
(be) divorced from	participate in	warn (someone) about
dream about/of	plan on	(be) worried about
(be) engaged to	pray to	worry about
(be) excited about	pray for	

Appendix I

Direct and Indirect Objects

> The order of direct and indirect objects depends on the verb you use. It also can depend on whether you use a noun or a pronoun as the object.

Group 1   Pronouns affect word order. The preposition used is *to*.

Patterns: He gave a present to his wife. (DO to IO)
He gave his wife a present. (IO/DO)
He gave it to his wife. (DO to IO)
He gave her a present. (IO/DO)
He gave it to her. (DO to IO)

Verbs:

bring	lend	pass	sell	show	teach
give	offer	pay	send	sing	tell
hand	owe	read	serve	take	write

Group 2   Pronouns affect word order. The preposition used is *for*.

Patterns: He bought a car for his daughter. (DO for IO)
He bought his daughter a car. (IO/DO)
He bought it for his daughter. (DO for IO)
He bought her a car. (IO/DO)
He bought it for her. (DO for IO)

Verbs:

bake	buy	draw	get	make
build	do	find	knit	reserve

Group 3   Pronouns don't affect word order. The preposition used is *to*.

Patterns: He explained the problem to his friend. (DO to IO)
He explained it to her. (DO to IO)

Verbs:

admit	introduce	recommend	say
announce	mention	repeat	speak
describe	prove	report	suggest
explain			

Group 4   Pronouns don't affect word order. The preposition used is *for*.

Patterns: He cashed a check for his friend. (DO for IO)
He cashed it for her. (DO for IO)

Verbs:

answer	change	design	open	prescribe
cash	close	fix	prepare	pronounce

Group 5   Pronouns don't affect word order. No preposition is used.

Patterns: She asked the teacher a question. (IO/DO)
She asked him a question. (IO/DO)

Verbs:

ask	charge	cost	wish	take (with time)

Capitalization Rules

- The first word in a sentence: **My** friends are helpful.
- The word "I": My sister and **I** took a trip together.
- Names of people: **J**ulia **R**oberts; **G**eorge **W**ashington
- Titles preceding names of people: **D**octor (**D**r.) **S**mith; **P**resident **L**incoln; **Q**ueen **E**lizabeth; **M**r. **R**ogers; **M**rs. **C**arter
- Geographic names: the **U**nited **S**tates; **L**ake **S**uperior; **C**alifornia; the **R**ocky **M**ountains; the **M**ississippi **R**iver

  NOTE: The word "the" in a geographic name is not capitalized.

- Street names: **P**ennsylvania **A**venue (**A**ve.); **W**all **S**treet (**S**t.); **A**bbey **R**oad (**R**d.)
- Names of organizations, companies, colleges, buildings, stores, hotels: the **R**epublican **P**arty; **H**einle **C**engage; **D**artmouth **C**ollege; the **U**niversity of **W**isconsin; the **W**hite **H**ouse; **B**loomingdale's; the **H**ilton **H**otel
- Nationalities and ethnic groups: **M**exicans; **C**anadians; **S**paniards; **A**mericans; **J**ews; **K**urds; **E**skimos
- Languages: **E**nglish; **S**panish; **P**olish; **V**ietnamese; **R**ussian
- Months: **J**anuary; **F**ebruary
- Days: **S**unday; **M**onday
- Holidays: **C**hristmas; **I**ndependence **D**ay
- Important words in a title: *Grammar in Context*; *The Old Man and the Sea*; *Romeo and Juliet*; *The Sound of Music*

  NOTE: Capitalize "the" as the first word of a title.

Glossary of Grammatical Terms

- **Adjective** An adjective gives a description of a noun.

    It's a *tall* tree.   He's an *old* man.   My neighbors are *nice*.

- **Adverb** An adverb describes the action of a sentence or an adjective or another adverb.

    She speaks English *fluently*.   I drive *carefully*.
    She speaks English *extremely* well.   She is *very* intelligent.

- **Adverb of Frequency** An adverb of frequency tells how often the action happens.

    I *never* drink coffee.   They *usually* take the bus.

- **Affirmative** means *yes*.

- **Apostrophe '** We use the apostrophe for possession and contractions.

    My *sister's* friend is beautiful.   Today *isn't* Sunday.

- **Article** The definite article is *the*. The indefinite articles are *a* and *an*.

    I have *a* cat.   I ate *an* apple.   *The* teacher came late.

- **Auxiliary Verb** Some verbs have two parts: an auxiliary verb and a main verb.

    He *can't* study.   We *will* return.

- **Base Form** The base form, sometimes called the "simple" form, of the verb has no tense. It has no ending (-s or -ed): *be, go, eat, take, write*.

    I didn't *go* out.   We don't *know* you.   He can't *drive*.

- **Capital Letter** A B C D E F G . . .

- **Clause** A clause is a group of words that has a subject and a verb. Some sentences have only one clause.

    She speaks Spanish.

Some sentences have **a main clause** and a **dependent clause**.

MAIN CLAUSE	DEPENDENT CLAUSE **(reason clause)**
She found a good job	because she has computer skills.

MAIN CLAUSE	DEPENDENT CLAUSE **(time clause)**
She'll turn off the light	before she goes to bed.

MAIN CLAUSE	DEPENDENT CLAUSE **(if clause)**
I'll take you to the doctor	if you don't have your car on Saturday.

(continued)

- Colon :

- Comma ,

- **Comparative Form** A comparative form of an adjective or adverb is used to compare two things.

    My house is *bigger* than your house.
    Her husband drives *faster* than she does.

- **Complement** The complement of the sentence is the information after the verb. It completes the verb phrase.

    He works *hard*.   I slept *for five hours*.   They are *late*.

- **Consonant** The following letters are consonants: *b, c, d, f, g, h, j, k, l, m, n, p, q, r, s, t, v, w, x, y, z*.

    NOTE: *y* is sometimes considered a vowel, as in the world *syllable*.

- **Contraction** A contraction is made up of two words put together with an apostrophe.

    He's my brother.   *You're* late.   They *won't* talk to me.
    (*He's* = he is)   (*You're* = you are)   (won't = will not)

- **Count Noun** Count nouns are nouns that we can count. They have a singular and a plural form.

    1 pen – 3 pens   1 table – 4 tables

- **Dependent Clause** See **Clause**.

- **Direct Object** A direct object is a noun (phrase) or pronoun that receives the action of the verb.

    We saw *the movie*.   You have *a nice car*.   I love *you*.

- **Exclamation Mark** !

- **Frequency Words** Frequency words are *always, usually, generally, often, sometimes, rarely, seldom, hardly ever, never*.

    I *never* drink coffee.   We *always* do our homework.

- **Hyphen** –

- **Imperative** An imperative sentence gives a command or instructions. An imperative sentence omits the word *you*.

    Come here.   *Don't be* late.   Please *sit* down.

- **Infinitive** An infinitive is *to* + base form.

    I want *to leave*.   You need *to be* here on time.

- **Linking Verb** A linking verb is a verb that links the subject to the noun or adjective after it. Linking verbs include *be, seem, feel, smell, sound, look, appear, taste*.

    She *is* a doctor.   She *seems* very intelligent.   She *looks* tired.

- **Modal** The modal verbs are *can, could, shall, should, will, would, may, might, must.*

  They *should* leave.   I *must* go.

- **Negative** means no.

- **Nonaction Verb** A nonaction verb has no action. We do not use a continuous tense (*be* + verb -*ing*) with a nonaction verb. The nonaction verbs are: *believe, cost, care, have, hear, know, like, love, matter, mean, need, own, prefer, remember, see, seem, think, understand, want,* and sense-perception verbs.

  She *has* a laptop.   We *love* our mother.   You *look* great.

- **Noncount Noun** A noncount noun is a noun that we don't count. It has no plural form.

  She drank some *water.*   He prepared some *rice.*
  Do you need any *money?*   We had a lot of *homework.*

- **Noun** A noun is a person (*brother*), a place (*kitchen*), or a thing (*table*). Nouns can be either count (*1 table, 2 tables*) or noncount (*money, water*).

  My *brother* lives in California.   My *sisters* live in New York.
  I get *advice* from them.   I drink *coffee* every day.

- **Noun Modifier** A noun modifier makes a noun more specific.

  fire department   *Independence* Day   *can* opener

- **Noun Phrase** A noun phrase is a group of words that form the subject or object of the sentence.

  A *very nice woman* helped me at registration.
  I bought *a big box of cereal.*

- **Object** The object of the sentence follows the verb. It receives the action of the verb.

  He bought *a car.*   I saw *a movie.*   I met *your brother.*

- **Object Pronoun** Use object pronouns (*me, you, him, her, it, us, them*) after the verb or preposition.

  He likes *her.*   I saw the movie. Let's talk about *it.*

- **Parentheses** ( )

- **Paragraph** A paragraph is a group of sentences about one topic.

- **Participle, Present** The present participle is verb + -*ing.*

  She is *sleeping.*   They were *laughing.*

- **Period** .

- **Phrase** A group of words that go together.

  Last month my sister came to visit.
  There is a strange car *in front of my house.*

(continued)

- **Plural** Plural means more than one. A plural noun usually ends with -s.

  She has beautiful *eyes*.   My *feet* are big.

- **Possessive Form** Possessive forms show ownership or relationship.

  Mary's coat is in the closet.   My brother lives in Miami.

- **Preposition** A preposition is a short connecting word: *about, above, across, after, around, as, at, away, back, before, behind, below, by, down, for, from, in, into, like, of, off, on, out, over, to, under, up, with.*

  The book is *on* the table.   She studies *with* her friends.

- **Pronoun** A pronoun takes the place of a noun.

  I have a new car. I bought *it* last week.
  John likes Mary, but *she* doesn't like *him*.

- **Punctuation** Period . Comma , Colon : Semicolon ; Question Mark ? Exclamation Mark !

- **Question Mark** ?

- **Quotation Marks** " "

- **Regular Verb** A regular verb forms its past tense with -ed.

  He *worked* yesterday.   I *laughed* at the joke.

- **-s Form** A present tense verb that ends in -s or -es.

  He *lives* in New York.   She *watches* TV a lot.

- **Sense-Perception Verb** A sense-perception verb has no action. It describes a sense. The sense perception verbs are: *look, feel, taste, sound, smell.*

  She *feels* fine.   The coffee *smells* fresh.   The milk *tastes* sour.

- **Sentence** A sentence is a group of words that contains a subject[1] and a verb (at least) and gives a complete thought.

  SENTENCE: She came home.
  NOT A SENTENCE: When she came home

- **Simple Form of Verb** The simple form of the verb, also called the base form, has no tense; it never has an -s, -ed, or -ing ending.

  Did you *see* the movie?   I couldn't *find* your phone number.

- **Singular** Singular means one.

  She ate a *sandwich*.   I have one *television*.

- **Subject** The subject of the sentence tells who or what the sentence is about.

  My *sister* got married last April. *The wedding* was beautiful.

---

[1]In an imperative sentence, the subject *you* is omitted: *Sit down. Come here.*

- **Subject Pronouns** Use subject pronouns (*I, you, he, she, it, we, you, they*) before a verb.

  They speak Japanese.   *We* speak Spanish.

- **Superlative Form** A superlative form of an adjective or adverb shows the number one item in a group of three or more.

  January is the *coldest* month of the year.
  My brother speaks English the *best* in my family.

- **Syllable** A syllable is a part of a word that has only one vowel sound. (Some words have only one syllable.)

  change (one syllable)   after (af·ter = two syllables)
  look (one syllable)   responsible (re·spon·si·ble = four syllables)

- **Tag Question** A tag question is a short question at the end of a sentence. It is used in conversation.

  You speak Spanish, *don't you?*   He's not happy, *is he?*

- **Tense** A verb has tense. Tense shows when the action of the sentence happened.

  SIMPLE PRESENT: She usually *works* hard.
  FUTURE: She *will work* tomorrow.
  PRESENT CONTINUOUS: She *is working* now.
  SIMPLE PAST: She *worked* yesterday.

- **Verb** A verb is the action of the sentence.

  He *runs* fast.   I *speak* English.

  Some verbs have no action. They are linking verbs. They connect the subject to the rest of the sentence.

  He *is* tall.   She *looks* beautiful.   You *seem* tired.

- **Vowel** The following letters are vowels: *a, e, i, o, u. Y* is sometimes considered a vowel (for example, in the word *mystery*).

Special Uses of Articles

No Article	Article

Personal names:
   John Kennedy
   Michael Jordan
	The whole family:
	   the Kennedys
	   the Jordans

Title and name:
   Queen Elizabeth
   Pope Benedict
	Title without name:
	   the Queen
	   the Pope

Cities, states, countries, continents:
   Cleveland
   Ohio
   Mexico
   South America
	Places that are considered a union:
	   the United States
	   the former Soviet Union
	   the United Kingdom
	Place names: the _____ of _____
	   the Republic of China
	   the District of Columbia

Mountains:
   Mount Everest
   Mount McKinley
	Mountain ranges:
	   the Himalayas
	   the Rocky Mountains

Islands:
   Coney Island
   Staten Island
	Collectives of islands:
	   the Hawaiian Islands
	   the Virgin Islands
	   the Philippines

Lakes:
   Lake Superior
   Lake Michigan
	Collectives of lakes:
	   the Great Lakes
	   the Finger Lakes

Beaches:
   Palm Beach
   Pebble Beach
	Rivers, oceans, seas, canals:
	   the Mississippi River
	   the Atlantic Ocean
	   the Dead Sea
	   the Panama Canal

Streets and avenues:
   Madison Avenue
   Wall Street
	Well-known buildings:
	   the Willis Tower
	   the Empire State Building

Parks:
   Central Park
   Hyde Park
	Zoos:
	   the San Diego Zoo
	   the Milwaukee Zoo

No Article	Article

Seasons:
    summer   fall
    spring   winter
    Summer is my favorite season.
NOTE: After a preposition, *the* may be used.
    In (the) winter, my car runs badly.
	Deserts:
	    the Mojave Desert
	    the Sahara Desert

Directions:
    north   south
    east   west
	Sections of a piece of land:
	    the Southwest (of the U.S.)
	    the West Side (of New York)

School subjects:
    history
    math
	Unique geographical points:
	    the North Pole
	    the Vatican

Name + *college* or *university*:
    Northwestern University
    Bradford College
	The University/College of _____:
	    the University of Michigan
	    the College of DuPage County

Magazines:
    Time
    Sports Illustrated
	Newspapers:
	    the *Tribune*
	    the *Wall Street Journal*

Months and days:
    September
    Monday
	Ships:
	    the *Titanic*
	    the *Queen Elizabeth*

Holidays and dates
    Thanksgiving
    Mother's Day
    July 4 (month + day)
	The day of the month:
	    the Fourth of July
	    the fifth of May

Diseases:
    cancer   AIDS
    polio   malaria
	Ailments:
	    a cold a toothache
	    a headache the flu

Games and sports:
    poker
    soccer
	Musical instruments, after *play*:
	    the drums
	    the piano
	NOTE: Sometimes *the* is omitted.
	    She plays (the) drums.

Languages:
    French
    English
	The _____ language:
	    the French language
	    the English language

Last month, year, week, etc. = the
one before this one:
    I forgot to pay my rent last month.
    The teacher gave us a test last week.
	The last month, the last year, the last
	week, etc. = the last in a series:
	    December is the last month of the year.
	    Summer vacation begins the last week in May.

(continued)

No Article	Article

In office = in an elected position:
    The president is in office for four years.
	In the office = in a specific room:
	    The teacher is in the office.

In back/front:
    She's in back of
    the car.
	In the back/the front:
	    He's in the back of the bus.

Appendix M

Alphabetical List of Irregular Verb Forms

Base Form	Past Form	Past Participle	Base Form	Past Form	Past Participle
be	was/were	been	drink	drank	drunk
bear	bore	born/borne	drive	drove	driven
beat	beat	beaten	eat	ate	eaten
become	became	become	fall	fell	fallen
begin	began	begun	feed	fed	fed
bend	bent	bent	feel	felt	felt
bet	bet	bet	fight	fought	fought
bid	bid	bid	find	found	found
bind	bound	bound	fit	fit	fit
bite	bit	bitten	flee	fled	fled
bleed	bled	bled	fly	flew	flown
blow	blew	blown	forbid	forbade	forbidden
break	broke	broken	forget	forgot	forgotten
breed	bred	bred	forgive	forgave	forgiven
bring	brought	brought	freeze	froze	frozen
broadcast	broadcast	broadcast	get	got	gotten
build	built	built	give	gave	given
burst	burst	burst	go	went	gone
buy	bought	bought	grind	ground	ground
cast	cast	cast	grow	grew	grown
catch	caught	caught	hang	hung	hung[2]
choose	chose	chosen	have	had	had
cling	clung	clung	hear	heard	heard
come	came	come	hide	hid	hidden
cost	cost	cost	hit	hit	hit
creep	crept	crept	hold	held	held
cut	cut	cut	hurt	hurt	hurt
deal	dealt	dealt	keep	kept	kept
dig	dug	dug	know	knew	known
dive	dove/dived	dove/dived	lay	laid	laid
do	did	done	lead	led	led
draw	drew	drawn	leave	left	left

[2]*Hanged* is used as the past form to refer to punishment by death. *Hung* is used in other situations:
She *hung* the picture on the wall.

Base Form	Past Form	Past Participle	Base Form	Past Form	Past Participle
lend	lent	lent	spit	spit/spat	spit/spat
let	let	let	split	split	split
lie[1]	lay	lain	spread	spread	spread
light	lit/lighted	lit/lighted	spring	sprang/sprung	sprung
lose	lost	lost	stand	stood	stood
make	made	made	steal	stole	stolen
mean	meant	meant	stick	stuck	stuck
meet	met	met	sting	stung	stung
mistake	mistook	mistaken	stink	stank/stunk	stunk
overcome	overcame	overcome	strike	struck	struck/stricken
overdo	overdid	overdone	strive	strove/strived	striven
overtake	overtook	overtaken	swear	swore	sworn
overthrow	overthrew	overthrown	sweep	swept	swept
pay	paid	paid	swell	swelled	swelled/swollen
plead	pled/pleaded	pled/pleaded	swim	swam	swum
prove	proved	proven/proved	swing	swung	swung
put	put	put	take	took	taken
quit	quit	quit	teach	taught	taught
read	read	read	tear	tore	torn
ride	rode	ridden	tell	told	told
ring	rang	rung	think	thought	thought
rise	rose	risen	throw	threw	thrown
run	ran	run	understand	understood	understood
say	said	said	uphold	upheld	upheld
see	saw	seen	upset	upset	upset
seek	sought	sought	wake	woke	woken
sell	sold	sold	wear	wore	worn
send	sent	sent	weave	wove	woven
set	set	set	wed	wedded/wed	wedded/wed
sew	sewed	sewed/sewn	weep	wept	wept
shake	shook	shaken	win	won	won
shed	shed	shed	wind	wound	wound
shine	shone/shined	shone/shined	withhold	withheld	withheld
shoot	shot	shot	withdraw	withdrew	withdrawn
show	showed	shown/showed	withstand	withstood	withstood
shrink	shrank/shrunk	shrunk/shrunken	wring	wrung	wrung
shut	shut	shut	write	wrote	written
sing	sang	sung			
sink	sank	sunk			
sit	sat	sat			
sleep	slept	slept			
slide	slid	slid			
slit	slit	slit			
speak	spoke	spoken			
speed	sped	sped			
spend	spent	spent			
spin	spun	spun			

Note: The past and past participle of some verbs can end in -ed or -t.

burn	burned or burnt
dream	dreamed or dreamt
kneel	kneeled or knelt
learn	learned or learnt
leap	leaped or leapt
spill	spilled or spilt
spoil	spoiled or spoilt

[1]When *lie* means to place, the forms are *lie, lay, lain*. When *lie* means to speak an untruth, the forms are *lie, lied, lied*.

Map of the United States of America

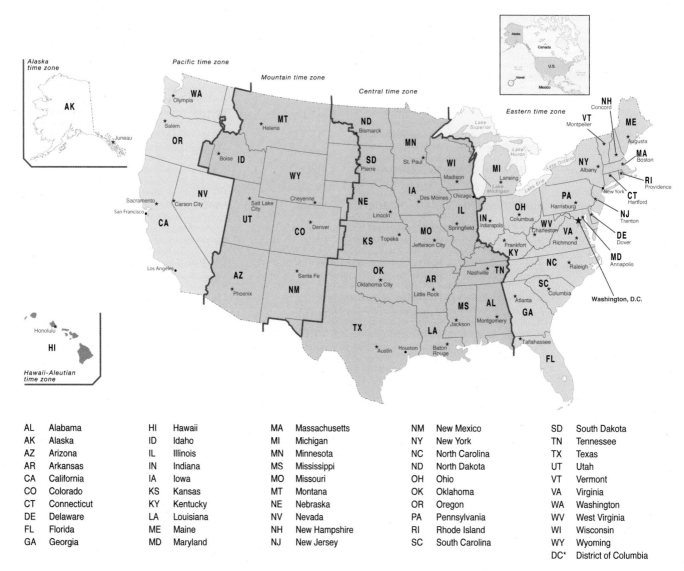

AL	Alabama	HI	Hawaii	MA	Massachusetts	NM	New Mexico	SD	South Dakota
AK	Alaska	ID	Idaho	MI	Michigan	NY	New York	TN	Tennessee
AZ	Arizona	IL	Illinois	MN	Minnesota	NC	North Carolina	TX	Texas
AR	Arkansas	IN	Indiana	MS	Mississippi	ND	North Dakota	UT	Utah
CA	California	IA	Iowa	MO	Missouri	OH	Ohio	VT	Vermont
CO	Colorado	KS	Kansas	MT	Montana	OK	Oklahoma	VA	Virginia
CT	Connecticut	KY	Kentucky	NE	Nebraska	OR	Oregon	WA	Washington
DE	Delaware	LA	Louisiana	NV	Nevada	PA	Pennsylvania	WV	West Virginia
FL	Florida	ME	Maine	NH	New Hampshire	RI	Rhode Island	WI	Wisconsin
GA	Georgia	MD	Maryland	NJ	New Jersey	SC	South Carolina	WY	Wyoming
								DC*	District of Columbia

*The District of Columbia is not a state. Washington, D.C., is the capital of the United States.
Note: Washington, D.C., and Washington state are not the same.

Index

Photo Credits